Course	Introduction to the Humanities
Course Number	**HUMA 1301**
	Ed Massey
	Coastal Bend College

D1466068

http://create.mcgraw-hill.com

ISBN-10: 1121649904   ISBN-13: 9781121649903

Contents

Credits

1

Powerful Ideas

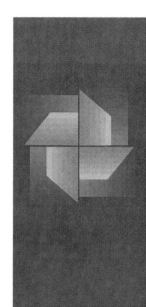

What I understand by "philosopher": a terrible explosive in the presence of which everything is in danger.   —Friedrich Nietzsche

Just before dawn on March 20, 2003, the United States unleashed an all-out missile and bomb attack on targets in Iraq. U.S. president George W. Bush then appeared on television before the world to state that the attack would free Iraqis from a terrible outlaw regime that threatened the world with weapons of mass murder. The Iraqi premier, Saddam Hussein, appeared on television a few hours later. The attack, he charged, was a criminal invasion in violation of international law. "It will be repelled by Iraqis through the grace of God," he declared.

Some beliefs are so important people are willing to kill and die for them. Among these are many beliefs that are philosophical, including, especially, opinions about values and principles. An important part of the rationale offered by George W. Bush for attacking Iraq was that Iraqis should be liberated from totalitarianism and should have freedom and democracy. At the time, most Americans assumed, without giving it much thought, that people universally want these things. Many Americans were surprised when supporters of Saddam Hussein, other Iraqi insurgents, and various religious leaders from the region actually denounced democracy, freedom of the press, and freedom of religion and referred to them as "Western perversions." Could it really be, some Americans wondered, that some people actually think totalitarianism is not evil and freedom and democracy are not good? Unfortunately, it became all too clear such "extremists" would stop at nothing to resist having what most Americans just assumed all people want and should have.

The American Civil War, which was fought over the institution of slavery, is another example of a clash in values that ended in bloodshed. And although the Cold War remained cold, it, too, pitted different belief systems—capitalism and communism—against each other. Wars often are fought for ideas. Philosophies matter.

Still, as you will discover when you read this book, many philosophical questions are abstract and theoretical, and few of us would resort to physical methods to defend them. Yet even abstract and theoretical issues can connect to ideas that people will go to extremes to enforce, defend, or spread. The philosophy department, as philosopher Van Meter Ames once said, works with potentially explosive material, dangerous stuff.

WHAT IS PHILOSOPHY?

The word **philosophy** comes from the Greek *philein,* which means "to love," and *sophia,* which means "knowledge" or "wisdom." Because knowledge can be discovered in many fields, the Greeks (who invented philosophy) thought of any person who sought knowledge in any area as a philosopher. Thus, philosophy once encompassed nearly everything that counted as knowledge.

This view of philosophy persisted for more than two thousand years. The full title of Sir Isaac Newton's *Principles,* in which in 1729 Newton set forth his famous theories of mechanics, mathematics, and astronomy, is *Mathematical Principles of Natural Philosophy.* At that time, physics was still thought of as a variety of philosophy. In fact, at some point nearly every subject currently listed in your university's catalog would have been considered philosophy. If you continue your studies and obtain the highest degree in psychology, mathematics, economics, sociology, history, biology, political science, or practically any other subject, you will be awarded a PhD, the doctorate of philosophy.

However, philosophy can no longer claim those subject areas that have grown up and moved out of it. What, then, is philosophy today?

PHILOSOPHICAL QUESTIONS

When we are confronted with a stark clash of values such as happened in the Iraq war, we might well wonder whether there are objective standards or criteria by which the opposed philosophies might be evaluated. Is democracy *really* a good? Does the United States do the right and proper thing in trying to spread freedom throughout the world? Well, of course we think so. George W. Bush referred to freedom as "almighty God's gift to each man and woman in this world," which fact, in his opinion, morally required America to spread it.[1] But the terrorists fighting America believe they are commanded by God to resist. Both sides cannot be correct, and if it is the other side that is mistaken, how do we know that? We might try to settle things by polling the world to see what most people think, but those who regard democracy as a "perversion" won't accept the democratic assumption on which that solution depends.

---

[1] See, for example, Bush's speech on April 4, 2004, in Buffalo, New York (http://www.whitehouse.gov/news/releases/2004/04/20040420-2.html).

To understand a subject, we should look at the questions it tries to answer. Is it good to spread freedom? How do we know that? And, by the way, what is freedom? These are questions of philosophy. As you can see, these questions are quite unlike those asked by economists, physicists, historians, communication studies experts, and so forth.

Here are a few other examples of philosophical questions.

- To what extent do we have a moral obligation to people we don't know? For that matter, to what extent do we have a moral obligation to nonhuman living things? How about the environment: do we have a moral obligation to it?

- What are the ethically legitimate functions and scope of government? What form of government is best? What is the proper connection between religion and the state? Questions like these separate Democrats from Republicans, conservatives from liberals, communists from capitalists, and theocrats from democrats.

- Do people have natural rights? If so, how do we know that? Where do they come from? What makes one person's list of rights superior to another person's?

- Is there a God? Perhaps just as important, Does it make any difference whether there is or isn't a God?

- Do ends justify means?

- What, if anything, is the self? Is a person more than a physical body? Do people really have free will?

- What is truth? Beauty? Art?

- Is it possible to know anything with absolute certainty?

- Does the universe have a purpose? Does life? Is there order in the cosmos independent of what the mind puts there?

- What is time?

- Could anything have happened before the Big Bang?

Clearly, it is *possible* to go through life without spending a moment wondering about such questions, but most of us have at least occasional moments of reflection about one or another of them. In fact, it is pretty difficult not to think philosophically from time to time. Whenever we think about a topic long enough, if our thinking is the least bit organized we may end up engaged in philosophy. Real-life ethical dilemmas provide an excellent illustration. For example, situations arise in which we must balance our own needs against the needs of others we care about—an aging parent might require care, for instance. Of course, we will try to determine the extent of our obligation. But we may go beyond this and ask what *makes* this our obligation, or even more generally, what makes *anything* our obligation. Is it simply that it strikes us that way? Or is there some feature of situations that requires a certain response? If we are led to questions like these, the rest of the university curriculum will be of little help. Other subjects tell us how things are or how they work or how they came about, but not what we should do or why we should do it. Unfortunately, when most people reach this point in their reflections, they really don't know what to think next.

Of course, ethical dilemmas are not the only questions that lead one into philosophy. For instance, these days a controversy exists as to whether Intelligent Design is a scientific theory on all fours with evolution.[2] Although many scientists are prepared (and qualified) to answer this question, in fact it is *not* a scientific question; you aren't likely to find an article about it in a scientific journal. It is, rather, a question in the *philosophy* of science.

To take quite a different example of how philosophical questions crop up in everyday contexts, in *The Matrix* movie trilogy, the hero discovers that the world humans live in is in fact a computer-generated simulated reality created by machines to keep people under their control. The movies raise the question, How do *you* know *you* are not in the matrix? Or, more generally, Can one really tell the difference between appearance and reality? This very question was asked by the first philosophers more than two thousand years ago and has been discussed in various forms by philosophers throughout the ages.

Other sci-fi movies portray robots that think like people. Arnold Schwarzenegger appears in some of these movies. Will it someday be possible to build a computer that can actually think? The question requires a *philosophical* response. Of course, you might say, "Well, let's just wait and see what they come up with." Unfortunately, you can't just go *observe* whether computers are thinking. Even if scientists succeeded in building a robot that walked and talked and acted like Arnold Schwarzenegger, one still might reasonably deny that the robot actually thought. "It isn't made out of flesh and blood," you might say. But then beings from other galaxies might think even though they are not made out of flesh and blood, so why must computers be made out of flesh and blood to think? Is it perhaps because computers don't have "souls" or aren't alive? Well, what *is* a soul, anyway? Why aren't computers alive? What is it to *be* alive? These are philosophical questions. Philosophers have spent a great deal of time analyzing and trying to answer them.

As can be gathered from what we have said so far, an important feature of philosophical questions is that they cannot be answered in any straightforward way by the discovery of some fact or collection of facts. Certainly, facts often are relevant to a philosophical question, but they cannot by themselves provide an answer. To illustrate this point, we might consider Matthew Nagle, a star athlete in high school whose spinal cord was severed when he was stabbed in the neck after a fireworks show on July 3, 2001. Researchers at New England Sinai Hospital and Rehabilitation Center in Rhode Island planted a small sensor on the surface of the motor cortex area of Nagle's brain. The sensor had tiny electrodes that penetrated the surface of his brain, where they picked up electrical signals from brain neurons and transmitted them to a pedestal protruding from Nagle's scalp. The pedestal was connected to computers, and over time Nagle learned how to turn a TV on and off, change channels and volume, play Pong, open e-mail, and do other things just by thinking about them. "I can't put it into words," he said. "It's just—I use my brain. I just thought it. I said, 'Cursor go up to the top right.' And it did."[3]

---

[2] Intelligent Design is the idea that some features of the universe and of living things can be explained only by an intelligent cause—God—not by a natural process.

[3] http://www.pbs.org/wnet/religionandethics/week846/feature.html.

Mr. Nagle died in 2007, from sepsis. His attacker, Nicholas Cirignano, currently is serving time for the attack and has recently been arraigned on a charge of second-degree murder for Nagle's death.[4]

Now, at the center of the controversy about whether a computer or a robot could think is the vexing philosophical problem of the relationship between thought and the brain. Experts from various fields, including computer science, cognitive science, and brain science, are grappling with this philosophical issue. A computer chip is a physical thing, and so is the brain; but a thought (many people would say) is something quite different. However, we need to remember, it is a *computer* that caused Matthew Nagle's TV set to change channels, and it was electrical activity in Mr. Nagle's brain that caused the computer to do that. Was Mr. Nagle's thought something *separate* from that electrical activity? This is a philosophical question that you cannot answer just by looking, and the research with Matthew Nagle does not answer it.

Often, too, philosophers ask questions about things that seem so obvious we might not wonder about them—for example, the nature of change. That things change is obvious, and we might not see anything puzzling in the fact. If something changes, it becomes different; so what?

For one thing, if we have a *different* thing, then we seem to be considering *two* things, the original thing and the new, different thing. Therefore, strictly speaking, shouldn't we say not that something changed but rather that it was *replaced?* If, over the course of years, you replaced every part in the Prius you bought—every part, the engine block, all door panels, each nut, bolt, and piece of steel, glass, rubber, vinyl, battery, or whatever—would you still have the same Prius? If you gathered up all the original pieces and put them together again, would that be the original Prius?

Perhaps these questions seem to be questions of nomenclature or semantics and of no practical interest. But over the course of a lifetime every molecule in a person's body may possibly (or probably!) be replaced. Thus, we might wonder, say, whether an old man who has been in prison for forty years for a murder he committed as a young man is really the same person as the young man. Since (let us assume) not a single molecule of the young man is in the old man, wasn't the young man in fact replaced? If so, can his guilt possibly pertain to the old man, who is in fact a different man? What is at stake here is whether the old man did in fact commit murder, and it is hard to see how this might be simply a matter of semantics.

Other times, philosophical questions come up when beliefs don't fit together the way we would like. We believe, for example, that anything that happens was caused to happen. We also believe that a cause *makes* its effect happen—if spoiled meat caused you to get sick, it *made* you sick. But we also believe that when we voluntarily decide to do something, nothing made us decide. And that belief seems to imply that our decision wasn't caused. So, which is it? Is every happening caused? Or are some happenings uncaused? Or is it perhaps that decisions aren't actually "happenings"? Do you see a way out of this dilemma? If so, congratulations. You are philosophizing.

---

[4] http://www.patriotledger.com/archive/x1082097278/Cirignano-charged-with-2nd-degree-murder-in-death-of-Matthew-Nagle.

Which Came First, the Chicken or the Egg?

What comes to mind for many people when they think of philosophy and of philosophical questions is either or both of these inquiries: "Which came first, the chicken or the egg?" and "If there is nobody around, does a tree falling in a forest make a sound?"

The first question is not particularly philosophical and, in the light of evolution, is not even especially difficult: the egg came first.

The second question is often supposedly resolved by distinguishing between sound viewed as the mental experience of certain waves contacting certain sensory organs and sound as the waves themselves. If sensory organs are absent, it is said, there can be no sound-as-experience, but there can still be sound-as-waves. Philosophy, however, asks not simply whether a tree falling in the forest makes a sound if no one is there but, rather, *If nobody is there, is there even a forest?* Is there even a universe? In other words, the question, for philosophers, is whether things depend for their existence on being perceived and, if so, how we know that. A somewhat similar question (equally philosophical) is debated by contemporary astrophysicists, who wonder whether the universe and its laws require the presence of intelligent observers for their existence.

MISCONCEPTIONS ABOUT PHILOSOPHY

A common misconception about philosophy, one that goes with the idea that philosophical questions are unanswerable, is expressed in the comment, "Philosophy never makes any progress." Now, progress comes in many forms. It doesn't happen only when questions are answered. Questions can be clarified, subdivided, and found to rest on confusions. They can be partially answered. These are all forms of progress. Even when a question is abandoned as unanswerable, that, too, is progress. Earlier answers to a question can be considered inadequate even if the final answer isn't in, and that's progress as well.

Another idea people have is that as soon as progress is made in a philosophical inquiry, the matter is turned over to (or becomes) another field of learning. It is true, as we have already observed, that many disciplines that today are independent of philosophy had their origin within philosophy. But philosophy doesn't always relegate its subjects to other disciplines. To take the most obvious example, logic is still a branch of philosophy, despite an enormous expansion in scope, complexity, and explanatory power during the last hundred years.

A couple of other ideas people have about philosophy ought to be discussed here at the outset.

First is the idea that *one person's philosophy is as correct as the next person's* and that *any philosophical position is as good, valid, or correct as any other opinion.* This idea is especially widespread when it comes to values. If one person thinks that one should contribute a major part of one's income to help support an aging parent, and another person thinks a much lower limit is called for, you might say something like, "Well, the first person's view is correct for that person, and the second person's view is correct for the second person." Or let's say you think there is nothing wrong with same-sex marriage, and your roommate doesn't agree. You might be tempted to say something like, "Well, my view is correct for me, and my roommate's view is correct for my roommate."

"My view is correct for me, and my roommate's view is correct for my roommate." What this means is far from clear. Does it mean it would be okay for you to marry someone of the same sex but wrong for your roommate to do so? That proposal probably would not be acceptable either to you or to your roommate. If your roommate thinks gay marriage is wrong, he or she probably thinks it is wrong for *you* as well as for him or her. He or she probably thinks gay marriage is wrong, period. And someone who believes there is nothing wrong with gay marriage probably doesn't think there is anything wrong with either you or your roommate marrying someone of the same sex.

In other words, if you and your roommate disagree as to whether there is anything wrong with two people of the same sex getting married, you cannot both be correct. You and your hypothetical roommate have contradictory opinions that *cannot* both be correct. So much, then, for thinking that one person's philosophy is as correct as the next person's or that any philosophical position is as good, valid, or correct as any other opinion. This may hold true for such matters as whether chocolate ice cream tastes good, but it does not hold true for a philosophical thesis.

Another misconception about philosophy is that it is *nothing but* opinion. In fact, we should distance ourselves from this notion, or at least from the "nothing but" part. This is because philosophy *requires opinions to be supported by good reasoning.* If you express your opinion without providing supporting reasoning, your philosophy teacher is apt to say something like, "Well, that is an interesting opinion," but he or she won't say that you have produced good philosophy. Philosophy requires supporting your opinions—which, by the way, can be hard work.

Another idea people sometimes have when they first enter into philosophy is that "truth is relative." Now, there are numerous things a person might mean by that statement. If he or she means merely that people's beliefs are relative to their perspectives or cultures, then there is no problem. If, however, the person means that the same sentence might be both true and not true depending on one's perspective or culture, then he or she is mistaken. The same sentence cannot be both true and not true, and whatever a person wishes to convey by the remark, "Truth is relative," it cannot be that. Of course, two different people from two different cultures or perspectives might *mean* something different by the same words, but that is a separate issue.

A different sort of misconception people have about philosophy is that it is light reading, something you relax with in the evening after all the serious work of the day is done. In reality, philosophical writing generally takes time and effort to understand. Often it seems to be written in familiar, everyday language, but that can be deceiving. It is best to approach a work in philosophy with the kind of mental preparedness and alertness appropriate for a textbook in mathematics or science. You should expect to be able to read *an entire novel* in the time it takes to understand just a *few pages* of philosophy! To understand philosophy, you have to reread a passage several times and think about it a lot. If your instructor assigns what seem to be short readings, don't celebrate. It takes much time to understand philosophy.

8   Chapter 1 · *Powerful Ideas*

Does a tree falling in the forest make a sound when nobody is around to hear it? Never mind that! Is there even a forest if there is nobody to observe it?

A PHILOSOPHICAL TOOL KIT

Philosophy isn't light reading, and it isn't mere expression of opinion. Philosophers support their positions with arguments, which (ideally) make it plain why the reasonable person will accept what they say.

Argument

When you support a position by giving a reason for accepting it, you are giving an **argument.**[5] **Logic,** the study of correct inference, is concerned with whether and to what extent a reason truly does support a conclusion. Giving and rebutting arguments (itself a form of argument) is the most basic philosophical activity; it distinguishes philosophy from mere opinion.

To illustrate, if you tell someone you believe that God exists, that's not philosophy. That's just you saying something about yourself. Even if you add, "I believe

[5] When you see a word or phrase in bold print in this book, it is defined in the index/glossary at the back of the book.

in God because I was raised a Catholic," that's still just biography, not philosophy. If, however, you say, "God must exist because the universe couldn't have caused itself," then you have given an *argument* that God exists (or existed). This remark counts as philosophy.

But if you want to be good at philosophy, you must also consider challenges to and criticisms of your arguments. Such challenges are known as **counterarguments.** Suppose, for example, someone challenges your argument with "Well, if God can be self-caused, then why can't the universe?" You are now being called upon to *defend* your assumption that the universe could not be self-caused. Good philosophizing requires the ability to reason correctly, to defend assumptions, and to anticipate and rebut rebuttals.

The Socratic Method

Philosophers have spent much time over the centuries trying to arrive at a proper understanding of several important concepts: truth, beauty, knowledge, justice, and others you will be reading about shortly. One of the most famous of all philosophers, the Greek philosopher Socrates [SOK-ruh-teez] (c. 470–399 B.C.E.), championed a method for doing this, which is now called the Socratic method. To see how this works, imagine that you and Socrates are discussing *knowledge:*

> *You:* You're asking me what knowledge is? Well, when you believe something very strongly, that's knowledge.
>
> *Socrates:* But that would mean that kids who believe in fairies actually know there are fairies, if they believe this strongly.
>
> *Y:* That's a good point. To know something, then, isn't just to believe it very strongly. The belief also must be true.
>
> *S:* That still doesn't sound quite right. That means a mere *hunch* is knowledge, if a person believes it strongly, and it turns out to be correct.
>
> *Y:* Well, you're right again. So, for one to know something, one must believe it strongly, it must be true, AND it must NOT be a mere hunch. In other words, it must be based on good evidence or solid reasoning. . . .

The exchange might continue until you offer an analysis of knowledge with which Socrates cannot take issue.

So, the **Socratic method** as practiced by Socrates involves proposing a definition, rebutting it by counterexample, modifying it in the light of the counterexample, rebutting the modification, and so forth. Needless to say, the method can be practiced by one person within his or her own mind. Clearly, the method can help advance understanding of concepts, but it can also be used to improve arguments or positions.

If you are reading this book as part of a class in philosophy, you may see your instructor utilizing the Socratic method with the class.

Thought Experiments

"Cassie, share! Would you like it if Jessica didn't give any of her candy to you?" Mom, here, is asking Cassie to do a **thought experiment**—to imagine a situation in order to extract a lesson about something (in this case about sharing and selfishness). Imagining yourself in someone else's shoes is a simple example of a thought experiment.

Thought experiments are not uncommon in science; in philosophy, they are among the most common methods used to try to establish something. You will encounter thought experiments in this book, and although some of them may seem far-fetched, you shouldn't discount them for that reason. For example, to establish whether time travel is possible, a philosopher might ask us to imagine someone stepping into a time machine, going back in time to before she was born and, while there, accidentally killing her parents. The thought experiment seems to show that, on one hand, the person existed at the time she entered the time machine; but, on the other hand, because her parents never gave birth to her, she could not have existed at that or any other time. The thought experiment thus shows, or seems to show, that time travel leads to contradictions and therefore is impossible.

Reductio ad Absurdum

Philosophers will often attempt to establish a thesis by using the ***reductio ad absurdum***—demonstrating that the contradictory of the thesis is or leads to (i.e., "reduces to") an absurdity. The thought experiment about time travel is an example of this method as well as an illustration of a thought experiment.

The most famous *reductio ad absurdum* in the history of philosophy is St. Anselm's ontological proof that God exists. As we shall see in detail in Chapter 13, St. Anselm (c. 1033–1109) began his famous proof by assuming—merely for the sake of argument—that God, a being "greater than which cannot be conceived," does *not* exist. This assumption, Anselm argued, leads to the absurd result that a being greater than which cannot be conceived is not a being greater than which cannot be conceived. In other words, the idea that God does not exist "reduces" to an absurdity; therefore, God exists. Likewise, in the foregoing dialogue between you and Socrates, Socrates argued that the assumption that knowledge is identical with strong belief leads to an absurd result; which means that knowledge is *not* identical with strong belief.

Fallacies

A **fallacy** is a mistake in reasoning. Some mistakes are so common they have earned names, many in Latin. You won't often find philosophers making these mistakes, but you will often find them referring to the mistakes, so you should at least be familiar with the more common specimens.

• **Switching the burden of proof:** Logically, you can't prove your position by asking an opponent to disprove it. You don't prove God exists by challenging a listener to prove God doesn't exist.

• **Begging the question:** These days, you frequently hear people assert that something "begs the question." Generally, when people say this they mean the thing *invites* some question. However, this is not what "begging the question" means to logicians or philosophers. To them, you *beg the question* when you *assume* the very thing you are trying to prove, which means your "proof" doesn't go anywhere. For example, if you want to give a reason for thinking that God exists, and your reason is that "It says so in the Bible, and the Bible is the word of God," you are assuming that God exists, when that is what you were supposed to prove. It's like trying to prove that someone committed a crime because "he was the one who did it."

• *Argumentum ad hominem* (argument against the person): This fallacy amounts to transferring the qualities of a spokesperson to his or her insights, arguments, beliefs, or positions. For example, thinking that a person's *position* is frightening because the person himself is frightening would be an obvious mistake in reasoning, an *argumentum ad hominem*.

It is especially important to note that when someone—Susan, let us say—has changed her mind about something, it doesn't mean that what she now thinks is incorrect. That *Susan* has contradicted herself doesn't mean that what she has just said is contradictory. If a critic of a war supported the war at an earlier time, that fact doesn't mean her criticism is defective. The earlier support and the present criticism are logically unrelated. That someone has changed positions is a fact about the *person*, not his or her position. Confusing these two things is perhaps the most common mistake in reasoning on this planet.

From time to time, you hear someone ask an opponent if he or she really believes what he or she has said. That question is irrelevant to the truth or falsity of what the person has said. In his book *Republic*, Plato portrays Socrates as conversing with the Athenian general Thrasymachus. Socrates asks Thrasymachus whether he really believes his own argument. Thrasymachus responds by saying,

> What difference does it make to you whether I believe it or not? Why don't you test the argument?"[6]

Thrasymachus's response is 100% correct, in response to a question like Socrates's.

• **Straw man:** This fallacy occurs when you think you have refuted a view by distorting, misrepresenting, or exaggerating it. When the Irish philosopher George Berkeley maintained that physical objects really exist only in the mind, the English writer Samuel Johnson "refuted" Berkeley by kicking a rock and proclaiming, "I refute him thus!" But Samuel Johnson misrepresented Berkeley, for Berkeley never maintained that rocks aren't solid; Berkeley's position was that solid things like rocks (and legs and boots) exist only in the mind.

Suppose we argue that there is no such thing as free will, because our decisions are predetermined by our heredity and environment. If an opponent then points

---

[6] Plato, *Plato in Twelve Volumes*, Vols. 5 & 6, translated by Paul Shorey. Cambridge, MA, Harvard University Press; London, William Heinemann Ltd. 1969.

Philosophy begins in amazement and curiosity.

out that people obviously can choose what they do, the opponent has brought in a straw man. Our position wasn't that people don't make choices but that choices were predetermined by heredity and environment. What we said was X; our opponent acts as if we had said Y.

- **False dilemma** (either–or fallacy): This is the fallacy of offering two choices when in fact more options exist. Suppose someone says, "Either God exists, or there is no explanation for the universe." This is a false dilemma because it ignores a third possibility, namely, that there is an explanation of the universe that does not involve God.

- **Appeal to emotion:** This is trying to establish a point by arousing pity, anger, fear, and so on. Suppose we try to "prove" that God exists with the "argument" that "if you don't believe in him, you will burn in hell." We haven't really given an argument; we are just trying to scare the listener into agreeing with us.

- **Red herring:** When someone brings an irrelevancy into a conversation, it is called a red herring. As you can see, many of the fallacies just discussed qualify as red herrings.

If you are reading this book as part of a course, there could be lots of discussion in class, and the discussion will involve disagreements. In addition, people will defend their positions with arguments. Perhaps you will find examples of these fallacies among the arguments you hear. You may even find an example or two in the arguments you read in this book.

THE DIVISIONS OF PHILOSOPHY

Most philosophical questions tend to fall into one of these four areas:

• *Questions related to being or existence.* **Metaphysics** is the branch of philosophy that is concerned with these questions. Two basic questions of metaphysics are: What is being? and What are its fundamental features and properties? Some of the questions listed earlier are questions of metaphysics, including: Is there a God? and Do people really have free will? Metaphysics has little to do with the occult or Tarot cards and the like.

• *Questions related to knowledge.* **Epistemology,** the theory of knowledge, is the branch of philosophy concerned with these questions. What is the nature of knowledge, and what are its criteria, sources, and limits? These are basic questions of epistemology, and thus it includes such questions from the list at the beginning of the chapter as: What is truth? and Is it possible to know anything with absolute certainty?

• Questions related to values. Included under this heading are primarily (1) **moral philosophy (ethics),** the philosophical study of moral judgments; (2) **social philosophy,** the philosophical study of society and its institutions; (3) **political philosophy,** which focuses on the state and seeks to determine its justification and ethically proper organization; and (4) **aesthetics,** the philosophical study of art and of value judgments about art.

• Questions pertaining to the theory of correct inference, otherwise known as **Logic,** which seeks to investigate and establish the criteria of valid reasoning and demonstration.

Part One of this book is devoted to metaphysics and epistemology, which are closely related. Part Two is concerned with questions of values, especially moral and political values. We talked a bit about logic earlier in this chapter.

Although philosophy has four main branches, they do not each contain an equal number of theories or concepts or words. Your library probably has more holdings under political philosophy than under the other areas and the fewest under epistemology or aesthetics.

There are other ways of dividing philosophy. Many universities offer philosophy courses that examine the fundamental assumptions and methods of other disciplines and areas of intellectual inquiry, such as science (philosophy of science), language (philosophy of language), and religion (philosophy of religion). Philosophy of science and philosophy of language are covered in Part One because most of the issues in these two areas are either metaphysical or epistemological issues. Part Three is devoted entirely to the philosophy of religion, especially to the question of whether God's existence can be proved.

14   Chapter 1 · *Powerful Ideas*

The fourth and last part of this book is called "Other Voices," and in it we consider various current themes in philosophy as well as influences and traditions beyond mainstream Western philosophy.

THE BENEFITS OF PHILOSOPHY

What can you do with a background in philosophy? As our friend Troy Jollimore said, the list of things you *can't* do with a background in philosophy is shorter than the list of things you can do. Life favors people who have the skills philosophy students tend to have in abundance. Take law school, for instance. You may have no intention of becoming a lawyer, but you know that, to be a lawyer, you must first be admitted to a law school, which requires no little mental ability. An interesting fact is that the Graduate Record Examination (GRE) scores of pre-law philosophy students tend to be considerably higher than the scores of other pre-law students, such as those majoring in, say, political science, communications, or public administration.[7] Or take the Medical College Admission Test (MCAT): Philosophy majors score higher, on average, than other humanities

---

[7] http://www.lclark.edu/~phil/gre.html.

majors.[8] Or the Graduate Management Aptitude Test (GMAT): the mean score for philosophy majors is better than the mean score of any of the various business majors (accounting, management, and so forth).[9] In other words, philosophy majors do better than business majors on the most important test for business and management schools.

According to one source, on the combined Verbal, Quantitative, and Analytical sections of the GRE,

> Philosophy students score higher than *every* other major in the Humanities and Arts, higher than *every* major in the Social Sciences, higher than *every* major in the Life Sciences, higher than *every* major in Education, higher than *every* major in Business, and higher than *every* major listed under "Other Fields." In fact, Philosophy students score higher than four out of the six majors listed in Physical Sciences, and five out of the seven listed in Engineering. . . . averaging the rank order in each of the areas of the GRE, Philosophy does better than *any other major* of the fifty listed.[10]

Such facts suggest philosophy students have exceptional aptitude for some of the most useful of all skills, including analytical thinking, critical thinking, careful reasoning, problem solving, and communication. Now, one of the things you learn when you study philosophy is that causal connections are difficult to establish, and it is an open question whether studying philosophy makes students better thinkers or whether better thinkers are attracted to philosophy in the first place. But philosophical training does emphasize the aforementioned skills. Finding answers to philosophical questions involves being good at exposition and logic, making nuanced distinctions, recognizing subtle similarities and differences, and detecting unstated assumptions.

More than this, those who have learned their philosophical lessons well may not be as prone as others to superficiality and dogmatism. Philosophy requires objectivity, reasonableness, and an open mind. These general attributes, along with the critical thinking skills that come with the practice of philosophizing, can stand one in good stead when faced with the problems life generously provides.

CHECKLIST

Key Terms and Concepts

aesthetics 13	begging the	false dilemma 12	*reductio ad*
appeal to emotion 12	question 11	logic 8	*absurdum* 10
argument 8	counterargument 9	metaphysics 13	social philosophy 13
argumentum ad	epistemology 13	moral philosophy	Socratic method 9
hominem 11	fallacy 10	(ethics) 13	straw man 11
		philosophy 2	switching the burden
		political	of proof 10
		philosophy 13	thought
		red herring 12	experiment 10

---

[8] http://falcon.tamucc.edu/~philosophy/pmwiki/pmwiki.php/PhilosophyProgram/WhyPhilosophy.

[9] http://falcon.tamucc.edu/~philosophy/pmwiki/pmwiki.php/PhilosophyProgram/WhyPhilosophy.

[10] http://www.lclark.edu/~phil/gre.html.

16   Chapter 1 · *Powerful Ideas*

QUESTIONS FOR DISCUSSION AND REVIEW

1. Why do you want to study philosophy?

2. Now that you've read this chapter, is philosophy what you expected it to be?

3. Why is it that the most advanced degree in so many fields is the doctor of philosophy?

4. Which of the questions raised in this chapter is most interesting to you? What do you think the answer is?

5. Can two people both be correct if one says, "Two members of the same sex should not have the right to get married," and the other says, "Two members of the same sex should have the right to get married"? Defend your answer with an argument.

6. If, by the time you become an adult, every molecule in your body has been replaced with a different one, are you-the-adult the same person as you-the-child?

7. Are all philosophical questions unanswerable? How about the question you mentioned in question 4?

8. Does it matter if God exists? Take a position, and defend it with an argument.

9. Does what is true depend on what your society believes is true? Was the world flat when people believed it was flat?

10. "2 + 2 = 4." Was this true before there were people (or other beings) around to think it? Explain.

LINKS

http://www.jimpryor.net/teaching/guidelines/writing.html
A guide to writing philosophy papers. We strongly encourage you to read it before you write your first paper.

http://www.ditext.com/encyc/frame.html
This resource enables you to compare topics listed in major Internet encyclopedias of philosophy.

http://plato.stanford.edu/contents.html
An excellent encyclopedia of philosophy. You can look up most philosophical topics here.

http://www.askphilosophers.org
Ask a question, get an answer, maybe.

SUGGESTED FURTHER READINGS

Here are some of the best reference books on philosophy in the English language.

Donald Abel, *Fifty Readings in Philosophy*, 2nd ed. (New York: McGraw-Hill, 2003). Readings by important philosophers on a broad range of subjects.

A. J. Ayer and Jane O'Grady, *A Dictionary of Philosophical Quotations* (Malden, Mass.: Blackwell, 1994). Essential quotations taken from the great Western philosophers.

Simon Blackburn, *The Oxford Dictionary of Philosophy* (New York: Oxford University Press, 1996). Concise and readable.

Stuart Brown, Diane Collinson, and Robert Wilkinson, eds., *Biographical Dictionary of Twentieth-Century Philosophers* (New York: Routledge, 2002). Brief reviews of twentieth-century philosophers.

A Buddhist Glossary, http://www.chezpaul.org.uk/buddhism/books/glossary.htm. Brief definitions of Buddhist terms.

Clive Cazeaux, *The Continental Aesthetics Reader* (New York: Routledge, 2000). Readings in European aesthetics from the phenomenologist, poststructuralist, psychoanalyst, and feminist traditions.

Diane Collinson, *Fifty Major Philosophers* (London: Routledge, 2006). A relatively accessible and short reference book.

Concise Routledge Encyclopedia of Philosophy (New York: Routledge, 2003). Short entries on philosophical terms and philosophers.

F. C. Copleston, *History of Philosophy*, 9 vols. (New York: Doubleday, 1965). Still the most complete history of philosophy available to English-only readers.

Eliot Deutsch and Ron Bontekoe, *A Companion to World Philosophies* (Malden, Mass.: Blackwell, 1999). Articles on philosophical issues concerning traditional ideas from around the world.

Dictionary of Philosophy of Mind, http://www.artsci.wustl.edu/~philos/MindDict/. Excellent resource in the philosophy of mind.

Paul Edwards, ed., *The Encyclopedia of Philosophy*, 8 vols. (New York: Macmillan, 1967). If you need to find out something about a philosopher or philosophical topic prior to 1967, begin here.

History of Philosophy, http://www.friesian.com/history.htm. Essays on many philosophical topics; the ones we have looked at seem pretty good and not too difficult.

Ted Honderich, *The Oxford Companion to Philosophy* (New York: Oxford University Press, 2005). A dictionary of short articles, definitions, and short biographies.

The Internet Encyclopedia of Philosophy, http://www.iep.utm.edu. Maintained by the University of Tennessee at Martin. A pretty good source of information on philosophical topics.

Frank Jackson and Michael Smith, eds., *The Oxford Handbook of Contemporary Philosophy* (New York: Oxford University Press, 2005). Good entries on recent thinking on the philosophy of mind, language, and science as well as moral and political philosophy.

Anthony Kenny, ed., *The Oxford History of Western Philosophy* (New York: Oxford University Press, 1994). An authoritative and beautifully illustrated history of Western philosophy, with articles by important contemporary philosophers.

Thomas Mautner, ed., *A Dictionary of Philosophy* (Cambridge, Mass.: Blackwell, 1996). Brief and useful.

Meta-Encyclopedia of Philosophy, http://www.ditext.com/encyc/frame.html. Enables you to compare the entries in various philosophy encyclopedias on various topics. A good place to start research.

Alex Neill and Aaron Ridley, *The Philosophy of Art: Readings Ancient and Modern* (New York: McGraw-Hill, 1995). Readings on aesthetics, starting with Plato.

Oxford Reference Online, http://www.oxfordreference.com/pub/views/home.html. Go here to subscribe to this premier service.

G. H. R. Parkinson, *An Encyclopaedia of Philosophy* (London: Routledge, 1988). A nice one-volume set of essays on most of the important topics in Anglo-American philosophy.

G. H. R. Parkinson and S. G. Shanker, gen. eds., *The Routledge History of Philosophy,* 10 vols. (London and New York: Routledge, various dates). A detailed chronological survey of the history of Western philosophy, together with chronologies and glossaries.

Philosophy Pages, from Garth Kemerling, http://www.philosophypages.com. A dictionary of philosophical terms and names.

Readings in Modern Philosophy, http://www.class.uidaho.edu/mickelsen/readings.htm. Writings of many modern philosophers from around 1500 to 1750. If you like the excerpts you read in this text, look here for more.

Reference.allrefer.com, http://reference.allrefer.com/encyclopedia/categories/philos.html. Another nice dictionary/encyclopedia that includes philosophy.

Bertrand Russell, *A History of Western Philosophy* (New York: Simon & Schuster, 1945). As readable as a novel, though critics find Russell brash and opinionated.

Stanford Encyclopedia of Philosophy, http://plato.stanford.edu/. Start here to access this authoritative source.

J. O. Urmson and Jonathan Rée, *The Concise Encyclopedia of Western Philosophy and Philosophers* (London: Routledge, 1995). A fine one-volume survey from a British viewpoint.

Mary Ellen Waithe, ed., *A History of Women Philosophers,* 4 vols. (Dordrecht: Martinus Nijhoff/Kluwer Press, 1987, 1989, 1991, 1995). Vol. 1: *Ancient Women Philosophers* (through A.D. 500); Vol. 2: *Medieval, Renaissance, and Enlightenment Women Philosophers* (500–1600); Vol. 3: *Modern Women Philosophers* (1600–1900); Vol. 4: *Contemporary* (twentieth century) *Women Philosophers.*

3

Socrates, Plato

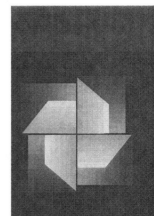

Thus the soul, since it is immortal and has been born many times, and has seen all things both here and in the other world, has learned everything that is.   —Plato, *Meno*

Love [is] between the mortal and the immortal. . . . [It is] a grand spirit which brings together the sensible world and the eternal world and merges them into one great whole.   —Diotima in Plato's *Symposium*, 202e

I [Socrates] affirm that the good is the beautiful.   —Plato's *Lysis*, 216d

I f you have heard of only one philosopher, it is probably one of the big three: Socrates, Plato, or Aristotle. These three were the most important philosophers of ancient Greece and in some respects the most important, period. Plato was the pupil of Socrates, and Aristotle was the pupil of Plato. This chapter covers Socrates and Plato; the following chapter, Aristotle.

SOCRATES

In the fifth century B.C.E., the center of Western civilization was Athens, a city-state and a democracy. This period of time was some three centuries after the first Olympic Games and the start of alphabetic writing, and approximately one century before Alexander the Great demonstrated that it is possible to conquer the world or what passed for it then. Fifty thousand citizens of Athens governed the city and the city's empire. Athenians did not settle disputes by brawling but rather by discussion and debate. Power was not achieved through wealth or physical strength or skill with weapons; it was achieved through words. Rhetoricians, men and women with sublime skill in debate, created plausible arguments for almost any assertion and, for a fee, taught others to do it too.

These rhetoricians, the Western world's first professors, were the **Sophists.** They were interested in practical things, and few had patience with metaphysical speculation. They demonstrated their rhetorical abilities by "proving" the seemingly unprovable—that is, by attacking commonly held views. The net effect was an examination and a critique of accepted standards of behavior within Athenian society. In this way, moral philosophy began. We will return to this topic in Chapter 10.

At the same time in the fifth century B.C.E., there also lived a stonemason with a muscular build and a keen mind, **Socrates** [SOK-ruh-teez] (470–399 B.C.E.). He wrote nothing, but we know quite a bit about him from Plato's famous dialogues, in which Socrates almost always stars. (Plato's later dialogues reflect Plato's own views, even though "Socrates" is doing the speaking in them. But we are able to extract a reasonably detailed picture of Socrates from the earlier dialogues.)

Given the spirit of the times, it is not surprising that Socrates shared some of the philosophical interests and practices of the Sophists. We must imagine him wandering about the city, engaging citizens in discussion and argument. He was a brilliant debater, and he was idolized by many young Athenians.

But Socrates did not merely engage in sophistry—he was not interested in arguing simply for the sake of arguing—he wanted to discover something important, namely, the *essential nature* of knowledge, justice, beauty, goodness, and, especially, traits of good character such as courage. The method of discovery he followed bears his name, the Socratic method. To this day, more than twenty centuries after his death, many philosophers equate proficiency within their own field with skill in the **Socratic** (or **dialectic**) **method.**

The method goes like this: Suppose you and Socrates wish to find out what knowledge is. You propose, tentatively, that knowledge is strong belief. Socrates then asks if that means that people who have a strong belief in, say, fairies must be said to *know* there are fairies. Seeing your mistake, you reconsider and offer a revised thesis: knowledge is not belief that is *strong* but belief that is *true.*

Socrates then says, "Suppose the true belief, which you say is knowledge, is based on a lucky guess. For instance, suppose I, Socrates, ask you to guess what kind of car I own, and you guess a Volvo. Even if your guess turns out to be right, would you call that knowledge?"

By saying this, Socrates has made you see that knowledge cannot be equated with true belief either. You must therefore attempt a better analysis. Eventually you may find a definition of knowledge that Socrates cannot refute.

So the Socratic/dialectic method is a search for the proper definition of a thing, a definition that will not permit refutation under Socratic questioning. The method does not imply that the questioner knows the essential nature of knowledge. It only demonstrates that the questioner is skilled at detecting misconceptions and at revealing them by asking the right questions. In many cases the process may not actually disclose the essence of the thing in question, and if

Socrates' prison—or what is left of it.

Plato's dialogues are an indication, Socrates himself did not have at hand many final, satisfactory definitions. Still, the technique will bring those who practice it closer to this final understanding.

The **Delphi Oracle** is said to have pronounced Socrates the wisest of people. (An oracle is a shrine where a priest delivers a god's response to a human question. The most famous oracle of all time was the Delphi Oracle, which was housed in the great temple to Apollo in ancient and Hellenistic Greece.) Socrates thought the pronouncement referred to the fact that he, unlike most people, was *aware* of his ignorance. Applying the Socratic method, one gets good at seeing misconceptions and learning to recognize one's own ignorance.

Socrates was not a pest who went around trapping people in argument and making them look idiotic. He was famous not only for his dialectical skill but also for his courage and stamina in battle. He staunchly opposed injustice, even at considerable risk to himself. His trial and subsequent death by drinking hemlock after his conviction (for "corrupting" young men and not believing in the city's gods) are reported by Plato in the gripping dialogues *Apology, Crito,* and *Phaedo.* These dialogues portray Socrates as an individual of impressive character and true grit. Although it would have been easy for him to escape from prison, he did not do so, because, according to Plato, by having chosen to live in Athens he had implicitly promised to obey the laws of the city.

Richard Robinson summarizes the greatest value of Socrates, as we perceive him through Plato, as lying in Socrates' clear conception of the demands placed on us by reason:

> [Socrates] impresses us, more than any other figure in literature, with the supreme importance of thinking as well as possible and making our actions conform to our thoughts. To this end he preaches the knowledge of one's own starting-points, the hypothetical entertainment of opinions, the exploration of their consequences and connections, the willingness to follow the argument wherever it leads, the public confession of one's thoughts, the invitation to others to criticize, the readiness to reconsider, and at the same time firm action in accordance with one's present beliefs. Plato's *Apology* has in fact made Socrates the chief martyr of reason as the gospels have made Jesus the chief martyr of faith.

PLATO

When we pause to consider the great minds of Western history, those rare individuals whose insight elevates the human intellect by a prodigious leap, we think immediately of Socrates' most famous student, **Plato** (c. 428–347 B.C.E.), and Plato's student, Aristotle (384–322 B.C.E.). Both Plato and Aristotle were interested in practically every subject, and each spoke intelligently on philosophical topics and problems. Platonic metaphysics formed the model for Christian theology for fifteen centuries. This model was superseded only when translations of Aristotle's works were rediscovered by European philosophers and theologians in the thirteenth century A.D. After this rediscovery, Aristotle's metaphysics came to predominate in Christian thinking, although Christianity is still Platonic in many, many ways.

Plato's Metaphysics: The Theory of Forms

Plato's metaphysics is known as the **Theory of Forms,** and it is discussed in several of the two dozen compositions we have referred to as **Plato's dialogues.** The most famous dialogue is the *Republic,* from the so-called middle period of Plato's writings, during which Plato reached the peak of his genius. The *Republic* also gives Plato's best-known account of the Theory of Forms.

According to Plato's Theory of Forms, what is truly real is not the objects we encounter in sensory experience but, rather, **Forms,** and these can only be grasped intellectually. Therefore, once you know what Plato's Forms are, you will understand the Theory of Forms and the essentials of Platonic metaphysics. Unfortunately, it is not safe to assume Plato had *exactly* the same thing in mind throughout his life when he spoke of the Forms. Nevertheless, Plato's concept is pretty clear and can be illustrated with an example or two.

The Greeks were excellent geometers, which is not surprising, because they invented the subject as a systematic science. Now, when a Greek geometer demonstrated some property of, say, *circularity,* he was not demonstrating the property of

PROFILE: Aristocles, a.k.a. Plato (c. 428–347 B.C.E.)

Plato was the nickname of an Athenian whose true name was Aristocles. The nickname, which means "broad shoulders," stuck, and so did this man's philosophy. Few individuals, if any, have had more influence on Western thought than Plato.

Plato initially studied with Cratylus, who was a follower of Heraclitus, and then with Socrates. He was also influenced by the Pythagoreans, from whom he may have derived his great respect for mathematics. Plato thought that the study of mathematics was a necessary introduction to philosophy, and it is said that he expelled from his Academy students who had difficulty with mathematical concepts.

Plato founded his Academy in 387, and it was the first multisubject, multiteacher institution of higher learning in Western civilization. The Academy survived for nine centuries, until the emperor Justinian closed it to protect Christian truth.

Plato's dialogues are divided into three groups. According to recent respected scholarship, the

Portrait of Plato. Eyes were not the artist's specialty, perhaps.

earliest include most importantly the *Apology*, which depicts and philosophically examines Socrates' trial and execution; the *Meno*, which is concerned with whether virtue can be taught; the *Gorgias*, which concerns the nature of right and wrong; and the first book of the *Republic*. The dialogues from the middle period include the remaining books of the *Republic*, *Phaedo*, *Symposium*, *Phaedrus*, *Cratylus*, *Parmenides*, and *Theaetetus*. In the most famous of these, the *Republic*, Plato explains and interrelates his conceptions of justice, the ideal state, and the Theory of Forms. Plato's later dialogues include most notably the *Timaeus*, which is Plato's account of the creation of the universe; the *Sophist*, which examines the nature of nonbeing; and the *Laws*, which is concerned with what laws a good constitution should contain. The *Laws* is Plato's longest dialogue and the only dialogue in which Socrates is not present.

something that could actually be found in the physical world. After all, you do not find circularity in the physical world: what you find are *things*—various round objects—that approach perfect circularity but are not *perfectly* circular. Even if you are drawing circles with an excellent compass and are paying close attention to what you are drawing, your "circle" is not perfectly circular. Thus, when a geometer discovered a property of circularity, for example, he was discovering something about an *ideal* thing. Circularity does not exist in the physical world. Circularity, then, is an example of a Form.

Here is another example. Consider two beautiful objects: a beautiful statue and a beautiful house. These are two very different objects, but they have *something* in common—they both qualify as beautiful. Beauty is another example of a Form. Notice that beauty, like circularity, is not something you encounter directly in the physical world. What you encounter in the physical world is always some object or other, a house or a statue or whatever, which may or may not be beautiful. But beauty itself is not something you meet up with; rather, you meet up with *objects* that to varying degrees *possess* beauty or, as Plato said, "participate" in the Form *beauty*. Beauty, like circularity, is an ideal thing, not a concrete thing.

You may be tempted to suppose that the Forms are just ideas or concepts in someone's mind. But this might be a mistake. Before any people were around, there were circular things, logs and round stones and so on—that is, things that came close in varying degrees to being perfectly circular. If there were circular things when there were no people around, or people-heads to have people-ideas in, it would seem that circularity is not just an idea in people's heads. It may be more difficult to suppose that there were beautiful things before there were people to think of things as beautiful, but this difficulty might only be due to assuming that "beauty is in the eyes of the beholder." Whether that assumption truly is justified is actually an unsettled question. (It is a question that belongs to the aesthetics branch of philosophy.)

Sometimes Plato's Forms are referred to as *Ideas,* and the Theory of Forms is also said to be the Theory of Ideas. But *Idea* is misleading because, as you can see, Plato's Forms are not the sort of ideas that exist in people. We will stick with the word *Forms.*

Forms have certain important and unusual features. We will begin by asking, How *old* is circularity? Immediately on hearing the question, you will realize that circularity is not any age. Circular things, sand dollars and bridge abutments and so on, are some age or other. But circularity itself has no age. The same thing is true of beauty, the Form. So we can see that the Forms are ageless, that is, *eternal.*

They are also *unchanging.* A beautiful house may change due to alterations or aging, but that couldn't happen to beauty itself. And you, having learned that the circumference of the circle is equal to π times twice the radius distance, aren't apt to worry that someday the circle may change and, when it does, the circumference will no longer equal $2\pi r$.

Finally, the Forms are *unmoving* and *indivisible.* Indeed, what sense would it make even to suppose that they might move or be physically divided?

When you think of these various characteristics of Forms and remember as well that Plato equated the Forms with true reality, you may begin to see why we stated that Plato's metaphysics formed the model for Christian theology. You may also be reminded, we hope, of what Parmenides said about true being (i.e., that it is eternal, unmoving, unchanging, and indivisible). Of course, you should also remember that for Parmenides there is only one being, but for Plato there are many Forms.

But why did Plato say that only the Forms are truly real? A thing is beautiful only to the extent it participates in the Form *beauty,* just as it is circular only if it participates in the Form *circularity.* Likewise, a thing is large only if it participates in the Form *largeness,* and the same principle would hold for all of a thing's properties. Thus, a large, beautiful, round thing—a beautiful, large, round oak table, for instance—couldn't be beautiful, large, or round if the Forms *beauty,* *largeness,* and *circularity* did not exist. Indeed, if the Forms *oak* and *table* did not exist, "it" wouldn't even be an oak table. Sensible objects—that is, the things we encounter in sensory experience—are what they are only if they sufficiently participate in their corresponding Forms. Sensible objects owe their reality to the Forms, so the ultimate reality belongs to the Forms.

Many people scold philosophers, mathematicians, and other thinkers for being concerned with abstractions and concepts. "That's all very interesting," they say about some philosophical or mathematical theory, "but I'm more interested in the *real* world." By "real world" they mean the world you experience with your senses. On the face of it, at least, Plato makes a convincing case that that world is *not* the real world at all.

The Cave

In the *Republic,* Plato uses a vivid allegory to explain his two-realms philosophy. He invites us to imagine a cave in which some prisoners are bound so that they can look only at the wall in front of them. Behind them is a fire whose light casts shadows of various objects on the wall in front of the prisoners. Because the prisoners cannot see the objects themselves, they regard the shadows they see as the true reality. One of the prisoners eventually escapes from the cave and, in the light of the sun, sees real objects for the first time, becoming aware of the big difference between them and the shadow images he had always taken for reality.

The cave, obviously, represents the world we see and experience with our senses, and the world of sunlight represents the realm of Forms. The prisoners represent ordinary people, who, in taking the sensible world to be the real world, are condemned to darkness, error, ignorance, and illusion. The escaped prisoner represents the philosopher, who has seen light, truth, beauty, knowledge, and true reality.

Of course, if the philosopher returns to the cave to tell the prisoners how things really are, they will think his brain has been addled. This difficulty is sometimes faced by those who have seen the truth and decide to tell others about it.

Plato was aware that there is a sense in which the objects we see and touch are real. Even appearances are *real* appearances. But Plato's position is that the objects we see and touch have a *lesser* reality because they can only approximate their Form and thus are always to some extent flawed. Any particular beautiful thing will always be deficient in beauty compared with the Form *beauty.* And, as any particular beautiful thing owes whatever degree of beauty it has to the Form *beauty,* the Form is the source of what limited reality as a beautiful thing the thing has.

Thus, Plato introduced into Western thought a *two-realms* concept. On one hand, there is the realm of particular, changing, sense-perceptible or "sensible" things. This realm Plato likened to a cave (see the box "The Cave"). It is the realm of flawed and lesser entities. Consequently, it is also, for those who concern themselves with sensible things, a source of error, illusion, and ignorance. On the other hand, there is the realm of Forms—eternal, fixed, and perfect—the source of all reality and of all true knowledge. This **Platonic dualism** was incorporated into Christianity and transmitted through the ages to our thought today, where it lingers still and affects our views on virtually every subject.

Now, Plato believed that some forms, especially the Forms *truth, beauty,* and *goodness,* are of a higher order than other Forms. For example, you can say of the Form *circularity* that it is beautiful, but you cannot say of the Form *beauty* that it is circular. So the Form *beauty* is higher than the Form *circularity.* This fact will turn out to be very important when we consider Plato's ethics in the second part of this book. Also, as we shall see in Part Two, Plato connected his Theory of Forms with a theory of the ideal state.

Plato's Theory of Knowledge

The first comprehensive theory of knowledge in philosophy was Plato's. Certainly many of his predecessors had implicit theories of knowledge, and some of them spoke explicitly on epistemological subjects. Some were quite skeptical. A **skeptic**

42   Part One · *Metaphysics and Epistemology: Existence and Knowledge*

Today's universities all descended from Plato's Academy.

is a doubter, a person who doubts that knowledge is possible. Xenophanes (c. 570–480 B.C.E.) declared that, even if truth were stated, it would not be known. Heraclitus (c. 535–475 B.C.E.), whom we talked about earlier, was a contemporary of Xenophanes. He had the idea that, just as you cannot step into the same river twice, everything is in flux; this theory suggests it is impossible to discover any fixed truth beyond what is expressed in the theory itself. (Heraclitus, however, apparently did not himself deduce skeptical conclusions from his metaphysical theory.) Cratylus, a younger contemporary of Socrates (470–399 B.C.E.), carried this flux theory even further, arguing that you cannot step even once into the "same" river, because with each passing moment there is a new river. And, for that matter, a new "you." As if that were not enough, he said that our words themselves change in their meaning as we speak them, and therefore true communication is impossible. Likewise impossible, one would think, would be knowledge. Cratylus, it is said, largely abstained from conversation and merely wiggled his finger when someone spoke to him, figuring that his understanding of words he heard must necessarily be different from the meaning the speaker intended.

Skeptical themes are also found in the pronouncements of the Sophists. If you were a citizen of Athens and wanted to be influential, you needed to be trained by a Sophist, who could devise an argument to back up any claim. Because the Sophists could make a plausible case for any position, they seemed to show that one idea is as valid as the next, a theory that supports skepticism.

Gorgias (c. 485–380 B.C.E.), one particularly famous Sophist, said: "There is no reality, and if there were, we could not know of it, and even if we could, we could not communicate our knowledge." This statement parallels that of Xenophanes just mentioned.

In Plato's Myth of the Cave, a group of prisoners are placed so they can see, on the wall of the cave, only reflections of objects carried back and forth in front of a fire behind them. Because the reflections are all they see, the prisoners assume the reflections to be reality.

The best-known Sophist philosopher of all, Protagoras (c. 485–410 B.C.E.), said that "man is the measure of all things." This can be interpreted—and was interpreted by Plato—as meaning that there is no absolute knowledge: one person's views about the world are as valid as the next person's. Plato argued strenuously against this theory. In his dialogue *Theaetetus*, Plato pointed out that, if Protagoras is correct, and one person's views really are as valid as the next person's, then the person who views Protagoras's theory as false has a valid view. To this day beginning philosophy students subscribe to Protagoras's theory (without knowing it is Protagoras's theory), and to this day philosophy instructors use Plato's argument against it.

In the *Theaetetus*, Plato also tried to show that another popular idea about knowledge is mistaken. This is the idea that knowledge may be equated with sense perception. Plato had several reasons for thinking this equation is false.

One reason for thinking that knowledge is not just sense perception is the fact that knowledge clearly involves more than sense perception. For example, sense perception by itself tells us a straight stick stuck in water is bent—*thinking* is required for us to know the stick is actually straight. Further, just to know the stick *exists* or is of a certain *length* involves thought. Visual sensations give you colored expanses, auditory sensations give you sounds, but existence itself is a concept that cuts across several senses simultaneously and is supplied by thought. Judgments of length, for example, involve making comparisons with rulers or tape measures, and comparing is a mental activity.

Another reason knowledge is not just sense perception is that you can retain knowledge even *after* you are no longer sensing a thing. Finally, and even more important, in Plato's view true knowledge is knowledge of what *is*. Because the objects of sense perception are always changing (remember Heraclitus?), sense perception and knowledge cannot be one and the same.

True knowledge, Plato was certain, must be concerned with what is *truly real*. This means, of course, that the objects of true knowledge are the Forms because the objects of sense perception are real only to the extent that they "participate" in the Forms.

This, then, is essentially Plato's theory of knowledge, and he elaborated on it in the *Republic*—especially in a passage known as the **Theory of the Divided Line** and in the **Myth of the Cave.**

The Theory of the Divided Line is used by Plato to contrast knowledge, on one hand, with mere belief or opinion, on the other. Plato illustrates his theory by dividing a line in two parts. The upper part of the line stands for knowledge, and the lower part stands for belief (opinion). Knowledge is concerned with absolutes—absolute beauty, absolute good, and so forth—in short, with the Forms. And this is not unreasonable of Plato. If your "knowledge" of beauty or goodness or circularity or the like is limited to this or that beautiful car or good deed or round plate, then you really do not have knowledge of *absolute* beauty, goodness, or circularity. At best you have a bunch of opinions that, as they are as likely as not to be riddled with error, come closer to *ignorance* than to true knowledge.

In Plato's Divided Line, the upper part of the line represents knowledge and the lower part represents opinion. Plato also subdivided the knowledge section of the line into two parts and did the same for the opinion section. (How these further subdivisions are to be understood is a matter of controversy.) What is essential to remember is that, according to Plato, the highest form of knowledge is that obtained through the *use of reason* because perfect beauty or absolute goodness or the ideal triangle cannot be perceived.

Plato's Theory of Love and Becoming

As mentioned earlier, knowledge is true ultimately because it is knowledge of what is. Plato believed that it is not enough to know the truth; rather, a person must also become that truth. This is where Plato's epistemology, or theory of truth, becomes a metaphysics, or theory of being. To know, for Plato, is to be. The more you know, the more you are and the better you are.

Plato began, as we saw, with the Myth of the Cave, which shows how and why human beings are in the dark about the truth of things. And this ignorance is almost universal—even Socrates admits that he has no knowledge. What allows humans eventually to come into the light of day regarding the truth of things is the Forms. Each individual has in his or her immortal soul a perfect set of Forms that can be remembered (*anamnesis*), and only this constitutes true knowledge. To remember the Forms is to know the absolute truth and simultaneously to become just and wise. Through the Forms, all skeptical doubts are laid to rest and the individual becomes good in the process. This way of thinking is so powerful and compelling that twentieth-century philosopher Martin Heidegger suggested that all Western philosophy since Plato is but a variety of Platonism.

Plato believed in two radically separate spheres: the realm of shadows or imperfect, changing beings and the realm of perfect, eternal, unchanging Forms. The problem is, how do we get out of the cave to the perfect world of Forms? In his dialogue *The Symposium,* Plato postulated the notion of love as the way in which a person can go from the state of imperfection and ignorance to the state of perfection and true knowledge. He defined love as a longing for and a striving to attain the object of longing. Love is that which seeks to possess the beautiful and to recreate in beauty. Human beings love to love: they truly come alive only in seeking a beloved, whether that beloved is another human being or an idea or health or money.

For Plato, love is meant to be the force that brings all things together and makes them beautiful. It is the way by which all beings, but especially human beings, can ascend to higher stages of self-realization and perfection. Plato's love begins as an experience of lacking something. Love provokes both thought and effort in the pursuit of what is lacking. The deeper the thought, the greater the love.

Plato initially mirrored the Athenian view that the deepest human relationships were between two men, usually an older man and a younger one. Women were not only considered the weaker sex but were also thought to be superficial, excitable, and superstitious. Marriage had as its purpose the reproduction and raising of children, and physical lovemaking was considered a low form of love. Plato's love does not exclude physical beauty, but "Platonic love" begins at a higher stage of development, namely, with the sharing of beautiful thoughts with a beautiful person. Plato believed that this kind of love should be experienced while a person is young. It is this intellectual or spiritual love that begins the ascent of love, which may eventually lead to the permanent possession of Absolute Beauty or Goodness.

The love for just one other human, even if that person is as noble as a Socrates, remains a limited form of intellectual eros. It is but the first step in the ascent of philosophical love to Absolute Beauty. To reach the higher stages of love means entering what are called the *mysteries.* Plato has Socrates recount a theory of love given to him by a woman named Diotima. Socrates implies that few may be able to follow this line of reasoning, which he himself has difficulty comprehending, but Diotima's theory of love was this: The higher forms of love express the will to immortality and the will to produce immortal "children," not merely physical children. All love seeks to possess beauty and to reproduce in beauty, but the creation of immortal children (like the writings of Homer) can grant the author immortality. A first step beyond merely loving a beautiful person and begetting beautiful thoughts lies in the realization that beauty in all things is one and the same and that all love is one. A further step involves the recognition of the superiority of intellectual or spiritual beauty over physical beauty. Then love must expand beyond preoccupations with a particular person to an appreciation of the beauty of moral practices and laws. An individual is part of larger social groupings, each with accompanying obligations. Love here takes the form of appreciating and aptly participating in organizations such as a city-state like Athens. Yet no matter how wide a person's involvement is in the moral and social spheres of love, this still does not represent the highest and most inclusive love. A person begins to glimpse the all-inclusive, all-uniting kind of love by first seeing the beauty of knowledge as a whole or at least many of the different forms of knowledge. This leads to an appreciation and love of the whole realm of beauty or the integrated beauty of everything there is. In the happiness of viewing such vast beauty, a person will have beautiful thoughts and be able to speak beautiful words. Eventually such a person may be able to make the final leap to the beauty and truth, which is beyond all mortal things.

The last and highest stage of love lies in the discovery of the ultimate mystery, Absolute Beauty itself. The beauty of this being contains no change of any kind. It was never born and will never die, nor will it increase or decrease. It is not good in one part and bad in another. It is perfect and one with itself forever. All imperfect things participate in this Beauty, thereby receiving a modicum of fulfillment and self-realization. Plato indicated that once a person has seen Absolute Beauty, then such a fortunate person would no longer be dazzled by mere physical beauty or the other rubbish of mortality. This, for human beings, is the ultimate kind of immortality, he thought.

Thus, love for Plato is the ultimate way of knowing and realizing truth. For mortals, love is a process of seeking higher stages of being: physical love begets mortal children; intellectual or spiritual love begets immortal children. The greater the love, the more it will contain an intellectual component. The lifelong longing and pursuit seeks ever higher stages of love so that it can eventually lead to the possession of Absolute Beauty. This is the pursuit that motivates the highest sorts of human beings and that transforms entire civilizations. To love the highest is to become the best.

SELECTION 3.1

Apology*

Plato

[*In 399 B.C.E., Socrates was sentenced to death by an Athenian court for impiety and corrupting the youth of Athens. This excerpt is from Plato's dialogue* Apology, *in which Socrates is seen defending himself.*]

I will make my defense, and I will try in the short time allowed to do away with this evil opinion of me

*From Christopher Biffle, *A Guided Tour of Five Works by Plato,* 3rd edition. Mountain View, CA: Mayfield, 2001, pp. 36–40. Based on the nineteenth-century translation by Benjamin Jowett. Copyright © 2001 by The McGraw-Hill Companies, Inc. Reprinted with permission from The McGraw-Hill Companies.

which you have held for such a long time. I hope I may succeed, if this be well for you and me, and that my words may find favor with you. But I know to accomplish this is not easy—I see the nature of the task. Let the event be as the gods will; in obedience to the law I make my defense.

I will begin at the beginning and ask what the accusation is which has given rise to this slander of me and which has encouraged Meletus to proceed against me. What do the slanderers say? They shall be my prosecutors and I will sum up their words in an affidavit. "Socrates is an evil-doer and a curious person, who searches into things under the earth and in the heavens. He makes the weaker argument defeat the stronger and he teaches these doctrines to others." That is the nature of the accusation and that is what you have seen in the comedy of Aristophanes. He introduced a man whom he calls Socrates, going about and saying he can walk in the air and talking a lot of nonsense concerning matters which I do not pretend to know anything about—however, I mean to say nothing disparaging of anyone who is a student of such knowledge. I should be very sorry if Meletus could add that to my charge. But the simple truth is, O Athenians, I have nothing to do with these studies. Very many of those here are witnesses to the truth of this and to them I appeal. Speak then, you who have heard me, and tell your neighbors whether any of you ever heard me hold forth in few words or in many upon matters of this sort. . . . You hear their answer. And from what they say you will be able to judge the truth of the rest.

There is the same foundation for the report I am a teacher and take money; that is no more true than the other. Although, if a man is able to teach, I honor him for being paid. There are Gorgias of Leontium, Prodicus of Ceos, and Hippias of Elis, who go round the cities and are able to persuade young men to leave their own citizens, by whom they might be taught for nothing, and come to them, whom they not only pay but are also thankful if they may be allowed to pay them.

There is actually a Parian philosopher residing in Athens who charges fees. I came to hear of him in this way: I met a man who spent a world of money on the sophists, Callias, the son of Hipponicus, and knowing he had sons, I asked him: "Callias," I said, "if your two sons were foals or calves, there would be no difficulty in finding someone to raise them. We would hire a trainer of horses, or a farmer probably, who would improve and perfect them in their own proper virtue and excellence. But, as they are human beings, whom are you thinking of placing over them? Is there anyone who understands human and political virtue? You must have thought about this because you have sons. Is there anyone?"

"There is," he said.

"Who is he?" said I. "And of what country? And what does he charge?"

"Evenus the Parian," he replied. "He is the man and his charge is five minae."

Happy is Evenus, I said to myself, if he really has this wisdom and teaches at such a modest charge. Had I the same, I would have been very proud and

conceited; but the truth is I have no knowledge like this, O Athenians.

I am sure someone will ask the question, "Why is this, Socrates, and what is the origin of these accusations of you; for there must have been something strange which you have been doing? All this great fame and talk about you would never have come up if you had been like other men. Tell us then, why this is, as we should be sorry to judge you too quickly."

I regard this as a fair challenge, and I will try to explain to you the origin of this name of "wise" and of this evil fame. Please attend then and although some of you may think I am joking, I declare I will tell you the entire truth. Men of Athens, this reputation of mine has come from a certain kind of wisdom which I possess. If you ask me what kind of wisdom, I reply, such wisdom as is attainable by man, for to that extent I am inclined to believe I am wise. Whereas the persons of whom I was speaking have a superhuman wisdom which I may fail to describe, because I do not have it. He who says I have, speaks false and slanders me.

O men of Athens, I must beg you not to interrupt me, even if I seem to say something extravagant. For the word which I will speak is not mine. I will refer you to a wisdom which is worthy of credit and will tell you about my wisdom—whether I have any and of what sort—and that witness shall be the god of Delphi. You must have known Chaerephon. He was a friend of mine and also a friend of yours, for he shared in the exile of the people and returned with you. Well, Chaerephon, as you know, was very impetuous in all his doings, and he went to Delphi and boldly asked the oracle to tell him whether—as I said, I must beg you not to interrupt—he asked the oracle to tell him whether there was anyone wiser than I was. The Pythian prophetess answered, there was no man wiser. Chaerephon is dead himself but his brother, who is in court, will confirm the truth of this story.

Why do I mention this? Because I am going to explain to you why I have such an evil name. When I heard the answer, I said to myself, "What can the god mean and what is the interpretation of this riddle? I know I have no wisdom, great or small. What can he mean when he says I am the wisest of men? And yet he is a god and cannot lie; that would be against his nature." After long consideration, I at last thought of a method of answering the question.

48   Part One • *Metaphysics and Epistemology: Existence and Knowledge*

MAKING PHILOSOPHY ACCESSIBLE: POP-UP PLATO

© Original Artist Reproduction rights obtainable from www.CartoonStock.com.

I reflected if I could only find a man wiser than myself, then I might go to the god with a refutation in my hand. I would say to him, "Here is a man who is wiser than I am, but you said I was the wisest." Accordingly I went to one who had the reputation of wisdom and observed him—his name I need not mention; he was a politician whom I selected for examination. When I began to talk with him I could not help thinking he was not really wise, although he was thought wise by many and wiser still by himself. I tried to explain to him that he thought himself wise but was not really wise. The result was he hated me, and his hatred was shared by several who were present and heard me. So I left him, saying to myself, as I went away: "Well, although I do not suppose either of us knows anything really beautiful and good, I am better off than he is—for he knows nothing and thinks that he knows. I neither know nor think that I know. In this latter, then, I seem to have an advantage over him." Then I went to another who had still higher philosophical pretensions, and my conclusion was exactly the same. I made another enemy of him and of many others besides him.

After this I went to one man after another, being aware of the anger that I provoked; and I lamented and feared this, but necessity was laid upon me. The word of the god, I thought, ought to be considered first. And I said to myself, "I must go to all who appear to know and find out the meaning of the oracle." And I swear to you Athenians, by the dog, I swear, the result of my mission was this: I found the men with the highest reputations were all nearly the most foolish and some inferior men were really wiser and better.

I will tell you the tale of my wanderings and of the Herculean labors, as I may call them, which I endured only to find at last the oracle was right. When I left the politicians, I went to the poets: tragic, dithyrambic, and all sorts. There, I said to myself, you will be detected. Now you will find out you are more ignorant than they are. Accordingly, I took them some of the most elaborate passages in their own writings and asked what was the meaning of them—thinking the poets would teach me something. Will you believe me? I am almost ashamed to say this, but I must say there is hardly a person present who would not have talked better about their poetry than the poets did themselves. That quickly showed me poets do not write poetry by wisdom, but by a sort of inspiration. They are like soothsayers who also say many fine things, but do not understand the meaning of what they say. The poets appeared to me to be much the same, and I further observed that upon the strength of their poetry they believed themselves to be the wisest of men in other things in which they were not wise. So I departed, conceiving myself to be superior to them for the same reason I was superior to the politicians.

At last I went to the artisans, because I was conscious I knew nothing at all, and I was sure they knew many fine things. In this I was not mistaken, for they did know many things of which I was ignorant, and in this they certainly were wiser than I was. But I observed even the good artisans fell into the same error as the poets. Because they were good workmen, they thought they also knew all sorts of high matters, and this defect in them overshadowed their wisdom. Therefore, I asked myself on behalf of the oracle whether I would like to be as I was, having neither their knowledge nor their ignorance, or like them in both. I answered myself and the oracle that I was better off as I was.

This investigation led to my having many enemies of the worst and most dangerous kind and has given rise also to many falsehoods. I am called wise because my listeners always imagine I possess the wisdom which I do not find in others. The truth is, O men of Athens, the gods only are wise and in this oracle they mean to say wisdom of men is little or nothing. They are not speaking of Socrates, only using my name as an illustration, as if they said, "He, O men, is the wisest who, like Socrates, knows his wisdom is in truth worth nothing." And so I go my way, obedient to the gods, and seek wisdom of anyone, whether citizen or stranger, who appears to be wise. If he is not wise, then in support of the oracle I show him he is not wise. This occupation quite absorbs me, and I have no time to give either to any public matter of interest or to any concern of my own, but I am in utter poverty by reason of my devotion to the gods.

There is another thing. Young men of the richer classes, who have little to do, gather around me of their own accord. They like to hear the pretenders examined. They often imitate me and examine others themselves. There are plenty of persons, as they soon enough discover, who think they know something, but really know little or nothing. Then those who are examined by the young men, instead of being angry with themselves, are angry with me. "This confounded Socrates," they say, "this villainous misleader of youth!" Then if somebody asks them, "Why, what evil does he practice or teach?," they do not know and cannot tell. But so they may not appear ignorant, they repeat the ready-made charges which are used against all philosophers about teaching things up in the clouds and under the earth, and having no gods, and making the worse argument defeat the stronger. They do not like to confess their pretense to knowledge has been detected, which it has. They are numerous, ambitious, energetic and are all in battle array and have persuasive tongues. They have filled your ears with their loud and determined slanders. This is the reason why my three accusers, Meletus and Anytus and Lycon, have set upon me. Meletus has a quarrel with me on behalf of the poets, Anytus, on behalf of the craftsmen, Lycon, on behalf of the orators. As I said at the beginning, I cannot expect to get rid of this mass of slander all in a moment.

This, O men of Athens, is the truth and the whole truth. I have concealed nothing. And yet I know this plainness of speech makes my accusers hate me, and what is their hatred but a proof that I am speaking the truth? This is the reason for their slander of me, as you will find out either in this or in any future inquiry.

SELECTION 3.2

Republic*

Plato

[*Plato's dialogue* Republic *is one of the most widely read Western books of all time. In this selection, Plato compares Goodness (or the Good) to the sun, sets forth his famous Theory of the Divided Line, and explains the Myth of the Cave.*]

Glaucon: But, Socrates, what is your own account of the Good? Is it knowledge, or pleasure, or something else? . . .

. . .

S: . . . First we must come to an understanding. Let me remind you of the distinction we drew earlier and have often drawn on other occasions, between the multiplicity of things that we call good or beautiful or whatever it may be

and, on the other hand, Goodness itself or Beauty itself and so on. Corresponding to each of these sets of many things, we postulate a single Form or real essence, as we call it.

G: Yes, that is so.

S: Further, the many things, we say, can be seen, but are not objects of rational thought; whereas the Forms are objects of thought, but invisible.

G: Yes, certainly.

S: And we see things with our eyesight, just as we hear sounds with our ears and, to speak generally, perceive any sensible thing with our sense-faculties.

G: Of course.

S: Have you noticed, then, that the artificer who designed the senses has been exceptionally lavish of his materials in making the eyes able to see and their objects visible?

*From *The Republic of Plato,* translated by Francis McDonald Cornford (Oxford: Clarendon Press, 1941). By permission of Oxford University Press.

50   Part One • *Metaphysics and Epistemology: Existence and Knowledge*

G: That never occurred to me.

S: Well, look at it in this way. Hearing and sound do not stand in need of any third thing, without which the ear will not hear nor sound be heard; and I think the same is true of most, not to say all, of the other senses. Can you think of one that does require anything of the sort?

G: No, I cannot.

S: But there is this need in the case of sight and its objects. You may have the power of vision in your eyes and try to use it, and colour may be there in the objects; but sight will see nothing and the colours will remain invisible in the absence of a third thing peculiarly constituted to serve this very purpose.

G: By which you mean   ?

S: Naturally I mean what you call light; and if light is a thing of value, the sense of sight and the power of being visible are linked together by a very precious bond, such as unites no other sense with its object.

G: No one could say that light is not a precious thing.

S: And of all the divinities in the skies is there one whose light, above all the rest, is responsible for making our eyes see perfectly and making objects perfectly visible?

G: There can be no two opinions: of course you mean the Sun.

S: And how is sight related to this deity? Neither sight nor the eye which contains it is the Sun, but of all the sense-organs it is the most sun-like; and further, the power it possesses is dispensed by the Sun, like a stream flooding the eye. And again, the Sun is not vision, but it is the cause of vision and also is seen by the vision it causes.

G: Yes.

S: It was the Sun, then, that I meant when I spoke of that offspring which the Good has created in the visible world, to stand there in the same relation to vision and visible things as that which the Good itself bears in the intelligible world to intelligence and to intelligible objects.

G: How is that? You must explain further.

S: You know what happens when the colours of things are no longer irradiated by the daylight, but only by the fainter luminaries of the night: when you look at them, the eyes are dim and seem almost blind, as if there were no unclouded vision in them. But when you look at things on which the Sun is shining, the same eyes see distinctly and it becomes evident that they do contain the power of vision.

G: Certainly.

S: Apply this comparison, then, to the soul. When its gaze is fixed upon an object irradiated by truth and reality, the soul gains understanding and knowledge and is manifestly in possession of intelligence. But when it looks towards that twilight world of things that come into existence and pass away, its sight is dim and it has only opinions and beliefs which shift to and fro, and now it seems like a thing that has no intelligence.

G: That is true.

S: This, then, which gives to the objects of knowledge their truth and to him who knows them his power of knowing, is the Form or essential nature of Goodness. It is the cause of knowledge and truth; and so, while you may think of it as an object of knowledge, you will do well to regard it as something beyond truth and knowledge and, precious as these both are, of still higher worth. And, just as in our analogy light and vision were to be thought of as like the Sun, but not identical with it, so here both knowledge and truth are to be regarded as like the Good, but to identify either with the Good is wrong. The Good must hold a yet higher place of honour.

G: You are giving it a position of extraordinary splendour, if it is the source of knowledge and truth and itself surpasses them in worth. You surely cannot mean that it is pleasure.

S: Heaven forbid. But I want to follow up our analogy still further. You will agree that the Sun not only makes the things we see visible, but also brings them into existence and gives them growth and nourishment; yet he is not the same thing as existence. And so with the objects of knowledge: these derive from the Good not only their power of being known, but their very being and reality; and Goodness is not the same thing as being, but even beyond being, surpassing it in dignity and power.

(Glaucon exclaimed with some amusement at my exalting Goodness in such extravagant terms.)

It is your fault; you forced me to say what I think.

G: Yes, and you must not stop there. At any rate, complete your comparison with the Sun, if there is any more to be said.

S: There is a great deal more.

G: Let us hear it, then; don't leave anything out.

S: I am afraid much must be left unspoken. However, I will not, if I can help it, leave out anything that can be said on this occasion.

G: Please do not.

S: Conceive, then, that there are these two powers I speak of, the Good reigning over the domain of all that is intelligible, the Sun over the visible world—or the heaven as I might call it; only you would think I was showing off my skill in etymology. At any rate you have these two orders of things clearly before your mind: the visible and the intelligible?

G: I have.

S: Now take a line divided into two unequal parts, one to represent the visible order, the other the intelligible; and divide each part again in the same proportion, symbolizing degrees of comparative clearness or obscurity. Then (A) one of the two sections in the visible world will stand for images. By images I mean first shadows, and then reflections in water or in close-grained, polished surfaces, and everything of that kind, if you understand.

G: Yes, I understand.

S: Let the second section (B) stand for the actual things of which the first are likenesses, the living creatures about us and all the works of nature or of human hands.

G: So be it.

S: Will you also take the proportion in which the visible world has been divided as corresponding to degrees of reality and truth, so that

the likeness shall stand to the original in the same ratio as the sphere of appearances and belief to the sphere of knowledge?

G: Certainly.

S: Now consider how we are to divide the part which stands for the intelligible world. There are two sections. In the first (C) the mind uses as images those actual things which themselves had images in the visible world; and it is compelled to pursue its inquiry by starting from assumptions and travelling, not up to a principle, but down to a conclusion. In the second (D) the mind moves in the other direction, from an assumption up towards a principle which is not hypothetical; and it makes no use of the images employed in the other section, but only of Forms, and conducts its inquiry solely by their means.

G: I don't quite understand what you mean.

S: Then we will try again; what I have just said will help you to understand. (C) You know, of course, how students of subjects like geometry and arithmetic begin by postulating odd and even numbers, or the various figures and the three kinds of angle, and other such data in each subject. These data they take as known; and, having adopted them as assumptions, they do not feel called upon to give any account of them to themselves or to anyone else, but treat them as self-evident. Then, starting from these assumptions, they go on until they arrive, by a series of consistent steps, at all the conclusions they set out to investigate.

	Objects		States of Mind
Intelligible World	*The Good*		
	Forms	Ⓓ	Intelligence (*noesis*) or Knowledge (*episteme*)
	Mathematical Objects	Ⓒ	Thinking (*dianoia*)
The Visible World	*The Sun*		
	Actual Things	Ⓑ	Belief (*pistis*)
	Images	Ⓐ	Imagining (*eikasia*)

G: Yes, I know that.

S: You also know how they make use of visible figures and discourse about them, though what they really have in mind is the originals of which these figures are images: they are not reasoning, for instance, about this particular square and diagonal which they have drawn, but about *the* Square and *the* Diagonal; and so in all cases. The diagrams they draw and the models they make are actual things, which may have their shadows or images in water; but now they serve in their turn as images, while the student is seeking to behold those realities which only thought can apprehend.

G: True.

S: This, then, is the class of things that I spoke of as intelligible, but with two qualifications: first, that the mind, in studying them, is compelled to employ assumptions, and, because it cannot rise above these, does not travel upwards to a first principle; and second, that it uses as images those actual things which have images of their own in the section below them and which, in comparison with those shadows and reflections, are reputed to be more palpable and valued accordingly.

G: I understand: you mean the subject-matter of geometry and of the kindred arts.

S: (D) Then by the second section of the intelligible world you may understand me to mean all that unaided reasoning apprehends by the power of dialectic, when it treats its assumptions, not as first principles, but as *hypotheses* in the literal sense, things "laid down" like a flight of steps up which it may mount all the way to something that is not hypothetical, the first principle of all; and having grasped this, may turn back and, holding on to the consequences which depend upon it, descend at last to a conclusion, never making use of any sensible object, but only of Forms, moving through Forms from one to another, and ending with Forms.

G: I understand, though not perfectly; for the procedure you describe sounds like an enormous undertaking. But I see that you mean to distinguish the field of intelligible reality studied by dialectic as having a greater certainty and truth than the subject-matter of the "arts," as they are

called, which treat their assumptions as first principles. The students of these arts are, it is true, compelled to exercise thought in contemplating objects which the senses cannot perceive, but because they start from assumptions without going back to a first principle, you do not regard them as gaining true understanding about those objects, although the objects themselves, when connected with a first principle, are intelligible. And I think you would call the state of mind of the students of geometry and other such arts, not intelligence, but thinking, as being something between intelligence and mere acceptance of appearances.

S: You have understood me quite well enough. And now you may take, as corresponding to the four sections, these four states of mind: *intelligence* for the highest, *thinking* for the second, *belief* for the third, and for the last *imagining*. These you may arrange as the terms in a proportion, assigning to each a degree of clearness and certainty corresponding to the measure in which their objects possess truth and reality.

G: I understand and agree with you. I will arrange them as you say.

S: Next, here is a parable to illustrate the degrees in which our nature may be enlightened or unenlightened. Imagine the condition of men living in a sort of cavernous chamber underground, with an entrance open to the light and a long passage all down the cave. Here they have been from childhood, chained by the leg and also by the neck, so that they cannot move and can see only what is in front of them, because the chains will not let them turn their heads. At some distance higher up is the light of a fire burning behind them; and between the prisoners and the fire is a track with a parapet built along it, like the screen at a puppet-show, which hides the performers while they show their puppets over the top.

G: I see.

S: Now behind this parapet imagine persons carrying along various artificial objects, including figures of men and animals in wood or stone or other materials, which project above the parapet. Naturally, some of these persons will be talking, others silent.

G: It is a strange picture, and a strange sort of prisoners.

S: Like ourselves; for in the first place prisoners so confined would have seen nothing of themselves or of one another, except the shadows thrown by the fire-light on the wall of the Cave facing them, would they?

G: Not if all their lives they had been prevented from moving their heads.

S: And they would have seen as little of the objects carried past.

G: Of course.

S: Now, if they could talk to one another, would they not suppose that their words referred only to those passing shadows which they saw?

G: Necessarily.

S: And suppose their prison had an echo from the wall facing them? When one of the people crossing behind them spoke, they could only suppose that the sound came from the shadow passing before their eyes.

G: No doubt.

S: In every way, then, such prisoners would recognize as reality nothing but the shadows of those artificial objects.

G: Inevitably.

S: Now consider what would happen if their release from the chains and the healing of their unwisdom should come about in this way. Suppose one of them set free and forced suddenly to stand up, turn his head, and walk with eyes lifted to the light; all these movements would be painful, and he would be too dazzled to make out the objects whose shadows he had been used to see. What do you think he would say, if someone told him that what he had formerly seen was meaningless illusion, but now, being somewhat nearer to reality and turned towards more real objects, he was getting a truer view? Suppose further that he were shown the various objects being carried by and were made to say, in reply to questions, what each of them was. Would he not be perplexed and believe the objects now shown him to be not so real as what he formerly saw?

G: Yes, not nearly so real.

S: And if he were forced to look at the fire-light itself, would not his eyes ache, so that he would try to escape and turn back to the things which he could see distinctly, convinced that they really were clearer than these other objects now being shown to him?

G: Yes.

S: And suppose someone were to drag him away forcibly up the steep and rugged ascent and not let him go until he had hauled him out into the sunlight, would he not suffer pain and vexation at such treatment, and, when he had come out into the light, find his eyes so full of its radiance that he could not see a single one of the things that he was now told were real?

G: Certainly he would not see them all at once.

S: He would need, then, to grow accustomed before he could see things in that upper world. At first it would be easiest to make out shadows, and then the images of men and things reflected in water, and later on the things themselves. After that, it would be easier to watch the heavenly bodies and the sky itself by night, looking at the light of the moon and stars rather than the Sun and the Sun's light in the day-time.

G: Yes, surely.

S: Last of all, he would be able to look at the Sun and contemplate its nature, not as it appears when reflected in water or any alien medium, but as it is in itself in its own domain.

G: No doubt.

S: And now he would begin to draw the conclusion that it is the Sun that produces the seasons and the course of the year and controls everything in the visible world, and moreover is in a way the cause of all that he and his companions used to see.

G: Clearly he would come at last to that conclusion.

S: Then if he called to mind his fellow prisoners and what passed for wisdom in his former dwelling-place, he would surely think himself happy in the change and be sorry for them. They may have had a practice of honouring and commending one another, with prizes for the man who had the keenest eye for the passing shadows and the best memory for the order in which they followed or accompanied one another, so that he could make a good guess as to which was going to come next. Would our released prisoner be likely to covet those prizes or to envy the men exalted to honour and power in the Cave? Would he not feel like Homer's Achilles, that he would far sooner "be on earth as a hired servant in the house of a landless man" or endure anything rather than go back to his old beliefs and live in the old way?

G: Yes, he would prefer any fate to such a life.

S: Now imagine what would happen if he went down again to take his former seat in the Cave. Coming suddenly out of the sunlight, his eyes would be filled with darkness. He might be required once more to deliver his opinion on those shadows, in competition with the prisoners who had never been released, while his eyesight was still dim and unsteady; and it might take some time to become used to the darkness. They would laugh at him and say that he had gone up only to come back with his sight ruined; it was worth no one's while even to attempt the ascent. If they could lay hands on the man who was trying to set them free and lead them up, they would kill him.

G: Yes, they would.

S: Every feature in this parable, my dear Glaucon, is meant to fit our earlier analysis. The prison dwelling corresponds to the region revealed to us through the sense of sight, and the fire-light within it to the power of the Sun. The ascent to see the things in the upper world you may take as standing for the upward journey of the soul into the region of the intelligible; then you will be in possession of what I surmise, since that is what you wish to be told. Heaven knows whether it is true; but this, at any rate, is how it appears to me. In the world of knowledge, the last thing to be perceived and only with great difficulty is the essential Form of Goodness. Once it is perceived, the conclusion must follow that, for all things, this is the cause of whatever is right and good; in the visible world it gives birth to light and to the lord of light, while it is itself sovereign in the intelligible world and the parent of intelligence and truth. Without having

had a vision of this Form no one can act with wisdom, either in his own life or in matters of state.

G: So far as I can understand, I share your belief.

S: Then you may also agree that it is no wonder if those who have reached this height are reluctant to manage the affairs of men. Their souls long to spend all their time in that upper world—naturally enough, if here once more our parable holds true. Nor, again, is it at all strange that one who comes from the contemplation of divine things to the miseries of human life should appear awkward and ridiculous when, with eyes still dazed and not yet accustomed to the darkness, he is compelled, in a law-court or elsewhere, to dispute about the shadows of justice or the images that cast those shadows, and to wrangle over the notions of what is right in the minds of men who have never beheld Justice itself.

G: It is not at all strange.

S: No; a sensible man will remember that the eyes may be confused in two ways—by a change from light to darkness or from darkness to light; and he will recognize that the same thing happens to the soul. When he sees it troubled and unable to discern anything clearly, instead of laughing thoughtlessly, he will ask whether, coming from a brighter existence, its unaccustomed vision is obscured by the darkness, in which case he will think its condition enviable and its life a happy one; or whether, emerging from the depths of ignorance, it is dazzled by excess of light. If so, he will rather feel sorry for it; or, if he were inclined to laugh, that would be less ridiculous than to laugh at the soul which has come down from the light.

G: That is a fair statement.

S: If this is true, then, we must conclude that education is not what it is said to be by some, who profess to put knowledge into a soul which does not possess it, as if they could put sight into blind eyes. On the contrary, our own account signifies that the soul of every man does possess the power of learning the truth and the organ to see it with; and that, just as one might have to turn the whole body round in order that the eye should see light instead of darkness, so the entire soul must be turned away from this changing world, until its eye can bear to contemplate reality and that supreme splendour which we have called the Good. Hence there may well be an art whose aim would be to effect this very thing, the conversion of the soul, in the readiest way; not to put the power of sight into the soul's eye, which already has it, but to ensure that, instead of looking in the wrong direction, it is turned the way it ought to be.

G: Yes, it may well be so.

S: It looks, then, as though wisdom were different from those ordinary virtues, as they are called, which are not far removed from bodily qualities, in that they can be produced by habituation and exercise in a soul which has not possessed them from the first. Wisdom, it seems, is certainly the virtue of some diviner faculty, which never loses its power, though its use for good or harm depends on the direction towards which it is turned. You must have noticed in dishonest men with a reputation for sagacity the shrewd glance of a narrow intelligence piercing the objects to which it is directed. There is nothing wrong with their power of vision, but it has been forced into the service of evil, so that the keener its sight, the more harm it works.

G: Quite true.

S: And yet if the growth of a nature like this had been pruned from earliest childhood, cleared of those clinging overgrowths which come of gluttony and all luxurious pleasure and, like leaden weights charged with affinity to this mortal world, hang upon the soul, bending its vision downwards; if, freed from these, the soul were turned round towards true reality, then this same power in these very men would see the truth as keenly as the objects it is turned to now.

G: Yes, very likely.

S: Is it not also likely, or indeed certain after what has been said, that a state can never be properly governed either by the uneducated who know nothing of truth or by men who are allowed to spend all their days in the pursuit of culture? The ignorant have no single mark before their eyes at which they must aim in all the conduct of their own lives and of affairs of state; and the others will not engage in action if they can help it, dreaming that while still alive, they have been translated to the Islands of the Blest.

G: Quite true.

S: It is for us, then, as founders of a commonwealth, to bring compulsion to bear on the noblest natures. They must be made to climb the ascent to the vision of Goodness, which we called the highest object of knowledge; and, when they have looked upon it long enough, they must not be allowed, as they now are, to remain on the heights, refusing to come down again to the prisoners or to take any part in their labours and rewards, however much or little these may be worth.

G: Shall we not be doing them an injustice, if we force on them a worse life than they might have?

S: You have forgotten again, my friend, that the law is not concerned to make any one class specially happy, but to ensure the welfare of the commonwealth as a whole. By persuasion or constraint it will unite the citizens in harmony, making them share whatever benefits each class can contribute to the common good; and its purpose in forming men of that spirit was not that each should be left to go his own way, but that they should be instrumental in binding the community into one.

G: True, I had forgotten.

S: You will see, then, Glaucon, that there will be no real injustice in compelling our philosophers to watch over and care for the other citizens. We can fairly tell them that their compeers in other states may quite reasonably refuse to collaborate: there they have sprung up, like a self-sown plant, in despite of their country's institutions; no one has fostered their growth, and they cannot be expected to show gratitude for a care they have never received. "But," we shall say, "it is not so with you. We have brought you into existence for your country's sake as well as for your own, to be like leaders and king-bees in a hive; you have been better and more thoroughly educated than those others and hence you are more capable of playing your part both as men of thought and as men of action. You must go down, then, each in his turn, to live with the rest and let your eyes grow accustomed to the darkness. You will then see a thousand times better than those who live there always; you will recognize every image for what it is and know what it represents, because you have seen justice, beauty, and goodness in their reality; and so you and we shall find life in our commonwealth no mere dream, as it is in most existing states, where men live fighting one another about shadows and quarrelling for power, as if that were a great prize; whereas in truth government can be at its best and free from dissension only where the destined rulers are least desirous of holding office."

G: Quite true.

S: Then will our pupils refuse to listen and to take their turns at sharing in the work of the community, though they may live together for most of their time in a purer air?

G: No; it is a fair demand, and they are fair-minded men. No doubt, unlike any ruler of the present day, they will think of holding power as an unavoidable necessity.

S: Yes, my friend; for the truth is that you can have a well-governed society only if you can discover for your future rulers a better way of life than being in office; then only will power be in the hands of men who are rich, not in gold, but in the wealth that brings happiness, a good and wise life. All goes wrong when, starved for lack of anything good in their own lives, men turn to public affairs hoping to snatch from thence the happiness they hunger for. They set about fighting for power, and this internecine conflict ruins them and their country. The life of true philosophy is the only one that looks down upon offices of state; and access to power must be confined to men who are not in love with it; otherwise rivals will start fighting. So whom else can you compel to undertake the guardianship of the commonwealth, if not those who, besides understanding best the principles of government, enjoy a nobler life than the politician's and look for rewards of a different kind?

G: There is indeed no other choice. One who holds a true belief without intelligence is just like a blind man who happens to take the right road, isn't he?

SELECTION 3.3

Meno*   *Plato*

[*In this selection from the dialogue* Meno, *"Socrates" explains another of Plato's theories about knowledge: Knowledge about reality comes from within the soul through a form of "recollection" rather than from without through being taught. The passage also serves to show that, in Plato's opinion, the soul is immortal. In the dialogue, Socrates has a boy who knows nothing of geometry construct a square twice the size of a given square. After one or two failed attempts, the boy succeeds without having been taught how to do it by Socrates. How could he succeed if knowledge of geometry were not already within his soul?*]

Meno: But how will you look for something when you don't in the least know what it is? How on earth are you going to set up something you don't know as the object of your search? To put it another way, even if you come right up against it, how will you know that what you have found is the thing you didn't know?

Socrates: I know what you mean. Do you realize that what you are bringing up is the trick argument that a man cannot try to discover either what he knows or what he does not know? He

*From *Plato, Protagoras and Meno,* translated by W. K. C. Guthrie (London: Penguin Press, 1956), pp. 128–139. Translation copyright © W. K. C. Guthrie, 1956. Reproduced by permission of Penguin Books Ltd.

would not seek what he knows, for since he knows it there is no need of the inquiry, nor what he does not know, for in that case he does not even know what he is to look for.

M: Well, do you think it a good argument?

S: No.

M: Can you explain how it fails?

S: I can. I have heard from men and women who understand the truths of religion—
(*Here he presumably pauses to emphasize the solemn change of tone the dialogue undergoes at this point.*)

M: What did they say?

S: Something true, I thought, and fine.

M: What was it, and who were they?

S: Those who tell it are priests and priestesses of the sort who make it their business to be able to account for the functions which they perform. Pindar speaks of it too, and many another of the poets who are divinely inspired. What they say is this—see whether you think they are speaking the truth. They say that the soul of man is immortal: at one time it comes to an end—that which is called death—and at another is born again, but is never finally exterminated. . . .

Thus the soul, since it is immortal and has been born many times, and has seen all things both here and in the other world, has learned everything that is. So we need not be surprised if it can recall the knowledge of virtue or anything else which, as we see, it once possessed. All nature is akin, and the soul has learned everything, so that when a man has recalled a single piece of knowledge—*learned* it, in ordinary language—there is no reason why he should not find out all the rest, if he keeps a stout heart and does not grow weary of the search; for seeking and learning are in fact nothing but recollection.

We ought not then to be led astray by the contentious argument you quoted. It would make us lazy, and is music in the ears of weaklings. The other doctrine produces energetic seekers after knowledge; and being convinced of its truth, I am ready, with your help, to inquire into the nature of virtue.

M: I see, Socrates. But what do you mean when you say that we don't learn anything, but that what we call learning is recollection? Can you teach me that it is so?

S: I have just said that you're a rascal, and now you ask me if I can teach you, when I say there is no such thing as teaching, only recollection. Evidently you want to catch me contradicting myself straight away.

M: No, honestly, Socrates, I wasn't thinking of that. It was just habit. If you can in any way make clear to me that what you say is true, please do.

S: It isn't an easy thing, but still I should like to do what I can since you ask me. I see you have a large number of retainers here. Call one of them, anyone you like, and I will use him to demonstrate it to you.

M: Certainly. (*To a slave-boy.*) Come here.

S: He is a Greek and speaks our language?

M: Indeed yes—born and bred in the house.

S: Listen carefully then, and see whether it seems to you that he is learning from me or simply being reminded.

M: I will.

S: Now boy, you know that a square is a figure like this?

(*Socrates begins to draw figures in the sand at his feet. He points to the square* ABCD.)

Boy: Yes.

S: It has all these four sides equal?

Boy: Yes.

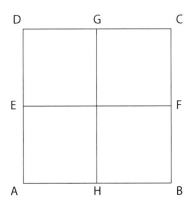

58   Part One · *Metaphysics and Epistemology: Existence and Knowledge*

S: And these lines which go through the middle of it are also equal? (*The lines* EF, GH.)

Boy: Yes.

S: Such a figure could be either larger or smaller, could it not?

Boy: Yes.

S: Now if this side is two feet long, and this side the same, how many feet will the whole be? Put it this way. If it were two feet in this direction and only one in that, must not the area be two feet taken once?

Boy: Yes.

S: But since it is two feet this way also, does it not become twice two feet?

Boy: Yes.

S: And how many feet is twice two? Work it out and tell me.

Boy: Four.

S: Now could one draw another figure double the size of this, but similar, that is, with all its sides equal like this one?

Boy: Yes.

S: How many feet will its area be?

Boy: Eight.

S: Now then, try to tell me how long each of its sides will be. The present figure has a side of two feet. What will be the side of the double-sized one?

Boy: It will be double, Socrates, obviously.

S: You see, Meno, that I am not teaching him anything, only asking. Now he thinks he knows the length of the side of the eight-feet square.

M: Yes.

S: But does he?

M: Certainly not.

S: He thinks it is twice the length of the other.

M: Yes.

S: Now watch how he recollects things in order— the proper way to recollect.

You say that the side of double length produces the double-sized figure? Like this I

mean, not long this way and short that. It must be equal on all sides like the first figure, only twice its size, that is eight feet. Think a moment whether you still expect to get it from doubling the side.

Boy: Yes, I do.

S: Well now, shall we have a line double the length of this (AB) if we add another the same length at this end (BJ)?

Boy: Yes.

S: It is on this line then, according to you, that we shall make the eight-feet square, by taking four of the same length?

Boy: Yes.

S: Let us draw in four equal lines (*i.e., counting* AJ, *and adding* JK, KL, *and* LA *made complete by drawing in its second half* LD), using the first as a base. Does this not give us what you call the eight-feet figure?

Boy: Certainly.

S: But does it contain these four squares, each equal to the original four-feet one? (*Socrates has drawn in the lines* CM, CN *to complete the squares that he wishes to point out.*)

Boy: Yes.

S: How big is it then? Won't it be four times as big?

Boy: Of course.

S: And is four times the same as twice?

Boy: Of course not.

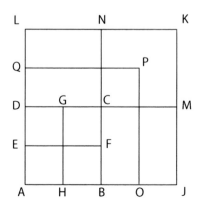

S: So doubling the side has given us not a double but a fourfold figure?

Boy: True.

S: And four times four are sixteen, are they not?

Boy: Yes.

S: Then how big is the side of the eight-feet figure? This one has given us four times the original area, hasn't it?

Boy: Yes.

S: And a side half the length gave us a square of four feet?

Boy: Yes.

S: Good. And isn't a square of eight feet double this one and half that?

Boy: Yes.

S: Will it not have a side greater than this one but less than that?

Boy: I think it will.

S: Right. Always answer what you think. Now tell me: was not this side two feet long, and this one four?

Boy: Yes.

S: Then the side of the eight-feet figure must be longer than two feet but shorter than four?

Boy: It must.

S: Try to say how long you think it is.

Boy: Three feet.

S: If so, shall we add half of this bit (BO, *half of* BJ) and make it three feet? Here are two, and this is one, and on this side similarly we have two plus one; and here is the figure you want.
(*Socrates completes the square* AOPQ.)

Boy: Yes.

S: If it is three feet this way and three that, will the whole area be three times three feet?

Boy: It looks like it.

S: And that is how many?

Boy: Nine.

S: Whereas the square double our first square had to be how many?

Boy: Eight.

S: But we haven't yet got the square of eight feet even from a three-feet side?

Boy: No.

S: Then what length will we give it? Try to tell us exactly. If you don't want to count it up, just show us on the diagram.

Boy: It's no use, Socrates, I just don't know.

S: Observe, Meno, the stage he has reached on the path of recollection. At the beginning he did not know the side of the square of eight feet. Nor indeed does he know it now, but then he thought he knew it and answered boldly, as was appropriate—he felt no perplexity. Now however he does feel perplexed. Not only does he not know the answer; he doesn't even think he knows.

M: Quite true.

S: Isn't he in a better position now in relation to what he didn't know?

M: I admit that too.

S: So in perplexing him and numbing him like the sting-ray, have we done him any harm?

M: I think not.

S: In fact we have helped him to some extent towards finding out the right answer, for now not only is he ignorant of it but he will be quite glad to look for it. Up to now, he thought he could speak well and fluently, on many occasions and before large audiences, on the subject of a square double the size of a given square, maintaining that it must have a side of double the length.

M: No doubt.

S: Do you suppose then that he would have attempted to look for, or learn, what he thought he knew (though he did not), before he was thrown into perplexity, became aware of his ignorance, and felt a desire to know?

M: No.

S: Then the numbing process was good for him?

M: I agree.

S: Now notice what, starting from this state of perplexity, he will discover by seeking the truth

60   Part One • *Metaphysics and Epistemology: Existence and Knowledge*

in company with me, though I simply ask him questions without teaching him. Be ready to catch me if I give him any instruction or explanation instead of simply interrogating him on his own opinions.

(*Socrates here rubs out the previous figures and starts again.*)

Tell me, boy, is not this our square of four feet? (ABCD.) You understand?

Boy: Yes.

S: Now we can add another equal to it like this? (BCEF.)

Boy: Yes.

S: And a third here, equal to each of the others? (CEGH.)

Boy: Yes.

S: And then we can fill in this one in the corner? (DCHJ.)

Boy: Yes.

S: Then here we have four equal squares?

Boy: Yes.

S: And how many times the size of the first square is the whole?

Boy: Four times.

S: And we want one double the size. You remember?

Boy: Yes.

S: Now does this line going from corner to corner cut each of these squares in half?

Boy: Yes.

S: And these are four equal lines enclosing this area? (BEHD.)

Boy: They are.

S: Now think. How big is this area?

Boy: I don't understand.

S: Here are four squares. Has not each line cut off the inner half of each of them?

Boy: Yes.

S: And how many such halves are there in this figure? (BEHD.)

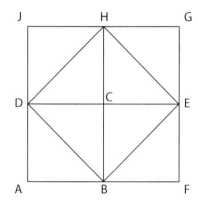

Boy: Four.

S: And how many in this one? (ABCD.)

Boy: Two.

S: And what is the relation of four to two?

Boy: Double.

S: How big is this figure then?

Boy: Eight feet.

S: On what base?

Boy: This one.

S: The line which goes from corner to corner of the square of four feet?

Boy: Yes.

S: The technical name for it is "diagonal"; so if we use that name, it is your personal opinion that the square on the diagonal of the original square is double its area.

Boy: That is so, Socrates.

S: What do you think, Meno? Has he answered with any opinions that were not his own?

M: No, they were all his.

S: Yet he did not know, as we agreed a few minutes ago.

M: True.

S: But these opinions were somewhere in him, were they not?

M: Yes.

S: So a man who does not know has in himself true opinions on a subject without having knowledge.

M: It would appear so.

S: At present these opinions, being newly aroused, have a dream-like quality. But if the same questions are put to him on many occasions and in different ways, you can see that in the end he will have a knowledge on the subject as accurate as anybody's.

M: Probably.

S: This knowledge will not come from teaching but from questioning. He will recover it for himself.

M: Yes.

S: And the spontaneous recovery of knowledge that is in him is recollection, isn't it?

M: Yes.

S: Either then he has at some time acquired the knowledge which he now has, or he has always possessed it. If he always possessed it, he must always have known; if on the other hand he acquired it at some previous time, it cannot have been in this life, unless somebody has taught him geometry. He will behave in the same way with all geometrical knowledge, and every other subject. Has anyone taught him all these? You ought to know, especially as he has been brought up in your household.

M: Yes, I know that no one ever taught him.

S: And has he these opinions, or hasn't he?

M: It seems we can't deny it.

S: Then if he did not acquire them in this life, isn't it immediately clear that he possessed and had learned them during some other period?

M: It seems so.

S: When he was not in human shape?

M: Yes.

S: If then there are going to exist in him, both while he is and while he is not a man, true opinions which can be aroused by questioning and turned into knowledge, may we say that his soul has been for ever in a state of knowledge? Clearly he always either is or is not a man.

M: Clearly.

S: And if the truth about reality is always in our soul, the soul must be immortal, and one must take courage and try to discover—that is, to recollect—what one doesn't happen to know, or (more correctly) remember, at the moment.

M: Somehow or other I believe you are right.

S: I think I am. I shouldn't like to take my oath on the whole story, but one thing I am ready to fight for as long as I can, in word and act: that is, that we shall be better, braver and more active men if we believe it right to look for what we don't know than if we believe there is no point in looking because what we don't know we can never discover.

M: There too I am sure you are right.

CHECKLIST

To help you review, here is a checklist of the key philosophers and terms and concepts of this chapter. The brief descriptive sentences summarize the philosophers' leading ideas. Keep in mind that some of these summary statements are oversimplifications of complex positions.

Philosophers

- **Plato** was most famous for his Theory of Forms and his two-realm doctrine: two separate worlds with two types of knowledge.   38

- **Socrates** was Plato's mentor and philosophy's most illustrious practitioner of the Socratic/dialectic method.   36

- **Sophists** were ancient Greek teachers of rhetoric. Through them and Socrates, moral philosophy began.   36

Key Terms and Concepts

Delphi Oracle 37	skeptic 41
Forms/Theory of	Socratic/dialectic
Forms 38	method 36
Myth of the Cave 44	Theory of the Divided
Platonic dualism 41	Line 44
Plato's dialogues 38	

62   Part One   ·   *Metaphysics and Epistemology: Existence and Knowledge*

QUESTIONS FOR DISCUSSION AND REVIEW

1. Can you step into the same river twice? Once?

2. Plato's metaphysics incorporates ideas from some of the earlier philosophers mentioned in Chapter 2. Identify those philosophers and their ideas.

3. Give an example of a Platonic Form not mentioned in the text. Explain whether it really exists, and why.

4. Does a world of Forms exist separately from the world of concrete, individual things? Explain.

5. What is the Myth of the Cave?

6. Is sense perception knowledge?

7. Can beauty be in more than one object at one time? Explain.

8. Are appearances real for Plato? Are they real in fact?

SUGGESTED FURTHER READINGS

J. L. Ackrill, *Essays on Plato and Aristotle* (New York: Oxford University Press, 1997). Selected essays by a famous classics scholar.

Julia Annas, *Ancient Philosophy: A Very Short Introduction* (New York: Oxford University Press, 2000). A brief look at some of the problems faced by the ancient Greeks and Romans.

Jonathan Barnes, R. M. Hare, and C. C. W. Taylor, *Greek Philosophers* (New York: Oxford University Press, 1999). Essays by three eminent scholars on Socrates, Plato, and Aristotle.

Christopher Biffle, *A Guided Tour of Five Works by Plato: Euthyphro, Apology, Crito, Phaedo (Death Scene), Allegory [Myth] of the Cave*, 2nd ed. (Mountain View, Calif.: Mayfield, 1994). The best introduction there is to these five dialogues.

Simon Blackburn, *Plato's Republic: A Biography* (London: Atlantic Books, 2006). The book shows how Plato's ideas concerning the perfect state and the perfect mind have helped shape modern Western culture.

Alan Bloom, trans., *The Republic of Plato*, 2nd ed. (New York: Basic Books, 1991). The famous translation by one of America's best-known intellectuals.

Thomas C. Brickhouse and Nicholas D. Smith, *Plato's Socrates* (New York: Oxford University Press, 1994). An analysis of the Socratic philosophy.

Ronna Burger, *The Phaedo, A Platonic Labyrinth* (South Bend, Ind.: St. Augustine's Press, 1999). A comprehensive study of Plato's *Phaedo,* which contains the Theory of Forms and Plato's ideas on the immortality of the soul.

David Gallop, trans., *Defence of Socrates, Euthyphro, Crito* (New York: Oxford University Press, 1999). This book gives access to the character of Socrates and the nature of his final trial.

E. Hamilton and H. Cairns, eds., *The Collected Dialogues of Plato* (New York: Bollingen Foundation, 1961). This is what you need to acquaint yourself firsthand with Plato's dialogues. Be sure to read the *Republic,* if you haven't already.

Richard Kraut, ed., *The Cambridge Companion to Plato* (New York: Cambridge University Press, 1996). A modern, convenient, accessible guide to Plato's thought.

Nicholas D. Smith, *The Philosophy of Socrates* (Boulder, Colo.: Westview Press, 1999). A comprehensive introduction to the life and thought of Socrates.

Harold Tarrant, *Plato's First Interpreters* (Ithaca, N.Y.: Cornell University Press, 2000). An exploration of ancient interpretations of Plato's writings.

A. E. Taylor, *Plato: The Man and His Works* (New York: Methuen, 1960). A standard introduction to Plato's philosophy.

C. C. W. Taylor, ed., *Oxford Studies in Ancient Philosophy* (New York: Oxford University Press, annually). Original articles by contemporary scholars on Aristotle, Plato, the Atomists, and others.

6

The Rise of Modern Metaphysics and Epistemology

Every part of the universe is body, and that which is not body is not part of the universe.   —Thomas Hobbes

Wood, stone, fire, water, flesh . . . are things perceived by my senses; and things perceived by the senses are immediately perceived; and things immediately perceived are ideas; and ideas cannot exist outside the mind.
    —George Berkeley

The transitional period between medieval and modern times was the Renaissance (fourteenth through sixteenth centuries). Through its emphasis on worldly experience and reverence for classical culture, the Renaissance helped emancipate Europe from the intellectual authority of the Church. The modern period in history (and philosophy) that followed lasted through the nineteenth century. Its interesting cultural and social developments include, among other things, the rise of nation-states, the spread of capitalism and industrialization, the exploration and settlement of the New World, the decline of religion, and the eventual domination of science as the most revered source of knowledge. The last development is the most important to a history of metaphysics and epistemology and is briefly described in the box "The Scientific Revolution."

The Scientific Revolution

Modern science began with the Scientific Revolution. That commenced when Copernicus (1473–1543) broke with long tradition and proposed (mid-sixteenth century) that the earth is not the center of the universe but in fact revolves, with the other planets, around the sun. The essence of the revolution lies in several ideas: (1) it is *important* to understand how the world works; (2) to do that, you have to *examine the world itself* rather than read Aristotle or consult scripture; (3) a fruitful way to examine the world is through *experimentation*— this is an idea expressed most clearly by Francis Bacon (1561–1626); and (4) the world is a *mechanical system* that can be *described mathematically*— this is an idea expressed most clearly by René Descartes (1596–1650). The details of the mechanistic Cartesian picture of the universe were filled in (to a degree) by the observations and findings of (among others) Tycho Brahe (1546–1601), Johannes Kepler (1571–1630), Galileo Galilei (1564–1642), and, most important, Sir Isaac Newton (1642–1727), who combined the various discoveries into a unified description of the universe based on the concept of gravitation.

Certain newly invented instruments aided the early scientists in their study of the world, including, most famously, the telescope, the microscope, the vacuum pump, and the mechanical clock. And by no means were the findings of the new science limited to astronomy and the dynamics of moving bodies. There were, for example, William Harvey's (1578–1657) discovery of the circulation of the blood, William Gilbert's (1540–1603) investigations of electricity and magnetism, and the various discoveries of Robert Boyle (1627–1691)— the father of chemistry—concerning gases, metals, combustion, acids and bases, and the nature of colors.

Another important idea that came to be characteristic of the Scientific Revolution was that the fundamental constituents of the natural world are basically corpuscular or atomistic—things are made out of tiny particles. The modern scientists (in effect) declared that Democritus had gotten things right.

To most educated Westerners today, it is a matter of plain fact that there exists a universe of physical objects related to one another spatiotemporally. These objects are composed, we are inclined to believe, of minute atoms and subatomic particles that interact with one another in mathematically describable ways.

We are also accustomed to think that in addition to the spatiotemporal *physical* universe there exist human (and perhaps other) observers who are able to perceive their corner of the universe and, within certain limits, to understand it. The *understanding,* we are inclined to suppose, and the *minds* in which this understanding exists, are not themselves physical entities, though we also tend to think that understanding and minds depend in some sense on the functioning of physical entities such as the brain and central nervous system. They, the understanding itself and the minds that have it—unlike physical things such as brains and atoms and nerve impulses and energy fields—exist in time but not in space. They, unlike physical things, are not bound by the laws of physics and are not made up of parts.

Thus, today it seems to be a matter of plain common sense that reality has a dual nature. The world or the universe, we believe, consists of physical objects on one hand and minds on the other. In a normal living person, mind and matter are intertwined in such a way that what happens to the body can affect the mind

Galileo being tried for heresy before a papal tribunal.

and what happens in the mind can affect the body. The clearest examples of mind–body interaction occur when the mind, through an act of will, causes the body to perform some action or when something that happens to the body triggers a new thought in the mind.

So this *commonsense metaphysics,* as we have been describing it, is dualistic. It supposes that two different kinds of phenomena exist: physical and mental (often called "spiritual"). *Dualism* is essentially the "two-realms view" invented by Plato, incorporated with changes into Christianity by Augustine and others and transmitted to us in its contemporary form by early modern philosophers.

Although our commonsense metaphysics is dualistic, it did not have to be that way; we might have adopted an alternative metaphysical perspective. Here are the main possibilities:

- **Dualism.** This view holds that what exists is either physical or mental ("spiritual"); some things, such as a human person, have both a physical component (a physical body) and a mental component (a mind).

- **Materialism,** or physicalism. This view holds that only the physical exists. Accordingly, so-called mental things are in some sense manifestations of an underlying physical reality. (Do not confuse metaphysical materialism with the doctrine that the most important thing is to live comfortably and acquire wealth.)

Chapter 6 · *The Rise of Modern Metaphysics and Epistemology* 99

- **Idealism.** This view holds that only the mental (or "spiritual") exists. Accordingly, so-called physical things are in some sense manifestations of the mind or of thought. (Do not confuse metaphysical idealism with the views of the dreamer who places ideals above practical considerations.)

- **Alternative views.** Some theorists have held that what exists is ultimately neither mental nor spiritual; still others have believed that what exists is ultimately both mental and physical. How could it be both mental and physical? According to this view, sometimes called **double aspect theory,** the mental and physical are just different *ways of looking at* the same things—things that in themselves are neutral between the two categories.

Thanks to the legacy of Greek and Christian influences on Western civilization, dualism continues to command the assent of common sense. Increasingly, however, the march of science seems philosophically to undermine metaphysical dualism in favor of materialism. At stake here are three important questions:

1. Does an immaterial God exist?
2. Do humans have free will?
3. Is there life after death?

Unfortunately for those who would prefer the answer to one or another of the questions to be "yes," a scientific understanding of the world tends to imply the materialist view that all that exists is matter. This is one major reason why modern metaphysics may be said to be concerned with powerful stuff: riding on the outcome of the competition among the perspectives just listed (dualism, materialism, idealism, and alternative views) is the reasonableness of believing in God, free will, and the hereafter.

Let us therefore consider each of these perspectives as it arose during the modern period of philosophy.

100   Part One · *Metaphysics and Epistemology: Existence and Knowledge*

Chronology of Postmedieval History

Here, for easy reference, are the dates of the major periods in postmedieval history mentioned in the text:

The Renaissance: the fourteenth through sixteenth centuries

The Reformation and Counter-Reformation: the sixteenth century

The Scientific Revolution: the seventeenth century (though that revolution still continues)

The Enlightenment or *Age of Reason:* the eighteenth century

The Industrial Revolution: the mid-eighteenth to mid-nineteenth centuries

The Romantic Period: the late eighteenth to very early nineteenth centuries

The Age of Technology: the twentieth century to the present

DESCARTES AND DUALISM

Many European thinkers of the sixteenth century began to question established precepts and above all to question the accepted authorities as arbiters of truth. That so-and-so said that something was true was no longer automatically accepted as proof of that something, no matter who said it or what the something was. This tendency to question authority effectively set the stage for the Scientific Revolution and modern philosophy, both of which are products of the seventeenth century. (For a chronology of postmedieval history, see the box above.)

Modern philosophy is usually said to have begun with **René Descartes** [day-KART] (1596–1650), mathematician, scientist, and, of course, philosopher. Descartes' importance to Western intellectual history cannot be overestimated. Other thinkers we have mentioned may have equaled him in significance, but none has surpassed him. He made important contributions to physiology, psychology, optics, and especially mathematics, in which he originated the Cartesian[1] coordinates and Cartesian curves. It is thanks to Descartes that students now study analytic geometry; he introduced it to the world.

Descartes was a Catholic, but he also believed there are important truths that cannot be ascertained through the authority of the Church. These include those truths that pertain to the ultimate nature of existing things.

But what, then, he wondered, is to be the *criterion* of truth and knowledge in such matters? What is to be the criterion by which one might separate *certain knowledge* about matters of fact from inferior products such as *mere belief?*

Such questions were not new to philosophy, of course. During the Renaissance, the classical skeptical works, notably those by Sextus, were "rediscovered," published, and taken quite seriously—even contributing to the controversies during the Protestant Reformation about the knowability of religious beliefs. In addition, in the sixteenth and seventeenth centuries, various new skeptical writings appeared. Especially noteworthy in this resurgent skeptical tradition were Pierre Gassendi (1592–1655) and Marin Mersenne (1588–1648), who separately used a variety of

---

[1] *Cartesian* is the adjective form of Descartes.

PROFILE: René Descartes (1596–1650)

Descartes had the great fortune to be able to transform his inheritance into a comfortable annual income on which he lived. And he did not waste his time. Before he died, he had made important advances in science, mathematics, and philosophy. Descartes founded analytic geometry and contributed to the understanding of negative roots. He wrote a text in physiology and did work in psychology. His work in optics was significant. His contributions in philosophy are of enormous importance.

As a youth, Descartes attended the Jesuit College at La Flèche and the University of Poitiers. When he was twenty-one, he joined the Dutch army and, two years later, the Bavarian army. His military experience allowed him to be a spectator of the human drama at first hand and granted him free time to think. In 1628 he retired to Holland, where he lived for twenty years in a tolerant country in which he was free from religious persecution.

Descartes was a careful philosopher and a cautious person. Although he took great issue with the medievalist thinking of his teachers, he did not make them aware of his reactions. Later, when he heard that the Church had condemned Galileo

for his writings, he decided that he would have his works published only one hundred years after his death. He subsequently changed his mind, though he came to wish that he had not. For when he did publish some of his ideas, they were bitterly attacked by Protestant theologians; Catholic denunciations came later. This caused Descartes to say that, had he been smarter, he would not have written anything, so he would have had more peace and quiet to think.

Two unconnected incidents in Descartes' life are always mentioned in philosophy texts. One is that the insights that underlay his philosophy came to him in dreams after he had spent a winter day relaxing in a well-heated room while in the army in Bavaria. The other is that he accepted an invitation, with some reluctance, to tutor Queen Christina of Sweden in 1649. This was a big mistake, for the cold weather and early hour of his duties literally killed him. We can only speculate what the queen learned from the episode.

Descartes' principal philosophical works are *Discourse on Method* (1637), *Meditations on First Philosophy* (1641), and *Principles of Philosophy* (1644).

skeptical arguments (which we do not have the space to discuss) to establish the unknowability of the true nature of things. Both believed, however, that a study of the appearances of things could yield information useful for living in this world.

Descartes was vitally concerned with skeptical questions as to the possibility of knowledge, but he was no skeptic. His interest in mathematics strongly affected his philosophical reflections, and it was his more or less lifelong intention to formulate a unified science of nature that was as fully certain as arithmetic.

He did, however, employ skepticism as a method of achieving certainty. His idea was simple enough: I will doubt everything that can possibly be doubted, he reasoned, and if anything is left, then it will be absolutely certain. Then I will consider what it is about this certainty (if there is one) that places it beyond doubt, and that will provide me with a *criterion* of truth and knowledge, a yardstick against which I can measure all other purported truths to see if they, too, are beyond doubt.

Skepticism as the Key to Certainty

Let's see how Descartes' *doubting methodology* worked.

To doubt every proposition that he possibly could, Descartes employed two famous conjectures, the **dream conjecture** and the **evil demon conjecture.** For all I know, Descartes said, I might now be dreaming—that is Descartes'

Descartes' Conjectures

For all I know, I might now be dreaming. This is Descartes' dream conjecture, and it is easy enough to disprove, correct? I just pinch myself. But then again . . . am I just dreaming that I pinched myself? Might not any evidence I have that I am now awake just be dream evidence? Can I really be certain that I won't find myself in a few moments waking up, realizing that I have been dreaming? And thus can I really be sure that the things I see around me, this desk and book, these arms and legs, have any existence outside my mind?

Well, you may say, even if I am dreaming, there are still many things I cannot doubt; even if I am dreaming, I cannot doubt, for instance, that two and three are five or that a square has four sides.

But then again—and this is where Descartes' evil demon conjecture comes in—of course, it

seems absolutely certain to me that two and three make five and that a square has four sides. But *some* propositions that have seemed absolutely certain to me have turned out to be false. So how can I be sure that *these* propositions (that two and three make five and that a square has four sides), or any other proposition that seems certain to me, are not likewise false? For all I know, a deceitful and all-powerful intelligence has so programmed me that I find myself regarding as absolute certainties propositions that in fact are not true at all.

Descartes thought that these two conjectures combined in this way to force him "to avow that there is nothing at all that I formerly believed to be true of which it is impossible to doubt."

---

dream conjecture. And further, he said, for all I know, some malevolent demon devotes himself to deceiving me at every turn so that I regard as true and certain propositions that are in fact false. That supposition is Descartes' evil demon conjecture.

Yes, these two conjectures are totally bizarre, and Descartes was as aware of that as you are. But that is just the point. What Descartes was looking for was a measure of certainty that escapes even the most incredible and bizarre possibilities of falsehood.

And what he discovered, when he considered everything he thought he knew in the light of one or the other of these two bizarre possibilities, is that he could doubt *absolutely everything, save one indubitable truth:* "I think, therefore I am"—**cogito, ergo sum.** Remember this phrase, which is from Descartes' *Discourse on Method.*

What Descartes meant is that any attempt to doubt one's existence as a thinking being is impossible because to doubt is to think and to exist. Try for a moment to doubt your own existence, and you will see what Descartes meant. The self that doubts its own existence must surely exist to be able to doubt in the first place. (For further description of this line of reasoning, see the box "Descartes' Conjectures.") Like Augustine, Descartes had found certain truth in his inability to doubt his own existence.

The "Clear and Distinct" Litmus Test

Descartes went much further than Augustine. Having supposedly found certain knowledge in his own existence as a thing that thinks, he reasoned as follows:

> I am certain that I am a thing that thinks; but do I not then likewise know what is required to make me certain of a truth? In this knowledge of my existence as a

I think, therefore I am, I think . . .

thinking thing there is nothing that assures me of its truth, excepting the clear and distinct perception of that which I state, which would not indeed suffice to assure me that what I say is true, if it could ever happen that a thing that I conceived so clearly and distinctly could be false. And accordingly it seems to me that already I can establish as a general rule that all things that I perceive very clearly and very distinctly are true.

In other words, Descartes examined his single indubitable truth to see what guaranteed its certainty and saw that any other proposition he apprehended with identical "clarity and distinctness" must likewise be immune to doubt. In short, he had discovered in the certainty of his own existence an essential characteristic of certain truth: anything that was as clear and distinct as his own existence would pass the litmus test and would also have to be certain.

Using this **clear and distinct criterion,** Descartes found to his own satisfaction that he could regard as certain much of what he had initially had cause to doubt. This doubting methodology was like geometry, in which a theorem whose truth initially only *seems* true is demonstrated as absolutely certain by deducing it from basic axioms by means of rules of logic. Descartes' axiom was, in effect, "I think, therefore I am," and his rule of logic was "Whatever I perceive clearly and distinctly is certain."

And so Descartes, having armed himself with an absolutely reliable litmus test of truth, discovers first that he has certain knowledge that God exists. (We shall go over the details of Descartes' proof of God's existence in Part Three.) Also, Descartes finds that he knows for certain, and that therefore it is the case, that God would not deceive the thinking mind with perceptions of an external world—a world of objects outside the mind—if such did not exist. Thus, for Descartes, there are, beyond God, two separate and distinct substances, and reality has a dual nature. On one hand is *material substance,* whose essential attribute is **extension** (occupancy of space), and on the other hand is *mind,* whose essential attribute is **thought.** Because a substance, according to

Oliva Sabuco de Nantes and the Body–Soul Connection

Descartes speculated that the mind interacts with the body in the pineal gland. Sixty or so years before Descartes, **Oliva Sabuco de Nantes** [sah-BOO-ko] (1562–?) proposed that, as the properties of the mind (or "soul," as she called it) are not physical properties, they cannot be physically located in some specific spot. Thus, she reasoned, the connection between body and soul occurs *throughout* the brain. The brain and the rest of the body "serve the soul like house servants serve the house," she maintained. She argued that a person is a microcosm (a miniature version) of the world, and this discloses that, in the same way as God activates, rules, and governs the world, the soul governs the "affects, movements, and actions of humans."

It is worth mentioning that Sabuco also believed that the intimate connection between soul and brain means there is a close relationship between psychological and physical health and between morality and medicine. For example, as soon as a negative emotion such as *sorrow* begins to affect our body, she said, we must control it before it becomes unmanageable *despair*. Virtuous passions promote good health, she said; immoral passions cause sickness and disease. As an illustration, she cited excessive sexual activity, which causes (she believed) excessive loss of an essential brain fluid, resulting in brainstem dehydration and the insanity found in advanced cases of syphilis and gonorrhea. There exists, she reasoned, a natural, medical basis for moral sanctions against sexual promiscuity. (It is pretty easy to think of a modern illustration of this thesis.)

Sabuco, born in Alcaraz, Spain, published her important book, *New Philosophy of Human Nature*, when she was only twenty-five years old. This was at the tail end of the Spanish Inquisition—not the most congenial of times for objective scholarship—and Sabuco was taking something of a risk as a woman writer of philosophy. Nevertheless, she was highly knowledgeable about ancient and medieval thinkers, and her book was cleared by the Church with only a few changes. It became quite influential and was published several times during her lifetime and in every century after her death.

Certainly, Sabuco did not solve the problem of mind–body interaction, but she anticipated by several hundred years today's holistic medicine with its emphasis on the intimate connection between mental and physical well-being.

Descartes, "requires nothing other than itself to exist," it follows that mind and matter are totally independent of each other. Still, he thought that in a living person the mind and the material body interact, the motion of the body being sometimes affected by the mind and the thoughts of the mind being influenced by physical sensations.

This is, of course, familiar stuff. Our commonsense metaphysics is pretty much the dualistic metaphysics of Descartes. (However, see the box on Oliva Sabuco.) Unfortunately, there are embarrassing difficulties in the Cartesian dualistic metaphysics. These difficulties vexed Descartes and have yet to be plausibly resolved. In Chapter 9 we explain these difficulties in some detail.

To anticipate what is said there, Descartes thought:

1. Material things, including one's own body, are completely subject to physical laws.

But he also thought:

2. The immaterial mind can move one's body.

The difficulty is that, if the immaterial mind can do this, then one's body evidently is *not* completely subject to physical laws after all. It seems contradictory to hold both (1) and (2). Do *you* hold both (1) and (2)?

Descartes also found it difficult to understand just how something immaterial *could* affect the movement of something material. He said that the mind interacts with the body through "vital spirits" in the brain, but he recognized that this explanation was quite obscure and almost wholly metaphorical. It was, in short, a dodge.

Some of Descartes' followers proposed a solution to the problem of how the immaterial mind interacts with the material body, given that the body is supposed to be subject to physical laws. The solution is called **parallelism.** The mind, they argued, does not *really* cause the body to move. When I will that my hand should move, my act of willing only *appears* to cause my hand to move.

What actually happens is two parallel and coordinated series of events: one a series of mental happenings, and the other a series that involves happenings to material things. Thus, my act of willing my hand to move does not cause my hand to move, but the act of willing and the movement of the hand *coincide*. Hence, it *appears* that the willing causes the moving.

Why do these events just happen to coincide? To account for the coinciding of the mental happenings with the physical happenings, Descartes' followers invoked God. God, they said, is the divine coordinator between the series of mental happenings and the series of material happenings. (In a variant of parallelism known as **occasionalism,** when I will my hand to move, that is the occasion on which God causes my hand to move.)

This theory of parallelism seems far-fetched, true. But perhaps that only illustrates how serious a difficulty it is to suppose both that material things, including one's body, are completely subject to physical laws and that the immaterial mind can move one's body.

To date, a satisfactory explanation of the problem of interaction still has not been found.

Despite these problems, Descartes thought he had succeeded in establishing metaphysical dualism as absolutely certain. He also thought he had shown that the mind, because it is not in space and hence does not move, is not in any sense subject to physical laws and therefore is "free." The metaphysical dualism that survives today as mere "common sense," though it originated with Plato and was incorporated into Christianity by Augustine, survives in the form developed by Descartes. Yesterday's philosophy became today's common sense.

Notice Descartes' overall approach to metaphysical issues. Instead of asking, "What is the basic stuff?" or "Of what does reality consist?" Descartes took an indirect approach and asked, in effect, "What do I know is the basic stuff?" and "Of what can I be certain about the nature of reality?" Descartes tried to discover *metaphysical* truth about what *is* through epistemological inquiry about *what can be known.*

We will call this approach to metaphysical truth the **epistemological detour.** After Descartes, and largely because of him, modern philosophy has attached considerable importance to epistemology, and metaphysical inquiry is often conducted via the epistemological detour.

Unfortunately, maybe the least debatable part of Descartes' overall reasoning is the two skeptical arguments (the dream conjecture and the evil demon conjecture) he advanced at the outset, which seem to make it a live issue whether what passes for knowledge genuinely is knowledge. After Descartes, the philosophers of the seventeenth century became divided about the power of reason in overcoming skepticism. This division is summarized in the box later in this chapter titled "Rationalism and Empiricism."

HOBBES AND MATERIALISM

Thomas Hobbes (1588–1679) read Descartes' *Meditations* before its publication and raised several criticisms, which, together with Descartes' rejoinders, were published by Descartes. About ten years later, in 1651, Hobbes published his own major work, *Leviathan.*

Hobbes was on close terms with many of the best scientists and mathematicians of the period, including most significantly Galileo, and their discoveries seemed to him to imply clearly that all things are made of material particles and that all change reduces to motion. Accordingly, the basic premise of Hobbes's metaphysics is that *all that exists is bodies in motion*, motion being a continual relinquishing of one place and acquiring of another. Because, according to Hobbes, there are two main types of bodies, physical bodies and political bodies, there are two divisions of philosophy, natural and civil. Here we are concerned with Hobbes's natural philosophy. Later we will examine his civil, or political, philosophy, which was enormously important.

Now, this business that all that exists is bodies in motion might sound plausible, until you consider such things as thoughts or acts of volition or emotion. Can it really be held that *thought* is just matter in motion? That *emotions* are? That *hatred* is? "Yes," said Hobbes.

Perception

Hobbes's strategy was to show that there is a basic mental activity, **perception,** or, as he called it, "sense," from which all other mental phenomena are derived and that perception itself reduces to matter in motion.

Perception, he maintained, occurs as follows: Motion in the external world causes motion within us. This motion within (which Hobbes called a "phantasm") is experienced by us as an external object (or group of objects) having certain properties. The properties do not *really* exist in the objects, Hobbes said; they are just the way the objects *seem* to us:

> The things that really are in the world outside us are those motions by which these seemings are caused.

So motion outside us causes motion within us, which is a perception. If the internal motion remains for a while even after the external object is no longer present, it is then *imagination* or *memory*. And *thinking,* he said, is merely a sequence of these perceptions. (There are subtleties in his account of thinking we won't now bother with.)

Now, humans, unlike animals (Hobbes said), are able to form signs or names (words) to designate perceptions, and it is this ability that allows humans to reason. In Hobbes's view, *reasoning* is nothing but "adding and subtracting of the consequences of general names." Reasoning occurs, for example, when you see that the consequences of the name *circle* are, among other things, that if a straight line is drawn through the center of a circle, the circle has been divided into two equal parts.

As for *decisions* and other voluntary actions, such as walking or speaking or moving our arms, these are all movements of the body that begin internally as "endeavors," caused by perceptions. When the endeavor is toward something that causes it, this is *desire;* when away from it, it is *aversion.* Love is merely desire, and hate merely aversion. We call a thing "good" when it is an object of desire and "bad" when it is an object of aversion. *Deliberation* is simply an alternation of desires and aversions, and *will* is nothing but the last desire or aversion remaining in a deliberation.

We've left out the finer details of Hobbes's account, but this should show you how Hobbes tried to establish that every aspect of human psychology is a derivative of perception and that perception itself reduces to matter in motion.

This theory that all is matter in motion may well strike you as implausible, maybe even ridiculous. Nevertheless, as you will see in Chapter 9, it expresses in a rudimentary form a view that is quite attractive to many contemporary philosophers and brain scientists, namely, that every mental activity is a brain process of one sort or another.

THE ALTERNATIVE VIEWS OF CONWAY, SPINOZA, AND LEIBNIZ

So much, then, for Descartes and dualism and Hobbes and materialism. We still need to discuss the remaining two perspectives listed at the beginning of this chapter, idealism and "alternative views." Since historically idealism was introduced last, we turn now to these alternative views—the three alternative metaphysical systems of Anne Conway, Benedictus de Spinoza, and Gottfried Wilhelm, Baron von Leibniz. It must be said that Spinoza and Leibniz had the greatest influence on subsequent developments, but we shall treat the three in chronological order.

The Metaphysics of Anne Conway

The metaphysical system that **Anne Conway** (1631–1679) developed is a *monadology:* a view that all things are reducible to a single substance that is itself irreducible. (This is roughly what atomic theory was until the discovery of subatomic particles in the twentieth century.) The most famous monadology in the history of philosophy is that of Leibniz. Leibniz was familiar with Conway's metaphysics, and scholars believe Conway's philosophy was a forerunner of Leibniz's.

In Conway's view, there is a kind of continuum between the most material and the most mental or "spiritual" substances. All created substances ("Creatures,"

108   Part One   ·   *Metaphysics and Epistemology: Existence and Knowledge*

PROFILE: Anne Finch, The Viscountess Conway (1631–1679)

Like most women of the seventeenth century, Anne Conway, as she is usually called, had no formal education. Her father, who was speaker of the House of Commons, died a week before Anne was born. But her family remained influential, her half-brother becoming lord high chancellor in England. So Anne Finch grew up knowing some of the most important and influential English intellectuals of her time. At home, she somehow managed to learn French, Latin, Hebrew, and Greek. She also studied mathematics and philosophy. She was critical of the work of Descartes (or "Cartes," as he was sometimes called), Hobbes, and Spinoza. And she discussed philosophy with some fairly well-known philosophers who lived in or visited England during her lifetime. The philosophical community was a small one there, and everybody in it seems to have known everybody else. She worked closely with some influential philosophers known as the Cambridge Platonists.

Anne Conway suffered from migraine headaches, and that is supposed to account for the unreadable scrawl with which she penciled her book, *The Principles of the Most Ancient and Modern Philosophy.* Depending on which scholar you read, she wrote it either between 1671 and 1674 or between 1677 and 1679. She died without having a chance to correct or revise it. Her husband was away in Ireland

at the time; and Francis Mercury von Helmont, her friend and one of the colleagues with whom she often discussed philosophy and religion, preserved her body in wine until her husband could return for the funeral.

Von Helmont had Conway's work translated into Latin and published in 1690. Two years later, it was translated back into English by somebody whose initials were J. C. Now, von Helmont was a good friend of Leibniz and showed him Conway's book. Scholars who have studied Conway's philosophy consider her to have been a forerunner of Leibniz in many ways. However, in the words of Sarah Hutton, writing in 2003 in the *Stanford Encyclopedia of Philosophy,*[1]

> although she was unusual as a female philosopher of the seventeenth century, by virtue of the fact that her philosophy achieved publication, the anonymity of her work has ensured that she has suffered the same neglect that has been the lot of most pre-modern female philosophers.

A digital copy of *The Principles of the Most Ancient and Modern Philosophy* is available online at http://digital.library.upenn.edu/women/conway/principles/principles.html.

[1] http://plato.stanford.edu/entries/conway.

Conway called them) are both mental and physical to some degree or other. Conway also argued that all created substances are dependent on God's decision to create them. Moreover, she said that all such Creatures have both an individual essence (what makes one thing different from another) and an essence that is common to all. This essence in common is what later came to be known as *de re* modality. The idea of *de re* essentially means that a property (in this case, the property of being both mental and physical) must be a property of anything that is created by God; otherwise, it ceases to be what it is. It could not exist except that it is necessarily both mental and physical. Everything—persons, animals, plants, inanimate objects (furniture)—is a substance. And everything is partly physical and partly mental, and could not be otherwise.

God, of course, is another matter, Conway believed. God is nonmaterial, non-physical; God is also all-perfect. Therefore, the one thing God cannot do is change his mind about being spiritual. To change his mind and be physical one moment, spiritual the next, and maybe back again, would imply that one state or the other was less than perfect. What possible reason could God have to want to change? What's not to like? Now, that does not mean that God cannot be physical; he just does not *want* to be and never would want to be because that would suggest that he was not perfect before the change. And we all know that if God is anything, he is perfect. God created Christ (making God older than Christ), and Christ, God's first physical manifestation of himself (his first Creature), always had some degree of physical essence and some degree of mental or spiritual essence.

Because God is perfect, Conway held, he is changeless and therefore exists outside the dimension of time. Conway's concept of time is less technical than, but philosophically much like, that articulated recently by the great contemporary physicist Stephen Hawking in his book *A Brief History of Time,* according to whom (roughly) time is the succession of events. Conway called events "motions" and "operations" of created objects (Creatures). Understood this way, time is the measure of changes in things. Because creating (making Creatures) is part of God's primary essence (a necessary property—the way God defines himself, as creator), Conway's God is an eternal creator. The universe is therefore not something that was made at some specific time: it always existed because God always existed and he was always creating. Past and future are all God's present.

Conway's book, *The Principles of the Most Ancient and Modern Philosophy,* reminds one of Spinoza's *Ethics* (see the following section) and Leibniz's *Monadology* (see pages 111–113) in that Conway begins with a series of assumptions or "axioms" (though she did not refer to them as such) and then derives from them various philosophical conclusions or "theorems" (though, again, she did not refer to them as such). If you read these three works, you are apt to be struck by how difficult it is to dispute the writer's conclusions if you accept the assumptions.

Spinoza

God also played an important role in the philosophy of **Benedictus de Spinoza** [spin-O-zuh] (1632–1677), even though Spinoza was considered an atheist. About the time Hobbes was sending his work to Amsterdam for publication, Spinoza was completing his major work, *Ethics,* in that city. Holland during this period of history was the most intellectually tolerant of all European countries, sort of a seventeenth-century Berkeley, California. It was probably also the only country in which the government would have tolerated Spinoza's opinions, which, like Hobbes's, were considered atheistic and repulsive.

Spinoza's *Ethics* consists of some 250 "theorems," each of which he attempted to derive by rigorous deductive logic from a set of eight basic definitions and seven self-evident axioms. Given his axioms and definition of substance (that which depends on nothing else for its conception, i.e., that which is self-subsistent), Spinoza is able to prove that there are no multiple substances, as Descartes thought, but

PROFILE: Benedictus de Spinoza (1632–1677)

The gentle Spinoza was among the most ethical men ever to have lived. "As a natural consequence," twentieth-century philosopher Bertrand Russell observed, "he was considered, during his lifetime and for a century after his death, a man of appalling wickedness."

Spinoza's family was one of many Jewish families that fled Portugal for Holland to escape the terrors of the Inquisition. His serious nature and love of learning were appreciated by all until he pointed out that the Old Testament and biblical tradition were full of inconsistencies. This produced a venomous wrath in the Jewish community. At first Spinoza was offered an annual pension for concealing his doubts. When this failed, the logical next step was taken: an attempt was made to murder him. He was finally, of course, excommunicated from the synagogue.

For a time, Spinoza lived in the house of his Latin teacher, though he later rented a room in a tiny house in Rhynsburg, now a suburb of Leyden, where he earned a sparse living by grinding glass lenses. He lived a modest and frugal existence and preferred to work on his philosophy than to do anything else.

Spinoza became known despite his quiet and retiring existence, and at one point he was offered a professorship at Heidelberg. He declined the appointment, realizing that there would be restrictions on his academic freedom and fearing that his philosophy might draw sharp reactions in German society. In that suspicion he was probably correct, if the fact that many German professors referred to him as "that wretched monster" is any indication.

Still, after his death, some of the greatest thinkers eventually came to appreciate his depth. Hegel went so far as to say that all subsequent philosophy would be a kind of Spinozism.

Spinoza died when he was forty-four, from tuberculosis. His condition was aggravated by the glass dust that he was forced to breathe in his profession. Today, the society for out-of-work American philosophers is called The Lensgrinders.

---

only one infinite substance. Spinoza equated this substance with God, but we must not be misled by his proof of God. Spinoza's "god" is simply *basic substance:* it is not the personal Judaeo-Christian God; rather, it is simply the sum total of everything that is. It is reality, nature. Although Spinoza was considered an atheist, he was not. On the contrary, he was a pantheist: god is all.

Because there is only one substance, according to Spinoza, thought and extension are not the attributes of two separate and distinct substances, mind and matter, as Descartes had thought. What they are, in Spinoza's system, are different attributes of the one basic substance—they are alternative ways of conceiving of it.

So a living person, from Spinoza's point of view, is not a composite of two different things. The living person is a single unit or "modification" of substance that can be conceived either as extension or as thought. Your "body" is a unit of substance conceived as extension; your "mind" is the selfsame unit of substance conceived as thought.

Because, according to Spinoza, the infinite substance is infinite in all respects, it necessarily has infinite attributes. Therefore, thought and extension are not the only attributes of substance. They are just the only attributes we know—they are the only ways available to us of characterizing or conceiving substance. They are, so to speak, the only "languages" in terms of which we can speak and think about reality or substance.

Accordingly, for Spinoza there is no problem in explaining how the mind interacts with the body, for they are one and the same thing. Wondering how the mind and the body interact is like wondering how your last glass of *wine* and your last glass of *vino* could mix with each other. The mind and the body are the same thing, conceptualized from different viewpoints.

In Spinoza's system, there is no personal immortality after death. Further, free will is an illusion; whatever happens is caused by the nature of substance. Material bodies are governed by the laws of physics, and what happens to them is completely determined by what happened before. Because the mental and the material are one and the same, what happens in minds is as inevitable as what happens in bodies. Everything was, is, and will be exactly as it must be.

There is certainly more to Spinoza's philosophy than this, but this is enough for our purposes here. Where Descartes had postulated two separate substances, both Hobbes and Spinoza postulated only one. For Hobbes, however, what exists is only material; a nonmaterial mental realm does not exist. For Spinoza, what exists is both material and mental, depending on how it is conceptualized. Thus, although neither Hobbes nor Spinoza is faced with Descartes' problem of explaining how two realms, the mental and the material, interact, Hobbes is faced with a different problem, that of *explaining away* the mental realm. We are inclined to ask Hobbes just how and why this illusory mental realm seems so clearly to be real when in fact it is not. For Spinoza, the mental realm is real, and there is nothing that he needs to explain away.

Before leaving Spinoza, we should mention that his philosophy is interesting not merely for its content but for its form as well. Spinoza attempted to geometrize philosophy to an extent unequaled by any other major philosopher.

Euclid began his *Elements* with a set of basic definitions and unproved postulates, and from them he logically derived a set of geometric theorems. Likewise, Spinoza began with definitions and seemingly self-evident axioms and proceeded to derive theorems or "propositions" from them.

For example, Spinoza's Proposition III states, "Things which have nothing in common cannot be one the cause of the other." And under that proposition Spinoza gives a proof that refers back to two of his axioms. Thus, giving Spinoza his definitions, and assuming his axioms are beyond doubt and that he made no mistakes in logic, every one of Spinoza's propositions—his *entire* philosophy—is beyond doubt! Spinoza, unlike Descartes, did not take the epistemological detour by explicitly asking, "What can be known?" But by geometrizing his philosophy, Spinoza attempted to provide a metaphysical system that could be known with certainty to be true.

Leibniz

Many recent scholars qualified to make such a judgment think that **Gottfried Wilhelm, Baron von Leibniz** [LIBE-nits] (1646–1716), was the most brilliant intellect of his age. This judgment is made specifically with the fact in mind that Leibniz was the contemporary of a very bright light, Sir Isaac Newton (1642–1727). Leibniz and Newton, independently of each other, developed the calculus—and at the time, there was bitter controversy over who did so first. Leibniz's calculus was

Newtonians, Metaphysicians, and Émilie du Châtelet

One of the important intellectual controversies of the eighteenth century was whether there could be such a thing as action at a distance. On one hand were the Cartesians (followers of Descartes), who said that, if an object is to move, another object must *come up against it and push it.* On the other hand were the Newtonians (followers of Sir Isaac Newton), who believed in action at a distance—for example, two objects will attract one another through the force of gravity, even though they are separated by space. Cartesians generally viewed the concept of action at a distance, and the forces postulated to explain such action, as mystical and bizarre.

This controversy was just a minor skirmish in a broader conceptual battle, that between Newtonian empirical physics, which was based on observation and experimentation, and speculative metaphysics, which was grounded to a large extent purely on reason and was represented by the Cartesians and, most important, the brilliant Leibniz. According to the metaphysicians, even if Newtonian science described *how* the universe operates, it did not show *why* the universe must operate in that way. The metaphysicians felt that Newtonian physics lacked the rational grounding or certainty found in the systems of a Descartes or a Leibniz.

The metaphysical group had other problems with Newtonianism, too, such as how God fit into the Newtonian picture of the universe. If the universe is a vast physical machine, couldn't God change his mind and destroy it—maybe make a different machine? How could there be human free will if the Newtonians were right and humans are just small parts in God's big machine? Do humans have free will, can they do what they choose, or are they nothing more than bodies, moving in reaction to immaterial forces?

A major participant in the disputes between science and metaphysics was **Émilie du Châtelet** [SHA-ta-lay] (1707–1749). Du Châtelet, a colleague (and lover) of Voltaire, was both a scientist and a philosopher, and her writings were respected by both camps. Her two-volume annotated translation of Newton's *Mathematical Principles of Natural Philosophy* (1759) remains to this day *the* French translation of Newton.

In her three-volume work, *Institutions de Physique* (1740), du Châtelet sought to answer some of the metaphysicians' complaints about Newtonianism. She did this essentially by adapting Leibniz's metaphysical principles (for example, the principle of sufficient reason and the principle of the identity of indiscernibles) to Newtonian science in such a way as to provide, she hoped, a vigorous metaphysical foundation for it and to allay fears that Newtonianism required abandoning important theological tenets. Although du Châtelet perhaps did not resolve all the problems, it is safe to say that she did as much as anyone to bring into focus exactly what the bones of contention were.

published in 1684, a few years before Newton's, but Newton had been slow in publishing his work. (Another controversy between the followers of both thinkers is discussed in the box "Newtonians, Metaphysicians, and Émilie du Châtelet.")

Because Leibniz's philosophy is highly technical and difficult to characterize or summarize in a brief passage, we won't go into it in detail. Basically, it is a complicated metaphysical system according to which the ultimate constituents of reality are indivisible atoms. But Leibniz's atoms are not indivisible units of matter, for, because matter is extended, a piece of matter, however tiny, is always further divisible. Instead, Leibniz's atoms are what he called **monads,** which are indivisible units of force or energy or activity. Here, Leibniz anticipated by a couple of centuries the views of contemporary physics, according to which material particles are a form of energy. Leibniz, however, believed the monads to be entirely *nonphysical* and often referred to them as "souls," though he distinguished them from souls in the ordinary sense.

Leibniz's philosophy is not just haphazard or idle speculation. His entire metaphysical system seems to follow from a few basic and plausible assumptions, or basic principles. One of these principles, for example, the **principle of the identity of indiscernibles,** says that, if two beings have exactly the same set of properties, then they are identical with one another. Another principle, known as the **principle of sufficient reason,** says that there is a sufficient reason why things are exactly as they are and are not otherwise. Leibniz also used this principle as a proof of God, as we shall see in Chapter 13.

Leibniz's most famous work is the *Monadology,* available online at http://www.rbjones.com/rbjpub/philos/classics/leibniz/monad.htm.

THE IDEALISM OF LOCKE AND BERKELEY

Descartes, Hobbes, Conway, and Spinoza all belonged to the lively seventeenth century, the century that produced not only great philosophy but also some of the most important scientific discoveries of all time. The seventeenth century, you may recall from your history books, was also the century of the Thirty Years' War (1618–1648), which was the most brutal European war before this century and the English Civil War. It also witnessed the Sun King (Louis XIV of France), the opening of Harvard, the founding of Pennsylvania, and the popularization of smoking.

In England the most important philosopher of the time was **John Locke** (1632–1704). In his great work, *An Essay Concerning Human Understanding,* Locke wished to inquire into the origin, certainty, and extent of human knowledge. Many of his views will almost certainly be shared by most readers of this book. Locke's epistemology is indeed so widely accepted that much of it is now thought to be so much common sense. You should be prepared, however—terrible philosophical difficulties attend Locke's basic position, as commonsensical as it will probably seem.

John Locke and Representative Realism

Locke's fundamental thesis is that all our ideas come from experience. The human mind at birth, he wrote (echoing Aristotle), is essentially a ***tabula rasa,*** or blank slate. On this blank slate, experience makes its imprint. External objects impinge on our senses, which convey into the mind ideas, or, as we might prefer to say today, perceptions, of these objects and their various qualities. In short, sensation furnishes the mind with all its contents. ***Nihil in intellectu quod prius non fuerit in sensu***—nothing exists in the mind that was not first in the senses. This, of course, is familiar and plausible.

These ideas or perceptions of some of the qualities of external objects are accurate copies of qualities that actually reside in the objects, Locke said. This is what he means. Think of a basketball. It has a certain size, shape, and weight, and when we look at and handle the ball, our sensory apparatus provides us with accurate pictures or images or ideas or perceptions of these "primary" qualities, as Locke called them.

114   Part One   •   *Metaphysics and Epistemology: Existence and Knowledge*

Locke's theory: According to Locke, when we say we are looking at an external object, what we are really doing is attending to the perceptions or "ideas" of the object in our mind. Some of these perceptions, such as those of a basketball's size and shape, accurately represent qualities in the object itself. Other perceptions, such as those of the basketball's color and odor, do not represent anything in the object.

The basketball also has the power to produce in us ideas of "secondary" qualities, such as the brown color, the leathery smell, the coolness we feel when we hold it, and so forth. Are these qualities really in the basketball? Well, not exactly, you will say. And that is exactly what Locke said. These secondary qualities exist in the basketball only as the power of the basketball to produce in us ideas of color and taste and so forth—but the color and taste are purely subjective and exist in us merely as ideas. In other words, in Locke's view—and we will bet that this is your view as well—if all sentient creatures were removed from the proximity of the basketball, there would not *be* any brownness, leathery odor, or coolness, but only an object of a certain size and shape and weight, composed of minute particles that collectively would smell leathery and feel cool and look brown if any creatures with sense organs then came into existence and held and looked at and sniffed the ball.

This theory that Locke accepted is often called **representative realism.** In a sentence, it is the theory that we perceive objects *indirectly* by means of our "representations" or ideas or perceptions of them, some of which are accurate copies or representations or reflections of the real properties of "external" objects, of objects "outside the mind." This theory is widely held and is probably regarded by most people as self-evident. Open almost any introductory psychology text, and you will behold implicit in its discussion of perception Locke's theory of representative realism.

Now, we said a moment ago that terrible philosophical difficulties attend to this very nice, down-to-earth, commonsense theory known as representative realism, and it is time for us to explain ourselves. As justifiable as Locke's theory may seem, it is subject to a powerful objection, stated most eloquently by the Irish bishop and philosopher George Berkeley.

George Berkeley and Idealism

If Locke is correct, then we experience sensible things, things like basketballs and garden rakes, *indirectly*—that is, through the intermediary of our ideas or perceptions. But if that is true, **George Berkeley** [BAR-klee] (1685–1753) said, then we cannot know that *any* of our ideas or perceptions accurately represent the qualities

Chapter 6 · *The Rise of Modern Metaphysics and Epistemology*   115

PROFILE: George Berkeley (1685–1753)

Berkeley was born in Ireland and studied at Trinity College, Dublin. He was made a Fellow of the College in 1707. His *Treatise Concerning the Principles of Human Knowledge* (1709) was a great success and gave Berkeley a lasting reputation, though few accepted his theory that nothing exists outside the mind.

Berkeley eventually obtained a post that included a lucrative stipend. But he gave up the post in what proved to be a futile attempt to establish a college in the Bermudas to convert the Indians in North America. He was made Bishop of Cloyne in 1734.

Berkeley was known for his generosity of heart and mind, and also for his enthusiasm for tar water (water made from pine tar). He especially liked the fact that tar water did not have the same effects as alcohol. His writings about the health benefits of drinking tar water actually caused it to become a fad in English society for a time.

Berkeley's main works, in addition to the one already mentioned, are *Essay Towards a New Theory of Vision* (1709) and *Three Dialogues between Hylas and Philonous* (1713).

of these sensible things. Why can't we know this? Because, Berkeley argued, if Locke is correct, we do not directly experience the basketball (or any other object) itself. Instead, what we directly experience is our *perceptions* and *ideas* of the basketball. And if we do not have direct experience of the basketball itself, then we cannot compare our perceptions or ideas of the basketball with the basketball itself to see if they "accurately represent" the basketball's qualities.

Indeed, given Locke's position, Berkeley said, we cannot really know that a thing like a basketball or a garden rake even *exists*. For according to Locke's theory, it is not the *object* we experience but rather our *perceptions* or *ideas* of it.

This, then, is Berkeley's criticism of Locke's theory. As satisfying as it might seem to common sense, Locke's position is the short road to skepticism. If we accept Locke's theory, then we cannot know that "sensible things," things like basketballs and rakes and even our own hands and feet, actually exist.

Berkeley began his criticism of Locke's theory by noting that the objects of human knowledge consist of "ideas" (1) conveyed to the mind through the senses (sense perceptions), (2) perceived by the mind when the mind reflects on its own operations, or (3) compounded or divided by the mind with the help of memory and imagination. "Light and colors, heat and cold, extension (length) and figures (shapes)—in a word the things we see and feel—what are they but so many sensations, notions, ideas, or impressions on the sense?"

There exist, therefore, Berkeley said, ideas and the minds that have them. However, Berkeley observed, people have the strange opinion that houses, mountains, rivers, and all sensible objects have an existence outside the mind. But that is a contradictory opinion, Berkeley suggested. "For what are the forementioned objects but the things we perceive by sense? And what do we perceive besides our own ideas or sensations? And is it not plainly contradictory that any one of these, or any combination of them, should exist unperceived?"

At this point, John Locke's theory kicks in and says that our ideas of *primary* qualities (extension, figure, motion, and so on) *represent* to us or *resemble* properties that exist outside the mind in an inert, senseless substance called matter. "But it is evident," Berkeley wrote, "that extension, figure, and motion are only ideas existing in the mind and consequently cannot exist in an unperceiving substance."

Common sense, of course, tells us that the so-called secondary qualities such as tastes, odors, and colors, exist only in the mind because, after all, what tastes sweet or smells good or seems red to one person will taste bitter or smell bad or seem green to another person. But, Berkeley argued, "let anyone consider those arguments which are thought to prove that colors and tastes exist only in the mind, and he shall find they may with equal force prove the same thing of extention, figure, and motion." In other words, extension, figure, and motion are relative to the observer, too. A cookie, for example, might taste sweet to one taster and bitter to another; but its shape will be elliptical to an observer viewing it from the side and round to an observer viewing it straight on, and its size will be smaller to an observer farther away.

Of course, our inclination is to distinguish the *perceived* size and shape of a cookie from the size and shape that are the cookie's "true" size and shape. But Berkeley pointed out that size and shape (and the other qualities) *are* perceived qualities. Talking about an *unperceived* size or shape is nonsense. It is like talking about unfelt pain. And thus sensible objects, because they are nothing more than their qualities, are themselves only ideas and exist only in the mind.

But, you may still insist (in frustration?), surely there are material things "out there" that have their own size, shape, texture, and the like! Well, Berkeley has already responded to this line of thought: it is contradictory to suppose that size, shape, texture, and so on could exist in unthinking things. Size, shape, texture, and so on are *ideas,* and it is silly to suppose that ideas could exist in unthinking things.

Material Things as Clusters of Ideas

This theory of Berkeley's is *idealism,* the last of the four metaphysical philosophies. There are other versions of idealism, but in Berkeley's version, sensible things, such as tables, chairs, trees, books, and frogs, are not material things that exist outside the mind. They are, in fact, groups of ideas and as such are perceived directly and exist only within the mind. Because they are ideas, we can no more doubt their existence than we can doubt our own aches and pains (which also, indeed, are ideas).

Berkeley's idealism does not mean, however, that the physical world is a mere dream or that it is imaginary or intangible or ephemeral. Dr. Samuel Johnson (1709–1784), the famous English literary critic and scholar, believed that he had refuted Berkeley by kicking a stone, evidently thinking that the solidity of the stone was solid disproof of Berkeley. In fact, Johnson succeeded only in hurting his foot and demonstrating that he did not understand Berkeley. A stone is just as hard an object in Berkeley's philosophy as it is to common sense, for the fact that a stone exists only in the mind does not make its hardness disappear.

Rationalism and Empiricism

A doctrine that St. Thomas Aquinas (see Chapter 5) accepted and attributed to Aristotle, and that John Locke also accepted, is *nihil in intellectu quod prius non fuerit in sensu;* that is, there is nothing in the intellect that was not first in the senses. This doctrine is called **empiricism.** Another doctrine, known as **rationalism,** holds that the intellect contains important truths that were not placed there by sensory experience. "Something never comes from nothing," for example, might count as one of these truths, because experience can tell you only that something has never come from nothing so far, not that it can never, ever happen (or so a rationalist might argue). Sometimes rationalists believe in a *theory of innate ideas,* according to which these truths are "innate" to the mind—that is, they are part of the original dispositions of the intellect.

The empiricist is, in effect, a type of modified skeptic—he or she denies that there is any knowledge that does not stem from sensory experience. Most rationalists, by contrast, do not deny that *some* knowledge about the world can be obtained through experience. But other rationalists, such as Parmenides (see Chapter 2), deny that experience can deliver up any sort of true knowledge. This type of rationalist is also a type of modified skeptic.

Classical rationalism and empiricism in modern philosophy were mainly a product of the seventeenth and eighteenth centuries. Rationalism is associated most significantly during that time period with Descartes (1596–1650), Spinoza (1632–1677), and Leibniz (1646–1716). These three are often called the *Continental rationalists* and are contrasted with Locke (1632–1704), Berkeley (1685–1753), and Hume (1711–1776), the *British empiricists.* (We discuss Hume in the next chapter.) Philosophers from other periods, however, are sometimes classified as rationalists or empiricists depending on whether they emphasized the importance of reason or experience in knowledge of the world. Those earlier philosophers treated in this book who are usually listed as rationalists are, among others, Pythagoras, Parmenides, and Plato. Those who are often listed as empiricists are Aristotle, Epicurus, and Aquinas. Immanuel Kant (1724–1804), also discussed in the next chapter, is said to have synthesized rationalism and empiricism because he believed that all knowledge *begins* with experience (a thesis empiricists agree with) but also believed that knowledge is not limited to what has been found in experience (a thesis rationalists agree with).

Modern epistemology, as you will see, has been predominantly empiricist. This is because the Continental rationalists, and later rationalists too, were primarily metaphysicians. That is, they were generally less concerned with discussing the possibility of knowledge and related issues than with actually coming to propose some philosophically important theory about reality. The great exception is Descartes, a rationalist who concerned himself explicitly with the possibility of knowledge.

As for the stones found in dreams, Berkeley distinguished unreal dream stones from real stones just the way you and we do. Stones found in dreams behave in an irregular and chaotic manner—they can float around or change into birds or whatever—compared with those found in waking life. And Berkeley distinguished stones that we conjure up in our imaginations from real stones by their lack of vividness and also by the fact that they, unlike real stones, can be brought into existence by an act of our will.

Berkeley and Atheism

So Berkeley's position is that sensible things cannot exist independent of perception—to be is to be perceived (***esse est percipi***). What, then, happens to

Telegraph Avenue in Berkeley, California. The city was named after George Berkeley because of his line of poetry, "Westward the course of empire takes its way."

this desk when everyone leaves the room? What happens to the forest when all the people go away? What happens to sensible things when no one perceives them?

Berkeley's answer is that the perceiving mind of God makes possible the continued existence of sensible things when neither you nor any other people are perceiving them. Because sensible things do not depend on the perception of humans and exist independently of them, Berkeley wrote, "There must be some other mind wherein they exist." This other mind, according to Berkeley, is God.

Berkeley believed that the greatest virtue of his idealist system was that it alone did not invite skepticism about God. Dualism, he thought, by postulating the existence of objects outside the mind, made these objects unknowable and was just an open invitation to skepticism about their existence; skepticism about the existence of sensible objects, he thought, would inevitably extend itself to skepticism about their creator, God. Materialism, he believed, made sensible objects independent of God; and thus it, too, led to skepticism about God. His own system, he thought, by contrast made the existence of sensible objects undeniable (they are as undeniable as your own ideas). This meant, for Berkeley, that the existence of the divine mind, in which sensible objects are sustained, was equally undeniable.

So, for Berkeley, the fact that sensible things continue to exist when we do not perceive them is a short and simple proof of God's existence. Another similar proof, in Berkeley's view, can be derived from the fact that we do not ourselves cause our ideas of tables, chairs, mountains, and other sensible things.

We would say the railroad tracks *appear* to grow smaller and closer together. Berkeley thought the tracks *really* did grow smaller and closer together.

"There is therefore," he reasoned, "some other will or spirit that produced them"—God.

Berkeley was aware that his theory that what we call material things are ideas both in God's mind and in our own raises peculiar questions about the relationship between our minds and the mind of God. For example, if a mountain is an idea in God's mind and we perceive the mountain, does that mean we perceive or have God's ideas?

With Berkeley, Hobbes, Descartes, and Spinoza, the four basic metaphysical perspectives of modern philosophy were set out: reality is entirely physical (Hobbes), *or* it is entirely nonphysical or "mental" (Berkeley), *or* it is an even split (Descartes), *or* "matter" and "mind" are just alternative ways of looking at one and the same stuff (Spinoza). See the box "Mind–Body Theories."

An alternative, epistemological classification of these philosophers was given in the box "Rationalism and Empiricism" earlier in this chapter.

Mind–Body Theories

Matter	Mind		
+	+	Both matter and mind	Descartes' dualism
+	−	Only matter, no mind	Hobbes's materialism
−	+	No matter, only mind	Berkeley's idealism
−	−	No matter, no mind	Spinoza's alternativism

120   Part One • *Metaphysics and Epistemology: Existence and Knowledge*

SELECTION 6.1

Meditations on First Philosophy*

René Descartes

[*Descartes'* Meditations on First Philosophy *is among the most widely read books of all time—right up there, almost, with Plato's* Republic. *In this selection, Descartes is trying to doubt everything that can be doubted and finds that almost everything that he previously thought he knew for certain is actually open to question.*]

Reason persuades me that I ought no less carefully to withhold my assent from matters which are not entirely certain and indubitable than from those which appear to me manifestly to be false. . . .

All that up to the present time I have accepted as most true and certain I have learned either from the senses or through the senses; [and], although the senses sometimes deceive us concerning things which are hardly perceptible, or very far away, there are yet many others to be met with as to which we cannot reasonably have any doubt. . . .

For example, there is the fact that I am here, seated by the fire, attired in a dressing gown, having this paper in my hands and other similar matters. And how could I deny that these hands and this body are "mine[?] . . ."

At the same time I must remember that . . . I am in the habit of sleeping and in my dreams representing to myself the same things. . . . How often has it happened to me that in the night I dreamt that I found myself in this particular place, that I was dressed and seated near the fire, while in reality I was lying undressed in bed! At this moment it does indeed seem to me that it is with eyes awake that I am looking at this paper. . . . But in thinking over this I remind myself that on many occasions I have in sleep been deceived by similar illusions, and in dwelling carefully on this reflection I see . . . that there are no certain indications by which we may clearly distinguish wakefulness from sleep. . . .

At the same time we must at least confess that . . . whether I am awake or asleep, two and three together always form five, and the square can never have more than four sides, and it does not seem possible that truths so clear and apparent can be suspected of any falsity.

Nevertheless . . . how do I know that I am not deceived every time that I add two and three, or count the sides of a square, or judge of things yet simpler, if anything simpler can be imagined? . . . Possibly God has not desired that I should be thus deceived, for He is said to be supremely good. . . . But let us . . . grant that all that is here said of a God is a fable. . . . I shall then suppose, not that God who is supremely good and the fountain of truth, but some evil genius not less powerful than deceitful, has employed his whole energies in deceiving me; I shall consider that the heavens, the earth, colors, figures, sound, and all other external things are nought but the illusions and dreams of which this genius has availed himself in order to lay traps for my credulity; I shall consider myself as having no hands, no eyes, no flesh, no blood, nor any senses, yet falsely believing myself to possess all these things. . . .

[Yet even if] there is some deceiver or other, very powerful and very cunning, who ever employs his ingenuity in deceiving me[,] then without a doubt I exist also if he deceives me, and let him deceive me as much as he will, he can never cause me to be nothing so long as I think that I am something. So that after having reflected well and carefully examined all things, we must come to the definite conclusion that this proposition: I am, I exist, is necessarily true each time that I pronounce it, or that I mentally conceive it.

But what am I, now that I suppose that there is a certain genius which is extremely powerful, and, if I may say so, malicious, who employs all his powers in deceiving me? Can I affirm that I possess the least of all those things which I have just said pertain to the nature of body? I pause to consider, I revolve all these things in my mind, and I find none of which I can say that it pertains to me. It would be tedious to

* René Descartes, "Meditations on First Philosophy" from *The Philosophical Works of Descartes,* translated by Elizabeth S. Haldane and G. R. T. Ross, Vol. 1 (Cambridge: The University Press, 1911).

stop to enumerate them. Let us pass to the attributes of soul and see if there is any one which is in me? What of nutrition or walking [the first mentioned]? But if it is so that I have no body it is also true that I can neither walk nor take nourishment. Another attribute is sensation. But one cannot feel without body, and besides I have thought I perceived many things during sleep that I recognised in my waking moments as not having been experienced at all. What of thinking? I find here that thought is an attribute that belongs to me; it alone cannot be separated from me. I am, I exist, that is certain. But how often? Just when I think; for it might possibly be the case if I ceased entirely to think, that I should likewise cease altogether to exist. I do not now admit anything which is not necessarily true: to speak accurately I am not more than a thing which thinks, that is to say a mind or a soul, or an understanding, or a reason, which are terms whose significance was formerly unknown to me. I am, however, a real thing and really exist; but what thing? I have answered: a thing which thinks. . . . What is a thing which thinks? It is a thing which doubts, understands, [conceives], affirms, denies, wills, refuses, which also imagines and feels. . . .

. . . [I]n the little that I have just said, I think I have summed up all that I really know, or at least all that hitherto I was aware that I knew. In order to try to extend my knowledge further, I shall now look around more carefully and see whether I cannot still discover in myself some other things which I have not hitherto perceived. I am certain that I am a thing which thinks; but do I not then likewise know what is requisite to render me certain of a truth? Certainly in this first knowledge there is nothing that assures me of its truth, excepting the clear and distinct perception of that which I state, which would not indeed suffice to assure me that what I say is true, if it could ever happen that a thing which I conceived so clearly and distinctly could be false; and accordingly it seems to me that already I can establish as a general rule that all things which I perceive very clearly and very distinctly are true.

[*At this point in the* Meditations, *Descartes proves to his own satisfaction that he perceives clearly and distinctly that God exists and that God would never permit Descartes to be deceived as long as Descartes forms no judgment except on matters clearly and distinctly represented to Descartes by his understanding. He then continues:*]

Because I know that all things which I apprehend clearly and distinctly can be created by God as I apprehend them, it suffices that I am able to apprehend one thing apart from another clearly and distinctly in order to be certain that the one is different from the other, since they may be made to exist in separation at least by the omnipotence of God . . . and therefore, just because I know certainly that I exist, and that meanwhile I do not remark that any other thing necessarily pertains to my nature of essence, excepting that I am a thinking thing, I rightly conclude that my essence consists solely in the fact that I am a thinking thing . . . [and as] I possess a distinct idea of body, inasmuch as it is only an extended and unthinking thing, it is certain that this I is entirely and absolutely distinct from my body, and can exist without it. . . .

There is certainly further in me a certain passive faculty of perception, that is, of receiving and recognising the ideas of sensible things, but this would be useless to me, if there were not either in me or in some other thing another active faculty capable of forming and producing these ideas. . . . [A]nd since God is no deceiver, [and since] He has given me . . . a very great inclination to believe that [these ideas] are conveyed to me by corporeal objects, I do not see how He could be defended from the accusation of deceit if these ideas were produced by causes other than corporeal objects. Hence we must allow that corporeal things exist. . . . [And] we must at least admit that all things which I conceive in them clearly and distinctly, that is to say, all things which, speaking generally, are comprehended in the object of pure mathematics, are truly to be recognised as external objects. . . .

[O]n the sole Ground that God is not a deceiver . . . there is no doubt that in all things which nature teaches me there is some truth contained. . . . But there is nothing which this nature teaches me more expressly than that I have a body which is adversely affected when I feel pain, which has need of food or drink when I experience the feelings of hunger and thirst, and so on; nor can I doubt there being some truth in all this.

Nature also teaches me by these sensations of pain, hunger, thirst, etc., that I am not only lodged in my body as a pilot in a vessel, but that I am very closely united to it, and so to speak so intermingled with it that I seem to compose with it one whole. For if that were not the case, when my body is hurt,

I, who am merely a thinking thing, would not feel pain, for I should perceive this wound by the understanding only, just as the sailor perceives by sight when something is damaged in his vessel. . . .

[T]here is a great difference between mind and body, inasmuch as body is by nature always divisible, and the mind is entirely indivisible. For, as a matter of fact, when I consider the mind, that is to say, myself inasmuch as I am only a thinking thing, I cannot distinguish in myself any parts, but apprehend myself to be clearly one and entire; and although the whole mind seems to be united to the whole body, yet if a foot, or an arm, or some other part, is separated from my body, I am aware that nothing has been taken away from my mind. And the faculties of willing, feeling, conceiving, etc.,

cannot be properly speaking said to be its parts, for it is one and the same mind which employs itself in willing and in feeling and understanding. But it is quite otherwise with corporeal or extended objects, for there is not one of these imaginable by me which my mind cannot easily divide into parts, and which consequently I do not recognise as being divisible. [T]his would be sufficient to teach me that the mind or soul of man is entirely different from the body, if I had not already learned it from other sources.

I further notice that the mind does not receive the impressions from all parts of the body immediately, but only from the brain, or perhaps even from one of its smallest parts, to wit, from that in which the common sense is said to reside.

SELECTION 6.2

Ethics*

Benedictus de Spinoza

[*This excerpt will give you a good idea of Spinoza's geometric method in which metaphysical certainties ("Proportions") are deduced from a short list of "Definitions" and self-evident "axioms."*]

Definitions and Axioms

Definitions   I. By that which is *self-caused*, I mean that of which the essence involves existence, or that of which the nature is only conceivable as existent.

II. A thing is called *finite after its kind*, when it can be limited by another thing of the same nature; for instance, a body is called finite because we always conceive another greater body. So, also, a thought is limited by another thought, but a body is not limited by thought, nor a thought by body.

III. By *substance*, I mean that which is in itself, and is conceived through itself: in other words, that of which a conception can be formed independently of any other conception.

IV. By *attribute*, I mean that which the intellect perceives as constituting the essence of substance.

V. By *mode*, I mean the modifications of substance, or that which exists in, and is conceived through, something other than itself.

VI. By *God*, I mean a being absolutely infinite—that is, a substance consisting in infinite attributes, of which each expresses eternal and infinite essentiality.

Explanation.—I say absolutely infinite, not infinite after its kind: for, of a thing infinite only after its kind, infinite attributes may be denied; but that which is absolutely infinite, contains in its essence whatever expresses reality, and involves no negation.

VII. That thing is called free, which exists solely by the necessity of its own nature, and of which the action is determined by itself alone. On the other hand, that thing is necessary, or rather constrained, which is determined by something external to itself to a fixed and definite method of existence or action.

VIII. By *eternity*, I mean existence itself, in so far as it is conceived necessarily to follow solely from the definition of that which is eternal.

* From *The Chief Works of Benedictus de Spinoza*, Vol. 2, revised edition, translated by R. H. M. Elwes (London: George Bell & Sons, 1901), 45–48.

Explanation.—Existence of this kind is conceived as an eternal truth, like the essence of a thing, and, therefore, cannot be explained by means of continuance or time, though continuance may be conceived without a beginning or end.

Axioms I. Everything which exists, exists either in itself or in something else.

II. That which cannot be conceived through anything else must be conceived through itself.

III. From a given definite cause an effect necessarily follows; and, on the other hand, if no definite cause be granted, it is impossible that an effect can follow.

IV. The knowledge of an effect depends on and involves the knowledge of a cause.

V. Things which have nothing in common cannot be understood, the one by means of the other; the conception of one does not involve the conception of the other.

VI. A true idea must correspond with its ideate or object.

VII. If a thing can be conceived as non-existing, its essence does not involve existence.

Seven Propositions on Substance

Propositions PROP. I. *Substance is by nature prior to its modifications.*

Proof.—This is clear from Defs. iii. and v.

PROP. II. *Two substances, whose attributes are different, have nothing in common.*

Proof.—Also evident from Def. iii. For each must exist in itself, and be conceived through itself; in other words, the conception of one does not imply the conception of the other.

PROP. III. *Things which have nothing in common cannot be one the cause of the other.*

Proof.—If they have nothing in common, it follows that one cannot be apprehended by means of the other (Ax. v.), and, therefore, one cannot be the cause of the other (Ax. iv.). *Q.E.D.*

PROP. IV. *Two or more distinct things are distinguished one from the other, either by the difference of the attributes of the substances or by the difference of their modifications.*

Proof.—Everything which exists, exists either in itself or in something else (Ax. i.),—that is (by Defs. iii. and v.), nothing is granted in addition to the understanding, except substance and its modifications. Nothing is, therefore, given besides the understanding, by which several things may be distinguished one from the other, except the substances, or, in other words (see Ax. iv.), their attributes and modifications. *Q.E.D.*

PROP. V. *There cannot exist in the universe two or more substances having the same nature or attribute.*

Proof.—If several distinct substances be granted, they must be distinguished one from the other, either by the difference of their attributes, or by the difference of their modifications (Prop. iv.): If only by the difference of their attributes, it will be granted that there cannot be more than one with an identical attribute. If by the difference of their modifications—as substance is naturally prior to its modifications (Prop. i.),—it follows that setting the modifications aside, and considering substance in itself, that is truly (Defs. iii. and vi.), there cannot be conceived one substance different from another,—that is (by Prop. iv.), there cannot be granted several substances, but one substance only. *Q.E.D.*

PROP. VI. *One substance cannot be produced by another substance.*

Proof.—It is impossible that there should be in the universe two substances with an identical attribute, i.e., which have anything common to them both (Prop. ii.), and, therefore (Prop. iii.), one cannot be the cause of another, neither can one be produced by the other. *Q.E.D.*

Corollary.—Hence it follows that a substance cannot be produced by anything external to itself. For in the universe nothing is granted, save substances and their modifications (as appears from Ax. i. and Defs. iii. and v.). Now (by the last Prop.) substance cannot be produced by another substance, therefore it cannot be produced by anything external to itself. *Q.E.D.* This is shown still more readily by the absurdity of the contradictory. For, if substance be produced by an external cause, the knowledge of it would depend on the knowledge of its cause (Ax. iv.), and (by Def. iii.) it would itself not be substance.

PROP. VII. *Existence belongs to the nature of substance.*

Proof.—Substance cannot be produced by anything external (Corollary Prop. vi.), it must, therefore, be its own cause—that is, its essence necessarily involves existence, or existence belongs to its nature.

124   Part One • *Metaphysics and Epistemology: Existence and Knowledge*

SELECTION 6.3

Treatise Concerning the Principles of Human Knowledge

George Berkeley

[*Berkeley's philosophy—that what we call material objects are really just ideas in the mind—strikes newcomers to philosophy as bizarre and preposterous. In this selection, Berkeley defends his view through a series of arguments and rebuttals to those who would disagree with him. Enjoy Berkeley's direct, powerful, elegant English.*]

It is evident to anyone who takes a survey of the objects of human knowledge, that they are either ideas (1) actually imprinted on the senses, or else such as are (2) perceived by attending to the passions and operations of the mind, or lastly (3) ideas formed by help of memory and imagination, either compounding, dividing, or barely representing those originally perceived in the aforesaid ways. By sight I have the ideas of lights and colors, with their several degrees and variations. By touch I perceive hard and soft, heat and cold, motion and resistance, and of all these more and less either as to quantity or degree. Smelling furnishes me with odors, the palate with tastes, and hearing conveys sounds to the mind in all their variety of tone and composition. And as several of these are observed to accompany each other, they come to be marked by one name, and so to be reputed as one thing. Thus, for example, a certain color, taste, smell, figure, and consistence, having been observed to go together, are accounted one distinct thing, signified by the name "apple." Other collections of ideas constitute a stone, a tree, a book, and the like sensible things. . . .

2. But besides all that endless variety of ideas or objects of knowledge, there is likewise something which knows or perceives them, and exercises divers operations, as willing, imagining, remembering, about them. This perceiving, active being is what I call mind, spirit, soul, or myself. By which words I do not denote any one of my ideas, but a thing entirely distinct from them wherein they exist, or, which is the same thing, whereby they are perceived; for the existence of an idea consists in being perceived.

3. That neither our thoughts, nor passions, nor ideas formed by the imagination, exist without the mind, is what everybody will allow. And it seems no less evident that the various sensations or ideas imprinted on the sense, however blended or combined together (that is, whatever objects they compose), cannot exist otherwise than in a mind perceiving them. . . .

4. It is indeed an opinion strangely prevailing amongst men, that houses, mountains, rivers, and in a word all sensible objects, have an existence, natural or real, distinct from their being perceived by the understanding. But with how great an assurance and acquiescence soever this principle may be entertained in the world, yet whoever shall find in his heart to call it in question may, if I mistake not, perceive it to involve a manifest contradiction. For what are the forementioned objects but the things we perceive by sense? and what do we perceive besides our own ideas or sensations? and is it not plainly repugnant that any one of these, or any combination of them, should exist unperceived?

5. Light and colors, heat and cold, extension and figures—in a word the things we see and feel—what are they but so many sensations, notions, ideas, or impressions on the sense? And is it possible to separate, even in thought, any of these from perception? . . .

8. But, say you, though the ideas themselves do not exist without the mind, yet there may be things like them, whereof they are copies or resemblances, which things exist without the mind in an unthinking substance. I answer, an idea can be like nothing but an idea; a color or figure can be like nothing but another color or figure. . . . Again, I ask whether those supposed originals or external things, of which our ideas are the pictures or representations, be themselves perceivable or no? If they are, then they are ideas and we have gained our point; but if

you say they are not, I appeal to anyone whether it be sense to assert a color is like something which is invisible; hard or soft, like something which is intangible; and so of the rest.

9. Some there are who make a distinction betwixt primary and secondary qualities. By the former they mean extension, figure, motion, test, solidity or impenetrability, and number; by the latter they denote all other sensible qualities, as colors, sounds, tastes, and so forth. The ideas we have of these they acknowledge not to be the resemblances of anything existing without the mind, or unperceived, but they will have our ideas of the primary qualities to be patterns or images of things which exist without the mind, in an unthinking substance which they call matter. By matter, therefore, we are to understand an inert, senseless substance, in which extension, figure, and motion do actually subsist. But it is evident from what we have already shown, that extension, figure, and motion are only ideas existing in the mind, and that an idea can be like nothing but another idea, and that consequently neither they nor their archetypes can exist in an unperceiving substance. Hence, it is plain that the very notion of what is called matter, or corporeal substance, involves a contradiction in it.

10. They who assert that figure, motion, and the rest of the primary or original qualities do exist without the mind in unthinking substances, do at the same time acknowledge that color, sounds, heat, cold, and such-like secondary qualities, do not; which they tell us are sensations existing in the mind alone. . . . Now, if it be certain that those original qualities are inseparably united with the other sensible qualities, and not, even in thought, capable of being abstracted from them, it plainly follows that they exist only in the mind. But I desire anyone to reflect and try whether he can, by any abstraction of thought, conceive the extension and motion of a body without all other sensible qualities. For my own part, I see evidently that it is not in my power to frame an idea of a body extended and moving, but I must withal give it some color or other sensible quality which is acknowledged to exist only in the mind. In short, extension, figure, and motion, abstracted from all other qualities, are inconceivable. Where therefore the other sensible qualities are, there must these be also, to wit, in the mind and nowhere else.

11. Again, great and small, swift and slow, are allowed to exist nowhere without the mind, being entirely relative, and changing as the frame or position of the organs of sense varies. The extension therefore which exists without the mind is neither great nor small, the motion neither swift nor slow, that is, they are nothing at all. . . .

12. That number is entirely the creature of the mind, even though the other qualities be allowed to exist without, will be evident to whoever considers that the same thing bears a different denomination of number as the mind views it with different respects. Thus, the same extension is one, or three, or thirty-six, according as the mind considers it with reference to a yard, a foot, or an inch. Number is so visibly relative, and dependent on men's understanding, that it is strange to think how anyone should give it an absolute existence without the mind. . . .

14. It is said that heat and cold are affections only of the mind, and not at all patterns of real beings, existing in the corporeal substances which excite them, for that the same body which appears cold to one hand seems warm to another. Now, why may we not as well argue that figure and extension are not patterns or resemblances of qualities existing in matter, because to the same eye at different stations, or eyes of a different texture at the same station, they appear various, and cannot therefore be the images of anything settled and determinate without the mind? Again, it is proved that sweetness is not really in the sapid (i.e. flavorful) thing, because the thing remaining unaltered the sweetness is changed into bitter, as in case of a fever or otherwise vitiated palate. Is it not as reasonable to say that motion is not without the mind, since if the succession of ideas in the mind become swifter, the motion, it is acknowledged, shall appear slower without any alteration in any external object?

15. In short, let anyone consider those arguments which are thought manifestly to prove that colors and tastes exist only in the mind, and he shall find they may with equal force be brought to prove the same thing of extension, figure, and motion. . . . The arguments foregoing plainly show it to be impossible that any color or extension at all, or other sensible quality whatsoever, should exist in an unthinking subject without the mind, or in truth, that

there should be any such thing as an outward object. . . .

18. But though it were possible that solid, figured, movable substances may exist without the mind, corresponding to the ideas we have of bodies, yet how is it possible for us to know this? Either we must know it by sense or by reason. As for our senses, by them we have the knowledge only of our sensations, ideas, or those things that are immediately perceived by sense, call them what you will; but they do not inform us that things exist without the mind. . . . It remains therefore that if we have any knowledge at all of external things, it must be by reason, inferring their existence from what is immediately perceived by sense. But what reason can induce us to believe the existence of bodies without the mind, from what we perceive. . . . It is granted on all hands (and what happens in dreams, frenzies, and the like, puts it beyond dispute) that it is possible we might be affected with all the ideas we have now, though there were no bodies existing without, resembling them. Hence, it is evident the supposition of external bodies is not necessary for the producing of our ideas; since it is granted that they are produced sometimes, and might possibly be produced always in the same order we see them in at present, without their concurrence. . . .

20. In short, if there were external bodies, it is impossible we should ever come to know it; and if there were not, we might have the very same reasons to think there were that we have now. Suppose (what no one can deny possible) an intelligence without the help of external bodies, to be affected with the same train of sensations or ideas that you are, imprinted in the same order and with like vividness in his mind. I ask whether that intelligence hath not all the reason to believe the existence of corporeal substances, represented by his ideas, and exciting them in his mind, that you can possibly have for believing the same thing?

22. I am content to put the whole upon this issue: if you can but conceive it possible for one extended movable substance, or, in general, for any one idea, or anything like an idea, to exist otherwise than in a mind perceiving it, I shall readily give up the cause. . . .

23. But, say you, surely there is nothing easier than for me to imagine trees, for instance, in a park, or books existing in a closet, and nobody by to perceive them. I answer, you may so, there is no difficulty in it; but what is all this, I beseech you, more than framing in your mind certain ideas which you call books and trees, and the same time omitting to frame the idea of anyone that may perceive them? But do not you yourself perceive or think of them all the while? . . . When we do our utmost to conceive the existence of external bodies, we are all the while only contemplating our own ideas.

CHECKLIST

To help you review, here is a checklist of the key philosophers and terms and concepts of this chapter. The brief descriptive sentences summarize the philosophers' leading ideas. Keep in mind that some of these summary statements are oversimplifications of complex positions.

Philosophers

• **George Berkeley**   was a British empiricist and idealist who denied the existence of material substance and held that sensible objects exist only in the mind.   114

• **Anne Conway**   argued against parts of the philosophies of Descartes, Hobbes, and Spinoza. An essentialist who argued that everything other than God has both physical and mental essences—God is totally mental—she had a big influence on Leibniz's monadology.   107

• **Oliva Sabuco de Nantes**   proposed that the connection between body and soul occurs throughout the brain.   104

• **René Descartes**   was the "father" of modern philosophy, a Continental rationalist, and a dualist. He said there are two separate and distinct substances: material substance and mind.   100

• **Benedictus de Spinoza**   was a Continental rationalist. He maintained that thought and extension are attributes of a single substance.   109

Chapter 6 · *The Rise of Modern Metaphysics and Epistemology*   127

- **Émilie du Châtelet**   adapted Leibniz's metaphysical principles to Newtonian science.   112

- **Thomas Hobbes**   was the first great modern materialist. He held that all that exists is bodies in motion.   106

- **Gottfried Wilhelm, Baron von Leibniz** was a Continental rationalist who held that the ultimate constituents of reality are monads, which are nonmaterial, indivisible units of force.   111

- **John Locke**   was a British empiricist who held that we perceive objects indirectly by means of our perceptions of them, some of which he believed were accurate copies of the real properties of objects.   113

Key Terms and Concepts

clear and distinct criterion   103
cogito, ergo sum   102
double aspect theory   99
dream conjecture   101
dualism   98
empiricism   117
epistemological detour   105
esse est percipi   117
evil demon conjecture   101
extension (as the essential attribute of material substance)   103
idealism   99
materialism   98

monads   112
nihil in intellectu quod prius non fuerit in sensu   113
occasionalism   105
parallelism   105
perception   106
principle of sufficient reason   113
principle of the identity of indiscernibles   113
rationalism   117
representative realism   114
tabula rasa   113
thought (as the essential attribute of mind)   103

QUESTIONS FOR DISCUSSION AND REVIEW

1. Define or explain dualism, materialism, and idealism.

2. Explain and critically evaluate either Descartes' dream conjecture or his evil demon conjecture.

3. Should Descartes have questioned whether there could be thinking without an "I" that does the thinking?

4. "We can think. This proves we are not just mere matter." Does it?

5. "Material things, including one's own body, are completely subject to physical laws." "The immaterial mind can move one's body." Are these two claims incompatible? Explain.

6. What is parallelism?

7. Explain Hobbes's idea that all mental activity reduces to matter in motion.

8. What does Spinoza claim is the relationship of the mind to the body?

9. Explain Anne Conway's concept of time and its relationship to her view of God and creatures.

10. Why does Berkeley say that sensible objects exist only in the mind?

11. Are the qualities of sensible objects (e.g., size, color, taste) all equally relative to the observer?

12. Does Berkeley's philosophy make everything into a dream?

13. If all our knowledge comes from experience, why might it be difficult to maintain that we have knowledge of external objects?

14. *Do* we have knowledge of external objects? Explain.

15. Is there really a difference between primary and secondary qualities?

16. Is your brain your mind? Explain.

17. Psychokinesis is the mental power by which psychics claim to make changes in the external physical world—to bend spoons, to cause balls to roll, and so on. Is there any difference between using your mind to bend a spoon and using your mind to bend your arm? Explain.

SUGGESTED FURTHER READINGS

Margaret Atherton, *Women Philosophers of the Early Modern Period* (Indianapolis: Hackett, 1994). Anthology of excerpts from Princess Elisabeth of Bohemia, Margaret Cavendish, Mary Astell, Damaris Cudworth Masham, Anne Conway, Catharine Trotter Cockburn, and Lady Mary Shepherd.

128   Part One · *Metaphysics and Epistemology: Existence and Knowledge*

George Berkeley, *Principles of Human Knowledge, Three Dialogues,* Howard Robinson, ed. (New York: Oxford University Press, 1999). Contains a useful introduction.

Christopher Biffle, *A Guided Tour of René Descartes' Meditations on First Philosophy* (New York: McGraw-Hill, 2000). Accessible translation of Descartes' *Meditations* I–VI with a guide to thinking about them critically.

Robert Black, ed., *Renaissance Thought: A Reader* (New York: Routledge, 2001). Essays by modern writers on Renaissance humanism, philosophy, and political thought.

E. O. Burtt, *The English Philosophers from Bacon to Mill* (New York: Modern Library, 1939). A general book on modern philosophy.

Anne Conway, *The Principles of the Most Ancient and Modern Philosophy* (Cambridge: Cambridge University Press, 1996). An affordable paperback edition of Conway.

John Cottingham, *The Rationalists* (New York: Oxford University Press, 1988). A brief introduction to the philosophies of the rationalists.

René Descartes, *Philosophical Works,* in two volumes, E. S. Haldane and G. R. T. Ross, trans. (Cambridge: The University Press, 1968). This is what you need to read Descartes.

Stephen Gaukroger, *Descartes: An Intellectual Biography* (Oxford: Clarendon Press, 1997). A first biography tracing Descartes' intellectual development and philosophical ideas.

A. C. Grayling, *Descartes* (New York: Pocket Books, 2005). A readable, lively study of Descartes' life and thought.

Errol E. Harris, *Spinoza's Philosophy: An Outline* (Atlantic Highlands, N.J.: Humanities Press, 1992). The title says it all.

S. Lamprecht, ed., *Locke Selections* (New York: Scribner's, 1928). If you want to read more than "Selections," you must turn to his *Essay Concerning Human Understanding,* in two volumes, A. C. Fraser, ed. (New York: Dover, 1959). This (the Fraser edition) is a heavily annotated work.

John Locke, *An Essay Concerning Human Understanding* (New York: Oxford University Press, 1979).

Benson Mates, *The Philosophy of Leibniz* (New York: Oxford University Press, 1986). An excellent exposition of the metaphysics of Leibniz.

Anthony Savile, *Routledge Philosophy Guidebook to Leibniz and the Monadology* (New York: Routledge, 2000). A brief exposition of Leibniz's idealism.

Tom Sorell, *Descartes: A Very Short Introduction* (New York: Oxford University Press, 2000). A short but accessible introduction to Descartes' life and thinking.

Tom Sorell, ed., *The Cambridge Companion to Hobbes* (Cambridge: Cambridge University Press, 1996). A review of Hobbes's life and the full range of his philosophical concerns.

Richard Tuck, *Hobbes: A Very Short Introduction* (New York: Oxford University Press, 1989). A quick look at Hobbes's life and key ideas.

J. O. Urmson and A. J. Ayer, *The British Empiricists* (New York: Oxford University Press, 1992). A set of introductory readings on the lives and thoughts of Locke, Berkeley, and Hume.

Mary Ellen Waithe, ed., *A History of Women Philosophers,* vol. 3, *Modern Women Philosophers: 1600–1900* (Dordrecht, Netherlands: Kluwer Academic Press, 1991). Chapters about thirty-one women philosophers of the period.

J. Wild, ed., *Spinoza Selections* (New York: Scribner's, 1930). This volume contains enough original material for the introductory student.

F. J. E. Woodbridge, ed., *Hobbes Selections* (New York: Scribner's, 1930). Here, too, we think that the selected original material will be sufficient for the introductory student.

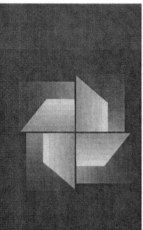

10

Moral Philosophy

Happiness, then, is something final and self-sufficient, and is the end of action.   —Aristotle

Morality is not properly the doctrine how we should make ourselves happy, but how we should become worthy of happiness.   —Immanuel Kant

Advice is something you never stop getting, although good, sound advice is perhaps not too common.

Most advice you get—and give—is of a practical nature: "If you want to live longer," someone will say, "you should stop smoking." Or: "If I were you, I would buy life insurance now while you are young."

But advice is not always intended to be merely practical. Sometimes it is moral advice. Someone—a friend, your minister, a relative—may suggest that you should do something not because it will be in your own best interest to do it but because doing it is *morally right*. "You should donate money to a charity," the person might say. Or: "You should be kind to animals." These suggestions express moral judgments.

Ethics, or moral philosophy, is the philosophical study of moral judgments— value judgments about what is virtuous or base, just or unjust, morally right or wrong, morally good or bad or evil, morally proper or improper. We say *morally* right and *morally* good and so on because terms like *right* and *good* and *proper* (and their negative correlates, *wrong* and *bad* and *improper*) can be used in *nonmoral* value judgments, as when someone speaks of a bad wine or of the right or proper way to throw a pass.

Many questions can be asked about moral judgments, so ethical philosophers discuss a wide array of issues. One basic question they ask is, What *is* a moral judgment? In other words, exactly what does it mean to describe something as

---

The Good Life

We view philosophy as valuable and applicable to real life. But then, we may be biased because we get paid to philosophize. Nevertheless, here is a case in favor of our view.

As you read about the moral philosophies of Plato, Aristotle, and almost every other thinker covered in Part Two, you might note their concern with the question, *In what does human happiness or well-being or the good life consist?* Maybe this question is not the *central* question of ethics, but it is close to the center. Almost every philosopher we cover in

this part of the book offers an alternative answer to this question. The question is also of considerable practical importance—and worth considering *now*. Ultimately, we all die, and sometimes, unfortunately, people die sooner, sometimes much sooner, than they expected. To get a clear focus on this question, only to learn that it is too late to do anything about it, could be a great tragedy.

Maybe you will find something in this and the next chapter to help you settle on your own definition of the good life.

---

morally right or wrong, good or evil? What is it to say that one thing ought to be done and another thing ought not be done? Or they might ask, What makes a moral judgment a *moral* judgment? How do moral judgments differ from other value judgments, factual assertions, and pieces of practical advice? What distinguishes reasoning about moral issues from reasoning about other things (from reasoning about the structure of matter, say, or about the qualities of good art)? These are some of the questions ethical philosophers ask.

The most important question of ethics, however, is simply, Which moral judgments are correct? That is, what is good and just and the morally right thing to do? What is the "moral law," anyway? This question is important because the answer to it tells us how we should conduct our affairs. Perhaps it is the most important question not of ethics but of philosophy. Perhaps it is the most important question, period.

A less obvious question of ethics, though logically more fundamental, is whether there is a moral law in the first place. In other words, do moral obligations even exist? Are there really such things as good and bad, right and wrong? And if there are, what is it that makes one thing right and another wrong? That is, what is the ultimate justification of moral standards?

In what follows, we will examine some of these issues and related questions as they have been treated throughout the history of philosophy. However, before we begin, we need to discuss several concepts that have been important throughout the history of moral philosophy.

SKEPTICISM, RELATIVISM, AND SUBJECTIVISM

Many beginning students in philosophy accept one or more of three important ideas about morals. The first, **ethical skepticism,** is the doctrine that moral knowledge is not possible. According to the skeptic, whether there are moral standards is not knowable, or, alternatively, if there are any moral standards, we cannot know what they are.

You should be aware that the beliefs that there is no right or wrong and that "everything is permissible" (which we encountered in the previous chapter) are not skeptical beliefs. A person who makes either of these claims implies that he or she does have moral knowledge.

Another popular idea about ethics is called **descriptive relativism,** according to which the moral standards people subscribe to are different from culture to culture. This idea might seem obviously true, but you must remember that different *practices* do not necessarily entail different *standards.* For example, it might seem that the pro-choice "culture" and the pro-life "culture" obviously have different moral standards, and perhaps they do. On the other hand, they might both accept the standard that it is wrong to kill a living person but just disagree about whether a fetus counts as a living person.

In any case, descriptive relativism is not an ethical doctrine. It says merely that people in different cultures have different beliefs about what is morally right and wrong. It says nothing about what *is* morally right and morally wrong. The idea that what a culture *believes* is morally right or wrong *is* morally right or wrong for people in that culture is known as **cultural relativism,** and it is a popular idea among beginning philosophy students. Many tend to think, for example, that whether or not you should act selfishly is entirely determined by whether or not your culture thinks you should act selfishly. Beginning philosophy students who are cultural relativists sometimes also advocate being accepting toward the practices of other cultures. However, it would be inconsistent for a cultural relativist to advocate being accepting toward another culture's practice if her or his own culture thought that practice was wrong.

Another relativist doctrine is known as **individual relativism,** according to which what is right or wrong is what each individual believes is right or wrong. If you hold this view, then you would have to say that nobody ever acts wrongly, provided he or she is doing what he or she thinks is right. Both individual relativism and cultural relativism are sometimes spoken of as **subjectivist** ethical philosophies, in that what is right or wrong depends entirely on what a person (i.e., a "subject") or a culture (i.e., a group of "subjects") thinks is right or wrong.

EGOISM

Egoism is another popular ethical doctrine, but there are two types of egoism. First, there is **descriptive egoism,** the doctrine that in all conscious action you seek to promote your self-interest above all else. Then there is **prescriptive egoism,** the doctrine that in all conscious action you *ought* to seek your self-interest above all else. The Epicurean ethical philosophy, for example, was a version of prescriptive egoism.

Often, beginning philosophy students accept descriptive egoism as almost self-evidently true. Many also favor prescriptive egoism as an ethical philosophy. Of course we always act to further our own ends! And that is exactly what we *ought* to do, right?

Does acting ethically mean squelching devilish selfish interests in favor of more high-minded objectives? Prescriptive egoism is the idea that you ought to act in your own self-interest.

But some philosophers see a difficulty in accepting both prescriptive and descriptive egoism in that it seems trivial or pointless to tell people they ought to do what you think they are *going to do anyway.* That is like advising someone that she or he has a moral obligation to obey the laws of physics or to remain visible at all times or to occupy space, these philosophers say.

A further comment: If you find yourself subscribing to prescriptive egoism (one ought to seek one's self-interest above all else), as many do, then you should consider this: Does it make sense for you to advocate your own egoistic philosophy? If you ought to seek your own self-interest above all else (as prescriptive egoism says), then should you really go around telling others to seek *their* self-interest above all else? Is telling them that in *your* best interests? Might it not be better for your interests to urge others to promote the *common* good?

HEDONISM

Hedonism is the pursuit of pleasure. Philosophers distinguish between the *descriptive* doctrine known as **psychological hedonism,** according to which the ultimate object of a person's desire *is* always pleasure, and the *ethical* doctrine known as **ethical hedonism,** according to which a person *ought* to seek pleasure over other things. You should remember these doctrines.

The descriptive doctrine may be plausible at first glance, but on closer inspection it appears somewhat doubtful. We do seem to seek things beside pleasure—for example, food, good health, relaxation, rest, rightness in our actions, success, friends, and many other things too. As the British moralist and clergyman Bishop Joseph Butler (1692–1752) observed, we could not seek pleasure at all unless we had desires for something other than pleasure, because pleasure consists in satisfying these desires. And then, too, "the pleasure of virtue," as Irish historian W. E. H. Lecky wrote, "is one which can only be obtained on the express condition of its not being the object sought." In other words, if your motive in acting virtuously is to obtain the pleasure that accompanies virtuous acts, then you are not being virtuous and will not get that pleasure.

As for ethical hedonism, there are two kinds: **egoistic ethical hedonism,** according to which one ought to seek his or her own pleasure over other things, and **universalistic ethical hedonism,** otherwise known as utilitarianism, according to which one ought to seek the greatest pleasure for the greatest number of people over other things.

One difficulty utilitarians face is in explaining why pleasure for others is something one should seek. One common answer is that only by seeking others' pleasure can you experience a full allotment of pleasure for yourself. But this answer seems to assume that one's primary ethical duty is to oneself after all.

THE FIVE MAIN ETHICAL FRAMEWORKS

Moral philosophers these days often regard ethical or moral theories as falling into one of the five following ethical frameworks or perspectives as to what one fundamentally ought to do. We list them in no particular order and mention philosophers who provide good examples of each category, to help you understand those philosophers when you read about them in this chapter.

- First, **divine-command ethics:** What ought I to do? What God ordains, I ought to do. Augustine and Aquinas are good examples.

- Second, **consequentialism:** What ought I to do? Whatever has the most desirable consequences. The Epicureans, Stoics, and utilitarians are good examples.

- Third, **deontological ethics:** What ought I to do? Whatever it is my moral duty to do (in at least some cases, regardless of consequences). Kant is a good example.

- Fourth, **virtue ethics:** What ought I to do? What the virtuous person would do. (For virtue ethics, the primary question is not, What ought I to do? but rather, What kind of person ought I to be?) Plato and Aristotle are good examples.

- Fifth, **relativism:** What ought I to do? What my culture or society thinks I ought to do. None of the philosophers covered in this chapter are relativists (though many students are).

Sometimes *contractarianism* (or *contractualism*) is mentioned as a basic ethical theory. However, more often it is treated as a theory of social justice, the theory that principles of justice are best constructed through negotiations among impartial, informed, and rational agents. We'll discuss this idea in Chapter 11, which deals with political philosophy.

Let's now take a closer look at these five various ethical perspectives as they debuted in the history of moral philosophy.

THE EARLY GREEKS

That moral judgments must be supported by reasons is an idea we owe to the **Sophists,** those professional teachers of fifth-century B.C.E. Greece, and to **Socrates** (c. 470–399 B.C.E.). The Sophists, who attacked the traditional moral values of the Greek aristocracy, demanded rational justification for rules of conduct, as did Socrates. Their demands, together with Socrates' skillful deployment of the dialectical method in moral discussions, mark the beginning of philosophical reasoning about moral issues.

Maybe it was not inevitable that a time would come when someone insisted that moral claims be defended by reasons. When children ask why they should do something their parents think is right, they may be content to receive, and their parents content to give, the simple answer, "Because that is what is done." In some societies, evidently, values are accepted without much question, and demands for justification of moral claims are not issued. In our society it is frequently otherwise, and this is the legacy of the Sophists and Socrates.

It was Socrates especially who championed the use of reason in moral deliberation and with it raised good questions about some still-popular ideas about morality, such as that good is what pleases, that might makes right, and that happiness comes only to the ruthless.

Socrates was also concerned with the meanings of words that signify moral virtues, words like *justice, piety,* and *courage.* Because a moral term can be correctly applied to various specific acts—many different types of deeds count as courageous deeds, for example—Socrates believed that all acts characterized by a given moral term *must have something in common.* He therefore sought to determine (without notable success, we are sorry to report) what the essential commonality is. Socrates' assumption that a virtue has an essential nature, an essence that may be disclosed through rational inquiry, is still made by many philosophers and is central to several famous ethical theories, including Plato's, as you will see shortly.

Socrates also assumed that any sane person who possessed knowledge of the essence of virtue could not fail to act virtuously. He thus believed that ignoble behavior, if not the result of utter insanity, is always the product of ignorance. This is also a view that Plato shared, and it has its adherents today.

Plato

Plato accepted the Socratic idea that all things named by a given term, including any given moral term, share a common essential or "defining" feature. For example, what is common to all actions called heroic, is that they all have a feature or property—heroic-ness—that makes it possible for us to refer to them by the same name. What is common to all brave deeds is that feature that qualifies them all as brave. This essential or defining characteristic Plato referred to as the **Form** of the things in question; and, for various plausible reasons, he regarded this Form as possessing more reality than the particular things that exemplified it. We talked

260   Part Two · *Moral and Political Philosophy*

What do these objects have in common that makes them all chairs? Arms? Legs? Wood? No. What makes them all Chairs is that they share the same Form.

about this in Chapter 3, but let's look into Plato's reasoning again, for this bears closely on Plato's ethics.

For a thing to be a chair, we think you must agree, it must possess that feature that qualifies a thing as a chair. That feature—let's call it *chairness*—is what Plato called the Form. And so, for a thing to qualify as a chair, it must possess chairness. Thus, the Form *chairness* must exist if anything at all is to qualify as a chair. So the Form is more fundamental and "real" than even the chair you are sitting on or any other chair.

Forms, Plato held, are not perceptible to the senses, for what the senses perceive are individual things: particular chairs, particular people, particular brave deeds, and so forth. We do not perceive the Forms through the senses. We cannot see chairness, and we cannot reach out and grasp bravery or humanity. Thus, Forms, he maintained, are known only through reason.

Further, according to Plato, the individual things that we perceive by sense are forever changing. Some things—rocks, for example—change very slowly. Other things, such as people, change a good bit more rapidly. That means that knowledge by sense perception is uncertain and unstable. Not so knowledge of the Forms. Knowledge of the Forms is certain and stable, for the objects known—the Forms—are eternal and unchanging.

Now the various Forms, Plato maintained (and here we will see what all of this has to do with ethics), constitute a *hierarchy* in terms of their inherent value or worth. It is easy enough to understand his point. For example, does not the Form *beauty* (i.e., the essence of beautiful things) seem to you to be inherently of more worth than the Form *wartness* (i.e., the essence of warts)?

At the apex of all Forms, Plato said, is the Form *goodness*, or (as it is often expressed) *the Good*, because it is the Form of highest value. Thus, for Plato, because

a. the Forms define true reality, and because
b. the Form of the Good is the uppermost of all Forms, it follows that
c. individual things are real only insofar as they partake of or exemplify this ultimate Form.

A corollary of (c) is that things are less "real" the less they partake of the Good. Another corollary is that evil is unreal. Make a mental note of the second corollary.

Because the Form of the Good is the source of all value and reality, Plato believed, we must strive to obtain knowledge and understanding of it. Therefore, he maintained, because (remember) Forms can be apprehended only by reason, we should govern ourselves by reason. Similarly, the state should be ruled by intellectuals, he said, but more of this in Chapter 11.

So, to summarize to this point, according to Plato, the true reality of individual things consists in the Forms they exemplify, Forms that are apprehended by reason and not by the senses; and the Form highest in value is the Form of the Good. One should, therefore, strive for knowledge of the Good and be ruled by reason.

But now consider this moral edict that Plato has in effect laid down: "Be governed by reason!" Is this not a little too abstract? Does it not fail to enjoin anything *specific* about what the individual should or should not do?

Plato would have answered "no" to both questions. The human soul, he said (a couple of thousand years before Freud proposed his analogous theory of the id, the ego, and the superego), has three different elements: an element consisting of raw appetites, an element consisting of drives (like anger and ambition), and an intellectual element (i.e., an element of thought or reason). For each of these elements, there is an excellence or virtue that obtains when reason is in charge of that element, as is the case when you govern yourself by reason. When our *appetites* are ruled by reason, we exhibit the virtue of *temperance;* when our *drives* are governed by reason, we exhibit *courage;* and when the *intellect* itself is governed by reason, we exhibit *wisdom.*

Thus, Plato held, the well-governed person, the person ruled by reason, exhibits the four cardinal virtues of temperance, courage, wisdom, and "justice." How did justice get in the list? Justice is the virtue that obtains when all elements of the soul function as they should in obedience to reason.

Given Plato's understanding of the soul, the principle "Be governed by reason," which follows from the theory of Forms, dictates that you be temperate, courageous, wise, and just. And what, in turn, these dictates mean more specifically was much discussed by Plato, though we will not go into the details. Further, he said, only by being virtuous—that is, by possessing these four virtues—can you have a well-ordered soul and thus have the psychological well-being that is true happiness. In this way Plato connected virtue with happiness, a connection we still acknowledge by saying, "Virtue is its own reward."

262   Part Two · *Moral and Political Philosophy*

Plato and Divine-Command Ethics

Plato examined the idea that what is morally right and good is determined by divine command, that is, by the edict or decree of God—a popular idea today in Western (and other) societies—and the result of that examination was a question: Is something right or good because the gods (or God) decree that it is, or is it decreed by the gods (or God) as right or good because it is right or good? (If the question interests you, you might wish to read Plato's very short dialogue *Euthyphro.*)

Some critics of "divine-command" theories of ethics argue that Plato's question puts the adherents of these theories in an awkward position. If you say

that God decrees something because it *is* good, then you seem to imply that God is not the ultimate authority or the ultimate source of goodness: you seem to imply that there is something beyond God that makes good things good things. But if you say that something is good because God decrees it, you seem to imply that God's decrees are arbitrary; he could just as well have decreed that the thing was not good.

In short, the question implies—so it is argued—either that God's moral prescriptions are arbitrary or that God is not the ultimate source of goodness.

But is a well-ordered or just or virtuous soul really required for happiness? Plato did not merely assert that it is and expect us to close our eyes and blindly swallow the assertion. He knew as well as anyone that exactly the opposite seems to be true: that the people who seem to be the best off often seem to be very unscrupulous. So Plato examined the matter rather carefully, especially in the *Republic*. In that dialogue, Plato has various characters explain and defend the view that the life of the person who cleverly and subtly promotes his own ends at the expense of other people is preferable to the life of the virtuous person. Plato (in the person of his Socrates character) does think that this view is mistaken and attempts (at considerable length) to explain what is wrong with it—this attempt actually is the main theme of the *Republic*. Whether he succeeds you may wish to consider for yourself at some point. In any case, a more powerful defense of being *unjust* and *unvirtuous* than the one Plato sets forth (and tries to refute) in the *Republic* has never been devised.

Sometimes beginning philosophy students have difficulty seeing how Plato's theories apply to their own lives. Here, though, there seems to be direct applicability. Chances are that from time to time you find yourself in a situation in which . . . In such a situation you may not be sure . . . you have not thought the situation through carefully enough. For Plato asserts that the virtuous course of action is the one most apt to produce your own well-being.

Of course, you may agree with Plato's conclusion, that the virtuous course of action is the one most apt to produce your own well-being, because you believe that God will reward you in an afterlife if you are virtuous here and now and punish you if you are not. Notice, though, what you are assuming if you accept this belief, namely, that virtuous activity does *not* promote its own reward (i.e., happiness) in *this* life. Plato, though, believed that your well-being in *this* life is best promoted by virtuous activity. (See the box "Plato and Divine-Command Ethics.")

The Go-for-It Philosophy of Aristippus

At about the time Plato lived in Athens, another Greek, Aristippus (435–366 B.C.E.), who lived in Cyrene, espoused an ethical doctrine quite different from Plato's. Aristippus said our lives should always be dedicated to the acquisition of as many pleasures, preferably as intense as possible, as we can possibly obtain. Even when intense pleasures lead to subsequent pain, they should still be sought, he said, for a life without pleasure or pain would be unredeemingly boring. Pleasures are best obtained, according to Aristippus, when one takes control of a situation and other people and uses them to one's own advantage.

Perhaps you know people who agree with Aristippus.

Cyrenaicism, which is the name of this hedonistic (pleasure-seeking) philosophy, was the historical antecedent of Epicureanism. As you can see from the text, Epicurus's pleasure-oriented philosophy is considerably more moderate than Aristippus'. Epicurus recommended avoiding intense pleasure as producing too much pain and disappointment over the long run.

Plato's moral philosophy is applicable in other ways. He was also very interested in such popular views (popular both then and now and perhaps forevermore) as that *goodness is the same thing as pleasure,* that *self-control is not the best way to get happiness,* and that *it is better to exploit others than to be exploited by them.* He found, when he considered these ideas carefully, that they are mistaken. So if you are tempted to agree with any of these ideas, we recommend that you read the *Republic* and another famous Platonic dialogue, the *Gorgias,* before arranging your affairs in the belief that they are true. You should also read the box "The Go-for-It Philosophy of Aristippus." We present a brief excerpt from the *Gorgias* at the end of the chapter.

Aesara, the Lucanian

A strong echo of Platonic ethical themes may be found in the work of **Aesara** [ai-SAH-ruh], a Greek philosopher from Lucania (in southern Italy), who probably lived around 350 B.C.E. Only a fragment of her original work survives. Aesara has been mentioned only rarely in textbooks in philosophy, perhaps because of the scanty remains of her work, perhaps due to other reasons. But she is interesting and worth reading.

Like Plato, Aesara was concerned with the nature of human well-being, or the good life. And like Plato, she saw the key to this to be the well-ordered or virtuous or "just" soul—the balanced and harmoniously functioning psyche. Also like Plato, she saw that the well-functioning state replicates the balance and order that exists in the well-functioning soul.

Aesara's analysis of the human psyche or soul was very similar to Plato's. She thought the soul has three parts: the mind, spiritedness, and desire. The *mind* analyzes ideas and reaches decisions. *Spiritedness* is the part of the soul that gives a person the ability to carry out decisions; we might call it the *will.* The element of *desire* contains moral emotions such as love.

It is worth noting that the role of women in ancient Greek society was to stay at home and raise virtuous, rational offspring, the male versions of whom would run the world of government and the marketplace—the world outside the home. As a woman, Aesara was keenly aware that men, even men philosophers, sometimes tended to think that justice applies only to the world outside the home. Are two different approaches to moral philosophy needed, one for inside the home and another for dealings with people outside the family and for public institutions? We will encounter this question again in the twentieth century, but it seems clear that Aesara's answer would be "no." All morally significant decisions, whether regarding our families or the state, should reflect the appropriate proportions of reason, will power, and such positive affective emotions as love.

Only a fragment of Aesara's original work remains. Even though Aesara's influence on the history of philosophy was less than that of, say, Plato or Aristotle, we remain convinced of the value of including Aesara's thoughts here. A more elegant statement than Aesara's cannot be found for two ancient Greek ideas—the idea that from the well-ordered soul, the soul characterized by the harmonious functioning and proper proportioning of its elements, springs virtue, and the idea that the human soul is the model for society. "Human nature," she said, "provides the standard for law and justice for both the home and the city." If you understand the nature of the soul, you understand how society and social justice ought to be.

Aristotle

The ultimate source of all value for Plato was the Form of the Good, an entity that is distinct from the particular things that populate the natural world, the world we perceive through our senses. This Platonic idea, that all value is grounded in a *nonnatural* source, is an element of Plato's philosophy that is found in many ethical systems and is quite recognizable in Christian ethics. But not every ethical system postulates a nonnatural source of value.

Those systems that do not are called *naturalistic ethical systems*. According to **ethical naturalism,** moral judgments are really judgments of fact about the natural world. Thus, **Aristotle,** for instance, who was the first great ethical naturalist, believed that the good for us is defined by our natural objective.

Now, what would you say is our principal or highest objective by nature? According to Aristotle, it is the attainment of happiness, for it is that alone that we seek for its own sake. And because the attainment of happiness is naturally our highest objective, it follows that happiness is our highest good.

In what does happiness, our highest good, consist? According to Aristotle, to answer we must consider the human being's function. To discover what goodness is for an ax or a chisel or anything whatsoever, we must consider its function, what it actually does. And when we consider what the human animal does, as a *human* animal, we see that, most essentially, it (a) lives and (b) reasons.

Thus, happiness consists of two things, Aristotle concluded: *enjoyment (pleasure)* and the *exercise and development of the capacity to reason.* It consists in part of enjoyment because the human being, as a living thing, has biological needs and impulses the satisfaction of which is pleasurable. And it consists in part of developing and exercising the capacity to reason, because only the human being, as distinct from other living things, has that capacity. Because this capacity differentiates humans from other living things, its exercise is stressed by Aristotle as the most important component of happiness. Pleasure alone does not constitute happiness, he insists.

The exercise of our unique and distinctive capacity to reason is termed by Aristotle *virtue*—thus Aristotle's famous phrase that happiness is activity in accordance with virtue. There are two different kinds of virtues. To exercise actively our reasoning abilities, as when we study nature or cogitate about something, is to be *intellectually* virtuous. But we also exercise our rational capacity by moderating our impulses and appetites, and when we do this, we are said by Aristotle to be *morally* virtuous.

The largest part of Aristotle's major ethical work, the *Nicomachean Ethics*, is devoted to analysis of specific moral virtues, which Aristotle held to be the **mean between extremes** (e.g., courage is the mean between fearing everything and fearing nothing). He emphasized as well that virtue is a matter of *habit:* just as an ax that is only occasionally sharp does not fulfill its function well, the human who exercises his rational capacities only occasionally does not fulfill his function, that is, is not virtuous.

Aristotle also had the important insight that a person's pleasures reveal his true moral character. "He who faces danger with pleasure, or, at any rate, without pain, is courageous," he observed, "but he to whom this is painful is a coward." Of course, we might object that he who is willing to face danger *despite* the pain it brings him is the most courageous, but this is a quibble.

Another distinction made by Aristotle is that between instrumental ends and intrinsic ends. An **instrumental end** is an act performed as a means to other ends. An **intrinsic end** is an act performed for its own sake.

For example, when we, Bruder and Moore, sat down to write this book, our end was to finish it. But that end was merely instrumental to another end—to provide our readers with a better understanding of philosophy.

But now notice that the last goal, the goal of providing our readers with a better understanding of philosophy, is instrumental to a further end, namely, an enlightened society.

Notice, too, that when your teacher grades you and the other students in the class, that act is instrumental to your learning, and that end also is instrumental to an enlightened society.

As a matter of fact, all the activities in the university are aimed at producing an enlightened society. For example, your teacher may recently have received a promotion. Promotions are instrumental to effective teaching in your university, and effective teaching also is instrumental to an enlightened society.

But notice that that end, an enlightened society, is merely instrumental to another end, at least according to Aristotle. For why even have an enlightened society? An enlightened society is good, Aristotle would say, because in such a society people will be able to fulfill their natural function as human beings. And therefore, he would say, when we understand what the natural function of people is, then we finally will know what is intrinsically good, good for its own sake. Then we will know what the "Good of Man" is.

So to sum up the main points, Aristotle's ethics were basically naturalistic: human good is defined by human nature. Plato's were nonnaturalistic: goodness in all its manifestations is defined by the Form of the Good. Despite these differences, Aristotle and Plato would doubtless have agreed to a great extent in their praise and condemnation of the activities of other people. Aristotle, too, deemed the cardinal moral virtues to be courage, temperance, justice, and wisdom, and both he and Plato advocated the intellectual life.

Notice, too, that Plato and Aristotle both conceive of ethics as focusing on good *character traits* of individuals—virtues—rather than on a set of *rules for actions* (such as "treat others as you would have others treat you"). In the last quarter of the twentieth century (as we shall see in Chapter 12), there was considerable interest among Anglo-American philosophers in this type of ethical theory, which is known as *virtue ethics*. From the point of view of virtue ethics, the fundamental ethical question is not so much, What ought one do? but rather, What kind of person ought one to be?

Despite these similarities, it must be kept in mind that the ultimate source of all moral value—that is, the Good—was for Plato a nonnatural "Form," whereas Aristotle sought to define the good for humans in terms of what the human organism in fact naturally seeks, namely, happiness.

Ever since Aristotle's time, ethical systems often fall into one of two categories: those that find the supreme moral good as something that *transcends* nature and thus follow the lead of Plato, and those that follow Aristotle by grounding morality in human nature.

EPICUREANISM AND STOICISM

In the Greek and Roman periods following Aristotle, there were four main "schools" of philosophy: the Epicureans, the Stoics, the Skeptics, and the Neoplatonists. The Neoplatonists and the Skeptics were discussed in Part One.

The Skeptics denied the possibility of any knowledge, and this denial included moral knowledge. They said that no judgments can be established and that it does not matter if the judgments are factual judgments or value judgments (a value judgment assigns a value to something). Accordingly, they advocated tolerance toward others, detachment from the concerns of others, and caution in your own actions. Whether the Skeptics were *consistent* in advocating toleration, detachment, and caution while maintaining that no moral judgment can be established, you might consider for yourself.

Epicureanism and Stoicism, which mainly concern us in this chapter, were both naturalistic ethical philosophies, and both had a lasting effect on philosophy and ethics. To this day, "taking things philosophically" means responding to disappointments as a Stoic would, and the word *epicure* has its own place in the everyday English found outside the philosophy classroom.

Epicureanism

Epicureanism, the theory that personal pleasure is the highest good, began with **Epicurus** [ep-uh-KYUR-us] (341–270 B.C.E.), flourished in the second and first centuries B.C.E., spread to Rome, and survived as a school until almost the third century C.E. Though few today would call themselves Epicureans, there is no question that many people still subscribe to some of the central tenets of this philosophy. You may do so yourself. We do.

According to Epicurus, it is natural for us to seek a pleasant life above all other things; it follows, he reasoned (as perhaps you will, too), that we ought to seek a pleasant life above all other things. In this sense, Epicurus was a naturalist in ethics.

The pleasant life, Epicurus said, comes to you when your desires are satisfied. And there are three kinds of desires, he maintained:

- Those that are *natural and must be satisfied* for one to have a pleasant life (such as the desire for food and shelter)
- Those that, *though natural, need not necessarily be satisfied* for a pleasant life (including, for example, the desire for sexual gratification)
- Those that are *neither natural nor necessary* to satisfy (such as the desire for wealth or fame)

The pleasant life is best achieved, Epicurus believed, by neglecting the third kind of desire and satisfying only desires of the first kind, although desires of the second kind may also be satisfied, he said, when doing so does not lead to discomfort or pain. It is *never* prudent to try to satisfy unnecessary/unnatural desires, he said, for in the long run trying to do so will produce disappointment, dissatisfaction, discomfort, or poor health. There is, surely, much that is reasonable in this philosophy, even though many people spend a good bit of time and energy trying to satisfy precisely those desires that, according to Epicurus, are both unnecessary and unnatural.

As is evident, Epicurus favored the *pleasant life* over momentary pleasures and attached great importance to the avoidance of pain as the prime ingredient in the pleasant life. It is one of the ironies of philosophy that the word *epicure* is often used to denote a fastidious person excessively fond of refined tastes—a snob. Epicurus was certainly not an epicure in this sense, for he recommended a life of relaxation, repose, and moderation, as well as avoidance of the pleasures of the flesh and passions. He would not have been fond of expensive champagne or caviar.

The Stoics

If Epicurus was not exactly an epicure (at least in one meaning of the word), were the Stoics stoical? A stoic is a person who maintains a calm indifference to pain and suffering, and yes, the Stoics were stoical.

The school was founded by **Zeno** (c. 335–c. 263 B.C.E.; not the same Zeno mentioned in Chapter 2), who met his students on the *stoa* (Greek for "porch"). **Stoicism** spread to Rome and survived as a school until almost the

268   Part Two · *Moral and Political Philosophy*

Athletes often subscribe to the idea that physical improvement requires stoical acceptance of physical discomfort. No pain, no gain.

third century C.E. Its most famous adherents, other than Zeno, were **Epictetus** [ep-ik-TEET-us] (c. 55–c. 135 C.E.), the Roman statesman Cicero (106–43 B.C.E.), and Marcus Aurelius (121–180 C.E.), the Roman emperor.

Like the Epicureans, the Stoics believed that it is only natural for a person to seek a pleasant life and that therefore a person ought to seek such a life. But the Stoics were much influenced by the Cynics (see the box "Diogenes the Cynic"), who went *out of their way* to find hardship. The Stoics saw that the Cynics, by actively pursuing hardship, acquired the ability to remain untroubled by the pains and disappointments of life. The Stoics thought there was some sense in this. It occurred to them that untroubledness or serenity is a desirable state indeed.

The Stoics, however, more than the Cynics, had a *metaphysical justification* for their ethics. All that occurs, the Stoics believed, occurs in accordance with natural law, which they equated with reason. **Natural law,** they said, is the vital force that activates or (as we might say) energizes all things. It follows that

1. Whatever happens is the inevitable outcome of the logic of the universe.
2. Whatever happens, happens with a reason and therefore is for the best.

So, according to the Stoic philosophy, you can do nothing to alter the course of events, because they have been fixed by the law of nature. Do not struggle against the inevitable, the Stoics said. Instead, understand that what is happening is for the best, and accept it.

If you are wise, according to the Stoics, you will approach life as an actor approaches his or her part. You will realize that you have no control over the plot or

Diogenes the Cynic

According to the **Cynics,** who were fiercely individualistic, the wise person avoids even the most basic comforts and seeks total self-reliance by reducing all wants to a minimum and by forgoing any convenience or benefit offered by society. The most famous Cynic, the fourth-century B.C.E. philosopher **Diogenes** [dy-AH-juh-neez], is said to have dressed in rags and lived in an empty tub and even to have thrown out his drinking cup when he observed a child drinking from his hands. Alexander the Great, who admired Diogenes, is said to have made his way to the latter and announced that he would fill Diogenes' greatest need. Diogenes replied that he had a great need for Alexander to stop blocking his sunlight.

Diogenes is also reported to have masturbated in public while observing that it was too bad that hunger could not be relieved in similar fashion merely by rubbing your stomach. His point in part was simply to flout conventions, but it was apparently also to contrast sexual needs with the need for food.

According to another story, Diogenes visited the home of a wealthy man. The man asked Diogenes to avoid spitting on the floor or furnishings because the home was expensively appointed. Diogenes responded by spitting in the man's face and commented that it was the only worthless thing in the room.

Whether these stories are true or not, the indifference to material things that they portray was appreciated by the Stoics. Yet even though the Stoics saw the advantages to scaling back needs in the manner of the Cynics, they were not nearly so flamboyant in what they said and did. The Cynics were often willing to do or say something just to shock people.

Incidentally, as the word is most commonly used today, a cynic is one who sneers at sincerity, helpfulness, and other virtuous activity as inspired by ulterior motives. It is clear how the word acquired this meaning, given the contempt the Cynics had for traditional institutions and practices.

---

assignment of roles, and therefore you will distance yourself psychologically from all that happens to the character you play. Does the character you play grow ill in the play? Well, you will *act* the part to the best of your ability, but you certainly will not permit yourself to suffer. Do your friends die in the play? Do you die? It is all for the best because it is dictated by the plot.

Now, perhaps you are thinking, Well, if I cannot control what happens to me, then how on earth can I control my attitude about what happens? If what happens is inevitable, then what happens to my attitudes is inevitable, too, right? Nevertheless, this was the Stoics' doctrine: *You can control your attitude. Remain uninvolved emotionally in your fate, and your life will be untroubled.*

The Stoic philosophy also had a political ethic according to which the Stoic had a duty to serve other people and respect their inherent worth as equals under natural law. So the Stoics thought that, although you should seek the untroubled life for yourself, your ethical concerns are not limited to your own welfare. Whether this social component of Stoicism is consistent with a philosophy of emotional noninvolvement, acceptance of the natural order, and seeking tranquility for yourself may be questioned, of course. In fact, whether a philosophy of self-interest is compatible with concern for the common good is one of the most important questions of ethics, and you know quite well that this is a very live issue even today.

Let's summarize this section: According to the Epicureans, one's ultimate ethical objective is to lead the pleasant life through moderate living. According to the

Stoics, the objective is to obtain the serene or untroubled life through acceptance of the rational or natural order of things while remembering that one is obligated to be of service to one's fellow creatures. Stoicism in particular had an impact on Christian thought, primarily through the philosophy of St. Augustine, to whom we shall turn next.

One of the selections at the end of this chapter is from Epictetus, among the most famous of Stoics. Epictetus also is unusual among philosophers in that he was sold as a slave when a child but was given an education and later freed, thereafter becoming an influential teacher of philosophy. As you might expect from what we have said about Stoicism and Epicureanism, the two philosophies are very similar (even though Epictetus thought he was recommending a way of life quite different from that of the Epicureans).

CHRISTIANIZING ETHICS

Let us next turn to the way the Christian religion shaped the ancient idea of ethics and to the figure most responsible for that transformation.

St. Augustine

St. Augustine (354–430 C.E.) is one of the towering figures of Christian philosophy. It is he who first gave Christianity philosophical weight and substance.

Augustine found philosophical justification for Christianity in the metaphysics of Plato, as reinterpreted by the Neoplatonist Plotinus (205–270 C.E.). Christianity rests on the belief in a transcendent God, and with the assistance of Platonic metaphysics, St. Augustine was able to make philosophically intelligible to himself the concept of a *transcendent realm*, a realm of being beyond the spatiotemporal universe that contains (or is) the source of all that is real and good. He also saw in Platonic and Neoplatonic doctrines the solution to the *problem of evil*. This problem can be expressed in a very simple question: How could evil have arisen in a world created by a perfectly good God?

One solution to this problem that Augustine considered was that evil is the result of a creative force other than God, a *force of darkness*, so to speak. But isn't there supposed to be just one and only one Creator? That is what Augustine believed, so this solution was not acceptable.

For Plato, remember, the Form of the Good was the source of all reality, and from this principle it follows that all that is real is good. Thus, given Plato's principle, evil *is not real*. St. Augustine found this approach to the problem of evil entirely satisfactory. Because evil is not something, it was not created by God.

This theory of evil is plausible enough as long as you are thinking of certain "physical" evils, such as blindness or droughts (though others, such as pain, seem as real as can be). Blindness, after all, is the absence of sight, and droughts are the absence of water.

Unfortunately, however, the absence theory does not plausibly explain *moral evil*, the evil that is the wrongdoing of men and women. How did Augustine account for moral evil? His explanation of moral evil was a variation of another idea of Plato's, the idea that a person never knowingly does wrong, that evil actions are the result of ignorance of the good, of misdirected education, so to say. But Augustine added a new twist to this idea. Moral evil, he said, is not exactly a case of misdirected *education* but, instead, a case of misdirected *love*. This brings us to the heart of Augustine's ethics.

For Augustine, as for the Stoics, a natural law governs all morality, and human behavior must conform to it. But for Augustine this is not an impersonal rational principle that shapes the destiny of the cosmos. The Augustinian natural law is, rather, the eternal law of God as it is written in the heart of man and woman and is apprehended by them in their conscience; and the eternal law is the "reason and will of God."

Thus, the ultimate source of all that is good, for Augustine, is God, and God alone is intrinsically good. Our overriding moral imperative is therefore to love God. The individual virtues are simply different aspects of the love of God.

Augustine did not mean that you must love *only* God. He meant that, although there is nothing wrong with loving things other than God, you must not love them as if they were good in and of themselves, for *only God is intrinsically good.* To love things other than God as if they were inherently good—for example, to love money or success as if these things were good in and of themselves—is *disordered* love: it is to turn away from God, and moral evil consists in just this disordered love.

Now, do not let any of this make you think that Augustine was unconcerned with happiness, for as a matter of fact he did indeed think we should seek happiness. But happiness, he argued, consists in having all you want and wanting no evil. This may seem to be an odd notion at first, but when you think about it, it is by no means absurd. In any event, the only conceivable way to have all you want and to want no evil, Augustine thought, is to make God the supreme object of your love.

So, for Augustine, moral evil arises when man or woman turns away from God. Thus, *God* is not the creator of moral evil; it is *we* who create evil. But does it not then follow that *we* can create good? No, for God, remember, is the source of all that is good. We can do good only *through* God, Augustine said.

In sum, Augustine borrowed a theme from Plato by maintaining that physical evil can always be explained as the absence of something, and his concept of moral evil as arising from misdirected love can be viewed as a variation of Plato's idea of moral evil as ignorance of the good. In this way, Augustine thought he had solved the problem of evil without doing damage to principles of Christian faith.

One other aspect of Augustine's moral philosophy must be emphasized. According to Augustine, our highest good, or virtue, consists in loving and having God. By contrast, sin is distorted or misdirected or disordered love. So virtue and sin, according to Augustine, are *conditions of the soul.* What counts, for Augustine, is living out of love for God; doing supposedly good deeds is of secondary importance. When it comes to appraising a person's moral worth, therefore, what matters is not the person's accomplishments but, rather, the *state of mind* from which the person acts. We shall see that this idea—that a person's intent is what matters morally—came to play an important role in moral philosophy.

272   Part Two   •   *Moral and Political Philosophy*

St. Hildegard of Bingen

Augustine was the last of the great late ancient philosophers. Between the sixth century and the eleventh, Europe went through the Dark Ages, as we discussed in Chapter 5. **Hildegard** (1098–1179) was a light at the end of the tunnel. Her ethical writings typify the beginning of a period of religious mysticism that never came to a complete end: religious mysticism just went out of fashion with the onslaught of rationalism that began with Descartes (see Chapter 6). Mysticism, we perhaps should mention, is belief in (or experience of) a form of higher, spiritual, mystical realm often found in trances or dreams.

Hildegard was unquestionably an important figure in the history of philosophy (see the Profile). It is true that she and other religious mystical philosophers are usually called "theologians," but what they have to say is important for both ethics and moral epistemology. They provided theories of the nature of moral knowledge.

For mystical philosophers, mystical experience provides as certain a form of knowledge as pure rational introspection ever could. Their mystical experiences often take the form of visions and sometimes take the form of ideas, thoughts, and even whole books that seemingly are dictated directly by some divine source during these experiences. We are not going to assess the validity of such claims here; we are just going to reproduce and talk about their contents.

In one of her books, Hildegard listed thirty-five vices and their opposite virtues. This kind of list of opposites is a traditional format for talking about virtue and vice and dates back to Pythagoras. One vice, *Immoderation* (lack of moderate desires), is opposed to the virtue *Discretion* (keeping things within appropriate bounds). Hildegard describes Immoderation in the following allegory:

> This one is just like a wolf. She is furiously cunning, in hot pursuit of all evils, without distinction. With flexed legs, she crouches, looking in all directions, in such a way that she would devour anything she could snatch. She has a tendency to anything low-grade, following the worst habits of her peculiar mind. She considers every empty, worthless thing.

Now, before you jump to conclusions about this medieval Benedictine nun, before you dismiss her views on virtue and vice as narrow and constricted, take a look at her accounts of human sexuality. In these excerpts from her philosophy of medicine in *Causa et Curae* (*Causes and Cures*), she gives the following accounts of what she considered to be healthy male and female sexuality:

> There are some men showing much virility, and they have strong and solid brains. The wind also which is in their loins has two tents to its command, in which it blows as if into a chimney. And these tents surround the stem of all manly powers, and are helpers to it, just like small buildings placed next to a tower which they defend. Therefore, there are two, surrounding the stem, and they strengthen and direct it so that the more brave and allied, they would attract the wind and release it again, just like two bellows which blow into a fire. When likewise they erect the stem in its manliness, they hold it bravely and thus at a later time the stem blossoms into a fruit.

PROFILE: St. Hildegard of Bingen (1098–1179)

Hildegard was born at the end of the eleventh century in the Rhine River valley in Germany. She was the tenth child and was therefore "tithed" to God; at age seven or eight, she was sent to live with a group of women in a hermitage that eventually became the Benedictine convent of Disibodenberg. Hildegard learned Latin and studied the Bible, and she read the philosophical works of early Church fathers, including St. Jerome and St. Augustine.

Even as a child, Hildegard experienced mystical visions. By the time Hildegard had been head of the convent at Disibodenberg for three years, God commanded her, during one of these visions, to begin writing them down and to teach others their content. This put Hildegard in a difficult position because women were considered by the Church as well as by society to have no religious, theological, or philosophical authority. But the Bishop of Mainz (Germany) was impressed by her writings and convinced Pope Eugene III to consider them. The pope was convinced that the visions were genuine messages from God and had part of Hildegard's messages read to the bishops, who had come from all over Europe to attend a conference called the Synod of Trier during the winter of 1147–1148.

Hildegard and her little convent were now better known than the adjoining monastery. As Hildegard's fame spread, more and more women flocked to her convent. When the monks at the monastery refused to give the nuns the additional living quarters and library space they needed, Hildegard moved the convent. The monks, who controlled the dowries of the nuns, tried to retain the money and valuables. But Hildegard had some power now and effectively convinced the bishops that the monks were obligated to turn the sizable dowries over to her. These funds and artifacts were needed to finance the construction of the new convent at Bingen and to provide support for her nuns. She was a formidable champion for the education of women, which at that time meant establishing convents (she founded two) where ancient copies of philosophical and religious texts were hand-copied by nuns who had been taught to read Latin.

Hildegard was a prolific writer. She wrote books on natural science and on medicine (she is credited with developing the theory that disease can be transmitted by dirty water—resulting in the construction of massive sewage systems in Germany), wrote music (recently released on CD!), and wrote lengthy works of religious philosophy that she had lavishly illustrated with replications of the visions upon which they were based.

She was a very influential thinker and traveled and "preached" the meaning of her visions throughout Germany. She was regularly consulted by a succession of four popes, and her many correspondents included two emperors, a king, and two queens. Hildegard lived to a ripe old age despite a lifetime of recurrent illnesses and the hardships of extended preaching tours.

And:

> Pleasure in a woman is compared to the sun which caressingly, gently, and continuously fills the earth with its heat, so that it can bear fruits, since if it would heat the earth more harshly in its constancy, it would hurt the fruits more than it would produce them. And so pleasure in a woman caressingly and gently, but nevertheless continuously, would have heat so that she can conceive and produce fruit. For when pleasure surges forth in a woman, it is lighter in her than it is in a man.

Clearly, sexual pleasure is not on this nun's list of vices.

Heloise and Abelard

An important thinker who lived at the same time as Hildegard was the French abbess **Heloise** [HEL-oh-eez] (1098–1164). Heloise, like Hildegard, was concerned with virtue and vice, although Heloise was especially concerned with a specific virtue.

For Heloise, philosophy was life. If you believed in the truth of a theory of morality, you lived according to its principles. End of story. Heloise's writings on moral philosophy are found in her *Problemata* (Problems) and *Epistolae* (Letters), written when Heloise was in her thirties and all addressed to **Peter Abelard** (1079–1144), another major figure in the history of ethical philosophy and the most important logician of his time. The famous love story of Abelard and Heloise is explained in the box "The Truth about Heloise and Abelard."

The ethics of Heloise has two primary components. The first component, adapted from the Roman Stoic philosopher Cicero, places high value on the virtue *Disinterested Love*. True love for another, whether or not sexual, is completely unselfish and asks nothing, Heloise believed. The lover loves the beloved for who the beloved is. A true lover supports the beloved in achieving his goals and realizing his highest moral potential. In an ideal loving relationship, the beloved has reciprocal feelings for the lover. He loves her for herself, for who she is. He aspires to help her realize her highest moral potential and the fulfillment of her goals. He has no selfish desires.

The other major component of Heloise's moral philosophy concerns the **morality of intent,** which she derived basically from Abelard's own teachings. Think back to the Augustinian theory: it is not *what you do* that matters but rather the *state of mind* with which you do it (virtue is essentially a matter of having a mind that is disposed to do right). This theory was accepted throughout the Dark Ages and into the Middle Ages. The one who explored this theory most carefully prior to St. Thomas Aquinas was Abelard.

Abelard drew a distinction between moral defects or imperfections and other defects or imperfections of the mind, such as being stupid or having a bad memory. Moral defects dispose you to do what you should not do—or not do what you should do. He also drew a distinction between moral defects and sin. Sin is "contempt of God"—failing to do or renounce what we should.

Armed with these distinctions, Abelard argued that sin does not consist in *acting* on evil desires. In fact, it does not even consist in *having* evil desires. Sin consists instead in *consenting* to act on evil desires. Further, a wrongful act—an act that ought not be done, such as killing someone—can be committed without an evil will, in which case, although the act is wrong, the person who acts is not morally reprehensible.

Thus, Abelard's position is that virtue consists not in having no evil desires but in not consenting to act on them. And "the evil will itself, when restrained, though it may not be quenched, procures the palmwreath for those who resist it."

Heloise, too, accepted this theory: "In a wicked deed, rectitude of action depends not on the effect of the thing but on the affections of the agent, not on what is done but with what dispositions it is done."

This conception of ethics certainly played an important role in the relationship between Abelard and Heloise. Heloise argued that, by voluntarily marrying Abelard, she would have been the cause of Abelard's being barred from final

The Truth about Heloise and Abelard

Heloise (1098–1164) was a French philosopher and poet who received an early education at the Benedictine convent of Argenteuil. By the time she was sixteen years old, she was known as the most learned woman in France. Heloise's uncle Fulbert, who was her guardian and also a canon at Notre Dame, hired an unordained cleric named Pierre Abelard (1079–1144) to teach Heloise philosophy.

The traditional literature tends to describe Heloise and Abelard's relationship as one of the great love affairs of all time, right up there with Romeo and Juliet. Now, that is true to a certain extent. Heloise certainly fell in love with her philosophy teacher— but she refused to have sex with him.

Abelard acknowledged that Heloise verbally refused to have sex and physically fought him off. In his words, "I frequently forced your consent (for after all you were the weaker) by threats and blows." Or, as we might say today if he were brought up on charges: on some occasions he beat her and raped her, and on other occasions he threatened to beat her again if she did not stop resisting.

Heloise became pregnant. Abelard offered to marry her. Heloise refused. As usual, Abelard would not take no for an answer. As her due date came near, he took her to his sister's farm in the country, where she gave birth. They named their son Astrolabe (after an astronomical instrument). Abelard convinced Heloise to marry him so that their son would not be a bastard. You see, illegitimate children could not be baptized back then, so if Heloise had not married Abelard, she would have been condemning their son to an eternity in limbo.

Now, saving your baby from eternal limbo might well be enough to make you marry someone who, incidentally, had already become an important medieval philosopher. But it is important, if you are going to understand Heloise's moral philosophy, to know about the other sordid details of their personal life. (Unfortunately, there are more.)

When the happy couple returned to Paris (leaving the baby at the farm), they lied to Uncle Fulbert about having gotten married. If the story got out that Abelard was married, Heloise knew, he would

Not a modern-day Heloise and Abelard, we hope.

not be permitted to continue studying for the priesthood. The Cathedral School of Notre Dame, where Abelard taught, was turning into the University of Paris. It would be the first institution of higher learning in France (the second in Europe) to accept students who were not studying to be priests.

Heloise thought it would be a waste of Abelard's talents for him to miss out on this new experiment in education: a university. Worse, Heloise would feel responsible for keeping Abelard from fulfilling his ambitions.

Fulbert, though, was no fool. He figured things out and announced that Abelard had gotten married. Heloise tried to protect Abelard by denying the marriage, so Uncle Fulbert started mistreating Heloise (who was living at his house). To make it appear as if Heloise were not lying, Abelard ordered her to return to the convent and become a nun, which she did. At this point, Uncle Fulbert, who evidently was not given to halfway measures, hired thugs to castrate Abelard. (Heloise, who was in Argenteuil at the convent, did not hear about this for years.) But now that having sex with Heloise was permanently out of the question, Abelard sought final ordination as a priest. He set up a convent called the Paraclete and made Heloise its abbess. For decades, she never knew why.

ordination to the priesthood. She did not want to be morally responsible for that outcome. She felt he forced and tricked her into marrying him and that this was a consequence of her pregnancy, for which she was not morally responsible. Abelard's *Historica Calamitatum* (*Story of My Calamities*), as well as Heloise's letters to Abelard, insists that she never agreed to have sex with him: he beat and raped her. She would not accept moral responsibility for the pregnancy because she had no evil intent to seduce him.

But because they actually were married, Abelard could order Heloise to enter a convent. After she did so, Abelard had almost no contact with her. Heloise did not understand why Abelard ignored her letters nor why he ignored the physical and spiritual welfare of her nuns. Decades later, she read his book and learned about his castration. She put two and two together.

Heloise might have loved Abelard in this ideal, disinterested type of love, but it was a one-way street. Although she loved him for himself and expressed that love by helping him achieve his goals (priesthood and a job as a philosopher at the emerging university), his love for her was predominantly sexual. After he was no longer able to have sex, she realized, Abelard had made her head of her own convent. Heloise had obeyed Abelard (who was both her husband and her religious superior), running the convent and teaching the nuns. All those years, Heloise had lived according to the moral theory she thought Abelard shared, loving him unselfishly, for himself.

St. Thomas Aquinas

Augustine fashioned a philosophical framework for Christian thought that was essentially Platonic. He found many Platonic and Neoplatonic themes that could be given a Christian interpretation and thus is sometimes said to have Christianized Plato. Eight centuries later, **St. Thomas Aquinas** [uh-QUINE-nuss] (1225–1274), in a somewhat different sense, Christianized the philosophy of Aristotle. Aquinas's task was perhaps the more difficult of the two, for the philosophy of Aristotle, with its this-worldly approach to things, was less congenial to a Christian interpretation. Thus, it is customary to speak of Aquinas as having *reconciled* Aristotelianism with Christianity. In Aquinas's ethical philosophy, this amounted by and large to accepting both Christianity and the philosophy of Aristotle wherever that could be done without absurdity.

Aristotle said that the good for each kind of thing is defined with reference to the function or the nature of that kind of thing and is in fact the goal or purpose of that kind of thing. In the case of humans, goodness is happiness. Aquinas agreed. The natural (moral) law, which is God's eternal law as it is applied to humans on earth, is apprehended by us in the dictates of our conscience and practical reasoning, which guide us to our natural goal, happiness on earth.

But there is also, according to Aquinas, an eternal, atemporal good—namely, happiness everlasting. The law that directs us to that end is God's divine law, which the Creator reveals to us through his grace.

Thus, the natural law of Aquinas is the law of reason, which leads us to our natural end insofar as we follow it. The **divine law** is God's gift to us, revealed through his grace. Therefore, according to Aquinas, there are two sets of virtues:

the "higher" virtues of faith, love, and hope; and the natural virtues, such as forti-
tude and prudence, which are achieved when the will, directed by the intellect, mod-
erates our natural drives, impulses, and inclinations. And Aquinas, like Aristotle,
thought of the virtues as matters of character or habit—in Aquinas's view, the
habit of acting according to the provisions of natural law.

Although Aquinas's ethics are thus a type of virtue-ethics, he does treat the
moral goodness of actions. When evaluating an act, and only voluntary acts are
subject to moral evaluation, we must consider not only what was done but also why
it was done and the circumstances under which it was done.

Now, suppose someone does something, or refrains from doing it, because the
person's conscience tells him or her that this would be the morally proper thing to
do or refrain from doing. And suppose, further, that in this case the individual's
conscience is mistaken. Yes, an erring conscience is possible, according to Aquinas,
despite the fact that it is through conscience that we become aware of natural law.
In such a case, if the person acts as he or she honestly thinks is morally right, and
the mistake in thinking is due to involuntary ignorance on the person's part, the
person has not really sinned, according to Aquinas.

Aquinas's ethical system is detailed and systematic, and it is difficult to convey
this in this brief summary. Aquinas treats highly general and abstract principles
such as the ultimate objective of human existence, the nature of goodness, and
the sources of action and also applies these principles to specific and concrete
moral questions.

HOBBES AND HUME

You have seen that the naturalism found in Aristotle's ethics and the nonnaturalistic ethics of Plato, with its conception of a transcendental source of ultimate value,
flowed in separate streams through the philosophy of the centuries until the time
of Aquinas. If it is not quite true to say that Aquinas channeled the waters from
each of these two streams into a common bed, it may at least be said that he con-
trived to have them flow side by side, though in separate channels.

But the next philosopher we wish to discuss, **Thomas Hobbes** (1588–1679),
drew exclusively from the Aristotelian channel. This is not surprising, for Hobbes
was one of the first philosophers of the modern period in philosophy, a period
marked by the emergence of experimental science, in which once again nature
itself was an object of study, just as it had been for Aristotle. (You should be aware,
nevertheless, that Hobbes, reacting to the Aristotelianism of his Oxford tutors, had
harsh things to say about Aristotle.)

Hobbes

Hobbes's metaphysics was a relentless materialism. All that exists, he said, are
material things in motion. Immaterial substance does not exist. There is no such
thing as the nonphysical soul. Thoughts, emotions, feelings—all are motions of the

Hobbes and the Beggar

The story is told of Hobbes that he was asked by a clergyman why he was giving alms to a beggar.

"Is it because Jesus has commanded you to do so?" the latter asked.

"No," came Hobbes's answer.

"Then why?"

"The reason I help the man," said Hobbes, "is that by doing so I end my discomfort at seeing his discomfort."

One moral that might be drawn from the story is that even the most altruistic and benevolent actions can be given an egoistic interpretation. Why did Hobbes help the beggar? To relieve his own discomfort. Why do saints devote their lives to relieving the suffering of others? Because it brings them pleasure to do so. Why did the soldier sacrifice his life to save his comrades? To end the distress he felt at thinking of his friends' dying—or maybe even because it

pleased him to think of others praising him after his demise.

In short, because those who act to relieve their own discomfort or to bring pleasure to themselves are acting for their own self-interest, all of these seemingly altruistic actions can be interpreted egoistically.

Are you convinced?

Well, if you are, you should know that many philosophers are uncomfortable with this egoistic analysis of altruistic behavior. After all (they argue), it brings the saint pleasure to help others only if the saint is genuinely motivated to help others, right? Thus, if egoism is equated with the doctrine that we are never motivated to help others, it is false. If it is equated with the doctrine that we only act as we are motivated to act, it is true, but not particularly interesting.

matter within the brain, caused by moving things outside the brain. Even our reasoning and volition are purely physical processes.

As for values, according to Hobbes the words *good* and *evil* simply denote that which a person desires or hates. And Hobbes, like Aristotle, the Epicureans, the Stoics, and Aquinas, believed that one has a natural "end" or objective toward which all activity is directed. Hobbes specified this object of desire as the preservation of one's life. One seeks personal survival above all other things, he held. Hobbes also said that one has a "natural right" to use all means necessary to defend oneself or otherwise ensure one's survival.

Thus, Hobbes was a descriptive egoist, in the sense we explained earlier in this chapter. That is, he believed that, in all conscious action, one seeks to promote one's self-interest (for Hobbes this meant seeking survival) above all else. A story is reported in the box "Hobbes and the Beggar" that Hobbes was asked by a clergyman why he was giving alms to a beggar; Hobbes reportedly said he did so to end his own discomfort at seeing the beggar's discomfort. Beginning students in philosophy often are tempted to give a similar "selfish" analysis of even the most apparently unselfish actions; a difficulty in that idea is explained in the box.

Was Hobbes also a prescriptive egoist? That is, did he also think that one *ought* to seek to promote one's self-interest above all else? In general, Hobbes did not attempt to determine how people ought to behave in some absolute sense; he seems intent on describing how they ought to behave *if* they want best to secure their natural objective. A question he left for subsequent philosophers, and one that has not been resolved to this day, is this: If the universe is material, can there really *be* absolute values? Do good and evil, justice and injustice, exist in some *absolute* sense, or must they be regarded, as Hobbes so regarded them, as expressions of desires or the products of human agreements?

Hobbes's major work, *Leviathan,* is a classic in moral and political philosophy and encompasses as well metaphysics, epistemology, ethics, and psychology. It secured for Hobbes a prime-time place in all histories of Western thought.

Hume

Hobbes maintained that the idea of incorporeal or immaterial substance was a contradiction in terms, but he denied being an atheist. Nevertheless, he certainly did not rest his ethics on the authority of the Church. And although most of the major philosophers of the modern period shrank from Hobbes's extreme materialism, they, too—most of them—sought to discover the basic principles of morality elsewhere than in scripture. Some, such as Locke, though believing that these principles are decreed by God, held, like Hobbes, that they are discoverable—and provable—by reason.

But in the eighteenth century, **David Hume** (1711–1776) argued with some force that moral principles are neither divine edicts nor discoverable by reason. Hume's general position regarding God, as we shall see in Part Three, was that the order in the universe does offer some slight evidence that the universe has or had a creative force remotely analogous to human intelligence. But we certainly cannot affirm anything about the moral qualities of the creator, he held; and we cannot derive guidelines for our own actions from speculating about his (its) nature. Christianity Hume regarded as superstition.

Value Judgments Are Based on Emotion, Not Reason

Hume held likewise that moral judgments are not the "offspring of reason." Scrutinize an act of murder as closely as you can, he said. Do you find anything in the *facts of the case* that reveal the act is morally wrong? The *facts,* he said, are simply that one person has terminated the life of another in a certain way at a particular time and place. Reasoning can disclose how long it took for death to occur, whether the victim suffered great pain, what the motives of the killer were, as well as the answers to many other factual questions such as these. But it will not show the *moral wrongfulness* of the act. The judgment that an act is immoral, Hume maintained, comes not from reason but from *emotion.* Perhaps this idea has occurred to you as well. For an example, see the box "Cold-Blooded Murder."

It is the same, Hume believed, with all value judgments. Is the judgment that a portrait is beautiful founded on reason? Of course not. Reason can disclose the chemical composition of the paints and canvas, the monetary value of the work, and many similar factual things. But whether the portrait is beautiful is an issue that cannot be settled by reason.

Thus, for Hume, moral judgments, and all value judgments, are based on emotion. Actions that we find morally praiseworthy or blameworthy create within us feelings of pleasure or displeasure, respectively. Now, obviously, these feelings are

---

Cold-Blooded Murder

A fundamental principle of Hume's philosophy is that moral judgments are not the offspring of reason.

A consideration that might favor Hume's thesis is that we tend to think of particularly heinous deeds—execution-style murders, for example—as "cold-blooded" and "heartless," not as "irrational."

This is an indication that we view the murderer as lacking in *feeling* rather than as deficient in *reason*.

Is it hard to believe that an absolutely brilliant mind could commit murder? We think not. But is it hard to believe that someone with normal sensibilities could commit murder? We think that it is. These considerations favor Hume's principle.

---

different in kind from aesthetic pleasures and pleasures of the palate. Humans clearly have a capacity for moral pleasure as well as for other types of pleasure: we are *morally sensitive creatures*. Behavior that pleases our moral sensibilities elicits our approval and is deemed good, right, just, virtuous, and noble. Behavior that offends our moral sense is deemed bad, wrong, unjust, base, and ignoble.

Benevolence

But just what is it about behavior that elicits our moral approval? *What do virtuous, good, right, and noble acts have in common?* Hume's answer was that the type of act we deem morally praiseworthy is one taken by an agent *out of concern for others*. The act that pleases our moral sensibilities is one that reflects a *benevolent character* on the part of the agent, he said. By "agent," philosophers mean the person who did the act.

Why does benevolence bring pleasure to us when we witness, read about, or contemplate it? A cynical answer is that we imagine ourselves benefiting from the benevolent activity, and imagining this is pleasant. Do you get a warm glow when you read about someone coming to the aid of a fellow person? Well, according to the cynical view, that is because you picture yourself on the receiving end of the exchange.

But this cynical theory is unnecessarily complex, said Hume. The reason you get that pleasant feeling when you read about or see someone helping someone else is that you *sympathize* with others. It just plainly upsets a normal person to see others suffering, and it pleases a normal person to see others happy. True, there are people who suffer from the emotional equivalent of color blindness and lack the capacity to sympathize with others. But these people are not the norm. The normal human being is a sympathetic creature, maintained Hume.

This aspect of Hume's moral philosophy may well have some significance for us today. On one hand, we tend to believe that you should care for others but, on the other hand, that you must also certainly look out for yourself. And we are inclined to think that there is a problem in this because self-concern and other-concern seem mutually exclusive. But if Hume is correct, they are not. Looking out for your own interests includes doing what brings you pleasure. And if Hume is correct, caring for others will bring you an important kind of pleasure. Indeed, if Hume is correct, when you praise an action as good, it is precisely because it brings you this kind of pleasure.

It is important to notice, finally, the emphasis Hume placed on character. As we said, according to Hume, the act that pleases our moral sensibilities is one that reflects a benevolent *character* on the part of the agent. Hume believed that when we morally praise (or condemn) someone, it is the person's character we praise (or condemn) primarily: his or her actions we find praiseworthy (or condemnatory) mainly as an indication of character. This idea—that we apply moral attributes primarily to a person's character and secondarily to the person's actions—is common in the virtue-ethics tradition of Plato, Aristotle, and Aquinas. In this respect, Hume is part of that tradition.

Can There Be Ethics after Hume?

"Morality," Hume said, "is more properly felt than judged of." Ethical standards are not fixed by reason, he held; further, even if there is a God, he maintained, it is impossible for us to gain moral guidance from him.

Loosely speaking, therefore, ethics after Hume seems generally to have had these options. First, it might seek to establish that, despite Hume, morality *can* be grounded on reason or God. As we shall see next, this was the option taken by Kant, who favored reason as the ultimate ground of morality. Second, ethics might try to find objective sources of moral standards other than reason and God. This is what the utilitarians tried to do, as we shall see shortly. Third, it might try to determine how one should conduct one's affairs given the absence of objective moral standards. This is a primary concern of contemporary existentialists, as we saw in Chapter 8. Fourth, ethics might abandon the search for moral standards altogether and concentrate instead on such factual questions as, What do people believe is good and right? What does it mean to say that something is good or right? How do moral judgments differ from other kinds of judgments? What leads us to praise certain actions as moral and condemn others as immoral? These are some of the issues that captured the attention of many twentieth-century philosophers, such as G. E. Moore, whom we will encounter in Chapter 12.

KANT

Immanuel Kant (1724–1804) disagreed entirely with Hume's discounting of the possibility that reason can settle whether an act is morally right. In Kant's opinion, reason and reason alone can settle this. Kant's argument, paraphrased and distilled, went like this:

1. *Scientific inquiry can never reveal to us principles that we know hold without exception.* Scientific inquiry is based on experience, and in the final analysis experience can show only how things have been to this point, not how they must be. For example, science reveals to us physical "laws" that hold true of the universe as it is now, but it cannot provide absolutely conclusive

282   Part Two · *Moral and Political Philosophy*

A scene from Königsburg today. The home of Immanuel Kant.

guarantees that these laws will forever hold true. (If you have difficulty understanding this point, rereading the section on Kant in Chapter 7 will help.)

2. *Moral principles, however, hold without exception.* For example, if it is wrong to torture helpless animals, then it would be wrong for anyone, at any time, to do so.

Thus, from these two premises—that moral principles hold without exception and that scientific investigations cannot reveal what holds without exception—it follows that

3. *Moral principles cannot be revealed through scientific investigation.* Because Kant believed that any principle that holds without exception is knowable only through reason, he maintained that *reason alone can ascertain principles of morality.*

The Supreme Principle of Morality

Further, according to Kant, because a moral rule is something that holds without exception—that is, holds universally—you should act only on principles that could hold universally. For example, if you think you must cheat to pass an exam, then the principle on which you would act (if you were to cheat) would be this: *To obtain a passing grade, it is acceptable to cheat.* But now consider: If this principle were a universal law, then a passing grade would be meaningless, right? And in that case the principle itself would be meaningless. In short, the principle logically could not hold universally, and (this comes to the same thing) it would be irrational for anyone to want it to hold universally.

Now, if it would be irrational for you to want the principle on which you act to be a universal law, then that principle is morally improper, and the act should not be done. Thus, for Kant, the supreme prescription of morality, which he calls the supreme **categorical imperative,** is *to act always in such a way that you could, rationally, will the principle on which you act to be a universal law.* In Kant's words, "Act only on that maxim whereby you can at the same time will that it should become a universal law."

Because, in Kant's view, a universal law would in effect be a sort of law of nature, he offers a second formulation of the categorical imperative: "Act as if the maxim of your action were to become by your will a Universal Law of Nature."

Why You Should Do What You Should Do

Moral principles, Kant observed, may always be expressed in the imperative form: Do not steal! Be kind to others! Further, because moral imperatives must hold without exception, they are different from **hypothetical imperatives,** which state, in effect, that one ought to do something *if* such-and-such an end is desired.

For example, the imperatives "If you wish to be healthy, then live moderately!" and "If you wish to secure your own survival, then surrender your rights to a sovereign power!" are both hypothetical imperatives. Neither is a **moral imperative,** for a moral imperative holds unconditionally, or *categorically.* This means that a moral imperative commands obedience for the sake of no other end than its own rightness.

Thus, for Kant, what I should do, I should do *because it is right.* Doing something for any other purpose—for the sake of happiness or the welfare of humankind, for example—is not to act morally. It is to act under the command of a hypothetical imperative, which is not unconditional, as a moral imperative must be. According to Kant, you should do your moral duty simply because it is your moral duty. You should be aware that duty-based ethical systems, like Kant's, are known as deontological ethical systems.

Furthermore, according to Kant, it's not the *effects or consequences* of your act that determine whether your act is good, for these are not totally within your control. What is within your control is the *intent* with which you act. Thus, what determines whether your act is good or bad is the intent with which it is undertaken. He wrote, "Nothing can possibly be conceived in the world, or even out of it, which can be called good, without qualification, except a good will."

And because a morally good will is one that acts solely for the sake of doing what is right, it follows, in Kant's opinion, that *there is no moral worth* in, say, helping others because you are sympathetic or inclined to do so. Moral worth lies only in helping others for the sake of doing the right thing.

Because to violate the supreme principle of morality, the supreme categorical imperative, is to be irrational, rationality may be said to be the source of all value. Hence, the rational will alone is deemed inherently good by Kant. Accordingly, Kant offers yet another formulation of the supreme categorical imperative: *Treat rational beings (i.e., humans) in every instance as ends and never just as means!*

That this is an alternative formulation of the same principle may be seen in the fact that, if you were to violate the categorical imperative and do something that you could not rationally will to be a law for all, then in effect you would be treating the interests of others as subordinate to your own; that is, you would be treating others as means and not as ends. Kant, it is often said (for obvious reasons), was the first philosopher to provide a *rational basis* for the golden rule found in many religions: Do unto others as you would have them do unto you.

Did Kant provide a viable response to Hume's idea that reason cannot determine whether an act is morally right? You decide.

THE UTILITARIANS

Kant, we have seen, may well have offered a sound refutation of Hume's idea that moral principles are not determined by reason. It is therefore perhaps strange that two of the most celebrated ethical philosophers of the nineteenth century, the Englishmen **Jeremy Bentham** (1748–1832) and **John Stuart Mill** (1806–1873), largely ignored the rationalistic ethics of Kant, Bentham perhaps more so than Mill. Bentham and Mill did not, however, ignore Hume. Instead, they developed further Hume's idea that traits and actions that are virtuous promote the welfare of people, the "general happiness."

Bentham and Mill were utilitarians, which means they believed that *the rightness of an action is identical with the happiness it produces as its consequence.* What is new or exciting about this? Didn't Aristotle and the Epicureans and Augustine and Aquinas also advocate pursuing happiness? The difference is that, according to those earlier philosophers, it is *your own happiness* that you should strive for.

By contrast, the utilitarians said that the morally best act is the one that produces the greatest amount of happiness *with everyone considered*. But this is ambiguous: should we aim at increasing the *average* happiness or the *total* happiness— even if this would reduce the happiness per person? Usually the utilitarians are interpreted as favoring increasing the average happiness. In any case, they believed that, when you are trying to produce happiness, it is not just your own happiness you should aim for but rather the happiness of people in general.

It is common to attribute to the utilitarians the view that the right act is the one that produces "the greatest happiness for the greatest number." That phrase—the greatest happiness for the greatest number—is unfortunate, because it tells us to maximize two different things. (Just try to plot the greatest happiness for the greatest number as a single line on a graph, with happiness as one variable and number as a second variable!) You can say, "The more people who have a given amount of happiness, the better," and you can say, "The more happiness a given number of people have, the better." But it is not clear what you could mean by saying, "The more happiness the greater number of people have, the better." We will interpret the utilitarians as favoring the view that the more happiness a given number of people have, the better (i.e., the higher the average happiness, the better). And again, according to this philosophy, your own happiness is *not* more important morally than that of others.

Notice, too, that for the utilitarians it is the *consequences* of an act that determine its rightness, a position that contrasts strongly with Kant's idea that the moral worth of an act depends on the *will* or *motive* with which it is taken.

Bentham

Bentham, the earlier of the two utilitarians, equated happiness with pleasure. "Nature," he wrote, "has placed mankind under the governance of two sovereign masters, *pain* and *pleasure*. It is for them alone to point out what we ought to do, as well as determine what we shall do."

The words *ought, right, good,* and the like have meaning only when defined in terms of *pleasure,* Bentham said. This fact is evident, he argued, in that all other intelligible moral standards either must be interpreted in terms of the pleasure standard or are simply disguised versions of the pleasure standard in the first place.

For example, suppose you maintain that the right act is the one that is preferred by God. Well, said Bentham, unless we know God's preferences—that is, unless we know what, exactly, pleases God—what you maintain is pretty meaningless, is it not? And the only way "to know what is His pleasure," he said, is by "observing what is our own pleasure and pronouncing it to be His."

Or consider the theory that a moral obligation to obey the law stems from a "social contract" among members of society. That theory, said Bentham, is unnecessarily complicated. For when we have a moral obligation to obey the law, he said, that obligation is more simply explained by the fact that obedience to the law would result in more pleasure for more people than disobedience would.

Bentham believed that the pain and pleasure an act produces can be evaluated solely with reference to *quantitative* criteria. Which of two or more courses of action you should take should be determined by considering the probable consequences of each possible act with respect to the certainty, intensity, duration, immediacy, and extent (the number of persons affected) of the pleasure or pain it produces, and with respect to the other kinds of sensations it is likely to have as a result over the long run. This "calculus" of pleasure, as it is often called, represents a distinctive feature of Bentham's ethics. Bentham believed that, by using these criteria, one could and should calculate which of alternative courses of action would produce the greatest amount of pleasure and which, therefore, ought morally to be taken.

Through all of this you should be asking: But why ought I seek the *general* happiness and not give higher priority to my own? Bentham's answer was that your own happiness *coincides* with the general happiness: what brings pleasure to you and what brings pleasure to others fortunately go together.

You may wish to consider whether this answer is fully satisfactory.

PROFILE: Jeremy Bentham (1748–1832)

You will find it easy to identify with Jeremy Bentham—if, that is, you studied Latin when you were four, started college when you were twelve, graduated by age fifteen, and finished law school and were admitted to the bar all while you were still a teenager.

Yes, Bentham was a sharp youth. When he was fifteen, he went to hear Sir William Blackstone, the famous English jurist. Bentham said that he instantly spotted errors in Blackstone's reasoning, especially on natural rights. Bentham came to believe that the whole notion of natural rights, including that found in the American Declaration of Independence, was just "nonsense on stilts." In 1776 he published his first book, *Fragment on Government*, a critique of Blackstone.

For David Hume and Hume's *Treatise on Human Nature*, however, Bentham had more respect, and he claimed that the work made the scales fall from his eyes about ethics. Bentham's own ethical philosophy reflects the great influence of Hume.

Though qualified to do so, Bentham never actually practiced law. He was much more interested in legal and social reform and wrote daily commentaries on English law and society. He advocated a simplified and codified legal system and worked for prison and education reform and extension of voting rights. Bentham also published numerous pamphlets on such abuses as jury packing and extortionate legal fees, and his followers, the "Benthamites," were an effective political force that endured after his death.

Bentham was in the habit of not finishing books that he started to write, and the only major philosophical treatise that he published himself is the *Introduction to the Principles of Morals and Legislation* (1789). The title states exactly Bentham's main concern in life: applying sound principles of morality to the law.

If you want to know what Bentham looked like, do not stop with a picture. Bentham's embalmed body, complete with a wax head and dressed just as he liked to, is there for you to see at University College, London.

Mill

John Stuart Mill, who claimed to have discovered in Bentham's ethical theory what he needed to give purpose to his own life, was also concerned with providing a philosophical justification for the utilitarian doctrine that it is the *general* happiness that one should aim to promote. The justification, according to Mill, lies in the fact that a moral principle by its very nature singles out no one for preferential treatment. Thus, Mill wrote, "as between his own happiness and that of others," the utilitarian is required "to be as strictly impartial as a disinterested and benevolent spectator." Compare Mill's justification with that of Bentham. Mill's justification is sounder, is it not?

Probably the most important difference between Mill and Bentham is that Mill believed that some pleasures are *inherently better* than others and are to be preferred even over a greater amount of pleasure of an inferior grade.

That some pleasures are better than others can be seen, Mill argued, in the fact that few people would be willing to trade places with an animal or even with a more ignorant person than themselves, even if the exchange guaranteed their having the fullest measure of an animal's or an ignoramus's pleasure. Here is what he meant. Would you trade places with a pig or a lunkhead? Would you do it even if you knew that as a pig or a lunkhead you would have more pig or lunkhead pleasures than you now have pleasure as an intelligent human being?

The cartoon points up the foolishness of the notion that we can seek pleasure *by itself.* Such a search has no direction. What we seek is food, shelter, companionship, sex, and so forth—we do not, strictly speaking, seek pleasure per se. And if you tried to seek pleasure, you would not know how to go about finding it. Your seeking must always be for something, such as food, that is not *itself* pleasure.

Thus, for Mill, in determining the pleasure for which we should strive, we must consider the *quality* of the pleasure as well as the quantity. Choose the pleasure of the highest quality.

Now, this is all very well, but what settles which of two pleasures is of higher quality? Mill's answer is quite simple: Of two pleasures, if there is one to which most who have experienced both give a decided preference, that is the more desirable pleasure.

Notice what this answer seems to entail. It seems to entail that the pleasures preferred by the *intellectual* will be found to be of superior quality, for nonintellectuals "only know their own side of the question. The other party to the comparison knows both sides," said Mill.

According to Mill, then, it is not simply the quantity of pleasure an act produces that determines its moral worth; the quality of the pleasure produced must also be taken into account. Mill is thus said to have recognized implicitly (though not in so many words) a factor other than pleasure by which the moral worth of actions should be compared: the factor of quality. In other words, he is said to have proposed, in effect, a standard of moral worth other than pleasure, a standard of "quality" by means of which pleasure itself is to be evaluated. So he sometimes is said not to be a "pure" utilitarian, if a utilitarian is one who believes that the pleasure an act produces is the only standard of good.

It is not unusual, therefore, to find philosophers who think of Bentham's philosophy as more consistently utilitarian than Mill's, though everyone refers to both Mill and Bentham as "the" utilitarians.

288   Part Two   •   *Moral and Political Philosophy*

There is one other, sort of fuzzy, difference between Bentham and Mill. Bentham's utilitarianism is what today is called **act utilitarianism:** the rightness of an *act* is determined by its effect on the general happiness. Mill also subscribed to act utilitarianism in some passages, but in other places he seems to have advocated what is called **rule utilitarianism.** According to this version of utilitarianism, we are to evaluate the moral correctness of an action not with reference to its impact on the general happiness but rather with respect to the impact on the general happiness of the *rule* or principle the action exemplifies.

Take this case, for example: Suppose that by murdering us you would increase the general happiness (maybe unknown to anyone, we harbor some awful contagious disease). Act utilitarianism would say that you should murder us. But a rule utilitarian, as Mill in some places seems to be, would say that if society accepted murder as a rule of conduct, ultimately the general happiness would be diminished, so you should not murder us. Rule utilitarianism is, in a way, much more Kantian than is act utilitarianism.

FRIEDRICH NIETZSCHE

Another important nineteenth-century philosopher, one who believed that all previous moral philosophy was tedious and soporific and who had no use at all for the utilitarians, was **Friedrich Nietzsche** (1844–1900). In Nietzsche's view, moralities are social institutions, and basically there are just two moralities: master morality and slave morality, the morality of the masses. Slave morality—for Nietzsche,

The paradox of hedonism. The British moralist Henry Sidgwick (1838–1900) noted the curious fact, which he called the *paradox of hedonism*, that the desire for pleasure, if too predominant, defeats its own aim. (Sidgwick also observed that "the pleasures of thought and study can only be enjoyed in the highest degree by those who have an ardour of curiosity which carries the mind temporarily away from self and its sensations.")

epitomized by Christian ethics—emphasizes such virtues as compassion, humility, patience, warmheartedness, and turning the other cheek. These "virtues" glorify weakness. Master morality, by contrast, is the morality of noble individuals, who are egoistic, hard, intolerant, but bound by a code of honor to their peers. Noble individuals define harm entirely in terms of what is harmful to themselves and despise altruism and humility.

According to Nietzsche, the enhancement of the species is always the result of aristocratic societies, which, he held, are the ultimate justification of human social existence. The primal life force, for Nietzsche, is the will-to-power, whose essence is the overpowering and suppression of what is alien and weaker and which finds its highest expression in the noble man, or *Übermensch* ("Superman" in German). The principle by which the *Übermensch* lives is "There is no god or human over me." He is the source of ethical truth.

Nietzsche followed the ancient Greek philosopher Heraclitus (Chapter 2) in holding that life is quintessentially strife or warfare. It is only within the dark eye of battle that human energies are truly stretched and fruit-bearing actions become possible. Battles make heroes, he thought; peace renders us weak and ineffectual. One of Nietzsche's most famous proverbs was, "What doesn't kill us makes us stronger."

The ultimate battle, Nietzsche thought, takes place within the human frame and is the battle between two forces, the Apollonian and the Dionysian. The Greek god Apollo represents the force of measure, order, and harmony. The Greek god Dionysius (or Bacchus in the Roman world) represents the counterforce of excess, destruction, and creative power, the ecstatic rush and rave of the original, formless will. In the human soul, these two forces contest each other for ascendancy. While both are necessary if one is to be fully and creatively alive, the creative Dionysian force has been lost almost entirely in the slave mentality, with its emphasis on humility, meekness, mediocrity, and the denial of life.

The selection from Nietzsche at the end of the chapter conveys many of these themes clearly and will make it obvious why attempts often are made to censor Nietzsche from schools and libraries.

SELECTION 10.1

Gorgias*

Plato

[*You may know someone—or may be someone—who thinks that one should fully indulge one's appetites, or that pleasure, whatever its nature, is the key to happiness. In this excerpt from the Dialogue* Gorgias, *Plato has the character Callicles advancing this view and Socrates rebutting it.*]

---

* From *Socratic Dialogues,* translated and edited by W. D. Woodhead (Edinburgh: Thomas Nelson & Sons, 1953).

Socrates: . . . You say we should not curb our appetites, if we are to be what we should be, but should allow them the fullest possible growth and procure satisfaction for them from whatever source, and this, you say, is virtue.

Callicles: That is what I say. . . .

S: Consider whether you would say this of each type of life, the temperate and the undisciplined.

290   Part Two • *Moral and Political Philosophy*

Imagine that each of the two men has several jars, in the one case in sound condition and filled, one with wine, another with honey, another with milk, and many others with a variety of liquids, but that the sources of these liquids are scanty and hard to come by, procured only with much hard labor. Imagine then that the one after filling his vessels does not trouble himself to draw in further supplies but as far as the jars are concerned is free from worry; in the case of the other man the sources, as in the first instance are procurable but difficult to come by, but his vessels are perforated and unsound and he is ever compelled to spend day and night in replenishing them, if he is not to suffer the greatest agony. If this is the character of each of the lives, do you still insist that the life of the uncontrolled man is happier than that of the orderly? Do I or do I not persuade you with this image that the disciplined life is better than the intemperate?

C: You do not, Socrates. The man who has filled his vessels can no longer find any pleasure, but this is what I just now described as living the life of a stone. Once the vessels are filled, there is neither pleasure nor pain any more. But a life of pleasure demands the largest possible influx.

S: Then if there is a big influx, must there not also be a great outflow, and must not the holes for the outflow be large?

C: Certainly.

S: It is the life of a plover you mean, not that of a corpse or a stone. And now tell me. You are thinking of some such thing as being hungry and, when hungry, eating?

C: I am.

S: And being thirsty and, when thirsty, drinking?

C: Yes, and experiencing all the other appetites and being able to satisfy them and living happily in the enjoyment of them.

S: Good, my worthy friend, just continue as you began, and mind you do not falter through shame. And I too, it seems, must throw all shame aside. First of all then, tell me whether one who suffers from the itch and longs to scratch himself, if he can scratch himself to his

heart's content and continue scratching all his life, can be said to live happily. . . .

C: Well then, I say that even one who scratches himself would live pleasantly.

S: And if pleasantly, happily?

C: Certainly.

S: If it was only his head that he wanted to scratch—or can I push the question further? Think what you will answer, Callicles, if anyone should ask all the questions that naturally follow. And as a climax of all such cases, the life of a catamite—is not that shocking and shameful and miserable? Will you dare to say that such people are happy, if they have what they desire in abundance?

C: Are you not ashamed, Socrates, to drag our discussion into such topics?

S: Is it I who do this, my noble friend, or the man who says so unequivocally that pleasure, whatever its nature, is the key to happiness, and does not distinguish between pleasures good and evil? But enlighten me further as to whether you say that the pleasant and the good are identical, or that there are some pleasures which are not good.

C: To avoid inconsistency if I say they are different, I assert that they are the same. . . .

S: Tell me, do you not think that those who fare well experience the opposite of those who fare ill?

C: I do.

S: Then if these things are opposites, the same must hold true of them as of health and sickness. A man cannot be both in health and sick at the same time, nor be rid of both conditions at the same time.

C: How do you mean?

S: Take, for example, any part of the body separately and consider it. A man perhaps has trouble with his eyes, which is called ophthalmia.

C: Of course.

S: Then his eyes are not at the same time sound.

C: By no means.

S: And what of when he is rid of ophthalmia? Does he then get rid of the health of his eyes, and is he finally quit of both conditions?

C: Certainly not.

S: For that would be miraculous and irrational, would it not?

C: Very much so.

S: But, I suppose, he acquires and gets rid of each in turn.

C: I agree.

S: And is it not the same with strength and weakness?

C: Yes.

S: And swiftness and slowness?

C: Certainly.

S: And good things and happiness, and their opposites, evils and wretchedness—does he possess and get rid of each of these in turn?

C: Assuredly, I think.

S: Then if we discover certain things which a man possesses and gets rid of simultaneously, it is obvious that these cannot be the good and the evil. Do we agree on this? Do not answer until you have considered it carefully.

C: I am in the most complete possible accord.

S: Back then to our previous admissions. Did you say hunger was pleasant or painful? Actual hunger, I mean.

C: Painful, but to satisfy hunger by eating is pleasant.

S: I understand. But hunger itself at least is painful, is it not?

C: I agree.

S: And thirst too?

C: Most certainly.

S: Am I to ask any further then, or do you admit that every deficiency and desire is painful?

C: I admit it; you need not ask.

S: Very well then, but to drink when thirsty you say is pleasant?

C: I do.

S: Now in this statement the word 'thirsty' implies pain, I presume.

C: Yes.

S: And drinking is a satisfaction of the deficiency and a pleasure?

C: Yes.

S: Then you say that in drinking there is pleasure?

C: Certainly.

S: When one is thirsty?

C: I agree.

S: That is, when in pain?

C: Yes.

S: Then do you realize the result—that you say a man enjoys pleasure simultaneously with pain, when you say that he drinks when thirsty? Does not this happen at the same time and the same place, whether in body or soul? For I fancy it makes no difference. Is this so or not?

C: It is.

S: Yes, but you say also that when one is faring well it is impossible for him at the same time to fare ill.

C: I do.

S: But you have agreed it is possible to experience pleasure at the same time as pain.

C: Apparently.

S: Then pleasure is not the same as faring well, nor pain as faring ill, and so the pleasant is different from the good.

C: I do not understand what your quibbles mean, Socrates.

S: You understand, Callicles, but you are playing coy. But push on a little further, that you may realize how cunning you are, you who admonish me. Does not each one of us cease at the same time from thirsting and from his pleasure in drinking?

C: I do not know what you mean.

292   Part Two · *Moral and Political Philosophy*

S: Do not behave so, Callicles, but answer for our sakes too, that the arguments may be concluded.

C: But Socrates is always the same, Gorgias. He asks these trivial and useless questions and then refutes.

S: What difference does that make to you? In any case you do not have to pay the price, Callicles, but suffer Socrates to cross-examine you as he will.

C: Well then, ask these petty little questions, since Gorgias so wishes.

S: You are lucky, Callicles, in having been initiated in the Great Mysteries before the Little; I did not think it was permitted. Answer then from where you left off, whether thirst and the pleasure of drinking do not cease for each of us at the same time.

C: I agree.

S: And does not one cease from hunger and other desires, and from pleasures at the same time?

C: That is so.

S: Does he not then cease from pains and pleasures at the same time?

C: Yes.

S: Yes, but he does not cease from experiencing the good and the ill simultaneously, as you yourself agreed. Do you not agree now?

C: I do. What of it?

S: Only this, that the good is not the same as the pleasant, my friend, nor the evil as the painful. For we cease from the one pair at the same time, but not from the other, because they are distinct. How then could the pleasant be the same as the good, or the painful as the evil? Let us look at it in a different way, if you like, for I think that even here you do not agree. But just consider. Do you not call good people by that name because of the presence in them of things good, just as you call beautiful those in whom beauty is present?

SELECTION 10.2

The Nicomachean Ethics*

Aristotle

[*This is an excerpt from one of the classics of Western philosophy. In it, Aristotle provides a "rough outline" of the good.*]

Let us again return to the good we are seeking, and ask what it can be. It seems different in different actions and arts; it is different in medicine, in strategy, and in the other arts likewise. What then is the good of each? Surely that for whose sake everything else is done. In medicine this is health, in strategy victory, in architecture a house, in any other sphere something else, and in every action and pursuit the end; for it is for the sake of this that all men do whatever else they do. Therefore, if there is an end for all that we do, this will be the good achievable by action, and if there are more than one, these will be the goods achievable by action.

So the argument has by a different course reached the same point; but we must try to state this even more clearly. Since there are evidently more than one end, and we choose some of these (e.g. wealth, flutes, and in general instruments) for the sake of something else, clearly not all ends are final ends;

* The author's footnotes have been deleted. From "Ethica Nicomachea," translated by W. D. Ross, from *The Works of Aristotle,* translated into English under the editorship of W. D. Ross, Vol. IX (Oxford: Oxford University Press, 1925). By permission of Oxford University Press.

but the chief good is evidently something final. Therefore, if there is only one final end, this will be what we are seeking, and if there are more than one, the most final of these will be what we are seeking. Now we call that which is in itself worthy of pursuit more final than that which is worthy of pursuit for the sake of something else, and that which is never desirable for the sake of something else more final than the things that are desirable both in themselves and for the sake of that other thing, and therefore we call final without qualification that which is always desirable in itself and never for the sake of something else.

Now such a thing happiness, above all else, is held to be; for this we choose always for itself and never for the sake of something else, but honour, pleasure, reason, and every virtue we choose indeed for themselves (for if nothing resulted from them we should still choose each of them), but we choose them also for the sake of happiness, judging that by means of them we shall be happy. Happiness, on the other hand, no one chooses for the sake of these, nor, in general, for anything other than itself.

From the point of view of self-sufficiency the same result seems to follow; for the final good is thought to be self-sufficient. Now by self-sufficient we do not mean that which is sufficient for a man by himself, for one who lives a solitary life, but also for parents, children, wife, and in general for his friends and fellow citizens, since man is born for citizenship. But some limit must be set to this; for if we extend our requirement to ancestors and descendants and friends' friends we are in for an infinite series. Let us examine this question, however, on another occasion; the self-sufficient we now define as that which when isolated makes life desirable and lacking in nothing; and such we think happiness to be; and further we think it most desirable of all things, without being counted as one good thing among others—if it were so counted it would clearly be made more desirable by the addition of even the least of goods; for that which is added becomes an excess of goods, and of goods the greater is always more desirable. Happiness, then, is something final and self-sufficient, and is the end of action.

Presumably, however, to say that happiness is the chief good seems a platitude, and a clearer account of what it is is still desired. This might perhaps be given, if we could first ascertain the func-

tion of man. For just as for a flute-player, a sculptor, or any artist, and, in general, for all things that have a function or activity, the good and the 'well' is thought to reside in the function, so would it seem to be for man, if he has a function. Have the carpenter, then, and the tanner certain functions or activities, and has man none? Is he born without a function? Or as eye, hand, foot, and in general each of the parts evidently has a function, may one lay it down that man similarly has a function apart from all these? What then can this be? Life seems to be common even to plants, but we are seeking what is peculiar to man. Let us exclude, therefore, the life of nutrition and growth. Next there would be a life of perception, but *it* also seems to be common even to the horse, the ox, and every animal. There remains, then, an active life of the element that has a rational principle; of this, one part has such a principle in the sense of being obedient to one, the other in the sense of possessing one and exercising thought. And, as 'life of the rational element' also has two meanings, we must state that life in the sense of activity is what we mean; for this seems to be the more proper sense of the term. Now if the function of man is an activity of soul which follows or implies a rational principle, and if we say 'a so-and-so' and 'a good so-and-so' have a function which is the same in kind, e.g. a lyre-player and a good lyre-player, and so without qualification in all cases, eminence in respect of goodness being added to the name of the function (for the function of a lyre-player is to play the lyre, and that of a good lyre-player is to do so well): if this is the case, [and we state the function of man to be a certain kind of life, and this to be an activity or actions of the soul implying a rational principle, and the function of a good man to be the good and noble performance of these, and if any action is well performed when it is performed in accordance with the appropriate excellence: if this is the case,] human good turns out to be activity of soul in accordance with virtue, and if there are more than one virtue, in accordance with the best and most complete.

But we must add 'in a complete life.' For one swallow does not make a summer, nor does one day; and so too one day, or a short time, does not make a man blessed and happy.

Let this serve as an outline of the good; for we must presumably first sketch it roughly, and then later fill in the details.

294   Part Two · *Moral and Political Philosophy*

SELECTION 10.3

Epicurus to Menoeceus*

Epicurus

[*Epicurus, like Callicles in the first selection, advocates living a life devoted to acquiring pleasure. But when you read this selection, you will see that Epicurus's concept of pleasure is much more sophisticated than Callicles'.*]

The things which I [unceasingly] commend to you, these do and practice, considering them to be the first principles of the good life. . . .

Become accustomed to the belief that death is nothing to us. For all good and evil consists in sensation, but death is deprivation of sensation. And therefore a right understanding that death is nothing to us makes the mortality of life enjoyable, not because it adds to it an infinite span of time, but because it takes away the craving for immortality. For there is nothing terrible in life for the man who has truly comprehended that there is nothing terrible in not living. . . . Death, the most terrifying of ills, is nothing to us, since so long as we exist, death is not with us; but when death comes, then we do not exist. It does not then concern either the living or the dead, since for the former, it is not, and the latter are no more. . . .

We must then bear in mind that the future is neither ours, nor yet wholly not ours, so that we may not altogether expect it as sure to come, nor abandon hope of it, as if it will certainly not come.

We must consider that of desires some are natural, others vain, and of the natural some are necessary and others merely natural; and of the necessary some are necessary for happiness, others for the repose of the body, and others for very life. The right understanding of these facts enables us to refer all choices and avoidance to the health of the body and the soul's freedom from disturbance, since this is the aim of the life of blessedness. For it is to obtain this end that we always act, namely, to avoid pain and fear. And when this is once secured for us, all the tempest of the soul is dispersed, since the living crea-

ture has not to wander as though in search of something that is missing, and to look for some other thing by which he can fulfill the good of the soul and the good of the body. For it is then that we have need of pleasure, when we feel pain owing to the absence of pleasure; but when we do not feel pain, we no longer need pleasure. And for this cause we call pleasure the beginning and end of the blessed life. For we recognize pleasure as the first good innate in us, and from pleasure we begin every act of choice and avoidance, and to pleasure we return again, using the feeling as the standard by which we judge every good.

And since pleasure is the first good and natural to us, for this very reason we do not choose every pleasure, but sometimes we pass over many pleasures, when greater discomfort accrues to us as the result of them: and similarly we think many pains better than pleasures, since a greater pleasure comes to us when we have endured pains for a long time. Every pleasure then because of its natural kinship to us is good, yet not every pleasure is to be chosen: even as every pain also is an evil, yet not all are always of a nature to be avoided. Yet by a scale of comparison and by the consideration of advantages and disadvantages we must form our judgment on all these matters. For the good on certain occasions we treat as bad, and conversely the bad as good.

And again independence of desire we think a great good—not that we may at all times enjoy but a few things, but that, if we do not possess many, we may enjoy the few in the genuine persuasion that those have the sweetest pleasure in luxury who least need it, and that all that is natural is easy to be obtained, but that which is superfluous is hard. And so plain savours bring us a pleasure equal to a luxurious diet, when all the pain due to want is removed; and bread and water produce the highest pleasure, when one who needs them puts them to his lips. To grow accustomed therefore to simple and not luxurious diet gives us health to the full, and makes a man alert for the needful employments of life, and when after long intervals we approach luxuries disposes us better towards them, and fits us to be fearless of fortune.

---

* From *Epicurus: The Extant Remains,* translated by Cyril Bailey (Oxford: Clarendon Press, 1926). By permission of Oxford University Press.

Chapter 10 · *Moral Philosophy* 295

When, therefore, we maintain that pleasure is the end, we do not mean the pleasures of profligates and those that consist in sensuality, as is supposed by some who are either ignorant or disagree with us or do not understand, but freedom from pain in the body and from trouble in the mind. For it is not continuous drinkings and revellings, nor the satisfaction of lusts, nor the enjoyment of fish and other luxuries of the wealthy table, which produce a pleasant life, but sober reasoning, searching out the motives for all choice and avoidance, and banishing mere opinions, to which are due the greatest disturbance of the spirit.

Of all this the beginning and the greatest good is prudence. Wherefore prudence is a more precious thing even than philosophy: for from prudence are sprung all the other virtues; and it teaches us that it is not possible to live pleasantly without living prudently and honourably and justly, not, again, to live a life of prudence, honour and justice without living pleasantly. For the virtues are by nature bound up with the pleasant life, and the pleasant life is inseparable from them. For indeed who, think you, is a better man than he who holds reverent opinions concerning the gods, and is at all times free from fear of death, and has reasoned out the end ordained by nature?

SELECTION 10.4

The Encheiridion*

Epictetus

[*Epictetus, like Epicurus and Callicles, advocates a life of pleasure. Epictetus advises us to get straight on what things are under our control and what things aren't. What happens isn't under our control, but our attitudes are. Therefore, the key to happiness is, when something bad happens, to take a stoical attitude.*]

1. Some things are under our control, while others are not under our control. Under our control are conception, choice, desire, aversion, and, in a word, everything that is our own doing; not under our control are our body, our property, reputation, office, and in a word, everything that is not our own doing. Furthermore, things under our control are by nature free, unhindered, and unimpeded; while the things not under our control are weak, servile, subject to hindrance, and not our own. Remember, therefore, that if what is naturally slavish you think to be free, and what is not your own to be your own, you will be hampered, will grieve, will be in turmoil,

and will blame both gods and men; while if you think only what is your own to be your own, and what is not your own to be, as it really is, not your own, then no one will ever be able to exert compulsion upon you, no one will hinder you, you will blame no one, will find fault with no one, will do absolutely nothing against your will, you will have no personal enemy, no one will harm you, for neither is there any harm that can touch you. . . .

Make it, therefore, your study at the very outset to say to every harsh external impression, "You are an external impression and not at all what you appear to be." After that examine it and test it by these rules which you have, the first and most important of which is this: Whether the impression has to do with the things which are under our control, or with those which are not under our control; and, if it has to do with some one of the things not under our control, have ready to hand the answer, "It is nothing to me."

2. Remember that the promise of desire is the attainment of what you desire, that of aversion is not to fall into what is avoided, and that he who fails in his desire is unfortunate, while he who falls into what he would avoid experiences misfortune. If, then, you avoid only what is unnatural among those things which are under your control, you will fall into none of the things which you avoid; but if you

try to avoid disease, or death, or poverty, you will experience misfortune. Withdraw, therefore, your aversion from all the matters that are not under our control, and transfer it to what is unnatural among those which are under our control. But for the time being remove utterly your desire; for if you desire some one of the things that are not under our control you are bound to be unfortunate; and, at the same time, not one of the things that are under our control, which it would be excellent for you to desire, is within your grasp. But employ only choice and refusal, and these too but lightly, and with reservations, and without straining. . . .

5. It is not the things themselves that disturb men, but their judgments about these things. For example, death is nothing dreadful, or else Socrates too would have thought so, but the judgment that death is dreadful, this is the dreadful thing. When, therefore, we are hindered, or disturbed, or grieved, let us never blame anyone but ourselves, that means, our own judgments. It is the part of an uneducated person to blame others where he himself fares ill; to blame himself is the part of one whose education has begun; to blame neither another nor his own self is the part of one whose education is already complete. . . .

8. Do not seek to have everything that happens happen as you wish, but wish for everything to happen as it actually does happen, and your life will be serene. . . .

11. Never say about anything, "I have lost it," but only "I have given it back." Is your child dead? It has been given back. Is your wife dead? She has been given back. "I have had my farm taken away." Very well, this too has been given back. "Yet it was a rascal who took it away." But what concern is it of yours by whose instrumentality the Giver called for its return? So long as He gives it to you, take care of it as of a thing that is not your own, as travellers treat their inn. . . .

15. Remember that you ought to behave in life as you would at a banquet. As something is being passed around it comes to you; stretch out your hand and take a portion of it politely. It passes on; do not detain it. Or it has not come to you yet; do not project your desire to meet it, but wait until it comes in front of you. So act toward children, so toward a wife, so toward office, so toward wealth; and

then some day you will be worthy of the banquets of the gods. But if you do not take these things even when they are set before you, but despise them, then you will not only share the banquet of the gods, but share also their rule. . . .

16. When you see someone weeping in sorrow, either because a child has gone on a journey, or because he has lost his property, beware that you be not carried away by the impression that the man is in the midst of external ills, but straightway keep before you this thought: "It is not what has happened that distresses this man (for it does not distress another), but his judgment about it." Do not, however, hesitate to sympathize with him so far as words go, and, if occasion offers, even to groan with him; but be careful not to groan also in the centre of your being.

17. Remember that you are an actor in a play, the character of which is determined by the Playwright; if He wishes the play to be short, it is short; if long, it is long; if He wishes you to play the part of a beggar, remember to act even this role adroitly; and so if your role be that of a cripple, an official, or a layman. For this is your business, to play admirably the role assigned you; but the selection of that role is Another's. . . .

20. Bear in mind that it is not the man who reviles or strikes you that insults you, but it is your judgment that these men are insulting you. Therefore, when someone irritates you, be assured that it is your own opinion which has irritated you. And so make it your first endeavour not to be carried away by the external impression; for if once you gain time and delay, you will more easily become master of yourself.

21. Keep before your eyes by day death and exile, and everything that seems terrible, but most of all death; and then you will never have any abject thought, nor will you yearn for anything beyond measure. . . .

33. Lay down for yourself, at the outset, a certain stamp and type of character for yourself, which you are to maintain whether you are by yourself or are meeting with people. And be silent for the most part, or else make only the most necessary remarks, and express these in few words. But rarely, and when occasion requires you to talk, talk indeed, but about no ordinary topics. Do not talk about gladiators, or

horse-races, or athletes, or things to eat or drink—topics that arise on all occasions; but above all, do not talk about people, either blaming, or praising, or comparing them. If, then, you can, by your own conversation bring over that of your companions to what is seemly. But if you happen to be left alone in the presence of aliens, keep silence.

Do not laugh much, nor at many things, nor boisterously.

Refuse, if you can, to take an oath at all, but if that is impossible, refuse as far as circumstances allow. . . .

In things that pertain to the body take only as much as your bare need requires, I mean such things as food, drink, clothing, shelter, and household slaves; but cut down everything which is for outward show or luxury.

In your sex-life preserve purity, as far as you can, before marriage, and if you indulge, take only those privileges which are lawful. However, do not make yourself offensive, or censorious, to those who do indulge, and do not make frequent mention of the fact that you do not yourself indulge.

If someone brings you word that So-and-so is speaking ill of you, do not defend yourself against what has been said; but answer: "Yes, indeed, for he did not know the rest of the faults that attach to me; if he had, these would not have been the only ones he mentioned." . . .

41. It is a mark of an ungifted man to spend a great deal of time in what concerns his body, as in much exercise, much eating, much drinking, much evacuating of the bowels, much copulating. But these things are to be done in passing; and let your whole attention be devoted to the mind. . . .

44. The following statements constitute a non-sequitur: "I am richer than you are, therefore I am superior to you"; or, "I am more eloquent than you are, therefore I am superior to you." But the following conclusions are better: "I am richer than you are, therefore my property is superior to yours"; or "I am more eloquent than you are, therefore my elocution is superior to yours." But you are neither property nor elocution. . . .

46. On no occasion call yourself a philosopher, and do not, for the most part, talk among laymen about your philosophic principles, but do what follows from your own principles.

SELECTION 10.5

Foundations of the Metaphysics of Morals*

Immanuel Kant

[*In the first paragraph Kant states the "categorical imperative," the supreme principle of morality. He then illustrates the principle by examining four concrete and specific examples.*]

There is, therefore, only one categorical imperative. It is: Act only according to that maxim by which you can at the same time will that it should become a universal law.

* From Beck, Lewis White, *Immanuel Kant: Foundations of the Metaphysics of Morals*, 2nd Edition, © 1990. Reprinted by permission of Pearson Education, Inc., Upper Saddle River, NJ.

Now if all imperatives of duty can be derived from this one imperative as a principle, we can at least show what we understand by the concept of duty and what it means, even though it remains undecided whether that which is called duty is an empty concept or not.

The universality of law according to which effects are produced constitutes what is properly called nature in the most general sense (as to form), i.e., the existence of things so far as it is determined by universal laws. [By analogy], then, the universal imperative of duty can be expressed as follows: Act as though the maxim of your action were by your will to become a universal law of nature.

We shall now enumerate some duties, adopting the usual division of them into duties to ourselves

298   Part Two · *Moral and Political Philosophy*

and to others and into perfect and imperfect duties.[1]

1. A man who is reduced to despair by a series of evils feels a weariness with life but is still in possession of his reason . . . sufficiently to ask whether it would not be contrary to his duty to himself to take his own life. Now he asks whether the maxim of his action could become a universal law of nature. His maxim, however, is: For love of myself, I make it my principle to shorten my life when by a longer duration it threatens more evil than satisfaction. But it is questionable whether this principle of self-love could become a universal law of nature. One immediately sees a contradiction in a system of nature whose law would be to destroy life by the feeling whose special office is to impel the improvement of life. In this case it would not exist as nature; hence that maxim cannot obtain as a law of nature, and thus it wholly contradicts the supreme principle of all duty.

2. Another man finds himself forced by need to borrow money. He well knows that he will not be able to repay it, but he also sees that nothing will be loaned him if he does not firmly promise to repay it at a certain time. He desires to make such a promise, but he has enough conscience to ask himself whether it is not improper and opposed to duty to relieve his distress in such a way. Now, assuming he does decide to do so, the maxim of his action would be as follows: When I believe myself to be in need of money, I will borrow money and promise to repay it, although I know I shall never do so. Now this principle of self-love or of his own benefit may very well be compatible with his whole future welfare, but the question is whether it is right. He changes the pretension of self-love into a universal law and then puts the question: How would it be if my maxim became a universal law? He immediately sees that it could never hold as a universal law of nature and be consistent with itself; rather, it must necessarily contradict itself. For the universality of a law which says that anyone who believes himself to be in need

could promise what he pleased with the intention of not fulfilling it would make the promise itself and the end to be accomplished by it impossible; no one would believe what was promised to him but would only laugh at any such assertion as vain pretense.

3. A third finds in himself a talent which could, by means of some cultivation, make him in many respects a useful . . . man. But he finds himself in comfortable circumstances and prefers indulgence in pleasure to troubling himself with broadening and improving his fortunate natural gifts. Now, however, let him ask whether his maxim of neglecting his gifts, besides agreeing with his propensity to idle amusement, agrees also with what is called duty. He sees that a system of nature could indeed exist in accordance with such a law, even though man (like the inhabitants of the South Sea Islands) should let his talents rust and resolve to devote his life merely to idleness, indulgence, and propagation—in a word, to pleasure. But he cannot possibly will that this should become a universal law of nature or that it should be implanted in us by a natural instinct. For, as a rational being, he necessarily wills that all his faculties should be developed, inasmuch as they are given to him for all sorts of possible purposes.

4. A fourth man, for whom things are going well, sees that others (whom he could help) have to struggle with great hardships, and he asks, "What concern of mine is it? Let each one be as happy as heaven wills, or as he can make himself; I will not take anything from him or even envy him; but to his welfare or to his assistance in time of need I have no desire to contribute." If such a way of thinking were a universal law of nature, certainly the human race could exist, and without doubt even better than in a state where everyone talks of sympathy and good will, or even exerts himself occasionally to practice them while, on the other hand, he cheats when he can and betrays or otherwise violates the rights of man. Now although it is possible that a universal law of nature according to that maxim could exist, it is nevertheless impossible to will that such a principle should hold everywhere as a law of nature. For a will which resolved this would conflict with itself, since instances can often arise in which he would need the love and sympathy of others, and in which he would have robbed himself, by such a law of nature springing from his own will, of all hope of the aid he desires.

The foregoing are a few of the many actual duties, or at least of duties we hold to be actual, whose

---

[1] It must be noted here that I reserve the division of duties for a future *Metaphysics of Morals* and that the division here stands as only an arbitrary one (chosen in order to arrange my examples). For the rest, by a perfect duty I here understand a duty which permits no exception in the interest of inclination; thus I have not merely outer but also inner perfect duties. This runs contrary to the usage adopted in the schools, but I am not disposed to defend it here because it is all one to my purpose whether this is conceded or not.

derivation from the one stated principle is clear. We must be able to will that . . . a maxim of our action become a universal law; this is the canon of the moral estimation of our action generally. Some actions are of such a nature that their maxim cannot even be *thought* as a universal law of nature without contradiction, far from it being possible that one could will that it should be such. In others this internal impossibility is not found, though it is still impossible to *will* that their maxim should be raised to the universality of a law of nature, because such a will would contradict itself. We easily see that the former maxim conflicts with the stricter or narrower (imprescriptible) duty, the latter with broader (meritorious) duty. Thus all duties, so far as the kind of obligation (not the object of their action) is concerned, have been completely exhibited by these examples in their dependence on the one principle.

SELECTION 10.6
Utilitarianism

John Stuart Mill

[*Here, John Stuart Mill states in plain English what utilitarianism is and corrects popular misconceptions of it.*]

What Utilitarianism Is
. . . The creed which accepts as the foundation of morals "utility" or the "greatest happiness principle" holds that actions are right in proportion as they tend to promote happiness; wrong as they tend to produce the reverse of happiness. By happiness is intended pleasure and the absence of pain; by unhappiness, pain and the privation of pleasure. To give a clear view of the moral standard set up by the theory, much more requires to be said; in particular, what things it includes in the ideas of pain and pleasure, and to what extent this is left an open question. But these supplementary explanations do not affect the theory of life on which this theory of morality is grounded—namely, that pleasure and freedom from pain are the only things desirable as ends; and that all desirable things (which are as numerous in the utilitarian as in any other scheme) are desirable either for pleasure inherent in themselves or as means to the promotion of pleasure and the prevention of pain.

Now such a theory of life excites in many minds, and among them in some of the most estimable in feeling and purpose, inveterate dislike. To suppose that life has (as they express it) no higher end than pleasure—no better and nobler object of desire and pursuit—they designate as utterly mean and groveling, as a doctrine worthy only of swine, to whom the followers of Epicurus were, at a very early period, contemptuously likened; and modern holders of the doctrine are occasionally made the subject of equally polite comparisons by its German, French, and English assailants.

When thus attacked, the Epicureans have always answered that it is not they, but their accusers, who represent human nature in a degrading light, since the accusation supposes human beings to be capable of no pleasures except those of which swine are capable. . . . It is quite compatible with the principle of utility to recognize the fact that some kinds of pleasure are more desirable and more valuable than others. It would be absurd that, while in estimating all other things quality is considered as well as quantity, the estimation of pleasure should be supposed to depend on quantity alone.

If I am asked what I mean by difference of quality in pleasures, or what makes one pleasure more valuable than another, merely as a pleasure, except its being greater in amount, there is but one possible answer. Of two pleasures, if there be one to which all or almost all of who have experience of both give a decided preference, irrespective of any feeling of moral obligation to prefer it, that is the more desirable pleasure. If one of the two is, by those who are competently acquainted with both, placed so far above the other that they prefer it, even though knowing it to be attended with a greater amount of discontent, and would not resign it for any quantity of the other pleasure which their nature is capable of, we are justified in ascribing to the preferred enjoyment a superiority in quality so far outweighing quantity as to render it, in comparison, of small amount.

Now it is an unquestionable fact that those who are equally acquainted with and equally capable of appreciating and enjoying both do give a most marked preference to the manner of existence which employs their higher faculties. Few human creatures would consent to be changed into any of the lower animals for a promise of the fullest allowance of a beast's pleasures; no intelligent human being would consent to be a fool, no instructed person would be an ignoramus, no person of feeling and conscience would be selfish and base, even though they should be persuaded that the fool, the dunce, or the rascal is better satisfied with his lot than they are with theirs. They would not resign what they possess more than he for the most complete satisfaction of all the desires which they have in common with him. If they ever fancy they would, it is only in cases of unhappiness so extreme that to escape from it they would exchange their lot for almost any other, however undesirable in their own eyes. A being of higher faculties requires more to make him happy, is capable probably of more acute suffering, and certainly accessible to it at more points, than one of an inferior type; but in spite of these liabilities, he can never really wish to sink into what he feels to be a lower grade of existence. . . . It is indisputable that the being whose capacities of enjoyment are low has the greatest chance of having them fully satisfied; and a highly endowed being will always feel that any happiness which he can look for, as the world is constituted, is imperfect. But he can learn to bear its imperfections, if they are at all bearable; and they will not make him envy the being who is indeed unconscious of the imperfections, but only because he feels not at all the good which those imperfections qualify. It is better to be a human being dissatisfied than a pig satisfied; better to be Socrates dissatisfied than a fool satisfied. And if the fool, or the pig, are of a different opinion, it is because they only know their own side of the question. The other party to the comparison knows both sides.

It may be objected that many who are capable of the higher pleasures occasionally, under the influence of temptation, postpone them to the lower. But this is quite compatible with a full appreciation of the intrinsic superiority of the higher. Men often, from infirmity of character, make their election for the nearer good, though they know it to be the less valuable; and this is no less when the choice is between two bodily pleasures than when it is between bodily and mental. They pursue sensual indulgences to the injury of health, though perfectly aware that health is the greater good. It may be further objected that many who begin with youthful enthusiasm for everything noble, as they advance in years, sink into indolence and selfishness. But I do not believe that those who undergo this very common change voluntarily choose the lower description of pleasures in preference to the higher. I believe that, before they devote themselves exclusively to the one, they have already become incapable of the other. Capacity for the nobler feelings is in most natures a very tender plant, easily killed, not only by hostile influences, but by mere want of sustenance; and in the majority of young persons it speedily dies away if the occupations to which their position in life has devoted them, and the society into which it has thrown them, are not favorable to keeping that higher capacity in exercise. Men lose their high aspirations as they lose their intellectual tastes, because they have not the time or opportunity for indulging them; and they addict themselves to inferior pleasures, not because they deliberately prefer them, but because they are either the only ones to which they have access or the only ones which they are any longer capable of enjoying. It may be questioned whether anyone who has remained equally susceptible to both classes of pleasures ever knowingly and calmly preferred the lower, though many, in all ages, have broken down in an ineffectual attempt to combine both.

From this verdict of the only competent judges, I apprehend there can be no appeal. On a question which is the best worth having of two pleasures, or which of two modes of existence is the most grateful to the feelings, apart from its moral attributes and from its consequences, the judgment of those who are qualified by knowledge of both, or, if they differ, that of the majority among them, must be admitted as final. And there needs to be the less hesitation to accept this judgment respecting the quality of pleasures, since there is no other tribunal to be referred to even on the question of quantity. What means are there of determining which is the acutest of two pains, or the intensest of two pleasurable sensations, except the general suffrage of those who are familiar with both? Neither pains nor pleasures are homogeneous, and pain is always heterogeneous with pleasure. What is there to decide whether a particular pleasure is worth purchasing at the cost of a particular pain, except the feelings and judgment of the experienced? When, therefore, those feelings and judgment declare the pleasures derived from the higher faculties to be preferable *in kind,* apart from the question of intensity, to those of which the animal nature, disjoined from the higher faculties, is susceptible, they are entitled on this subject to the same regard.

I have dwelt on this point as being a necessary part of a perfectly just conception of utility or happiness considered as the directive rule of human conduct. But it is by no means an indispensable condition to the acceptance of the utilitarian standard; for that standard is not the agent's own greatest happiness, but the greatest amount of happiness altogether; and if it may possibly be doubted whether a noble character is always the happier for its nobleness, there can be no doubt that it makes other people happier, and that the world in general is immensely a gainer by it. Utilitarianism, therefore, could only attain its end by the general cultivation of nobleness of character, even if each individual were only benefited by the nobleness of others, and his own, so far as happiness is concerned, were a sheer deduction from the benefit. But the bare enunciation of such an absurdity as this last renders refutation superfluous.

According to the greatest happiness principle, as above explained, the ultimate end, with reference to and for the sake of which all other things are desirable—whether we are considering our own good or that of other people—is an existence exempt as far as possible from pain, and as rich as possible in enjoyments, both in point of quantity and quality; the test of quality and the rule for measuring it against quantity being the preference felt by those who, in their opportunities of experience, to which must be added their habits of self-consciousness and self-observation, are best furnished with the means of comparison. This, being according to the utilitarian opinion the end of human action, is necessarily also the standard of morality, which may accordingly be defined "the rules and precepts for human conduct," by the observance of which an existence such as has been described might be, to the greatest extent possible, secured to all mankind; and not to them only, but, so far as the nature of things admits, to the whole sentient creation.

. . . The utilitarian morality does recognize in human beings the power of sacrificing their own greatest good for the good of others. It only refuses to admit that the sacrifice itself is a good. A sacrifice which does not increase or tend to increase the sum total of happiness, it considers as wasted. The only self-renunciation which it applauds is devotion to the happiness, or to some of the means of happiness, of others, either of mankind collectively or of individuals within the limits imposed by the collective interests of mankind.

I must again repeat what the assailants of utilitarianism seldom have the justice to acknowledge, that the happiness which forms the utilitarian standard of what is right in conduct is not the agent's own happiness but that of all concerned. As between his own happiness and that of others, utilitarianism requires him to be as strictly impartial as a disinterested and benevolent spectator. In the golden rule of Jesus of Nazareth, we read the complete spirit of the ethics of utility. "To do as you would be done by," and "to love your neighbor as yourself," constitute the ideal perfection of utilitarian morality.

SELECTION 10.7

Beyond Good and Evil*

Friedrich Nietzsche

[*This passage contains a succinct, orderly, and easy-to-read statement by Friedrich Nietzsche of his conception of morality and the two types of morality (master morality and slave morality).*]

Every enhancement of the type "man" has so far been the work of an aristocratic society—and it will be so again and again—a society that believes in the long ladder of an order of rank and differences in value between man and man, and that needs slavery in some sense or other. . . . Let us admit to ourselves, without trying to be considerate, how every higher culture on earth so far has *begun.* Human beings whose nature was still natural, barbarians in every

302   Part Two · *Moral and Political Philosophy*

terrible sense of the word, men of prey who were still in possession of unbroken strength of will and lust for power, hurled themselves upon weaker, more civilized, more peaceful races, perhaps traders or cattle raisers, or upon mellow old cultures whose last vitality was even then flaring up in splendid fireworks of spirit and corruption. In the beginning, the noble caste was always the barbarian caste: their predominance did not lie mainly in physical strength or in strength of the soul—they were more whole human beings (which also means, at every level, "more whole beasts").

. . . The essential characteristic of a good and healthy aristocracy, however, is that it experiences itself *not* as a function (whether of the monarchy or the commonwealth) but as their *meaning* and highest justification—that it therefore accepts with a good conscience the sacrifice of untold human beings who, *for its sake,* must be reduced and lowered to incomplete human beings, to slaves, to instruments. Their fundamental faith simply has to be that society must *not* exist for society's sake but only as the foundation and scaffolding on which a choice type of being is able to raise itself to its higher task and to a higher state of *being*—comparable to those sun-seeking vines of Java—they called *Sipo Matador*—that so long and so often enclasp an oak tree with their tendrils until eventually, high above it but supported by it, they can unfold their crowns in the open light and display their happiness.

Refraining mutually from injury, violence, and exploitation and placing one's will on a par with that of someone else—this may become, in a certain rough sense, good manners among individuals if the appropriate conditions are present (namely, if these men are actually similar in strength and value standards and belong together in *one* body). But as soon as this principle is extended, and possibly even accepted as the *fundamental principle of society,* it immediately proves to be what it really is—a will to the *denial* of life, a principle of disintegration and decay.

Here we must beware of superficiality and get to the bottom of the matter, resisting all sentimental weakness: life itself is *essentially* appropriation, injury, overpowering of what is alien and weaker; suppression, hardness, imposition of one's own forms, incorporation and at least, at its mildest, exploitation—but why should one always use those words in which a slanderous intent has been imprinted for ages?

Even the body within which individuals treat each other as equals, as suggested before—and this happens in every healthy aristocracy—if it is a living and not a dying body, has to do to other bodies what the individuals within it refrain from doing to each other: it will have to be an incarnate will to power, it will strive to grow, spread, seize, become predominant—not from any morality or immorality but because it is *living* and because life simply *is* will to power. But there is no point on which the ordinary consciousness of Europeans resists instruction as on this: everywhere people are now raving, even under scientific disguises, about coming conditions of society in which "the exploitative aspect" will be removed—which sounds to me as if they promised to invent a way of life that would dispense with all organic functions. "Exploitation" does not belong to a corrupt or imperfect and primitive society: it belongs to the *essence* of what lives, as a basic organic function; it is a consequence of the will to power, which is after all the will of life. . . .

Wandering through the many subtler and coarser moralities which have so far been prevalent on earth, or still are prevalent, I found that certain features recurred regularly together and were closely associated—until I finally discovered two basic types and one basic difference.

There are *master morality* and *slave morality*—I add immediately that in all the higher and more mixed cultures there also appear attempts at mediation between these two moralities, and yet more often the interpenetration and mutual misunderstanding of both, and at times they occur directly alongside each other—even in the same human being, with a *single* soul. The moral discrimination of values has originated either among a ruling group whose consciousness of its difference from the ruled group was accompanied by delight—or among the ruled, the slaves and dependents of every degree.

In the first case, when the ruling group determines what is "good," the exalted, proud states of the soul are experienced as conferring distinction and determining the order of rank. The noble human being separates from himself those in whom the opposite of such exalted, proud states finds expression: he despises them. It should be noted immediately that in this first type of morality the opposition of "good" and *"bad"* means approximately the same as "noble" and "contemptible."

(The opposition of "good" and *"evil"* has a different origin.) One feels contempt for the cowardly, the anxious, the petty, those intent on narrow utility; also for the suspicious with their unfree glances, those who humble themselves, the doglike people who allow themselves to be maltreated, the begging flatterers, above all the liars; it is part of the fundamental faith of all aristocrats that the common people lie. "We truthful ones"—thus the nobility of ancient Greece referred to itself.

It is obvious that moral designations were everywhere first applied to *human beings* and only later, derivatively, to actions. Therefore it is a gross mistake when historians of morality start from such questions as: why was the compassionate act praised? The noble type of man experiences *itself* as determining values; it does not need approval; it judges, "what is harmful to me is harmful in itself"; it knows itself to be that which first accords honor to things; it is *value-creating*. Everything it knows as part of itself it honors: such a morality is self-glorification. In the foreground there is the feeling of fullness, of power that seeks to overflow, the happiness of high tension, the consciousness of wealth that would give and bestow: the noble human being, too, helps the unfortunate, but not, or almost not, from pity, but prompted more by an urge begotten by excess of power. The noble human being honors himself as one who is powerful, also as one who has power over himself, who knows how to speak and be silent, who delights in being severe and hard with himself and respects all severity and hardness. . . . Noble and courageous human beings who think that way are furthest removed from that morality which finds the distinction of morality precisely in pity, or in acting for others . . . faith in oneself, pride in oneself, a fundamental hostility and irony against "selflessness" belong just as definitely to noble morality as does a slight disdain and caution regarding compassionate feelings and a "warm heart." . . .

A morality of the ruling group, however, is most alien and embarrassing to the present taste in the severity of its principle that one has duties only to one's peers; that against beings of a lower rank, against everything alien, one may behave as one pleases or "as the heart desires," and in any case "beyond good and evil." . . .

It is different with the second type of morality, *slave morality*. Suppose the violated, oppressed, suffering, unfree, who are uncertain of themselves and

weary, moralize: what will their moral valuations have in common? Probably, a pessimistic suspicion about the whole condition of man will find expression, perhaps a condemnation of man along with his condition. The slave's eye is not favorable to the virtues of the powerful: he is skeptical and suspicious, *subtly* suspicious, of all the "good" that is honored there—he would like to persuade himself that even their happiness is not genuine. Conversely, those qualities are brought out and flooded with light which serve to ease existence for those who suffer: here pity, the complaisant and obliging hand, the warm heart, patience, industry, humility, and friendliness are honored—for these are the most useful qualities and almost the only means for enduring the pressure of existence. Slave morality is essentially a morality of utility.

Here is the place for the origin of that famous opposition of "good" and "evil": into evil one's feelings project power and dangerousness, a certain terribleness, subtlety, and strength that does not permit contempt to develop. According to slave morality, those who are "evil" thus inspire fear; according to master morality it is precisely those who are "good" that inspire, and wish to inspire, fear, while the "bad" are felt to be contemptible.

The opposition reaches its climax when, as a logical consequence of slave morality, a touch of disdain is associated also with the "good" of this morality—this may be slight and benevolent—because the good human being has to be *undangerous* in the slaves' way of thinking: he is good-natured, easy to deceive, a little stupid perhaps, *un bonhomme* [a "good person"]. Wherever slave morality becomes preponderant, language tends to bring the words "good" and "stupid" closer together.

One last fundamental difference: the longing for *freedom*, the instinct for happiness and the subtleties of the feeling of freedom belong just as necessarily to slave morality and morals as art and enthusiastic reverence and devotion are the regular symptom of an aristocratic way of thinking and evaluating. . . .

A *species* comes to be, a type becomes fixed and strong, through the long fight with essentially constant *unfavorable* conditions. Conversely, we know from the experience of breeders that species accorded superabundant nourishment and quite generally extra protection and care soon tend most strongly toward variations of the type and become rich in marvels and monstrosities (including monstrous vices).

304   Part Two · *Moral and Political Philosophy*

Now look for once at an aristocratic common-wealth—say, an ancient Greek *polis*, or Venice—as an arrangement, whether voluntary or involuntary, for breeding: human beings are together there who are dependent on themselves and want their species to prevail, most often because they *have to* prevail or run the terrible risk of being exterminated. Here that boon, that excess, and that protection which favor variations are lacking; the species needs itself as a species, as something that can prevail and make itself durable by virtue of its very hardness, uniformity, and simplicity of form, in a constant fight with its neighbors or with the oppressed who are rebellious or threaten rebellion. Manifold experience teaches them to which qualities above all they owe the fact that, despite all gods and men, they are still there, that they have always triumphed: these qualities they call virtues, these virtues alone they cultivate. They do this with hardness, indeed they want hardness; ever aristocratic morality is intolerant—in the education of youth, in their arrangements for women, in their marriage customs, in the relations of old and young, in their penal laws (which take into account deviants only)—they consider intolerance itself a virtue, calling it "justice."

In this way a type with few but very strong traits, a species of severe, warlike, prudently taciturn men, closemouthed and closely linked (and as such possessed of the subtlest feeling for the charms and nuances of association), is fixed beyond the changing generations; the continual fight against ever constant *unfavorable* conditions is, as mentioned previously, the cause that fixes and hardens a type.

Eventually, however, a day arrives when conditions become more fortunate and the tremendous tension decreases; perhaps there are no longer any enemies among one's neighbors, and the means of life, even for the enjoyment of life, are superabundant. At one stroke the bond and constraint of the old discipline are torn: it no longer seems necessary, a condition of existence—if it persisted it would only be a form of *luxury*, an archaizing *taste*. Variation, whether as deviation (to something higher, subtler, rarer) or as degeneration and monstrosity, suddenly appears on the scene in the greatest abundance and magnificence; the individual dares to be individual and different.

At these turning points of history we behold beside one another, and often mutually involved and entangled, a splendid, manifold, junglelike growth and upward striving, a kind of *tropical* tempo in the competition to grow, and a tremendous ruin and self-ruination, as the savage egoisms that have turned, almost exploded, against one another wrestle "for sun and light" and can no longer derive any limit, restraint, or consideration from their previous morality. It was this morality itself that dammed up such enormous strength and bent the bow in such a threatening manner; now it is "outlived." The dangerous and uncanny point has been reached where the greater, more manifold, more comprehensive life transcends and *lives beyond* the old morality; the "individual" appears, obliged to give himself laws and to develop his own arts and wiles for self-preservation, self-enhancement, self-redemption.

All sorts of new what-fors and wherewithals; no shared formulas any longer; misunderstanding allied with disrespect; decay, corruption, and the highest desires gruesomely entangled; the genius of the race overflowing from all cornucopias of good and bad; a calamitous simultaneity of spring and fall, full of new charms and veils that characterize young, still unexhausted, still unwearied corruption. Again danger is there, the mother of morals, great danger, this time transposed into the individual, into the neighbor and friend, into the alley [sic], into one's own child, into one's own heart, into the most personal and secret recesses of wish and will: what may the moral philosophers emerging in this age have to preach now?

These acute observers and loiterers discover that the end is approaching fast, that everything around them is corrupted and corrupts, that nothing will stand the day after tomorrow, except *one* type of man, the incurably *mediocre*. The mediocre alone have a chance of continuing their type and propagating—they are the men of the future, the only survivors: "Be like them! Become mediocre!" is now the only morality that still makes sense, that still gets a hearing.

But this morality of mediocrity is hard to preach: after all, it may never admit what it is and what it wants. It must speak of measure and dignity and duty and neighbor love—it will find it difficult *to conceal its irony*.

CHECKLIST

To help you review, here is a checklist of the key philosophers and terms and concepts of this chapter. The brief descriptive sentences summarize the philosophers' leading ideas. Keep in mind that some of these summary statements are oversimplifications of complex positions.

Philosophers

- **Peter Abelard** set forth one of medieval philosophy's most careful analyses of the morality of intent. 274

- **Aesara of Lucania** was a Pythagorean philosopher from southern Italy who held that, by introspecting about the nature and structure of the human soul, we can identify a standard of personal and public morality. 263

- **St. Thomas Aquinas** reconciled Aristotelian ethical naturalism with Christianity. 276

- **Aristotle** was an ethical naturalist who held that moral judgments are judgments of fact about the natural world. He said that happiness is our highest good. 264

- **St. Augustine** used Platonic concepts to solve "the problem of evil," held moral evil to be misdirected love, and identified God as the supreme moral authority and source of all goodness. 270

- **Jeremy Bentham,** a utilitarian, held that the rightness of an action is identical with the pleasure it produces as its consequence and said that pleasure can be evaluated quantitatively. 284

- **Diogenes** was the most famous Cynic, who taught by shocking example that the wise person reduces all wants and avoids all comforts. 269

- **Epictetus,** a leading Stoic, held that one's highest objective is to find a serene or untroubled life through acceptance of the rational natural order of things. 268

- **Epicurus,** an ethical egoist, held that one's highest objective is to lead the pleasant life through moderate living. 267

- **Heloise** was a medieval French philosopher who held that the morality or immorality of an action is determined by the intention with which it is done. 274

- **St. Hildegard of Bingen** was a medieval German mystic philosopher who held that the moral powers of the soul come from its three faculties: understanding, insight, and execution. 272

- **Thomas Hobbes** held that "good" and "evil" denote what a person desires or hates; he maintained that our natural end is preservation of self. 277

- **David Hume** held that moral principles are neither divine edicts nor discoverable by reason and that value judgments are based on emotion. He said that the act that pleases our moral sensibilities is one that reflects the agent's benevolent character. 279

- **Immanuel Kant** held that the supreme prescription of morality is to act always in such a way that you could rationally will the principle on which you act to be a universal law. He believed that what you should do, you should do, not because it promotes some end but simply because it is right. 281

- **John Stuart Mill,** a utilitarian, held that the rightness of an action is identical with the happiness that it produces as its consequence and said that pleasure—a part of happiness— must be measured in terms of quality as well as quantity. 284

- **Friedrich Nietzsche** distinguished between slave morality (the morality of the masses) and master morality (the morality of the nobleman). The former represents the denial of life; the latter represents the will-to-power. 288

- **Plato** also sought the essences of moral virtues, identifying these with the unchanging Forms, the highest of which he held to be the Form of the Good, the ultimate source of all value and reality. 259

- **Socrates** sought to discover the essences of moral virtues and championed the use of reason in moral deliberation. 259

- **Sophists** were professional teachers of fifth-century B.C.E. Greece whose attack on traditional moral values marks the beginnings of ethical philosophy. 259

- **Zeno** was the founder of Stoicism. 267

306   Part Two · *Moral and Political Philosophy*

Key Terms and Concepts

act utilitarianism   288
categorical
   imperative   283
consequentialism   258
cultural relativism   256
Cynicism   269
Cyrenaicism   263
deontological
   ethics   258
descriptive egoism   256
descriptive
   relativism   256
divine law   276
divine-command
   ethics   258
egoistic ethical
   hedonism   258
egoism   256
Epicureanism   267
ethical hedonism   257
ethical naturalism   264
ethical
   skepticism   255
ethics   254
Form   259

hedonism   257
hypothetical
   imperative   283
individual
   relativism   256
instrumental versus
   intrinsic ends   265
mean between
   extremes   265
moral imperative   283
morality of intent   274
natural law   268
paradox of
   hedonism   288
prescriptive
   egoism   256
psychological
   hedonism   257
relativism   258
rule utilitarianism   288
Stoicism   267
subjectivism   256
universalistic ethical
   hedonism   258
virtue ethics   258

QUESTIONS FOR DISCUSSION AND REVIEW

1. Is there some single thing that all morally good actions have in common? Defend your view.

2. "What is right is what you yourself believe is right." Critically evaluate this statement.

3. What is the connection between virtue and happiness in the philosophy of Plato?

4. What is the connection among the structure of the soul, personal morality, and justice, according to Aesara of Lucania?

5. In what does happiness consist, according to Aristotle? When can we be said to be virtuous?

6. What is the connection between habit and moral character, for Aristotle?

7. Compare and contrast the ethical philosophies of Epicureanism and Stoicism. Which do you think is the superior philosophy, and why?

8. Is it a sound policy to reduce all wants to a minimum and to achieve utter self-reliance by avoiding all the comforts of society?

9. Can you control your attitude if you cannot control your fate?

10. What is Hildegard's concept of the structure and faculties of the soul? How does it compare to Aesara of Lucania's views on the soul?

11. Explain Heloise's view of the morality of intent and her view of the nature of disinterested love.

12. Explain Augustine's solution to the problem of evil, and determine whether it is sound.

13. Explain and evaluate Aquinas's reasons for believing that ultimate human happiness does not consist in wealth, worldly power, or anything in this life.

14. Do we seek personal survival above all other things?

15. Do we always act selfishly? Explain.

16. Explain and critically evaluate prescriptive egoism.

17. Can reasoning disclose the moral wrongfulness of an act of murder?

18. Is Hume correct in saying that the type of act we deem morally praiseworthy is one done out of concern for others?

19. Is it abnormal not to have sympathy for others? Are selfish people really admired in today's society?

20. Is it true that moral principles hold without exception? Explain.

21. Is it true that moral principles cannot be revealed through scientific investigation?

22. Suppose you stole something that did not belong to you. Could you rationally will the principle on which you acted to be a universal law? Explain.

23. Explain the difference between a hypothetical imperative and a categorical imperative.

24. Which is it: Does the nature of an act or its consequences determine whether it is good, or is it the intent with which the act has been undertaken? Or is it something else altogether?

25. What does it mean to say that rational beings should be treated as ends and not as means?

Give an example of treating another as a means.

26. Is your own happiness more important morally than that of others? ("It is to me" does not count as an answer.)

27. Was Bentham correct in saying that *ought, right, good,* and the like have meaning only when defined in terms of pleasure?

28. Explain the difference between psychological hedonism and ethical hedonism.

29. Is it true that the ultimate object of a person's desire is always pleasure? Explain.

30. Was Mill correct in saying that some pleasures are inherently better than others?

31. How does Mill propose to establish which of two pleasures is qualitatively better? Can you think of a better way of establishing this?

32. Leslie, who is in the Peace Corps, volunteers to aid starving Ethiopians. She travels to Ethiopia and, risking her own health and safety, works herself nearly to exhaustion for two years, caring for as many people as she can. Meanwhile, her father, Harold, dashes off a huge check for the Ethiopian relief fund. In fact, his check helps more people than Leslie's actions do. But, morally speaking, is Harold more praiseworthy than Leslie? What would Bentham say? Mill? You?

33. What does Nietzsche mean when he says life is the will to power?

34. "There cannot be moral values if there is no God." Critically evaluate this assertion.

SUGGESTED FURTHER READINGS

Julia Annas, *The Morality of Happiness* (New York: Oxford University Press, 1993). An analysis of ancient ethical theory.

Julia Annas, *Platonic Ethics, Old and New* (Ithaca, N.Y.: Cornell University Press, 1999). A detailed and widely acclaimed analysis of Plato's ethical thought.

Aristotle, *The Nichomachean Ethics,* Martin Ostwald, ed. (Indianapolis: Bobbs-Merrill, 1962).

James Baillie, *Routledge Philosophy Guidebook to Hume on Morality* (New York: Routledge, 2000). A relatively clear presentation of Hume's thought on passions, taste, virtue, and other related topics.

Jeremy Bentham, *An Introduction to the Principles of Morals and Legislation,* J. J. Burns, H. L. A. Hart, and F. Rosen, eds. (New York: Oxford University Press, 1996). This is the edition you should own. Includes an important essay by Hart.

Simon Blackburn, *Ethics: A Very Short Introduction* (New York: Oxford University Press, 2003). A brief look at the basic issues and development in moral philosophy.

R. Bracht Branham and Marie-Odile Goulet-Cazé, eds., *The Cynics* (Berkeley: University of California Press, 1996). These essays provide a good overview of this movement and its significance.

Sarah Broadie, *Ethics with Aristotle* (New York: Oxford University Press, 1991). A respected treatment of the subject.

Thomas Cleary, trans., *Living a Good Life* (Boston: Shambhala, 1997). Practical advice on life in short quotations from Plato, Aristotle, Pythagoras, and Diogenes.

Martin Cohen, *The Essentials of Philosophy and Ethics* (New York: Hodder Arnold, 2006). A wide-ranging reference work on ethics with more than 500 entries.

David E. Cooper, ed., *Ethics: The Classic Readings* (Malden, Mass.: Blackwell, 1997). A collection of critical texts concerning ethics, including contributions by Indian and Chinese philosophers.

F. C. Copleston, *Aquinas* (Baltimore: Penguin Books, 1955). See Chapter 5 of this text.

Epictetus, *Discourses, Book 1,* Robert F. Dobbin, trans. (New York: Oxford University Press, 1998). A recent translation with background information.

Epictetus, *The Handbook of Epictetus,* Nicholas P. White, trans. (Indianapolis: Hackett, 1983). If you enjoyed the Epictetus selection, here is where you can find more.

Epicurus, *The Extant Remains,* C. Bailey, trans. (Oxford: Clarendon Press, 1962). For those who wish to read more from Epicurus.

John Gaskin, ed., *The Epicurean Philosophers* (Rutland, Vt.: Charles Tuttle Co., 1995). A comprehensive collection of their surviving works.

J. Gould, *The Development of Plato's Ethics* (London: Cambridge University Press, 1955). Explains the important principles and concepts in Plato's ethics.

E. Hamilton and H. Cairns, eds., *The Collected Dialogues of Plato* (New York: Bollingen Foundation, 1961). This, as we said before, is what you need to acquaint yourself firsthand with Plato's dialogues. Be sure to read *The Republic.* The other dialogues

308   Part Two · *Moral and Political Philosophy*

especially relevant to ethics are *Gorgias, Meno,* and *Philebus.*

W. F. R. Hardie, *Aristotle's Ethical Theory* (Oxford: Clarendon Press, 1968). There are several reliable books on Aristotle's ethics. This is one of the most popular.

R. M. Hare, *The Language of Morals* (Oxford: Clarendon Press, 1952). An important treatise on the logic of moral discourse.

R. D. Hicks, *Stoic and Epicurean* (New York: Russell and Russell, 1962). Chapters 3, 4, and 5 are especially relevant to our discussion here.

Hildegard of Bingen, *Book of Divine Works,* Matthew Fox, ed. (Santa Fe, N.M.: Bear & Co., 1987).

Hildegard of Bingen, *Scivias,* Bruce Hozeki, trans. (Santa Fe, N.M.: Bear & Co., 1986).

Thomas Hobbes, *Leviathan,* J. C. A. Gaskin, ed. (New York: Oxford University Press, 1998). Includes annotations and an introduction by the editor.

David Hume, *An Enquiry Concerning the Principles of Morals,* Tom L. Beauchamp, ed. (New York: Oxford University Press, 1998). Hume's major work on ethics.

Terrence Irwin, *Plato's Ethics* (New York: Oxford University Press, 1995). An analysis.

Immanuel Kant, *Foundations of the Metaphysics of Morals,* R. P. Wolff, ed. (Indianapolis: Bobbs-Merrill, 1959). Contains Kant's most important moral philosophy together with commentary by Kant on assorted problems.

S. Korner, *Kant* (Baltimore: Penguin Books, 1955). See Chapters 6 and 7. A standard work on Kant.

Hugh La Folette, ed., *The Blackwell Guide to Ethical Theory* (New York: Blackwell, 2003). Survey of the major issues in contemporary moral philosophy.

A. A. Long, *Hellenistic Philosophy* (Berkeley: University of California Press, 1986). A readable account of Epicureanism, Skepticism, and Stoicism.

A. A. Long and P. N. Sedley, eds., *The Hellenistic Philosophers* (Cambridge: Cambridge University Press, 1987). Translations of texts from the Stoic, Epicurean, and Skeptic schools of thought.

J. S. Mill, *On Liberty and Other Essays,* John Gray, ed. (New York: Oxford University Press, 1998). The other essays include *Utilitarianism, Considerations on Representative Government,* and *The Subjection of Women.*

J. S. Mill, *Utilitarianism,* Roger Crisp, ed. (New York: Oxford University Press, 1998). Uses the 1871 edition of Mill's text, the last edition to be published in Mill's lifetime.

Friedrich Nietzsche, *Beyond Good and Evil,* Marion Faber and Robert C. Holub, eds. and trans. (New York: Oxford University Press, 1999). A new translation, with an introduction by an eminent Nietzsche scholar.

James Rachels, *The Right Thing to Do, Basic Readings in Moral Philosophy* (New York: McGraw-Hill, 2002). A selection of readings in moral philosophy from some of the great historical figures.

Betty Radice, trans., *The Letters of Abelard and Heloise* (New York: Penguin Books, 1974).

John Rawls, *Lectures on the History of Moral Philosophy,* Barbara Herman, ed. (Cambridge, Mass.: Harvard University Press, 2000). Lectures on the history of moral philosophy by one of the leading philosophers of our times.

W. D. Ross, *Kant's Ethical Theory* (Oxford: Oxford University Press, 1954). Brief; excellent.

Nancy Sherman, *The Fabric of Character, Aristotle's Theory of Virtue* (New York: Oxford University Press, 1989). Explains and examines Aristotle's theory of virtue.

Henry Sidgwick, *Outlines of the History of Ethics* (Boston: Beacon, 1960) and *The Methods of Ethics* (New York: Dover, 1974). These are classic works in ethics. Many standard ethical concepts, principles, and distinctions originated with Sidgwick, and his treatment of utilitarianism is complete and penetrating.

Mary Ellen Waithe, *A History of Women Philosophers,* vol. 2, *Medieval, Renaissance, and Enlightenment Women Philosophers: 500–1600* (Dordrecht: Kluwer Academic Publishers, 1989).

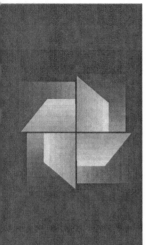

13

Philosophy and Belief in God

It is morally necessary to assume the existence of God.   —Immanuel Kant

God is dead.   —Friedrich Nietzsche

What is the difference between a theologian and a philosopher of religion? Let's back up about four steps and get a running start at the question.

If you subscribe to a religion, and the opinion polls say you most likely do, then you also accept certain purely philosophical doctrines. For example, if you believe in a nonmaterial God, then you believe that not all that exists is material, and that means you accept a metaphysics of immaterialism. If you believe you should love your neighbor because God said you should, then you are taking sides in the debate among ethical philosophers concerning ethical naturalism. You have committed yourself to a stand against naturalism.

Your religious beliefs commit you as well to certain epistemological principles. A lot of people who make no claim to have seen, felt, tasted, smelled, or heard God still say they know God exists. So they must maintain that humans can have knowledge not gained through sense experience. To maintain this is to take sides in an important epistemological issue, as you know from Part One.

These and many other metaphysical, ethical, and epistemological points of view and principles are assumed by, and incorporated in, religion, and it is the business of the philosophy of religion to understand and rationally evaluate them.

Of course, *theology* also seeks clear understanding and rational evaluation of the doctrines and principles found in religion, including those that are metaphysical, ethical, and epistemological. But, for the most part, theologians start from premises and assumptions that are themselves religious tenets. The philosopher of religion, in contrast, does not make religious assumptions in trying to understand and evaluate religious beliefs.

The Black Cat

An old saying goes that the difference between a metaphysician and a theologian is this: The metaphysician looks in a dark room for a black cat that is not there. The theologian looks in the same place for the same thing.

And finds it.

The religions of the world differ in their tenets, of course. Therefore, a philosopher of religion usually focuses on the beliefs of a specific religion or religious tradition, and in fact it is the beliefs of the Judaeo-Christian religious tradition that have received the most discussion by Western philosophers. Philosophers of religion may focus on the beliefs of a specific religion, but they will not proceed in their inquiries from the *assumption* that these beliefs are true, even though they may in fact accept them as a personal matter.

What are some of the metaphysical, ethical, and epistemological beliefs of the Judaeo-Christian tradition that philosophers have sought to understand and evaluate? Many of these beliefs have to do with *God:* that he exists, that he is good, that he created the universe and is the source of all that is real, that he is a personal deity, that he is a transcendent deity, and so forth. Many have to do with *humans:* that humans were created in the image of God, that they have free will, that they can have knowledge of God's will, that the human soul is immortal, and so on. Other beliefs have to do with *features of the universe:* for example, that there are miracles, that there is supernatural reality, that there is pain and suffering (a fact thought to require reconciliation with the belief in a good and all-powerful God). And still others have to do with *language:* that religious language is intelligible and meaningful, that religious utterances are (or are not) factual assertions or are (or are not) metaphorical or analogical, that terminology used in descriptions of God means the same (or does not mean the same) as when it is used in descriptions of other things.

This is a long list of issues. To simplify things, we will concentrate here only on the philosophical consideration of the Christian belief in the existence of God. Let's begin with two Christian greats, St. Anselm and St. Aquinas.

TWO CHRISTIAN GREATS

Other chapters have begun with discussions of ancient Greek philosophers, and we could have begun this chapter, too, with the ancient Greeks. Many modern religious beliefs contain ideas that were discussed by, and in some cases originated with, the Greeks. But we have narrowed the focus here to the philosophical consideration of the Judaeo-Christian belief in God's existence, and it is appropriate to begin with the man who was abbot of Bec and, later, archbishop of Canterbury.

Anselm

St. Anselm (c. 1033–1109) was among the first to evaluate the belief in the Christian God from a purely philosophical perspective, that is, from a perspective that does not make religious assumptions from the outset. Nonetheless, Anselm never entertained the slightest doubt that God exists. Further, he made no distinction between philosophy and theology, and he thought it impossible for anyone to reason about God or God's existence without already believing in him.

Still, Anselm was willing to evaluate *on its own merit and independently of religious assumptions* the idea that God does *not* exist.

The Ontological Argument   This idea, that God does not exist, is attributed in Psalms 14:1 to the "fool," and Anselm thought it plain that anyone who would deny God's existence is *logically* mistaken and is indeed an utter fool. Anselm reasoned that the fool is in a self-contradictory position. The fool, Anselm thought, is in the position of saying *that he can conceive of a being greater than the greatest being conceivable.* This may sound like a new species of doubletalk, so we must consider Anselm's reasoning carefully. You may find it helpful to read the box "*Reductio* Proofs" before we begin.

Anselm began with the premise that by *God* is meant "the greatest being conceivable," or, in Anselm's exact words, "a being than which nothing greater can be conceived."

Now, the fool who denies that God exists at least understands what he denies, said Anselm charitably. Thus, God at least exists in the fool's understanding. But, Anselm noted, a being that exists both in the understanding and outside in reality is greater than a being that exists only in the understanding. (That is why people prefer real houses and cars and clothes and vacations to those they just think about.)

But this means, Anselm said, that the fool's position is absurd. For his position is that God exists only in the understanding but not in reality. So the fool's position, according to Anselm, is that "the very being, than which nothing greater can be conceived, is one, than which a greater can be conceived." And yes, this silliness is something like doubletalk, but Anselm's point is that the denial of God's existence leads to this silliness. Hence, God exists: to think otherwise is to be reduced to self-contradiction and mumbo-jumbo.

This line of argument, according to which it follows from the very concept of God that God exists, is known as the **ontological argument.** It represents Anselm's most important contribution to the philosophy of religion. If Anselm's argument is valid, if Anselm did establish that it is self-contradictory to deny that God exists and hence established that God does exist, then he did so without invoking any religious premises or making any religious presuppositions. True, he made, in effect, an assumption about the concept of God, but even a non-Christian or an atheist, he thought, must concede that what is meant by *God* is "the greatest being conceivable." Thus, if the argument is valid, even those who are not moved by faith or are otherwise religious must accept its conclusion. Anselm, in effect, argued that the proposition "God exists" is *self-evident* and can no more be denied than can the proposition "A square has four sides," and anyone who thinks otherwise is either a fool or just does not grasp the concept of God.

Reductio **Proofs**

If a claim logically entails something that is absurd, nonsensical, or just plain false, you reject the claim, correct?

For example, if the claim that the butler killed Colonel Mustard in the kitchen means that the butler was in two different places at the same time (because it is known that he was in the library at the time of the murder), then you reject the claim that the butler killed Colonel Mustard in the kitchen.

This type of proof of a claim's denial is known as *reductio ad absurdum:* by demonstrating that a claim reduces to an absurdity or just to something false, you prove the denial of the claim. By showing that claim *C* entails falsehood *F*, you prove *not-C*.

Reductios, as they are called, are encountered frequently in philosophy and in real life. Anselm's ontological argument is a ***reductio* proof.** Here the claim, *C*, is that

God does not exist.

This claim, argued Anselm, entails the falsehood, *F,* that

the very being than which nothing greater can be conceived is one than which a greater can be conceived.

The conclusion of the argument is thus *not-C*, that

God does exist.

Anselm gave another version of the ontological argument that goes like this: Because God is that than which nothing greater can be conceived, God's nonexistence is inconceivable. For anyone whose nonexistence *is* conceivable is not as great as anyone whose nonexistence is *not* conceivable, and thus is not God.

Are you convinced? Many are not. Many regard the ontological argument in any version as a cute little play on words that proves absolutely nothing.

Gaunilo's Objection   One who found the argument unconvincing was a Benedictine monk from the Abbey of Marmontier, a contemporary of Anselm whose name was **Gaunilo** [GO-nee-low]. One of Gaunilo's objections was to the first version of the argument, which, he argued, could be used to prove ridiculous things. For example, Gaunilo said, consider the most perfect island. Because it would be more perfect for an island to exist both in reality and in the understanding, the most perfect island must exist in reality, if Anselm's line of reasoning is sound. For if this island did not exist in reality, then (according to Anselm's reasoning) any island that did exist in reality would be more perfect than it—that is, would be more perfect than the most perfect island, which is impossible. In other words, Gaunilo used Anselm's reasoning to demonstrate the necessary existence of the most perfect island, implying that any pattern of reasoning that can be used to reach such an idiotic conclusion must obviously be defective.

Anselm, however, believed that his reasoning applied only to God: because God is that than which a greater cannot be conceived, God's nonexistence is inconceivable; whereas, by contrast, the nonexistence of islands and all other things is conceivable.

As you will see in the selection from Anselm at the end of the chapter, which contains the first version of his ontological argument, Anselm was able to express his thought with elegant simplicity. Please accept our invitation to figure out what, if anything, is wrong with his reasoning.

Do not be confused when Anselm says that God is "something than which nothing greater can be thought." He just means, in plain English, "God is the being with the following characteristic: when you try to think of a greater or higher being, you cannot do it."

Aquinas

About a century and a half after Anselm died, **St. Thomas Aquinas** (c. 1225–1274), whom we have discussed in earlier chapters, interpreted Aristotelian philosophy from a Christian perspective. Aristotle, as we have had occasion to mention, emphasized the importance to philosophy of direct observation of nature. In keeping with his empiricist, Aristotelian leanings, Aquinas regarded the ontological argument as invalid. You cannot prove that God exists, he said, merely by considering the word *God*, as the ontological argument in effect supposes. For that strategy to work, you would have to presume to know God's essence. The proposition "God exists," he said, unlike "A square has four sides," is not self-evident to us mere mortals. Although you can prove God's existence in several ways, he asserted, you cannot do it just by examining the concept of God. You have to consider what it is about nature that makes it manifest that it requires God as its original cause.

The ways in which the existence of God can be proved are in fact five, according to Aquinas. Although Aquinas's theological and philosophical writings fill many volumes and cover a vast range of topics, he is most famous for his **Five Ways** (but some philosophers—discussed later—do not regard Aquinas's proofs of God as his best philosophy). It would be surprising if you were not already familiar with one or another of Aquinas's Five Ways in some version. In any case, they are included as a reading selection at the end of the chapter.

The First Way   The first way to prove that God exists, according to Aquinas, is to consider the fact that natural things are in motion. As we look around the world and survey moving things, it becomes clear that they did not put themselves into motion. But if every moving thing were moved by another moving thing, then there would be no **first mover;** if no first mover existed, there would be no other mover, and nothing would be in motion. Because things are in motion, a first mover must therefore exist that is moved by no other, and this, of course, is God.

We should note here that Aquinas is usually understood as meaning something quite broad by *motion*—something more like "change in general"—and as including under the concept of movement the coming into, and passing out of, existence. Thus, when he says that things do not put themselves into motion, do not suppose that he thought that you cannot get up out of your chair and walk across the room. He means that things do not just bring themselves into existence.

The Second Way   Aquinas's second way of proving God's existence is very similar to the first. In the world of sensible things, nothing causes itself. But if everything were caused by something else, then there would be no first cause, and if no first cause existed, there would be no first effect. In fact, there would be no

PROFILE: St. Thomas Aquinas (c. 1225-1274)

Aquinas, the son of a count of Aquino in Italy, studied for many years with Albertus Magnus ("Albert the Great"). Albertus, who had the unusual idea that Christian thinkers should be knowledgeable about philosophy and science, wished to make all of Aristotle's writings available in Latin. His fondness for Aristotle was a strong influence on his pupil, Aquinas.

Aquinas eventually received his doctorate from the University of Paris in his late twenties and soon acquired a substantial reputation as a scholar. For ten years in his thirties and early forties, he was a professor for the Papal Court and lectured in and around Rome.

Now, the thirteenth century was a time of considerable intellectual controversy between the Platonists and the Aristotelians. Some theologians believed that the teachings of Aristotle could not be harmonized with Christian doctrines. This belief was in part a reaction to Averroës (1126–1198), a brilliant Arabian philosopher, and his followers, whose philosophy was built entirely around the ideas of Aristotle. The Averroist philosophy conflicted with Church doctrine on creation and personal immortality, making Aristotle odious to some Christian theologians.

But Aquinas was no Averroist and defended his own version of Aristotle with inexorable logic. He returned to Paris in 1268 and became involved in a famous struggle with the Averroists, which he won. Although some factions within the Church voiced strong opposition to his philosophy, opposition that lasted for many years after his death, slowly but surely Aquinas's thinking became the dominant system of Christian thought. He was canonized (officially declared a saint) in 1323.

Aquinas was a stout fellow, slow and deliberate in manner. He was thus nicknamed the Dumb Ox. But he was a brilliant and forceful thinker, and his writings fill many volumes and cover a vast array of theological and philosophical topics. His most famous works are the *Summa Contra Gentiles* (1258–1260) and the *Summa Theologica* (1267–1273), a systematic theology grounded on philosophical principles. He was, in addition, a most humane and charitable man.

In 1879, Pope Leo XIII declared Aquinas's system to be the official Catholic philosophy.

second, third, or fourth effect either: if no first cause existed, there would be no effects, period. So we must admit a first cause, to wit, God. (This is a good time to read the box on the next page, "The Big Bang.")

Note that Aquinas did not say anything in either of the first two proofs about things being moved or caused by *earlier* motions or causes. The various motions and causes he is talking about are simultaneous. His argument is not the common one, that things must be caused by something earlier, which must be caused by something earlier, and so on, and that because this chain of causes cannot go back infinitely, there must be a first cause, God. In Aquinas's opinion, there is no philosophical reason that the chain of causes could not go back infinitely. But there cannot be an infinite series of *simultaneous* causes or movers, he thought.

The Third Way Aquinas's third way is easily the most complicated of the Five Ways. Many consider it his finest proof, though Aquinas himself seemed to prefer the first.

Many paraphrasings of the third proof are not faithful to what Aquinas actually said, which is essentially this: In nature some things are such that it is possible for them not to exist. Indeed, everything you can lay your hands on belongs to this "need-not-exist" category; whatever it is, despite the fact that it does exist, it need

The Big Bang

The view now accepted by most scientists is that the universe is an explosion, known as the **Big Bang.** Unlike other explosions, the Big Bang does not expand outward into space, like a dynamite or bomb explosion, nor does it have a duration in external time, as do all other explosions, because all space and all time are located within it. The beginning of the Big Bang is the beginning of space and time and of matter and energy, and it is, in fact, the beginning of our expanding universe.

The most prevalent view among the qualified experts who have an opinion on the matter is that it is impossible to know what transpired in the Big Bang before 10^{-43} seconds after zero time, when the Big Bang began. But for various reasons that we need not go into here, most of these experts do apparently believe that there was a zero time, that the universe did have an absolute beginning, that there was a first physical event.

Now, either the first physical event, assuming that such a thing did take place, is explainable, or it is not. On one hand, it is difficult to believe that the first physical event has no explanation, for that amounts to saying that the entire universe, with its incredible size and complexity, was just a chance occurrence, a piece of good luck. But on the other hand, if the first physical event is explicable, then it would seem that the explanation must refer to some sort of nonphysical phenomenon, which certainly could be called "God."

Thus, the Big Bang theory, if true—and there seems to be much reason for supposing that it is true—may require philosophers to make a hard choice between an unexplainable universe and one explainable only by reference to something nonphysical.

not have existed. Now, that which need not exist, said Aquinas, at some time did not exist. Therefore, if everything belongs to this category, then at one time nothing existed, and then it would have been impossible for anything to have begun to exist—and thus even now nothing would exist. Thus, Aquinas reasoned, not everything is such that it need not exist: "There must exist something the existence of which is *necessary*."

This is not quite the end of the third proof, however, for Aquinas believed that he had not yet ruled out the possibility that the necessity of this necessary being might be caused by another necessary being, whose necessity might be caused by another, and so on and so on. So, he asserted, "It is impossible to go on to infinity in necessary things which have their necessity caused by another." Conclusion: There must be some necessary being that has its own necessity, and this is God.

We said the third way was complicated.

The Fourth and Fifth Ways Aquinas's fourth way to prove God is to consider the fact that all natural things possess degrees of goodness, truth, nobility, and all other perfections. Therefore, there must be that which is the source of these perfections, namely, pure goodness and truth, and so on, and this is what we call God.

And the fifth way or proof of God's existence is predicated on the observation that natural things act for an end or purpose. That is, they function in accordance with a plan or design. Accordingly, an intelligent being exists by which things are directed toward their end, and this intelligent being is God.

Aquinas's first three proofs of God's existence are versions of what today is called the **cosmological argument.** The cosmological argument is actually not

Space Station over the earth. The cosmological and teleological arguments suppose that Fine. With life on it could not have arisen by chance.

one argument but a type of argument. Proponents of arguments of this type think that the existence of *contingent* things, things that could possibly not have existed, points to the existence of a noncontingent or *necessary* being, God, as their ultimate cause, creator, ground, energizer, or source of being. Note the difference between the cosmological argument and ontological arguments, which endeavor to establish the existence of God just by considering his nature or analyzing the concept of God, as we saw attempted by Anselm.

Aquinas's fourth proof, which cites the existence of goodness or good things, is called the **moral argument.** Here again, the term does not refer to just one argument but rather to a type of argument, and, as we will see, some of the "versions" of the moral argument resemble one another only vaguely.

Arguments like Aquinas's fifth proof, according to which the apparent purposefulness or orderliness of the universe or its parts or structure points to the existence of a divine designer, are called **arguments from design,** or **teleological arguments.**

Let's summarize all of this. Between them, Anselm and Aquinas introduced what have turned out to be the four principal arguments for God's existence. These are

- the ontological argument
- the cosmological argument
- the teleological or design argument
- the moral argument

Notice that none of these four arguments rests on any religious assumptions. They should therefore require the assent of every nonreligious person, if they are sound.

To a certain extent, the history of the philosophy of religion is a continuing discussion of various versions and aspects of these four arguments. Therefore, understanding each type of argument provides you with a good grasp of the basics of the philosophy of religion.

Now, before we leave Aquinas, we should call your attention to the fact that the distinction we drew at the beginning of this chapter between theology and the philosophy of religion is pretty much the same as the distinction Aquinas drew between theology and philosophy.

According to Aquinas, if your thinking proceeds from principles that are revealed to you in religion and that you accept on religious faith, then your thinking is theological, though he did not often use the word *theology*. If your reasoning proceeds from what is evident in sensory experience, then your thinking is philosophical.

According to Aquinas, some theological truths, truths of revelation, are such that philosophy could never discover them. For example, philosophy cannot establish that the universe had a beginning and is not eternal. And not everything discovered by philosophy is important for salvation. But philosophy and theology, although separate disciplines, are not incompatible; in fact, they complement each other, he thought (in contrast to some other Christian thinkers who thought that philosophy could lead to religious errors).

From the standpoint of theology, that God exists is a given, a truth that you start out knowing. From the standpoint of philosophy, that God exists is not a given but may be inferred from your experience.

Thus, Aquinas's proofs of God's existence are philosophical proofs. They do not depend for their soundness on any religious principles.

MYSTICISM

Quite a different approach to God may be found in the writings of the anchoress **Julian of Norwich** (1342–1414?), one of the great mystics of all time.

Anchoress? That is a person who had the great fortune to be anchored for life to a church. You will find more information on this in the nearby Profile on Julian.

Why do you believe in God, if you do? Perhaps at some point you had a "mystical experience"—you experienced God directly; God *came* to you. If you have had this type of experience, you may be unable to offer a justification or argument for your belief, and your inability to do so may not bother you in the slightest. If you have had a mystical experience of God, this whole business of debating the strengths and weaknesses of arguments about God may strike you as just so much mental exercise.

It is, however, one thing to say, "God came to me" and quite another to explain why this mystical experience is a reliable form of knowledge. Before we go any further, let's be clear. We are not talking about *hunches*—as in when you have a hunch that something good or bad will happen, and it does. We are talking about serious

PROFILE: The Anchoress, Julian of Norwich (1342–1414?)

Her name was Julian, but sometimes she is called Juliana. She lived in the English cathedral city of Norwich during a nasty time in history. The Hundred Years' War, the Great Schism in the Church, the ruthless suppression of the Peasant's Revolt in Norwich, and the condemnation of John Wycliffe for heresy made the mid-fourteenth century a rough time for Norwich. The fact that the Black Plague hit Norwich when Julian was six, again when she was nineteen, and again when she was twenty-seven did not exactly make Norwich a fun place to live.

Julian became an anchoress. It was the custom at that time to "anchor" someone to a church. Anchoring was a kind of permanent grounding of a scholarly nun or priest (it was an honor, not a punishment). The lucky person, someone known for saintly behavior and devotion to theology, was walled up alive in a small cell within the outer wall of the church. Food, books, and other items would be passed through a window, and occasionally the anchoress would be allowed to talk through the window to important clergy and nobility. She spent her life there, and when she died, she was entombed in a crypt in the church.

Julian wrote two versions (one short and one long) of her *Booke of Showings* (revelations). The short version is a partial description of a series of visions she had in 1373 when she was seriously ill. She became an anchoress soon after that experience. That left her lots of time for study, thought, and religious discussion. Many theologians and philosophers visited her to discuss the "showings" she described in the short version. She spent the next twenty years revising the manuscript, including fuller details and much analysis of what she thought the revelations meant.

Back then, women were not supposed to claim to have any religious or philosophical authority (or any other kind of authority, for that matter). To avoid criticism for having the crust to act as if she knew something, a woman writer typically began her text with a "humility formula." Here is Julian's as she wrote it:

Botte god for bede that ʒe schulde saye or take it so that I am a techere, for I meene nouʒt soo, no I mente nevere so; for I am a womann, leued, febille and freylle.

Some of Julian's words had special religious and philosophical meanings that her readers would have understood. What she is saying is: "God says do not you act like I am a teacher. I do not mean to claim to be, and I never meant so. For I am a woman, ordinary ('lewd'), morally weak ('feeble'), and likely to fall from virtue ('frail')." Having disclaimed any authority, Julian went on to write seven hundred pages of philosophy.

Julian's interests are in the nature and certainty of religious knowledge. She held that there were three sources of religious knowledge: natural reason, teachings of religious leaders, and visions given by God. As God gives visions to whomever God chooses, and God loves everyone, in theory everyone is a candidate for mystical revelations. Julian of Norwich lived during the Crusades, when heretics were claiming that the Catholic religion was based on false ideas. How can someone tell true religious claims from false ones? Might God make revelations to ordinary people? Julian and many other mystics, including Hildegard of Bingen, St. John of the Cross, and his teacher St. Teresa of Avila (all of whom are known as philosophers), thought so. To claim that only religious leaders have a direct line to God suggests that God has limited ability to communicate. Julian called God "Christ, Our Mother" and "God, our Father." In her mind, God was both male and female, mother and father. God made us and nurtures us through the hard times.

beliefs people hold on the basis of this peculiar form of experience, beliefs like "God is real" or "Jesus has touched me."

In a very rich mystical experience, one that comes with all the accessories, the mystic is often unconscious, appears to be delirious, or seems to be having what today is sometimes called an out-of-body experience. The mystic may be dreaming, awake, or in a trance. He or she may see visions or hear voices. Commonly, those who have such experiences report being told things by God. Sometimes they are told to write down what they experience or to teach others. Before the development of rationalism in the seventeenth century, back before philosophers mostly believed that reason was the premier tool for acquiring knowledge, mystical experiences like this were given more credence. Today, there is something of a tendency, at least among sophisticates, to discount such experiences as malfunctions in brain chemistry or temporal lobe disturbances or the like.

Julian of Norwich was a mystic, but she also *analyzed* her mystical experiences, or "showings," as she called them. Her analysis focused on the nature of personal religious and moral knowledge as well as on whether it is possible to know God. She denied that there is any meaningful difference in the validity of mystical revelations made directly to one's soul and knowledge derived through reason. She held, indeed, that it is mistaken to divorce reason from experience, especially from mystical experience.

Basilica of Saint Peter, Vatican City, Rome, Italy.

Julian also emphasized the importance of the "not showns"—what logically should have been part of the vision but was missing. She believed God intended her to use insight, instinct, and reason to figure out what was not being communicated directly and to piece together the missing parts of the puzzle.

In Julian's view, God lives in us and we in God; we are one with God and are nurtured and fed knowledge of God and of ourselves by our divine parent. Thus, she believed we could know God only partly through revelation; further knowledge comes through loving God. In addition, she maintained we could come to love God by loving our own souls.

Thomas Aquinas (who had recently been made a saint) had analyzed visions as the language God uses to convey God's meaning. Julian went beyond analysis to attempt to make the experiences of visionaries relevant to others. She believed that ordinary people could learn from visionaries and find comfort and reason to hope in their visions. Hope, we can imagine, must have been a valuable commodity in mid-fourteenth-century England, faced with seemingly endless outbreaks of plague, war, and religious disputation.

SEVENTEENTH-CENTURY PERSPECTIVES

For our purposes here, we can now pass lightly over some three hundred years from the Middle Ages through the Renaissance to the seventeenth century. This is not to suggest that the time was unimportant for the history of religion. Europe had seen a mixture not only of enlightenment and religious revolution but also of reaction and intolerance; it had brought forth not only printed books and open discussion but also gunpowder and the stake. Luther had challenged the very foundations of Catholic doctrine, and Protestantism had spread throughout Europe. In England, Henry VIII had forced creation of the Anglican Church so that he could marry young Anne Boleyn and then, through a liberal use of execution, secured a loyal following. A new disorder had been rung in by the time of Descartes' birth, and before his death modern science was offering its own challenge to the established orthodoxy.

But all of this, though of great significance to the history of religion, was only indirectly important to the history of the philosophy of religion. The main point for our purposes is that the seventeenth century was the age of scientific discovery amid intellectual uncertainty and political and religious instability, an age in which past authorities, institutions, and truths were questioned and often rejected or discarded.

Descartes

The next figure with whom you should be familiar in the philosophy of religion is **René Descartes** (1596–1650). Descartes, longing for an unshakable intellectual footing, made it his primary business to devise what he thought was a new method for attaining certainty in his turbulent age. When he employed his new method, however, it revealed to him the certain existence of God.

408   Part Three · *Philosophy of Religion: Reason and Faith*

As we saw in Chapter 6, Descartes' method was to challenge every belief, no matter how plausible it seemed, to ascertain which of his beliefs, if any, were absolutely unassailable. Employing this method, Descartes found that he could not doubt his existence as a thing that thinks: *cogito, ergo sum* (I think, therefore I am). He also found that he could not doubt the existence of God, for basically three reasons. These three reasons are Descartes' proofs of God.

Descartes' First Proof   Having established as absolutely certain his own existence as a thinking thing, Descartes found within his mind the idea of God, the idea of an infinite and perfect being. Further, he reasoned, because there must be a cause for his idea, and because there must be as much reality or perfection in the cause of an idea as there is in the content of the idea, and because he himself therefore certainly could not be the cause of the idea, it follows, he concluded, that God exists.

Let's call this Descartes' first proof. It is a simple proof, although Descartes makes it seem somewhat complicated because he has to explain *why* his idea of God could not have arisen from a source other than God, and, of course, it is difficult to do this.

As you can see, Descartes' first proof is sort of a combination ontological–cosmological argument. It is ontological in that the mere idea of God is held by Descartes to entail that God exists. It is cosmological in that the existence of some contingent thing—Descartes' idea of God—is considered by Descartes to require God as its ultimate cause.

Descartes' Second Proof   Descartes had two other proofs of God's existence. His second proof is only subtly different from the first and is basically this:

1. I exist as a thing that has an idea of God.
2. Everything that exists has a cause that brought it into existence and that sustains it in existence.
3. The only thing adequate to cause and sustain me, a thing that has an idea of God, is God.
4. Therefore, God exists.

In this second proof, God is invoked by Descartes as the cause of *Descartes,* a being that has the idea of God; whereas in the first proof, God is invoked by Descartes as the cause of Descartes' *idea* of God. In the second proof, Descartes also utilizes the important notion that a thing needs a cause to *conserve* or *sustain* it in existence. You will encounter this idea again.

Descartes' Third Proof   In contrast with the first two, Descartes' third proof is a straightforward and streamlined version of the ontological argument:

1. My conception of God is the conception of a being that possesses all perfections.
2. Existence is a perfection.
3. Therefore, I cannot conceive of God as not existing.
4. Therefore, God exists.

According to Descartes, when you think it through, you see that you couldn't have an idea of God unless God existed.

Now, assuming that this argument successfully gets you to conclusion (3), how about that move from (3) to (4)? Descartes had no difficulty with that move and said simply, "From the fact that I cannot conceive God without existence, it follows that existence is inseparable from Him, and hence that He really exists." He also offered what he thought was a parallel argument to support the move, and it was to this effect: Just as the fact that you cannot conceive of a triangle whose angles do not equal 180° means that a triangle must have angles that equal 180°, the fact that you cannot conceive of God as not existing means that God must exist.

Descartes' three proofs may be novel, but certain objections instantly spring to mind. A common criticism made of the first two proofs is that it seems possible to devise plausible alternative explanations for one's having an idea of God, explanations other than that given by Descartes. Descartes himself anticipates this objection and endeavors to show why the most likely alternative explanations fail.

The third proof—Descartes' version of the ontological argument—is more difficult to criticize, but about one hundred fifty years later, Immanuel Kant formulated what became the classic refutation of ontological arguments. More about this when we turn to Kant.

A different sort of objection to Descartes' proofs is that, given Descartes' method—according to which he vowed not to accept any claim that is in the least bit doubtable—Descartes should not have accepted without question either the principle that he and his ideas must be caused or the principle that there must be as much perfection and reality in the cause as in the effect. Although Descartes regarded his proofs of God as providing certainty, they seem to rest on principles that many people would think of as less than certain. Yet Descartes seems to accept these principles without hesitation.

Nevertheless, Descartes' proofs are important in the history of our subject, for they raise the important question—at least the first two proofs raise this question—just how *does* a person come to have the idea of an *infinite* being?

Leibniz

You may recall the name of Gottfried Wilhelm, Baron von Leibniz, or at least the "Leibniz" part, from our discussion in Chapter 6. **Leibniz** (1646–1716) was one of the Continental rationalists of the seventeenth century (Descartes and Spinoza were the other two). He is remembered for developing calculus independently of Newton and for his metaphysical doctrine of **monads**—the individual nonphysical units of activity that, he said, are the ultimate constituents of reality. Remember also that the Leibnizian metaphysical system is, or so Leibniz believed, derivable logically from a few basic principles, including, perhaps most famously, the principle of sufficient reason.

Leibniz and the Principle of Sufficient Reason   The **principle of sufficient reason** is used by Leibniz as a proof of God. According to this principle, there is a sufficient reason why things are exactly as they are and are not otherwise. To see how the proof works, consider any occurrence whatsoever, say, the leaves falling from the trees in autumn. According to the principle in question, there must be a sufficient reason for that occurrence. Now, a *partial* reason for any occurrence is that something else happened, or is happening, that caused or is causing the occurrence—in our example, the days turning cold. But that happening is only a *partial* reason for the occurrence in question because it, too, requires a sufficient reason for happening. Why did the days turn cold?

So it is plain, thought Leibniz, that as long as you seek the sufficient reason for an occurrence from within the sequence of happenings or events, you never get the complete, final, sufficient reason for the occurrence. You only get to some other event, and that itself needs a reason for having happened. (The days turned cold because of a shift southward in the jet stream. The jet stream shifted southward because of a reduction in solar radiation. The solar radiation was reduced because of changes in the earth's orientation relative to the sun. And so forth.) So, unless there is something *outside* the series of events, some reason for the *entire series itself,* there is no sufficient reason for *any* occurrence.

Therefore, reasoned Leibniz, because there is a sufficient reason for every occurrence, it follows that there is something outside the series of events that is its own sufficient reason. And this "something outside," of course, is God. Further, because God is a sufficient reason for God's own existence, God is a *necessary* being, argued Leibniz.

In this way, then, the principle of sufficient reason, coupled with the fact that something has occurred or is occurring, leads straightaway to a necessary being, God—at least according to Leibniz.

This proof is yet another cosmological argument, and it is very much like Aquinas's third way. In fact, there is a tendency in the literature to interpret Aquinas's third way in this Leibnizian mode. Further, Leibniz's "argument from sufficient reason" is thought by many contemporary philosophers to be the soundest cosmological argument and the soundest proof of God of any type ever put forward. As you will see directly when we turn to David Hume, however, not everyone is impressed with the argument.

Later, we will mention that Kant thought that the cosmological argument depended on the ontological argument. Kant thought this, apparently, because Leibniz's version ends up seeming to prove the existence of a necessary being, and it is the concept of God as a necessary being that is the foundation of the ontological argument. But it does seem doubtful that Leibniz's argument *depends* on the ontological argument or in any way *assumes* the existence of a necessary being. Instead, the argument seems to *prove* the existence of a necessary being.

Leibniz thought other proofs of God were sound, including an amended version of Descartes' ontological argument and a couple of others that rest on Leibniz's metaphysics. Leibniz, however, is most noted for the cosmological argument we have explained here.

Leibniz and the Problem of Evil   Unfortunately, pain and suffering are undeniably real. Cancer, natural disasters, war, poverty, racism, murder, animal cruelty—the list of causes is almost endless. How can it be said that the Creator is good, when little animals freeze to death or are incinerated in forest fires, when innocent men are tortured or beheaded by their fellow men, or when innocent women and children burn to death in atomic bomb attacks. Yes, much of the problem is due to evil in man; but the question then arises, Why would a good Creator create men who are evil? After all, He knew in advance, when he created people, that some of them would do such things.

This is the Problem of Evil, perhaps first posed by Epicurus, though not in these exact words. Obviously, if you believe that God is good and the all-knowing, all-powerful Creator of All, you need to confront this problem. **Theodicy** was Leibniz's word for an argument in defense of God's goodness despite the existence of evil, though the first to wrestle with this problem in a detailed way was St. Augustine (354–430 C.E.). Augustine's line of defense is widely accepted even today and includes the following elements:

- Human evil results when humans use their free will to turn away from God.
- Evil is the privation, or lack of good, that results from this turning away.
- Because a lack of something is not something, this evil is not something God created.
- Human sin is canceled out in the end by divine retribution.
- Our view of the world is limited and finite, meaning that we are not in a position to judge its overall goodness.

Now, Leibniz, remember, subscribed to the principle of sufficient reason, which logically entails (he thought) that God exists. It also requires that this must be the most perfect of all possible worlds, for otherwise God would not have chosen this world for existence. So Leibniz owed his readers an explanation of how evil got into the picture.

Leibniz's explanation, briefly, is that, for God to create things other than himself, the created things logically must be limited and imperfect. Thus, to the extent that creation is imperfect, it is not wholly good, and thus it is "evil."

This, of course, is a variation of the Problem of Evil (discussed in the text in the section on Leibniz) from a Republican's viewpoint.

Further, Leibniz argues, you have to look at the entire painting. You cannot pronounce it bad if you look at this or that small part, for if you do that, all you will see is a confused mass of colors. Likewise, you have to look at the world from a global perspective and not focus on this or that unpleasant aspect of it.

Not everyone, of course, finds this explanation of evil satisfactory. The optimism expressed in Leibniz's dictum that this is the best of all possible worlds was skewered with dripping sarcasm by Voltaire (1694–1778) in his famous novel *Candide*. Leibniz was of the opinion that one must look at evil from a global perspective, from which unfortunate events might be perceived as part of a larger fabric that, taken as a whole, is a perfect creation. This notion, in Voltaire's opinion, is meaningless from the standpoint of the individual who suffers a dreadful misfortune, and Voltaire had no difficulty in ridiculing it. If you look at the events of the world with a sober eye, Voltaire suggested, you will see anything but a just, harmonious, and ordered place. What you are more likely to see is injustice, strife, and rampant disorder.

"When death crowns the ills of suffering man, what a fine consolation to be eaten by worms," he wrote. You get the idea.

EIGHTEENTH- AND NINETEENTH-CENTURY PERSPECTIVES

Recall now Aquinas's fifth way, a version of the teleological argument, which also often is called the argument from design. The basic idea of this type of proof of God's existence is that the world and its components act for a purpose and thus exhibit design; therefore, the world was created by an intelligent designer. One of the most famous criticisms of the design argument was made by the British empiricist David Hume.

Hume

David Hume (1711–1776) was born some sixty years after Descartes died, during a period of European history that saw the clear emergence of two rivals, science and religion. Between Descartes' *Meditations* and Hume's writings on religion, science had made strong advances, especially in 1687 with the publication of Sir Isaac Newton's *Principia Mathematica*. Although Newton himself did not question God's existence, his system seemed to confirm scientifically what Hobbes earlier had concluded philosophically (see Chapter 6) and what Descartes seemed most to fear: that the universe is an aggregate of matter in motion that has no need of, and leaves no room for, God. Hume's case-hardened doubts about religion could make blood pressures soar, but by the time Hume put them in print, they were by no means considered capital offenses.

Hume's empiricist epistemological principles (if valid) in fact rule out the possibility of any meaningful ontological argument. But this is complicated business and need not detain us, because it is Hume's harsh criticisms of the cosmological and especially the teleological arguments that have been most influential in the philosophy of religion. The most important criticism of the ontological argument comes from Kant, anyway. (Hume's thinking on the subject of miracles has also been influential; we discuss it in the box "Miracles.")

Hume and the Argument from Design   Hume stated the teleological argument (that is, the argument from design) and then went on to criticize it severely. Here is his fair and balanced statement of the argument:

> Look round the world; contemplate the whole and every part of it: you will find it to be nothing but one great machine, subdivided into an infinite number of lesser machines, which again admit of subdivisions, to a degree beyond what human senses and faculties can trace and explain. All these various machines, and even their most minute parts, are adjusted to each other with an accuracy, which ravishes into admiration all men, who have ever contemplated them. The curious adapting of means to ends, throughout all nature, resembles exactly, though it

---

Miracles

Some Christians regard miracles as evidence of divine action. Hume, however, was highly skeptical of reports of miracles.

A miracle, he reasoned, is a violation of a natural law, such as that water flows downhill or that fire consumes wood. Thus, before it is reasonable to accept a report of a miracle as true, the evidence that supports the report must be even stronger than that which has established the natural law.

Because the evidence that a natural law holds is the uniform experience of humankind, it is almost inconceivable that any report of a miracle could be true. Therefore, before it would be reasonable to accept such a report, it would have to be a miracle in its own right for the report to be false. In fact, the report's being false would have to be a *greater* miracle than the miracle it reports.

"No testimony," wrote Hume, "is sufficient to establish a miracle, unless the testimony be of such a kind, that its falsehood would be more miraculous than the fact that it endeavors to establish."

much exceeds, the productions of human contrivance; of human design, thought, wisdom, and intelligence. Since therefore the effects resemble each other, we are led to infer, by all the rules of analogy, that the causes also resemble; and that the Author of Nature is somewhat similar to the mind of men; though possessed of much larger faculties, proportioned to the grandeur of the work, which he has executed. By this argument a posteriori, and by this argument alone, we do prove at once the existence of a Deity, and his similarity to human mind and intelligence.

Now note that in this proof of God, as stated by Hume, the reasoning is from an *effect* (the "world," i.e., the universe) and its parts to its *cause* (God). Further, this is an **argument by analogy,** in which the effect (the world or universe) is likened to a human contrivance, the cause is likened to a human creator, and the mechanism of creation is likened to human thought and intelligence. Hume's criticisms of the proof are mainly related to (1) the appropriateness of these analogies, and (2) the legitimacy of this particular instance of effect-to-cause reasoning.

Hume began his criticism by noticing that, in an effect-to-cause proof, we cannot attribute to the supposed cause any qualities over and beyond those required for the effect. For example, is the world absolutely perfect? Is it free from every error, mistake, or incoherence? No? Then you cannot say that its cause is absolutely perfect either. Does the world reflect infinite wisdom and intelligence? Hume's own opinion is that, at best, the world reflects these qualities to *some degree;* and, therefore, though we perhaps can infer that the cause has these qualities to a similar degree, we are unauthorized to attribute to it these qualities in a higher degree, and we certainly are not authorized to attribute to it these qualities in an *infinite* degree.

We also are not authorized to attribute to it other qualities, such as pure goodness or infinite power. The existence of evil and misery, in Hume's opinion, certainly does *not* indicate that the cause of the world is pure goodness coupled with infinite power. His point was not that the existence of pain and misery necessarily means that the creator of the world is *not* good or omnipotent. Rather, his point was just that, given the existence of evil and misery in the world, we cannot legitimately try to prove that the creator is all-good and all-powerful *by looking at the world.* To do that is to attribute something other to the cause than is found in the effect.

Hume also questioned whether we even *know* how perfect or good the world is. Given the limitations of our position, given that we have no basis for a comparison, can we be sure that the world does not contain great faults? Are we entitled to say that the world deserves considerable praise? If an ignorant chucklehead pronounces the only poem he has ever heard to be artistically flawless, does his opinion count for much?

Further, he noted, in the design proof of God, a cause is inferred from a single effect, namely, the world. But, Hume asked, is it legitimate to infer a cause from a *single* effect? If I learn (to take a modern illustration of the point) that a certain weird kind of sound is caused by a new type of electronic instrument, then when I hear that kind of sound again, I can infer that it was caused by a similar instrument. But if it is the first time I hear the sound, I cannot say much at all about its cause, save perhaps that it was not made by a trombone or guitar. In other words, if we have experience of only a single instance of the effect, as seems to be the case with the world, then it is not clear "that we could form any conjecture or inference at all concerning its cause."

Of course, we have had experience with the building of machines and ships and houses and so forth. But can the world really be compared to any of these? Can we pretend to show much similarity between a house and the universe? To speak of the origin of *worlds,* wrote Hume, "It is not sufficient, surely, that we have seen ships and cities arise from human art and contrivance."

Hume laid a great deal of emphasis on the limitedness of our viewpoint. We, who are but a part of the universe, use our intelligence and thought to build cities and machines. And so we suppose there must be a divine creator who used thought and intelligence to create the universe. But we and our creations are but a tiny aspect of the universe, and human thought and intelligence are just one of hundreds of known principles of activity. Is it legitimate, Hume asked, for us to suppose that the mechanism by which one small aspect of the universe rearranges little bits of wood and steel and dirt is the same mechanism by which *the entire universe* was originally created?

Further, even if we can liken the creation of the world to the building of a house or boat, there is this further problem, said Hume: If we survey a ship, we would be tempted to attribute a great deal of ingenuity to its builder, when in fact its builder may be a beef-brained clod who only copied an art that was perfected over the ages by hundreds of people working through a series of trials, mistakes, corrections, and gradual improvements. Can we be sure the world was not the result of a similar process of trial and error and even intermittent bungling, involving a multitude of lesser "creators"?

For that matter, Hume asked, is it even proper to liken the world to a ship or watch or machine or other human artifact? Is not the world arguably as much like a living organism as a machine? And are not living organisms produced by processes radically different from those by which human artifacts are made?

This, then, is the substance of Hume's complaints about the design argument. Given what seemed to him to be its several difficulties, Hume's own conclusion was just this: There is an apparent order in the universe, and this apparent order provides some slight evidence of a cause or causes bearing some remote analogy to human intelligence. But that is all the evidence warrants, Hume thought.

Hume and the Cosmological Argument   A cosmological argument, in the version Hume examines, says that anything that exists must have a cause (or reason or explanation) that is different from itself. But because the series of causes cannot go to infinity, there must be a first uncaused cause, God. A variation of the basic argument allows that the causal series can go to infinity but still stands in need of an uncaused cause that causes the whole infinite series. In either case, the uncaused cause cannot *not* exist. Thus, the uncaused cause is a **necessary being.**

Hume's objections to these lines of argument are that, *first,* as far as we can make out, the universe may itself be "the necessarily existent being"; *second,* if you maintain that everything has a prior cause, it is *contradictory* also to maintain that there was a first cause; and *third,* if I explain the cause of each member of a series of things, there is no further need for an explanation of the *series itself* as if it were some *further* thing.

A Verbal Dispute?   Hume also had the startling idea that the dispute between theists and atheists might be only a verbal dispute. This was his reasoning:

416   Part Three · *Philosophy of Religion: Reason and Faith*

Hume suggested that atheists and true believers are not all that different in their views.

Theists say that the universe was created by the divine will. But they concede that there is a great and immeasurable difference between the creative activity of the divine mind and mere human thought and its creative activity.

But what do atheists say? They concede that there is some original or fundamental principle of order in the universe, but they insist that this principle can bear only some remote analogy to everyday creative and generative processes or to human intelligence.

Thus, atheist and theist are very close to saying the same thing!

The main difference between them seems to lie only in this, Hume said: The theist is most impressed by the necessity of there being or having been a fundamental principle of order and generation in the universe, whereas the atheist is most impressed by how wildly different such a principle must be from any creative activity with which we are familiar. But then the more pious the theist, the more he will emphasize the difference between divine intelligence and human intelligence; the more he will insist that the workings of God are incomprehensible to mere mortals. The more pious the theist, in short, the more he will be like the atheist!

Kant

This brings us to **Immanuel Kant** (1724–1804), whose contribution to the philosophy of religion equals in importance his work in epistemology and ethics. Kant invented one of the most famous moral arguments for God's existence. But Kant's criticisms of traditional proofs of God have seemed to many commentators to be more cogent than his proof, and in any case they are among the most important criticisms in the literature.

According to Kant, there are only three (traditional) ways of proving God's existence, and none of them works.

What Is Wrong with the Ontological Proof? First is the ontological argument. Remember that, according to Anselm's version of the argument, God is the greatest being conceivable. Hence, if you suppose that God does not exist, you are supposing that the greatest being conceivable is not the greatest being conceivable, and that is nonsense. According to Descartes' version, God possesses all perfections, and because existence is a perfection, God exists.

Now, we are sure you will agree there is something very sneaky about the ontological argument, in any version. It seems intuitively wrong, somehow; yet it is difficult to pin down exactly what the problem is.

Kant provided a criticism that has withstood the test of time, though in recent years there have been challenges to it. What is wrong with the argument, Kant said, is that it assumes that *existence is a* predicate, *that is, a characteristic or an attribute.* Because Anselm assumed that existence is a characteristic, he could argue that a being that lacked existence lacked an important characteristic and thus could not be the greatest being conceivable. Because Descartes assumed that existence is a characteristic, he could argue that God, who by definition possesses all perfections, necessarily possesses the characteristic of existence.

But existence, said Kant, is not a characteristic at all. Rather, it is a *precondition* of having characteristics. Is there any difference between a warm day and an *existing* warm day? If you state that the potato salad is salty, do you further characterize the salad if you state that it is salty *and exists?* If you tell the mechanic that your tire is flat, do you further enlighten him if you add that the tire also *exists?* The answer to all such questions, in Kant's view, is obviously "no." To say of something that it exists is not to characterize it: existence is not a predicate.

So, to apply this lesson first to Descartes: Existence is *not* a perfection or any other kind of characteristic. Certainly, *if* there *is* a being that possesses all perfections,

Our cars are all mechanically sound, come with a six-month written guarantee, and exist.

Kant argued that existence is not a characteristic and that you do not enlarge a description of a thing to say that it exists. Of course, you may wish to assert that something—God, say, or ghosts—exists, but that sort of assertion is not really a description, Kant would maintain.

then God exists, for existence is a precondition of something's having any perfections at all. But this fact does not mean that God actually exists.

And to apply this lesson to Anselm: Existence is not a characteristic, and so it is not one that belongs to greatness. Certainly, *if* the greatest being conceivable exists, then God exists, because God by definition is that being, and something cannot possess any aspect of greatness without existing. But that fact does not mean that such a being exists.

What Is Wrong with the Cosmological and Teleological Proofs?   The second way of proving God's existence, according to Kant, is the cosmological argument, which, he asserts, reduces to this: If something exists, an absolutely necessary being must likewise exist. I, at least, exist. Therefore, an absolutely necessary being exists.

This is certainly a simple and streamlined version of the cosmological argument compared with the arguments set forth by Aquinas, Descartes, Leibniz, and Hume. Unfortunately, Kant, who generally did not try to make things easy for his reader, made up for this unusual lapse into simplicity and clarity by submitting the argument to several pages of exceedingly subtle and confusing analysis.

Kant's basic criticisms of the cosmological argument, however, are two: First, the argument really rests on the ontological argument. His explanation of why and how this is so is notoriously obscure and probably unsound; let's just let it go. Second, and more important anyway, the argument employs a principle (that everything contingent has a cause) that has significance only in the *experienced* world. The argument then uses that principle, Kant maintained, to arrive at a conclusion that goes beyond experience. (Kant, as we tried to make clear in Chapter 7, believed that causality is a concept applicable only to things-as-experienced. Why Kant held this position is too complicated to repeat here, but his case against the cosmological argument rests on his being correct about causality, which some people are inclined to doubt.)

The third and final way of trying to prove God's existence, according to Kant, is the teleological argument, the argument that cites the purposiveness and harmonious adaptation of nature as proof of the divine designer. Kant's main criticism is that at best the argument proves only the existence of an *architect* who *works* with the matter of the world, and not a creator. A similar line of thinking was found in Hume, as we saw.

Belief in God Rationally Justified   Despite Kant's criticisms of the three traditional proofs for God's existence, Kant believed in God. Further, amazingly to some, he thought this belief is rationally justified for any moral agent. Here, as almost always, his thinking is complicated, but what he had in mind was this:

Although we do not have theoretical or metaphysical knowledge of God, although we cannot prove or demonstrate that God exists, we must view the world *as if* it were created by God. Why? Because, Kant said, only if we assume the existence of God can we believe that virtue will be rewarded with happiness. Virtue, Kant held, is worthiness to be happy and is the supreme good. But without believing in God, the virtuous individual cannot be certain that the happiness of which he is worthy will in fact be his or that, in general, a person's happiness will be proportionate to his moral worth.

Thus, in Kant's opinion, God's existence cannot be proved but can and must rationally be assumed by a moral agent. That God exists, Kant said, is a postulate of *practical* reason. This particular argument for assuming that God exists is another version of the moral argument that we first encountered with Aquinas.

Kierkegaard

It is interesting to contrast Kant's philosophy with that of the Danish philosopher **Søren Kierkegaard** (1813–1855), who was born a little before Kant died. Neither philosopher thought you could rationally prove God exists. But the similarity between the two ends there.

For Kierkegaard, "to exist" is to be engaged in time and history. Because God is an eternal and immutable being, "existence" does not even apply to God. But God as Christ existed, for Kierkegaard. Christ, however, is a paradox that the human intellect cannot comprehend, for in Christ the immutable became changing, the eternal became temporal, and what is beyond history became historical.

In short, Kierkegaard thought that God is beyond the grasp of reason and that the idea that God came to us as a man in the person of Jesus is intellectually absurd. Yet, at the same time, Kierkegaard's primary mission was to show what it is to be a Christian, and he himself was totally committed to Christianity. How can this be?

First, the notion that we can sit back and weigh objectively the evidence about God's existence pro and contra, that we can conduct an impartial investigation of the issue and arrive at the "truth," is totally rejected by Kierkegaard. He would not have bothered reading this chapter.

In fact, Kierkegaard mocks the whole idea of objective truth as giving meaning to life. Truth, he said, is subjective. Truth lies not in *what* you believe, but in *how you live.* Truth is passionate commitment. For example, think of a person who worships the "true" God but does so merely as a matter of routine, without passion or commitment. Compare this person with one who worships a mere idol but does so with the infinite commitment of his soul. In fact, said Kierkegaard, "The one prays in truth to God though he worships an idol; the other prays falsely to the true God, and hence worships in fact an idol."

Second, Kierkegaard rejected completely the Aristotelian idea that the essential attribute of humans is their capacity to reason. For Kierkegaard, the most important attribute of man is not thought but *will.* Man is a being that *makes choices.*

But if truth is not objective, then there are no external principles or criteria that are objectively valid and against which one might judge one's choices. How, then, are we to choose, if there are no objective, rational criteria, and we have only our own judgment to rely on? This problem—the problem of knowing how and what to choose in the absence of objective truth—became, after Kierkegaard, the central problem of existentialism.

Kierkegaard's answer is that we must commit ourselves totally to God. Salvation can be had only through a **leap of faith,** through a nonintellectual, passionate, "infinite" commitment to Christianity. "Faith constitutes a sphere all by itself, and every misunderstanding of Christianity may at once be recognized by its transforming it into a doctrine, transferring it to the sphere of the intellectual."

God's Foreknowledge and Free Will

God supposedly knows everything. So whatever you did, he knew before you did it that you would do it. Did you sleep late this morning? God knew that you would.

And that means that you could not have *not* slept late this morning, because God knew that you would sleep late. And if you could not have not slept late, then in what sense did you sleep late of your own free will? See the problem? It seems that the view that God knows everything conflicts with the idea that you have free will.

This problem is sometimes dismissed by beginning philosophy students as "merely verbal" or as "easily solved." If this is true, it will come as news to the heavyweight philosophers and theologians who have grappled with it, including Paul, Augustine, Luther, Calvin, and others. It is because they saw the logical implications of crediting God with omniscience (all-knowingness) that Calvinists (followers of the great sixteenth-century Protestant theologian John Calvin), for example, believed that God must preordain who will be saved and who will be damned.

What Kierkegaard said must not be confused with what earlier Christian thinkers had maintained. Earlier Christian thinkers had said that faith precedes understanding and had held that you must have faith in God before rational thought about him can begin. But thinkers such as Augustine and Anselm had still looked for, and had fully expected there to be, rational grounds for confirming what they already accepted by faith. Kierkegaard, in contrast, thought that no such rational grounds exist: God is an intellectual absurdity.

Further, he held that rational grounds for believing in God, if there were any, would actually be *incompatible* with having faith. "If I wish to preserve myself in faith I must constantly be intent upon holding fast to the *objective uncertainty* [of God]," he said. The objective uncertainty of God, for Kierkegaard, is thus essential to a true faith in him. Only if there is objective uncertainty, he wrote, can "[I] remain out upon the deep, over seventy thousand fathoms of water, still preserving my faith."

Nietzsche

"God is dead," said Nietzsche. By this infamous remark, **Friedrich Nietzsche** (1844–1900) did not mean that God once existed and now no longer does. He meant that all people with an ounce of intelligence would now perceive that there is no intelligent plan to the universe or rational order in it: they would now understand that there is no reason why things happen one way and not another and that the harmony and order we imagine to exist in the universe is merely pasted on by the human mind.

Nietzsche, however, would have regarded very few people as having this required ounce of intelligence, and he in fact had a way of denigrating everyone in sight. For the mass of people, Nietzsche thought, God certainly is not dead. But these people, in Nietzsche's opinion, are pathetic wretches governed by a worldview inculcated by religion, science, and philosophy, a worldview that in Nietzsche's opinion makes them feeble losers who are motivated mainly by

Religion: Illusion with a Future

Religion, according to the founder of psychoanalysis, Sigmund Freud (1856–1939), is an exercise in mass delusion and serves mainly to keep people in a state of psychological infantilism. Religion is wish-fulfillment; it offers up the "figure of an enormously exalted father" who reassures us as our own fathers did. The infallible and omnipotent father in heaven assures us that there is meaning and purpose in life and that all will be well in the end. However, although religion enables us to retain our status as children throughout our lives, it is a dangerous illusion. Religion intimidates intelligence with its demands for unconditional submission to inscrutable laws and keeps us from distinguishing between fact and wishful thinking. It does this even when philosophers and theologians try to salvage the illusion by redefining God as an "impersonal, shadowy and abstract principle."

Sometimes belief in religion is fostered by the psychological feeling of the oneness of everything. Such "oceanic feelings," according to Freud, are just a recurrence of the limitless narcissism typical of early childhood. Freud thought human beings would be happier if they retained a modicum of reality in their thinking and cultivated their own gardens, as Voltaire had suggested.

resentment. They view the world as a rational, law-governed place and adhere to a slave morality that praises the man who serves his fellow creatures with meekness and self-sacrifice.

In Nietzsche's opinion, the negative morality of these pitiful slaves—the mass of humankind, ordinary people—must be reevaluated and replaced by life-affirming values. The new morality will be based on the development of a new kind of human being, whom Nietzsche calls the *Übermensch* ("overman" or "superman"). Such a one not only accepts life in all its facets, including all its pain, but also makes living into an art. Among the forerunners of the overman, Nietzsche cites Alexander the Great and Napoleon.

Nietzsche's thesis that there is no God and its apparent corollary, that there are no absolute and necessary criteria of right and wrong, were accepted by such twentieth-century existentialist philosophers as Albert Camus and Jean-Paul Sartre. For these thinkers, the fundamental problem of philosophy is how to live one's life, given the absence of absolutely valid standards by which to evaluate one's choices and decisions.

Nietzsche, Kierkegaard, and some existentialists would all have agreed that the various rational discussions about God's existence to which this chapter is devoted are impotent and meaningless. (However, for an interesting alternative view, you might like to read the box "Religion: Illusion with a Future," which discusses the views of Sigmund Freud.)

James

William James (1842–1910) published his first major work, *The Will to Believe and Other Essays,* in 1897. By the year 1900, there was a marked increase in agnosticism and antagonism between the religious view of the world as a divinely created paradise planned for the sake of human spiritual growth and the supposedly scientific

422   Part Three · *Philosophy of Religion: Reason and Faith*

PROFILE: William James (1842–1910)

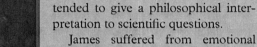

Few philosophers have been better writers than William James, whose catchy phrases gave life and succulence to even the driest philosophical subjects. James had a knack for words, and he was able to state complex ideas with easy elegance. This might be expected because James was the older brother of Henry James, the great American novelist.

The James children were raised by their wealthy and eccentric theologian father in an intellectually stimulating atmosphere that promoted their mental development. The Jameses benefited from diverse educational experiences in several schools both in America and in Europe and were largely free to pursue their own interests and develop their own capacities. They became refined and cosmopolitan.

William James had wide-ranging interests. Though fascinated with science, he decided, at age eighteen, to try to become a painter. But he was also wise enough to see very soon that his artistic urge exceeded his ability.

So James went off to Harvard and studied science. Then he entered the college's medical school, though he did not intend to practice medicine, and in his late twenties he received his medical degree. A few years later, he joined the Harvard faculty as a lecturer on anatomy and physiology and continued to teach at Harvard until 1907. From 1880 on, he was a member of the Harvard Department of Philosophy and Psychology. You should not think that James got interested in philosophy all of a sudden. He had always been fond of the subject and tended to give a philosophical interpretation to scientific questions.

James suffered from emotional crises until he was able to resolve the question of free will and to answer the compelling arguments for determinism. Around 1870, in the ideas of the French philosopher Charles Renouvier, he found philosophical justification for believing in free will, and with it, apparently, the cure to his episodes of emotional paralysis.

In 1890, James published his famous *Principles of Psychology*, thought by many to be his major work. Equally important from a purely philosophical standpoint was his *The Will to Believe and Other Essays in Popular Philosophy* (1897). In this work is James's solution to the problem of free will, in the essay "The Dilemma of Determinism." Other important works include *The Varieties of Religious Experience* (1902), *Pragmatism* (1907), *A Pluralistic Universe* (1909), *The Meaning of Truth* (1909), *Some Problems in Philosophy* (1911), and *Essays in Radical Empiricism* (1912).

William James was perhaps the most famous American intellectual of his time. Yet today some philosophers think of him as a lightweight—a popularizer of philosophical issues who failed to make a substantial contribution to technical philosophy (whatever that is). He is thought to bear the same relation to Hume or Kant, say, that Tchaikovsky bears to Mozart or Bach, the philosophical equivalent of the composer who only cranks out pretty melodies. But this is all a mistake. The discerning reader will find in James a great depth of insight.

view of the cosmos as a blind churning of material particles in accordance with physical laws. Over the past two hundred years, the blind-churning view had become more and more congenial to Western intellectuals. Around mid-century, Darwin had explained how the origin of species need not be divine, and Karl Marx had pronounced religion to be the opiate of the people. Hume and Kant did not force philosophers to question the old proofs of God, the times did. Before the end of the century, Friedrich Nietzsche could proclaim that God was dead.

But God was not, and is not, dead for everyone. In fact, for very many, the question of God's existence was at the time, and still is (1) a *live* issue and furthermore (2) a *momentous* one. For William James it is both. It is also, according to James, (3) *forced*, which means you cannot suspend judgment in the matter. For James, to profess agnosticism and to pretend to suspend judgment is in fact "backing the field against the religious hypothesis" (that is, deciding against God).

James argued for deciding the issue of God's existence in favor of God. He began his argument, not a simple one, by noting that "*our nonintellectual nature does influence our convictions.*" Indeed, usually our convictions are *determined* by our nonintellectual or "passional" nature, rather than by reason, he maintained. Sometimes we even deliberately will what we believe, James held.

Having argued that our nonintellectual nature influences our opinions, James next distinguished between the *two commandments* of rational thinkers. These are

1. to believe the truth
2. to avoid errors

Some individuals, James noted, favor (2) over (1): they would rather avoid errors than find the truth. "Better go without belief forever than believe a falsehood" is the creed dictated to them by their passional nature: better dead than misled. But favoring (2) over (1) is not James's creed. There are worse things than falling into error, he said. In some cases, he argued, it is best to regard "the chase for truth as paramount, and the avoidance of error as secondary."

It is this way in religious matters, he said. When it comes to religion it is better to yield to the hope that all of it may be true than to give way to the fear of being in error. If you permit the fear of error to rule you and say to yourself, "Avoid error at any cost!" then you will withhold assent to religious beliefs. Doing so will, of course, *protect* you from being in error—if the religious beliefs are incorrect. But if you withhold your assent to religious beliefs, then you will also *lose the benefits* that come from accepting those beliefs. And it is worse, James thought, to lose the benefits than to gain the protection from erring.

Further, if the religious beliefs are *true* but the evidence for them is insufficient, then the policy "Avoid error at any cost!" effectively cuts you off from an opportunity to make friends with God. Thus, in James's opinion, the policy "Avoid error at all cost!"—when applied to religion—is a policy that keeps you from accepting certain propositions even if those propositions are really true, and that means that it is an irrational policy.

James stressed that he was *not* saying that you should believe what, as he put it, "you know ain't true." His strategy applies, he said, only to *momentous* and *living* issues that cannot be resolved by the intellect itself. It applies only to issues like God's existence.

Applying the same strategy to the question of whether we have free will, James focused not directly on the question itself but rather on the outcomes that attend acceptance of the alternative viewpoints. Acceptance of determinism is unsatisfactory, James believed, because it entails never regretting what happens (what happened had to happen, according to determinism, so it is illogical to feel that it should not have happened). Thus, acceptance of determinism is inconsistent with the practices of moral beings, who perceive themselves as making genuine choices that can affect the world for better or for worse.

TWENTIETH-CENTURY PERSPECTIVES

James's reasoning elicited much criticism. Skeptics and believers both took issue with it. Skeptics thought James had elevated wishful thinking to the status of proof, and believers questioned James's implicit assumption that God's existence cannot be established. Still others said that belief grounded in James's way was not the uncompromising and unqualified faith in God demanded by religion. From their perspective, James's belief in God amounted to a gamble akin to **Pascal's wager** (see the box on the next page) rather than to true religious acceptance of God.

James in any event takes us into the twentieth and twenty-first centuries, and we shall now consider more recent discussions of God's existence. The first is something like an argument that God does not exist, but in actuality it is an argument that the whole issue is pretty meaningless to begin with.

God and Logical Positivism

In the late 1920s, a group of philosophers, mathematicians, and scientists led by Moritz Schlick, a philosopher at the University of Vienna, set forth a group of ideas known as **logical positivism.** A central tenet of this **Vienna Circle** and of logical positivism, as we saw in Chapter 9, is the **verifiability principle,** according to which the factual meaning of a proposition is the experience you must have to know it is true. What does it mean to say, "The sprinkler is on"? Well, to find out whether that proposition is true, you would have to look out the window or go out into the yard or otherwise do some checking. The experience required to do the checking is what the proposition means, according to the verifiability principle.

What this principle entails is that a pronouncement that is not verifiable has no factual meaning. Take the remark "The sprinkler stopped working due to fate." What kind of checking would you do to see whether this was true? There is no experience a person might have that would verify this remark. Therefore, it is factually meaningless, the logical positivists would say.

Of course, some propositions are true by virtue of what their words mean: for example, "You are older than everyone who is younger than you." Such *analytic propositions,* as they are called, are rendered true by definition rather than by experience, according to the logical positivists. But the proposition "The sprinkler stopped working due to fate" is not like that. It is not an analytic proposition, so it has to be verifiable in experience if it is to have factual meaning. And because it is not, it does not.

So, according to the logical positivists, the many philosophical assertions from metaphysics, epistemology, and ethics that are neither analytic nor verifiable are factually meaningless. These assertions may perhaps express emotional sentiments, but they are neither true nor false. Rudolph Carnap (1891–1970), one of the most famous members of the Vienna Circle, even declared, "We reject *all* philosophical questions, whether of Metaphysics, Ethics or Epistemology."

Today, few philosophers would call themselves logical positivists, for reasons mentioned in Chapter 9. But most philosophers would still maintain that *empirical* or *factual* propositions must in *some* sense and to *some* extent be verifiable by experience.

Pascal's Wager

The French mathematician and philosopher Blaise Pascal (1623–1662) is famous, among other reasons, for his wager–argument for God. Either God exists or he does not. By believing that he does exist, you lose nothing if he does not, and you gain a lot, namely, happiness and eternal life, if he does. So believing that God exists is a prudent wager; you will not lose anything, and you might gain much.

James denied that he was offering a version of Pascal's wager in his argument for the existence of God. You may wish to consider whether his denial is warranted.

So what, then, about assertions such as "God exists" or "God loves us"? These look like factual propositions. But are they in any sense verifiable? A reading by Antony Flew at the end of the chapter addresses the issue from a positivist perspective, according to which the utterances "God exists" and "God does not exist" are both meaningless.

In recent years Professor Flew abandoned his "atheistic" position. His recent book *There Is a God*, published in 2007 and written with Roy Abraham Varghese, is what Flew called his last will and testament. In it he proclaimed, "I now believe there is a God!" His major reasons? God provides the best explanation of how the laws of nature came to be, how life originated from nonlife, and how the universe came into existence.

Unfortunately, controversy exists as to how much of the book represents Flew's own thinking and how much represents the opinion of his coauthor. The arguments presented in the book stand or fall on their own merits, however.[1]

Mary Daly: The Unfolding of God

An entirely different line of thinking about God is evident in what contemporary feminist scholar **Mary Daly** (1928–2010) said on the subject in *Beyond God the Father* (1973).

The biblical and popular image of God as a *great father in heaven*, Daly wrote, a father who rewards and punishes according to his mysterious and seemingly arbitrary will, arose in patriarchal societies. Furthermore, according to Daly, the image serves patriarchal society by making mechanisms for the oppression of women seem right and fitting. "If God in 'his' heaven is a father ruling 'his' people, then it is in the 'nature' of things and according to divine plan and the order of the universe that society be male-dominated." Given the biblical and popular image of God, "the husband dominating his wife represents God himself." "If God is male, then the male is God."

This image of God as Lord and Father, which has been sustained "by the usual processes of producing plausibility such as preaching and religious indoctrination," perpetuates the artificial polarization of human qualities into the traditional sexual stereotypes, Daly maintained. This image of the person in authority and the popular

---

[1] For supposed evidence that Flew was in a state of mental decline when he wrote the book, see http://www.nytimes.com/2007/11/04/magazine/04Flew-t.html?_r=1.

426   Part Three · *Philosophy of Religion: Reason and Faith*

Mary Daly.

understanding of "his" role continually renew the eternal masculine stereotypes. They also nourish and justify domination and manipulation both toward persons and toward the environment. They perpetuate the eternal female stereotypes of emotionalism, passivity, self-abnegation, and the like.

Of course, a defender of the traditional image of God will probably protest that God is popularly conceived also as love. But, according to Mary Daly, the concept of God as love is split with the image of the "vengeful God who represents his chosen people." This split has perpetuated a double standard of behavior. God, she wrote, is like Vito Corleone of *The Godfather*, a "marriage of tenderness and violence blended in the patriarchal ideal." Given this image, worshipers feel justified in being intolerant. Thus, we should not be surprised by the numerous examples of fanatical believers who cruelly persecute "those outside the sacred circle." Nor should we be surprised when those who are anointed by society—scientists and leaders, for example—are given the blessings of priests for inventing and using napalm and the like to perpetrate atrocities.

Now, when Daly's view is compacted as it is here, it may perhaps seem like an angry and exaggerated diatribe. But Daly countered that it would surely be unrealistic *not* to believe that the instruments for symbolism and communication, which include the whole theological tradition in world religions, have been formulated by males under the conditions of patriarchy. It is therefore "inherent in these symbolic and linguistic structures that they serve the purposes of patriarchal social arrangements." If further proof is needed, one need merely consider (she said) the blatant misogynism of religious "authorities" from Augustine to Aquinas, Luther, Knox, and Barth, which has "simply been ignored or dismissed as trivial."

The problem, then, Daly said, is how to transform "the collective imagination so that this distortion of the human aspiration to transcendence loses its credibility." The

---

God Is Coming, and She Is Furious

So says the bumper sticker.

Most people who believe in God think of God as, in some sense or another, a male.

But in what sense is God a male? Certainly not in the sense that he possesses male genetic or anatomic features. And it seems doubtful that the qualities we attribute to him are uniquely male. For example, God, it is said, is knowing, loving, caring. But these are not uniquely male characteristics.

Even the qualities associated with God when he is viewed as like an earthly roler are not uniquely male qualities. Queens, too, can be beneficent, just, powerful, and wise rulers. And the concept of God as the creator of the heavens and earth—that concept seems to call to mind nonhuman properties as much as anything else.

So our custom of speaking of God in the masculine voice is largely honorific. We honor God by speaking and thinking of him as a male: God is the best there is; therefore, God is not female or neuter.

But honoring God by referring to him as "he" implies we think there is something inferior about not being a male. If God is defined as male, everything outside maleness is automatically inferior. For this reason, various feminist philosophers have been more than casually interested in the question, Why is God thought to be a male?—and in the possible harmful social consequences of our internalized ideas about **God's gender.**

---

question is how to "cut away the Supreme Phallus": "God"—the word, the image—must be *castrated*. Why, indeed, Daly wrote, must "God" even be a *noun?* Why not a verb—the "most active and dynamic verb of all," the "Verb of Verbs," the verb infinitely more personal than a mere static noun, the verb that conveys that God is "Be-ing"? "God," as an intransitive verb, she wrote, would not be conceived as an object—which implies limitation—for God as Be-ing is contrasted only with nonbeing.

But the confrontation with "the structured evil of patriarchy" must go beyond mere tinkering with the language used to talk about God, she said. To stop at that level, she wrote, would be to trivialize the "deep problem of human becoming in women."

And just what *is* the "deep problem of becoming"? It is a striving toward psychic wholeness, toward self-realization, toward self-transcendence—becoming who we really are. This becoming of women requires existential courage, Daly wrote, to confront the experience of *nothingness*. It is a "radical confrontation" with nothingness. We are all threatened by nonbeing, she wrote, and the only solution is self-actualization—not denial of self. An example of such denial of self provided by Daly is the woman who "singlemindedly accepts the role of housewife." This individual "may to some extent avoid the experience of nothingness, but she also avoids a fuller participation in being which would be her only real security." "Submerged in such a role, she cannot achieve a breakthrough to creativity." The women's revolution must, therefore, ultimately be religious. It must reach "outward and inward toward the God beyond and beneath the gods who have stolen our identity."

According to Daly, three false "demons dressed as God" especially need expurgation: the God of "explanation," who legitimizes suffering as due to God's will; God the Judge, whose chief activity lies in issuing after-death rewards and promises compensation for women's subjugation in this life; and, closely related, God the Judge of Sin, who maintains "false consciences and self-destructive guilt feelings." This last god enforces the rules of the patriarchal game (and is most blatant in arch-conservative religions, Daly wrote).

Does this seem angry? From Daly's perspective, women are dealing with "demonic power relationships" and "structured evil"; therefore, rage is *required* as a positive creative force. Anger, she wrote, "can trigger and sustain movement from the experience of nothingness to recognition of participation in being." According to Daly,

> When women take positive steps to move out of patriarchal space and time, there is a surge of new life. I would analyze this as participation in God the Verb who cannot be broken down simply into past, present, and future time, since God is form-destroying, form-creating, transforming power that makes all things new.

Intelligent Design or Evolution?

The publication in 1859 of Charles Darwin's *On the Origin of Species by Means of Natural Selection; or, the Preservation of Favoured Races in the Struggle for Life* (usually referred to as *On the Origin of Species*) provoked responses from within Catholicism and conservative Protestantism. Pope Pius IX declared evolution a heresy in 1870 (though in 1996, in a message to the Pontifical Academy of Sciences, Pope John Paul II observed that, while the occurrence of evolution is more than a theory, "theories of evolution which, in accordance with the philosophies inspiring them, consider the mind as emerging from the forces of living matter . . . are incompatible with the truth about man"). In 1874 Princeton theologian Charles Hodge, a Presbyterian, asked, "What is Darwinism?" and answered, "It is atheism."

Historian George Marsden, writing in 1984, found that, twenty years after the publication of *On the Origin of Species*, Bible-believing American Protestant scientists and even conservative theologians did not make opposition to all forms of evolution a necessary test of faith. But reconciliationist positions began to lose favor in the evangelical community after the Scopes "monkey trial," July 10–21, 1925, in Dayton, Tennessee.

Many fundamentalists retreated to a Christian subculture. Bible schools flourished, and many taught human origins from a perspective dubbed "creation-science."

Contemporary defenders include John D. Morris of the Institute for Creation Research (ICR) in El Cajon, California, who wrote in a 1992 newsletter article that evolution "embraces strict naturalism, an anti-God philosophy, and results in a denial of the major doctrines of Scripture. . . . If no supernatural agency has been at work throughout history, then creation is dead. But if evolutionists even allow a spark of supernatural design in history, then evolution is dead, for evolution necessarily relies on solely natural processes."

In the 1990s, three controversial books were published, spearheading the intelligent design movement. **Intelligent design** is the idea that a complete explanation of the universe requires positing an intelligent designer. The three books were: *Darwin on Trial* (first published in 1991) by Phillip E. Johnson (a graduate of Harvard University who has taught law at University of California, Berkeley, for more than three decades); *Darwin's Black Box: The Biochemical Challenge to Evolution* (1996) by Lehigh University biochemist Michael J. Behe; and *Intelligent Design: The Bridge between Science and Theology* (1999) by William A. Dembski, holder of a doctorate in mathematics from the University of Chicago and a doctorate in philosophy from the University of Illinois at Chicago, whose more technical treatment of the subject had been published by Cambridge University Press the year before.

Johnson, Behe, and Dembski, leaders of the intelligent design movement, rejected the "young earth" position of ICR in favor of a more academically engaged critique of Darwinian foundations. In an essay published in the *New York Times* in 1996, Behe wrote that the theory of evolution founders in explaining cellular development. "Many cellular systems are what I term 'irreducibly complex.' That means the system needs several components before it can work properly. An everyday example of irreducible complexity is a mousetrap, built of several pieces (platform, hammer, spring and so on). Such a system probably cannot be put together in a Darwinian manner, gradually improving its function. You can't catch a mouse with just the platform and then catch a few more by adding the spring. All the pieces have to be in place before you catch any mice."

For Dembski, irreducible complexity is a specific case of a more general understanding of how to detect intelligent, as opposed to mere natural, causes: "Whenever we infer design, we must establish three things: *contingency, complexity* and *specification*. Contingency ensures that the object in question is not the result of an automatic and therefore unintelligent process that had no choice in its production. Complexity ensures that the object is not so simple that it can readily be explained by chance. Finally, specification ensures that the object exhibits the type of pattern characteristic of intelligence."

Evolutionary biologist Richard Dawkins, in *The Blind Watchmaker* (1986) and other works, responded that any appearance of purpose in biological systems is merely the result of time and chance. "To 'tame' chance means to break down the very improbable into less improbable small components arranged in series. No matter how improbable it is that an X could have arisen from a Y in a single step, it is always possible to conceive of a series of infinitesimally graded intermediates between them. However improbable a large-scale change may be, smaller changes are less improbable."

Johnson, focused on a critique of evolutionism's materialist assumptions, what he called "methodological naturalism." The chemical or physical laws of nature, he wrote, "produce simple repetitive order, and chance produces meaningless disorder. When combined, law and chance work against each other to prevent the emergence of a meaningful sequence. In all human experience, only intelligent agency can write an encyclopedia or computer program." Dawkins's blind watchmaker (natural selection and mutation) cannot, Johnson insisted, create complex *new* genetic information. Johnson also presented a version of the claim that materialism is self-refuting. (The argument was popularized by the British writer C. S. Lewis and adopted by the American analytic philosopher Alvin Plantinga.) Johnson asked sarcastically, "If unthinking matter causes the thoughts the materialists *don't* like, then what causes the thoughts they *do* like?" This takes us back to the problem of explanation. The materialist must explain human reason, and indeed the existence of anything at all, in terms of "unthinking matter." If, for Dawkins, the appearance of purpose in evolution is merely an illusion, then what is the status of purposive human reason? If that, too, is an illusion, then there is no good reason to accept the argument. If it is not illusion, how can Dawkins explain the rise of genuine purpose or meaning from a purposeless flow of cause and effect?

430   Part Three · *Philosophy of Religion: Reason and Faith*

In recent years, proponents of intelligent design and creationism have won and lost battles to make inroads in public education. Most notably, in 1999, the Kansas Board of Education, reflecting the views of its conservative majority, wrote new state science standards that ushered creationism back into mainstream debate. The board mandated the teaching of so-called microevolution (changes within species) as illustrative of the working of natural selection. But the teaching of macroevolution (the origin of new organs or species) was made optional at the district level. In the revised document, science was no longer defined as human activity that seeks natural explanations but as one that seeks logical explanations.

Two years later, however, in 2001, after an election that changed its composition, the Kansas school board reversed its earlier course. Evolution was reinstated "as a broad, unifying theoretical framework in biology." But then elections in 2002 and 2004 changed the board again, and it again became more conservative. In 2005, the board approved science standards declaring that basic Darwinian theory is challenged by fossil evidence and molecular biology and rewrote the definition of science so that it was no longer limited to the search for natural explanations. The vote was regarded as a victory for advocates of intelligent design. But in the summer of 2006, when five of the ten seats on the board were up for election in the state's primary election, the conservatives who had approved the standards again lost control of the Board of Education.

In another famous school board case, in October 2004 the board of the Dover (Pennsylvania) Area School District, about twenty-five miles from Philadelphia, became the first in the nation to require high school science teachers to teach the concept of intelligent design as an alternative to the theory of evolution. The next month, however, voters in the district ousted the eight school board members who were up for reelection. And right after that, in December, eleven parents filed a lawsuit challenging the policy. U.S. District Judge John Jones, an appointee of President George W. Bush (who backed the teaching of intelligent design) ruled that teaching intelligent design would violate the constitutional separation of church and state. Intelligent design, Jones held, is an untestable hypothesis grounded in religion and has no place in the science classroom. He described the school board's decision as "breathtaking inanity" and those on the board who supported it as an "ill-informed faction."

In 2009, the Texas Board of Education made changes in the language in the state's curriculum that are thought to make it harder for creationism to be taught in Texas public schools.

God, the Fine-Tuner

In a recent book, Martin Rees, the Royal Astronomer of England, identifies six numbers that are a "recipe for the universe." $\mathcal{N}$, for example, represents the strength of the forces that hold atoms together divided by the force of gravity between them. This and the other five numbers have an unusual property: they are precisely tuned for our universe to be. If any of them were the teensiest bit different, the universe could not have existed and observers would not be here to talk about them.[2]

---

[2] Martin Rees, *Just Six Numbers* (New York, Basic Books, 2000), pp. 1–4. See also John Leslie's *Universes* (New York: Routledge, 1989), Chapters 2 and 3.

On the face of it, it might seem unlikely that such remarkable fine-tuning could happen simply by chance. It is as if the six fundamental control knobs of the universe were set exactly right for stars, life, and observers to evolve. The knobs seem to have been set for our eventual arrival. The best explanation of this fine-tuning, according to some philosophers and scientists, is that the universe was created by a cosmic intelligence.

At the end of this chapter is an excerpt from Richard Dawkins's book, *The God Delusion,* in which Dawkins considers this fine-tuning argument.

Who Needs Reasons for Believing in God?

For a belief to be rational, must we have supporting evidence for its truth? Maybe not, if the belief is a **basic belief,** a belief that is not inferred from evidence or from other beliefs but rather itself provides the rational foundation from which other beliefs are derived. For example, it seems rational to believe that there is an external world, that the past existed, and that other people have minds. Yet do we believe these things on the basis of evidence? On the contrary (it might be argued), we accept these beliefs just straight out and without evidence. Further, it is because we accept these things that we can even talk of evidence and rational inference in the first place. For example, unless we assume there was a past, the "evidence" we have that the car *now* has a flat because it ran over a nail does not make any sense— because without a past, there was no past for the car to have done anything.

Contemporary analytic philosopher **Alvin Plantinga** [PLAN-tin-guh] (1932–) has argued that the theist may accept the belief in God as a "basic belief," a belief that it is rational to hold without supporting evidence and that is foundational for the entire system of the theist's beliefs. Rationally speaking, the theist has the right, Plantinga suggests, to *start from* belief in God. The belief need not be an *end product* of justification and inference.

Interested? An easy-to-read essay by Plantinga titled "Advice to Christian Philosophers" may be found in the journal *Faith and Philosophy,* vol. 1, no. 3 (July 1984), pp. 253–271.

SELECTION 13.1

Proslogion*

St. Anselm

[*This passage is St. Anselm's famous ontological argument.*]

* From *Problems in Philosophical Inquiry,* 1st edition, by Julius R. Weinberg and Keith E. Yandell. Copyright © 1971. Reprinted with permission of Wadsworth, a division of Thomson Learning: www.thomsonrights.com. Fax 800 730-2215.

Lord, who gives understanding to faith give to me as much as you deem suitable, that I may understand that You are as we believe You to be, and that You are what we believe You to be. Now we believe that You are something than which nothing greater can be thought. But perhaps there is no such nature since "the fool hath said in his heart: There is no

God"? But surely this very same fool, when he hears what I say: "something than which nothing greater can be thought," understands what he hears, and what he understands is in his mind, even if he does not understand that it exists. For it is one thing for a thing to be in the mind, but something else to understand that a thing exists. For when a painter pre-thinks what is about to be made, he has it in mind but he does not yet understand that it exists because he has not yet made it. But when he has already painted it, he both has it in his mind and also understands that it exists because he has already made it. Hence, even the fool is convinced that something exists in the mind than which nothing greater can be thought, because when he hears this he understands and whatever is understood is in the mind. But surely that than which a greater cannot be thought cannot exist merely in the mind. For if it exists merely in the mind, it can be thought to exist also in reality which is greater. So if that than which a greater cannot be thought exists merely in the mind, that very same thing than which a greater cannot be thought is something than which a greater can be thought. But surely this cannot be. Hence, without doubt, something than which a greater cannot be thought exists both in the mind and in reality.

Indeed, it exists so truly that it cannot be thought not to be. For something can be thought to exist which cannot be thought not to exist, which is greater than what can be thought not to exist. So, if that than which a greater cannot be thought can be thought not to exist, that very thing than which a greater cannot be thought, is not that than which a greater cannot be thought; which is impossible. So there exists so truly something than which a greater cannot be thought that it cannot be thought not to exist.

You are that very thing, Lord our God.

SELECTION 13.2

Summa Theologica*

St. Thomas Aquinas

[*Aquinas's five proofs of God's existence are set forth here in his Five Ways.*]

The existence of God can be proved in five ways.

The first and more manifest way is the argument from motion. It is certain, and evident to our senses, that in the world some things are in motion. Now whatever is moved is moved by another, for nothing can be moved except it is in potentiality to that towards which it is moved; whereas a thing moves inasmuch as it is in act. For motion is nothing else than the reduction of something from potentiality to actuality. But nothing can be reduced from potentiality to actuality, except by something in a state of actuality. Thus that which is actually hot, as fire, makes wood, which is potentially hot, to be actually hot, and thereby moves and changes it. Now it is not possible that the same thing should be at once in actuality and potentiality in the same respect, but only in different respects. For what is actually hot cannot simultaneously be potentially hot; but it is simultaneously potentially cold. It is therefore impossible that in the same respect and in the same way a thing should be both mover and moved, *i.e.*, that it should move itself. Therefore, whatever is moved must be moved by another. If that by which it is moved be itself moved, then this also must needs be moved by another, and that by another again. But this cannot go on to infinity, because then there would be no first mover, and, consequently, no other mover, seeing that subsequent movers move only inasmuch as they are moved by the first mover; as the staff moves only because it is moved by the hand. Therefore it is necessary to arrive at a first mover, moved by no other; and this everyone understands to be God.

The second way is from the nature of efficient cause. In the world of sensible things we find there is an order of efficient causes. There is no case known (neither is it, indeed, possible) in which a thing is found to be the efficient cause of itself; for so it would be prior to itself which is impossible. Now in efficient causes it is not possible to go on to infinity, because in all efficient causes following in order, the first is the cause of the intermediate cause, and the intermediate is the cause of the ultimate cause, whether the intermediate cause be several, or one only. Now to take away the cause is to take away the effect. Therefore, if there be no first cause among efficient causes, there will be no ultimate, nor any intermediate, cause. But if in efficient causes it is possible to go on to infinity, there will be no first efficient cause, neither will there be an ultimate effect, nor any intermediate efficient causes; all of which is plainly false. Therefore it is necessary to admit a first efficient cause, to which everyone gives the name of God.

The third way is taken from possibility and necessity, and runs thus. We find in nature things that are possible to be and not to be, since they are found to be generated, and to be corrupted, and consequently, it is possible for them to be and not to be. But it is impossible for these always to exist, for that which can not-be at some time is not. Therefore, if everything can not-be, then at one time there was nothing in existence. Now if this were true, even now there would be nothing in existence, because that which does not exist begins to exist only through something already existing. Therefore, if at one time nothing was in existence, it would have been impossible for anything to have begun to exist; and thus even now nothing would be in existence—which is absurd. Therefore, not all beings are merely possible, but there must exist something the existence of which is necessary. But every necessary thing either has its necessity caused by another, or not. Now it is impossible to go on to infinity in necessary things which have their necessity caused by another, as has been already proved

in regard to efficient causes. Therefore we cannot but admit the existence of some being having of itself its own necessity, and not receiving it from another, but rather causing in others their necessity. This all men speak of as God.

The fourth way is taken from the gradation to be found in things. Among beings there are some more and some less good, true, noble, and the like. But *more* and *less* are predicated of different things according as they resemble in their different ways something which is the maximum, as a thing is said to be hotter according as it more nearly resembles that which is hottest; so that there is something which is truest, something best, something noblest, and consequently, something which is most being, for those things that are greatest in truth are greatest in being. . . . Now the maximum in any genus is the cause of all in that genus, as fire, which is the maximum of heat, is the cause of all hot things, as is said in the same book. Therefore there must also be something which is to all beings the cause of their being, goodness, and every other perfection; and this we call God.

The fifth way is taken from the governance of the world. We see that things which lack knowledge, such as natural bodies, act for an end, and this is evident from their acting always, or nearly always, in the same way, so as to obtain the best result. Hence it is plain that they achieve their end, not fortuitously, but designedly. Now whatever lacks knowledge cannot move towards an end, unless it be directed by some being endowed with knowledge and intelligence; as the arrow is directed by the archer. Therefore some intelligent being exists by whom all natural things are directed to their end; and this being we call God.

SELECTION 13.3

Monadology*

G. W. Leibniz

[*Leibniz explains the principle of sufficient reason and then uses the principle to prove that God exists.*]

* From G. W. Leibniz, *Philosophical Texts*, translated by Richard Francks and R.S. Woolhouse, with introduction and notes by R. S. Woolhouse (Oxford: Oxford University Press, 1998), pp. 272–273. By permission of Oxford University Press.

. . . 31. Our reasonings are founded on two great *principles: the principle of contradiction*, in virtue of which we judge to be false anything that involves contradiction, and as true whatever is opposed or contradictory to what is false. . . .

32. And that *of sufficient reason*, in virtue of which we hold that no fact could ever be true or

existent, no statement correct, unless there were a sufficient reason why it was thus and not otherwise—even though those reasons will usually not be knowable by us. . . .

33. There are also two kinds of *truth:* those of *reasoning,* and those of *fact.* Truths of reasoning are necessary, and their opposite is impossible; those of fact are contingent, and their opposite is possible. When a truth is necessary, the reason for it can be founded by analysis, by resolving it into simpler ideas and truths until we arrive at the basic ones. . . .

34. Thus mathematicians use analysis to reduce speculative *theorems* and practical *canons* to *definitions, axioms,* and *postulates.*

35. And finally there are the simple ideas, which cannot be given a definition; and there are axioms and postulates—in a word, *basic principles,* which can never be proved, but which also have no need of proof: these are *identical propositions,* the opposite of which contains an explicit contradiction.

36. But a *sufficient reason* must also be found for *contingent truths,* or *truths of fact*—for the series of things which fills the universe of created things, that is. Here the resolution into particular reasons could be continued endlessly, because of the immense variety of things in nature, and because of the infinite divisibility of bodies. There are an infinite number of shapes and of motions, present and past, which play a part in the efficient cause of my present writing; and there are an infinite number of tiny inclinations and dispositions of my soul, present and past, which play a part in its final cause. . . .

37. But since all this detail only involves other prior and more detailed contingencies, each one of which also stands in need of a similar analysis in order to give an explanation of it, we are no further forward: the sufficient or final reason must lie outside the succession or *series* in this detailed specification of contingencies, however infinite it may be.

38. And that is why the final reason for things must be in a necessary substance, in which the detailed specification of changes is contained only eminently, as in their source; and that is what we call *God.* . . .

39. Now, since this substance is a sufficient reason for all this detail, which is interconnected throughout, *there is only one God, and that God is enough.*

40. We can also see that this supreme substance, which is unique, universal, and necessary (because there is nothing outside it which is independent of it, and it is a straightforward consequence of possible being), must be incapable of limits, and must contain fully as much reality as is possible.

41. From which it follows that God is absolutely perfect, since *perfection* is nothing but the total amount of positive reality taken in the precise sense, leaving aside the limitations or boundaries of things that have them. And there, in something which has no boundaries—in God, that is—perfection is absolutely infinite. . . .

42. It also follows that created things have their perfections from the influence of God, but that they have their imperfections from their own natures, which are necessarily bounded. For that is what distinguishes them from God. . . . This original imperfection of created things is shown by the natural inertia of bodies. . . .

SELECTION 13.4

The Gay Science*

Friedrich Nietzsche

[*Nietzsche said, "God is dead." Here he elaborates.*]

The Meaning of Our Cheerfulness

The greatest recent event—that "God is dead," that the belief in the Christian god has become unbelievable—is already beginning to cast its first shadows over Europe. For the few at least, whose eye—the *suspicion* in whose eyes is strong and subtle enough for this spectacle, some sun seems to have set and some ancient and profound trust has been turned into doubt; to them our old world must appear daily more like evening, more mistrustful, stranger, "older." But in the main one may say: The event itself is far too great, too distant, too remote from the multitude's capacity for comprehension even for the tidings of it to be thought of as having *arrived* as yet. Much less may one suppose that many people know as yet *what* this event really means—and how much must collapse now that this faith has been undermined because it was built upon this faith, propped by it, grown into it; for example, the whole of our European morality. This long plenitude and sequence of breakdown, destruction, ruin, and cataclysm that is now impending—who could guess enough of it today to be compelled to play the teacher and advance proclaimer of this monstrous logic of terror, the prophet of a gloom and an eclipse of the sun whose like has probably never yet occurred on earth?

Even we born guessers of riddles who are, as it were, waiting on the mountains, posted between today and tomorrow, stretched in the contradiction between today and tomorrow, we firstlings and premature births of the coming century, to whom the shadows that must soon envelop Europe really *should* have appeared by now—why is it that even we look forward to the approaching gloom without any real sense of involvement and above all without any worry and fear for *ourselves?* Are we perhaps still too much under the impression of the *initial consequences* of this event—and these initial consequences, the consequences for *ourselves*, are quite the opposite of what one might perhaps expect: They are not at all sad and gloomy but rather like a new and scarcely describable kind of light, happiness, relief, exhilaration, encouragement, dawn.

Indeed, we philosophers and "free spirits" feel, when we hear the news that "the old god is dead," as if a new dawn shone on us; our heart overflows with gratitude, amazement, premonitions, expectation. At long last the horizon appears free to us again, even if it should not be bright; at long last our ships may venture out again, venture out to face any danger; all the daring of the lover of knowledge is permitted again; the sea, *our sea*, lies open again; perhaps there has never yet been such an "open sea."

SELECTION 13.5

Theology and Falsification*

Antony Flew

[*In this famous selection, British philosopher Antony Flew challenges those who believe in God to specify what they would accept as evidence that God does not exist or does not love us. Why should a believer try to do this? Flew explains why. In recent years, Flew has expressed more sympathy toward deism.*]

Let us begin with a parable. It is a parable developed from a tale told by John Wisdom in his haunting and revelatory article "Gods." Once upon a time two explorers came upon a clearing in the jungle. In the clearing were growing many flowers and many weeds. One explorer says, "Some gardener must tend this plot." The other disagrees, "There is no gardener." So they pitch their tents and set a watch. No gardener is ever seen. "But perhaps he is an invisible gardener." So they set up a barbed-wire fence. They electrify it. They patrol with bloodhounds. (For they remember how H. G. Wells's "invisible man" could be both smelt and touched though he could not be seen.) But no shrieks ever suggest that some intruder has received a shock. No movements of the wire ever betray an invisible climber. The bloodhounds never give cry. Yet still the Believer is not convinced. "But there is a gardener, invisible, intangible, insensible to electric shocks, a gardener who has no scent and makes no sound, a gardener who comes secretly to look after the garden which he loves." At last the

436   Part Three · *Philosophy of Religion: Reason and Faith*

Sceptic despairs, "But what remains of your original assertion? Just how does what you call an invisible, intangible, eternally elusive gardener differ from an imaginary gardener or even from no gardener at all?"

In this parable we can see how what starts as an assertion, that something exists or that there is some analogy between certain complexes of phenomena, may be reduced step by step to an altogether different status, to an expression perhaps of a "picture preference." The Sceptic says there is no gardener. The Believer says there is a gardener (but invisible, etc.). One man talks about sexual behavior. Another man prefers to talk of Aphrodite (but knows that there is not really a superhuman person additional to, and somehow responsible for, all sexual phenomena). The process of qualification may be checked at any point before the original assertion is completely withdrawn and something of that first assertion will remain (Tautology). Mr. Wells's invisible man could not, admittedly, be seen, but in all other respects he was a man like the rest of us. But though the process of qualification may be, and of course usually is, checked in time, it is not always judiciously so halted. Someone may dissipate his assertion completely without noticing that he has done so. A fine brash hypothesis may thus be killed by inches, the death by a thousand qualifications.

And in this, it seems to me, lies the peculiar danger, the endemic evil, of theological utterance. Take such utterances as "God has a plan," "God created the world," "God loves us as a father loves his children." They look at first sight very much like assertions, vast cosmological assertions. Of course, this is no sure sign that they either are, or are intended to be, assertions. But let us confine ourselves to the cases where those who utter such sentences intend them to express assertions. (Merely remarking parenthetically that those who intend or interpret such utterances as crypto-commands, expressions of wishes, disguised ejaculations, concealed ethics, or as anything else but assertions, are unlikely to succeed in making them either properly orthodox or practically effective.)

Now to assert that such and such is the case is necessarily equivalent to denying that such and such is not the case. Suppose then that we are in doubt as to what someone who gives vent to an utterance is asserting, or suppose that, more radically, we are sceptical as to whether he is really asserting anything at all, one way of trying to understand (or perhaps it will be to expose) his utterance is to attempt to find what he would regard as counting against, or as being incompatible with, its truth. For if the utterance is indeed an assertion, it will necessarily be equivalent to a denial of the negation of that assertion. And anything which would count against the assertion, or which would induce the speaker to withdraw it and to admit that it had been mistaken, must be part of (or the whole of) the meaning of the negation of that assertion. And to know the meaning of the negation of an assertion is, as near as makes no matter, to know the meaning of that assertion. And if there is nothing which a putative assertion denies then there is nothing which it asserts either: and so it is not really an assertion. When the Sceptic in the parable asked the Believer, "Just how does what you call an invisible, intangible, eternally elusive gardener differ from an imaginary gardener or even from no gardener at all?" he was suggesting that the Believer's earlier statement had been so eroded by qualification that it was no longer an assertion at all.

Now it often seems to people who are not religious as if there was no conceivable event or series of events the occurrence of which would be admitted by sophisticated religious people to be a sufficient reason for conceding "There wasn't a God after all" or "God does not really love us then." Someone tells us that God loves us as a father loves his children. We are reassured. But then we see a child dying of inoperable cancer of the throat. His earthly father is driven frantic in his efforts to help, but his Heavenly Father reveals no obvious sign of concern. Some qualification is made—God's love is "not a merely human love" or it is "an inscrutable love," perhaps—and we realize that such sufferings are quite compatible with the truth of the assertion that "God loves us as a father (but, of course . . .)." We are reassured again. But then perhaps we ask: what is this assurance of God's (appropriately qualified) love worth, what is this apparent guarantee really a guarantee against? Just what would have to happen not merely (morally and wrongly) to tempt but also (logically and rightly) to entitle us to say "God does not love us" or even "God does not exist?" I therefore put to the succeeding symposiasts the simple central question: "What would have to occur or to have occurred to constitute for you a disproof of the love of, or of the existence of, God?"

SELECTION 13.6

After the Death of God the Father*

Mary Daly

[*How is "God" an instrument of oppression? How do religious texts dehumanize women? Mary Daly offers her arguments in* Beyond God the Father, *from which this brief passage is excerpted.*]

The biblical and popular image of God as a great patriarch in heaven, rewarding and punishing according to his mysterious and seemingly arbitrary will, has dominated the imagination of millions over thousands of years. The symbol of the Father God, spawned in the human imagination and sustained as plausible by patriarchy, has in turn rendered service to this type of society by making its mechanisms for the oppression of women appear right and fitting. If God in "his" heaven is a father ruling "his" people, then it is in the "nature" of things and according to divine plan and the order of the universe that society be male-dominated.

Within this context a mystification of roles takes place: the husband dominating his wife represents God "himself." The images and values of a given society have been projected into the realm of dogmas and "Articles of Faith," and these in turn justify the social structures which have given rise to them and which sustain their plausibility. The belief system becomes hardened and objectified, seeming to have an unchangeable independent existence and validity of its own. It resists social change that would rob it of its plausibility. Despite the vicious circle, however, change can occur in society, and ideologies can die, though they die hard.

As the women's movement begins to have its effect upon the fabric of society, transforming it from patriarchy into something that never existed before—into a diarchal situation that is radically new—it can become the greatest single challenge to the major religions of the world, Western and Eastern. Beliefs and values that have held sway for thousands of years will be questioned as never before. This rev-olution may well be also the greatest single hope for survival of spiritual consciousness on this planet. . . .

Beyond the Inadequate God

The various theologies that hypostatize transcendence, that is, those which in one way or another objectify "God" as *a being*, thereby attempt in a self-contradictory way to envisage transcendent reality as finite. "God" then functions to legitimate the existing social, economic, and political status quo, in which women and other victimized groups are subordinate.

"God" can be used oppressively against women in a number of ways. First, it occurs in an overt manner when theologians proclaim women's subordination to be God's will. This of course has been done throughout the centuries, and residues remain in varying degrees of subtlety and explicitness in the writings of twentieth-century thinkers such as Barth, Bonhoeffer, Reinhold Niebuhr, and Teilhard de Chardin.

Second, even in the absence of such explicitly oppressive justification, the phenomenon is present when one-sex symbolism for God and for the human relationship to God is used. The following passage illustrates the point:

> To believe that God is Father is to become aware of oneself not as a stranger, not as an outsider or an alienated person, but as a son who belongs or a person appointed to a marvelous destiny, which he shares with the whole community. To believe that God is Father means to be able to say "we" in regard to all men.

A woman whose consciousness has been aroused can say that such language makes her aware of herself as a stranger, as an outsider, as an alienated person, not as a daughter who belongs or who is appointed to a marvelous destiny. She cannot belong to *this* without assenting to her own lobotomy.

Third, even when the basic assumptions of God-language appear to be nonsexist, and when language is somewhat purified of fixation upon maleness, it is damaging and implicitly compatible with sexism if it encourages detachment from the

---

* Author's footnotes have been omitted. From *Beyond God the Father* by Mary Daly. Copyright © 1973, 1985 by Mary Daly. Reprinted by permission of Beacon Press, Boston.

438   Part Three · *Philosophy of Religion: Reason and Faith*

reality of the human struggle against oppression in its concrete manifestations. That is, the lack of explicit relevance of intellection to the fact of oppression in its precise forms, such as sexual hierarchy, is itself oppressive. This is the case when theologians write long treatises on creative hope, political theology, or revolution without any specific acknowledgment of or application to the problem of sexism or other specific forms of injustice. Such irrelevance is conspicuous in the major works of "theologians of hope" such as Moltmann, Pannenberg, and Metz. This is not to say that the vision of creative eschatology is completely irrelevant, but that it lacks specific grounding in the concrete experiences of the oppressed. The theorizing then has a quality of unreality. Perhaps an obvious reason for this is that the theologians themselves have not shared in the experience of oppression and therefore write from the privileged distance of those who have at best a "knowledge about" the subject. . . .

Women's Liberation and Revelatory Courage
I have already indicated that it would be unrealistic to dismiss the fact that the symbolic and linguistic instruments for communication—which include essentially the whole theological tradition in world religions—have been formulated by males under the conditions of patriarchy. It is therefore inherent in these symbolic and linguistic structures that they serve the purposes of patriarchal social arrangements. Even the usual and accepted means of theological dissent have been restricted in such a way

that only some questions have been allowed to arise. Many questions that are of burning importance to women now simply have not occurred in the past (and to a large extent in the present) to those with "credentials" to do theology. Others may have been voiced timidly but quickly squelched as stupid, irrelevant, or naïve. Therefore, attempts by women theologians now merely to "up-date" or to reform theology within acceptable patterns of question-asking are not likely to get very far.

Moreover, within the context of the prevailing social climate it has been possible for scholars to be aware of the most crudely dehumanizing texts concerning women in the writings of religious "authorities" and theologians—from Augustine to Aquinas, to Luther, to Knox, to Barth—and at the same time to treat their unverified opinions on far more imponderable matters with utmost reverence and respect. That is, the blatant misogynism of these men has not been the occasion of a serious credibility gap even for those who have disagreed on this "point." It has simply been ignored or dismissed as trivial. By contrast, in the emerging consciousness of women this context is beginning to be perceived in its full significance and as deeply relevant to the worldview in which such "authorities" have seen other seemingly unrelated subjects, such as the problem of God. Hence the present awakening of the hitherto powerless sex demands an explosion of creative imagination that can withstand the disapproval of orthodoxy and overreach the boundaries cherished by conventional minds.

SELECTION 13.7

The God Delusion*

Richard Dawkins

[*British science expositor Richard Dawkins here considers the "Anthropic Principle," according to which, because observers of the universe exist, the universe had to be such as to permit their eventual emergence.*]

* From *The God Delusion* by Richard Dawkins, New York, Houghton Mifflin Company, 2006, 169–180.

**The Anthropic Principle:
Cosmological Version**
We live not only on a friendly planet but also in a friendly universe. It follows from the fact of our existence that the laws of physics must be friendly enough to allow life to arise. It is no accident that when we look at the night sky we see stars, for stars are a necessary prerequisite for the existence of most of the chemical elements, and without chemistry

there could be no life. Physicists have calculated that, if the laws and constants of physics had been even slightly different, the universe would have developed in such a way that life would have been impossible. Different physicists put it in different ways, but the conclusion is always much the same.[1] Martin Rees, in *Just Six Numbers*, lists six fundamental constants, which are believed to hold all around the universe. Each of these six numbers is finely tuned in the sense that, if it were slightly different, the universe would be comprehensively different and presumably unfriendly to life.[2] . . .

I won't go through the rest of Rees's six numbers. The bottom line for each of them is the same. The actual number sits in a Goldilocks band of values outside which life would not have been possible. How should we respond to this? Yet again, we have the theist's answer on the one hand, and the anthropic answer on the other. The theist says that God, when setting up the universe, tuned the fundamental constants of the universe so that each one lay in its Goldilocks zone for the production of life. It is as though God had six knobs that he could twiddle, and he carefully tuned each knob to its Goldilocks value. As ever, the theist's answer is deeply unsatisfying, because it leaves the existence of God unexplained. A God capable of calculating the Goldilocks values for the six numbers would have to be at least as improbable as the finely tuned combination of numbers itself, and that's very improbable indeed. This is exactly the premise of the whole discussion we are having. It follows that the theist's answer has utterly failed to make any headway towards solving the problem at hand. I see no alternative but to dismiss it, while at the same time marvelling at the number of people who can't see

the problem and seem genuinely satisfied by the 'Divine Knob-Twiddler' argument. . . .

Hard-nosed physicists say that the six knobs were never free to vary in the first place. When we finally reach the long-hoped-for Theory of Everything, we shall see that the six key numbers depend upon each other, or on something else as yet unknown, in ways that we today cannot imagine. The six numbers may turn out to be no freer to vary than is the ratio of a circle's circumference to its diameter. It will turn out that there is only one way for a universe to be. Far from God being needed to twiddle six knobs, there are no knobs to twiddle.

Other physicists (Martin Rees himself would be an example) find this unsatisfying, and I think I agree with them. It is indeed perfectly plausible that there is only one way for a universe to be. But why did that one way have to be such a set-up for our eventual evolution? Why did it have to be the kind of universe which seems almost as if, in the words of the theoretical physicist Freeman Dyson, it 'must have known we were coming'? The philosopher John Leslie uses the analogy of a man sentenced to death by firing squad. It is just possible that all ten men of the firing squad will miss their victim. With hindsight, the survivor who finds himself in a position to reflect upon his luck can cheerfully say, 'Well, obviously they all missed, or I wouldn't be here thinking about it.' But he could still, forgivably, wonder why they all missed, and toy with the hypothesis that they were bribed, or drunk.

This objection can be answered by the suggestion, which Martin Rees himself supports, that there are many universes, co-existing like bubbles of foam, in a 'multiverse' (or 'megaverse,' as Leonard Susskind prefers to call it).[3] The laws and constants of any one universe, such as our observable universe, are by-laws. The multiverse as a whole has a plethora of alternative sets of by-laws. The anthropic principle kicks in to explain that we have to be in one of those universes (presumably a minority) whose by-laws happened to be propitious to our eventual evolution and hence contemplation of the problem. . . .

It is tempting to think (and many have succumbed) that to postulate a plethora of universes is a profligate luxury which should not be allowed. If

---

[1] The physicist Victor Stenger (in e.g. *God, the Failed Hypothesis*) dissents from this consensus, and is unpersuaded that the physical laws and constants are particularly friendly to life. Nevertheless, I shall bend over backwards to accept the 'friendly universe' consensus, in order to show that, in any case, it cannot be used to support theism.

[2] I say 'presumably,' partly because we don't know how different alien forms of life might be, and partly because it is possible that we make a mistake if we consider only the consequences of changing one constant at a time. Could there be other *combinations* of values of the six numbers which would turn out to be friendly to life, in ways that we do not discover if we consider them only one at a time? Nevertheless, I shall proceed, for simplicity, as though we really do have a big problem to explain in the apparent fine-tuning of the fundamental constants.

[3] Susskind (2006) gives a splendid advocacy of the anthropic principle in the megaverse. He says the idea is hated by most physicists. I can't understand why. I think it is beautiful—perhaps because my consciousness has been raised by Darwin.

we are going to permit the extravagance of a multiverse, so the argument runs, we might as well be hung for a sheep as a lamb and allow a God. Aren't they both equally uparsimonious ad hoc hypotheses, and equally unsatisfactory? People who think that have not had their consciousness raised by natural selection. The key difference between the genuinely extravagant God hypothesis and the apparently extravagant multiverse hypothesis is one of statistical improbability. The multiverse, for all that it is extravagant, is simple. God, or any intelligent, decision-taking, calculating agent, would have to be highly improbable in the very same statistical sense as the entities he is supposed to explain. The multiverse may seem extravagant in sheer *number* of universes. But if each one of those universes is simple in its fundamental laws, we are still not postulating anything highly improbable. The very opposite has to be said of any kind of intelligence.

Some physicists are known to be religious (Russell Stannard and the Reverend John Polkinghorne are the two British examples I have mentioned). Predictably, they seize upon the improbability of the physical constants all being tuned in their more or less narrow Goldilocks zones, and suggest that there must be a cosmic intelligence who deliberately did the tuning. I have already dismissed all such suggestions as raising bigger problems than they solve. But what attempts have theists made to reply? How do they cope with the argument that any God capable of designing a universe, carefully and foresightfully tuned to lead to our evolution, must be a supremely complex and improbable entity who needs an even bigger explanation than the one he is supposed to provide?

The theologian Richard Swinburne, as we have learned to expect, thinks he has an answer to this problem, and he expounds it in his book *Is There a God?* He begins by showing that his heart is in the right place by convincingly demonstrating why we should always prefer the simplest hypothesis that fits the facts. Science explains complex things in terms of the interactions of simpler things, ultimately the interactions of fundamental particles. I (and I dare say you) think it a beautifully simple idea that all things are made of fundamental particles which, although exceedingly numerous, are drawn from a small, finite set of *types* of particle. If we are sceptical, it is likely to be because we think the idea too simple. But for Swinburne it is not simple at all, quite the reverse.

Given that the number of particles of any one type, say electrons, is large, Swinburne thinks it too much of a coincidence that so many should have the same properties. One electron, he could stomach. But billions and billions of electrons, *all with the same properties*, that is what really excites his incredulity. For him it would be simpler, more natural, less demanding of explanation, if all electrons were different from each other. Worse, no one electron should naturally retain its properties for more than an instant at a time; each should change capriciously, haphazardly and fleetingly from moment to moment. That is Swinburne's view of the simple, native state of affairs. Anything more uniform (what you or I would call more simple) requires a special explanation. 'It is only because electrons and bits of copper and all other material objects have the same powers in the twentieth century as they did in the nineteenth century that things are as they are now.'

Enter God. God comes to the rescue by deliberately and continuously sustaining the properties of all those billions of electrons and bits of copper, and neutralizing their otherwise ingrained inclination to wild and erratic fluctuation. That is why when you've seen one electron you've seen them all; that is why bits of copper all behave like bits of copper, and that is why each electron and each bit of copper stays the same as itself from microsecond to microsecond and from century to century. It is because God constantly keeps a finger on each and every particle, curbing its reckless excesses and whipping it into line with its colleagues to keep them all the same.

But how can Swinburne possibly maintain that this hypothesis of God simultaneously keeping a gazillion fingers on wayward electrons is a *simple* hypothesis? It is, of course, precisely the opposite of simple. Swinburne pulls off the trick to his own satisfaction by a breathtaking piece of intellectual *chutzpah*. He asserts, without justification, that God is only a *single* substance. What brilliant economy of explanatory causes, compared with all those gigazillions of independent electrons all just happening to be the same! . . .

. . . What could be simpler than that?

Well, actually, almost everything. A God capable of continuously monitoring and controlling the individual status of every particle in the universe *cannot* be simple. His existence is going to need a mammoth explanation in its own right. Worse (from the point of view of simplicity), other corners of God's giant consciousness are simultaneously preoccupied with the doings and emotions and prayers of every single human being—and whatever intelligent aliens there might be on other planets in this and 100 billion other galaxies. He even, according to Swinburne, has to decide continuously *not* to intervene miraculously to save us when we get cancer. That would never do, for, 'If God answered most prayers for a relative to recover from cancer, then cancer would no longer be a problem for humans to solve.' And *then* what would we find to do with our time?

Not all theologians go as far as Swinburne. Nevertheless, the remarkable suggestion that the God Hypothesis is *simple* can be found in other modern theological writings. Keith Ward, then Regius Professor of Divinity at Oxford, was very clear on the matter in his 1996 book *God, Chance and Necessity:*

> As a matter of fact, the theist would claim that God is a very elegant, economical and fruitful explanation for the existence of the universe. It is economical because it attributes the existence and nature of absolutely everything in the universe to just one being, an ultimate cause which assigns a reason for the existence of everything, including itself. It is elegant because from one key idea—the idea of the most perfect possible being—the whole nature of God and the existence of the universe can be intelligibly explicated.

Like Swinburne, Ward mistakes what it means to explain something, and he also seems not to understand what it means to say of something that it is simple. I am not clear whether Ward really thinks God is simple, or whether the above passage represented a temporary 'for the sake of argument' exercise. Sir John Polkinghorne, in *Science and Christian Belief,*

quotes Ward's earlier criticism of the thought of Thomas Aquinas: 'Its basic error is in supposing that God is logically simple—simple not just in the sense that his being is indivisible, but in the much stronger sense that what is true of any part of God is true of the whole. It is quite coherent, however, to suppose that God, while indivisible, is internally complex.' Ward gets it right here. Indeed, the biologist Julian Huxley, in 1912, defined complexity in terms of 'heterogeneity of parts,' by which he meant a particular kind of functional indivisibility.

Elsewhere, Ward gives evidence of the difficulty the theological mind has in grasping where the complexity of life comes from. He quotes another theologian-scientist, the biochemist Arthur Peacocke (the third member of my trio of British religious scientists), as postulating the existence in living matter of a 'propensity for increased complexity.' Ward characterizes this as 'some inherent weighting of evolutionary change which favours complexity.' He goes on to suggest that such a bias 'might be some weighting of the mutational process, to ensure that more complex mutations occurred.' Ward is sceptical of this, as well he should be. The evolutionary drive towards complexity comes, in those lineages where it comes at all, not from any inherent propensity for increased complexity, and not from biased mutation. It comes from natural selection: the process which, as far as we know, is the only process ultimately capable of generating complexity out of simplicity. The theory of natural selection is genuinely simple. So is the origin from which it starts. That which it explains, on the other hand, is complex almost beyond telling: more complex than anything we can imagine, save a God capable of designing it.

CHECKLIST

To help you review, here is a checklist of the key philosophers and terms and concepts of this chapter. The brief descriptive sentences summarize the philosophers' leading ideas. Keep in mind that some of these summary statements are oversimplifications of complex positions.

Philosophers

- **St. Anselm**   was the author of the ontological argument.   398

- **St. Thomas Aquinas**   was the author of the Five Ways of proving God's existence.   400

- **Mary Daly**   was a contemporary feminist analyst/critic of traditional conceptions of God.   425

- **René Descartes**   offered three proofs of God, including a streamlined version of the ontological argument.   407

- **Gaunilo,**   a Benedictine monk, was a contemporary of Anselm and a critic of the ontological argument.   399

442   Part Three   · *Philosophy of Religion: Reason and Faith*

- **David Hume,** a religious skeptic, provided classic criticisms of the teleological and cosmological arguments.   413
- **William James** held that it is rationally justifiable to yield to your hope that a God exists.   421
- **Julian of Norwich,** an English anchoress and mystic, argued that we are in God and God is in us. We learn about God by learning about ourselves.   404
- **Immanuel Kant** criticized the ontological, cosmological, and teleological proofs of God and thought that God's existence cannot be proved, yet he believed that God's existence must be assumed by the rational, moral individual.   416
- **Søren Kierkegaard** held that God is beyond reason's grasp, that truth is subjective, and that salvation can be attained only through a leap of faith to Christianity.   419
- **Gottfried Wilhelm, Baron von Leibniz,** proposed one of the most effective versions of the cosmological argument.   410
- **Friedrich Nietzsche** believed that the masses are ruled by a slave morality inculcated by religion, science, and philosophy. His statement "God is dead" meant that there is no rational order, not that people do not believe in God.   420
- **Alvin Plantinga** holds that theists may accept the belief in God as a "basic belief," one that is rational to hold without supporting evidence and that is a foundation for the entire system of the theists' beliefs.   431

Key Terms and Concepts

argument by
  analogy   414
argument from
  design/teleological
  argument   403
basic belief   431
Big Bang   402
cosmological
  argument   402
first mover   400
Five Ways   400
God's gender   427
intelligent
  design   428
leap of faith   419

logical
  positivism   424
monads   410
moral argument   403
necessary being   415
ontological
  argument   398
Pascal's wager   424
principle of sufficient
  reason   410
reductio proof   399
theodicy   411
verifiability
  principle   424
Vienna Circle   424

QUESTIONS FOR DISCUSSION AND REVIEW

1. Explain in your own words Anselm's two ontological proofs of God.

2. What is a *reductio* proof? Give an example other than the one mentioned in the text.

3. Summarize Gaunilo's objection to Anselm's argument. What is Anselm's response to that objection?

4. State, in your own words, Aquinas's first, second, and third ways. Which of these arguments seems to you the soundest, and why?

5. In your own words, state Julian of Norwich's arguments for knowing that God exists, for knowing what God's nature is, and for knowing what God wants of us.

6. Critically evaluate Leibniz's solution to the problem of evil.

7. In your own words, summarize Hume's criticisms of the teleological argument. Are these criticisms sound? Why or why not?

8. Explain Hume's reasoning for remaining skeptical of reports of miracles. Is this reasoning sound?

9. Hume maintained that, if you explain the cause of each event in a series by reference to earlier events in the series, there is no sense in then trying to find a single cause for the entire series of events. Is this right? What does it have to do with the question of God's existence?

10. Does the world/universe—or something in it—give evidence of divine design? Explain.

11. Does the theory of evolution undermine the design argument?

12. Explain James's argument for God. Is it a version of Pascal's wager? Is it sound? Why?

13. Is James correct in saying that you cannot really suspend judgment about God's existence?

14. Is the question of God's existence live and momentous, as James says?

15. Which is "better," to doubt everything that is less than certain or highly probable, or to believe falsehoods?

16. "It is impossible for normal people to believe that free will does not exist. Therefore, it does exist." Evaluate this remark.

17. "Most people believe in God; therefore, God must exist." Evaluate this claim.

18. Is the fact that the world is intelligible evidence of divine design?

19. "He died because God called on him." "The sprinkler stopped working due to fate." Are these claims equally meaningless? Explain. Is the claim "God exists" verifiable or falsifiable? Are any (other) claims made about God verifiable?

20. Assuming there is scientific evidence that the universe had an absolute beginning, does that evidence also prove the existence of God? Explain.

21. "The features of the world add to the probability that God exists but do not automatically make it probable that God exists." Explain this remark.

22. Can you logically believe both that God knows everything and that there is free will? Explain the difficulty.

23. How valid as proof of God's existence are purported eyewitness reports of miracles?

24. "Even assuming that the existence of God explains why there is a world, what explains why there is a God?" Does this question contain a valid criticism of the cosmological proof of God?

25. Would universal acceptance of atheism be morally disastrous for society?

26. In what sense is it legitimate rationally to think of God as male?

SUGGESTED FURTHER READINGS

Anselm, *Basic Writings*, S. N. Deane, trans. (La Salle, Ill.: Open Court, 1974). This work contains Anselm's basic writings, though what we have already given you in this text may well be sufficient for most purposes.

Aquinas, *Basic Writings of Saint Thomas Aquinas*, 2 vols., A. C. Pegis, ed. (New York: Random House, 1945). You have read the Five Ways, but you might also wish to consult the sections of *Summa Theologica* that deal with the nature and attributes of God and also part 1, questions 48 and 49, and the first part of part 2, question 79, for the classical Christian discussion of evil.

D. R. Burrill, ed., *The Cosmological Argument* (Garden City, N.Y.: Doubleday Anchor, 1967). Selected readings on the cosmological arguments, for and against.

John D. Caputo, *Philosophy and Theology* (Nashville, Tenn.: Abingdon Press, 2006). An essay on the way philosophy and theology have interacted in the history of Western thought.

Mary Daly, *Beyond God the Father* (Boston: Beacon Press, 1973). A fiery examination of sexism in theology and religious belief.

A. Flew, *Hume's Philosophy of Belief: A Study of His First Inquiry* (London: Routledge & Kegan Paul, 1961). Contains an analysis of Hume's treatment of the "religious hypothesis."

C. W. Hendel Jr., *Hume Selections* (New York: Scribner's, 1927). See especially pp. 143–282 and 284–401.

J. Hick, "Theology and Verification," in *Theology Today*, vol. 17, no. 1 (April 1960). A response to verificationist attacks on religious language.

W. James, *The Will to Believe and Other Essays in Popular Philosophy*, Frederick H. Burkhardt, ed. (Cambridge, Mass.: Harvard University Press, 1979). James is among the most pleasurable of philosophers to read.

Julian of Norwich, *A Book of Showings to the Anchoress Julian of Norwich*, 2 vols., Colledge and Walsh, eds. (Toronto: Pontifical Institute of Medieval Studies, 1978). The early English version. You have to read it aloud to understand it.

Julian of Norwich, *Revelations of Divine Love*, Clifton Wolters, trans. (Harmondsworth, England: Penguin, 1966, 1985). A good, cheap paperback version of "Showings" in modern English.

I. Kant, *Critique of Practical Reason*, L. W. Beck, trans. (New York: Liberal Arts, 1956). See book II, chapter II, sect. V.

I. Kant, *Critique of Pure Reason*, N. K. Smith, trans. (New York: St. Martin's, 1965). Check the index under "God." The most important material is in the chapter "The Ideal of Pure Reason."

W. Kaufmann, *Nietzsche* (New York: Meridian, 1956). A good introduction to Nietzsche's philosophy.

A. Kenny, *Five Ways: St. Thomas Aquinas's Proofs of God's Existence* (London: Routledge & Kegan Paul, 1969). Good critical discussion of the Five Ways.

G. Leibniz, *Theodicy*, E. M. Huggard, trans., and A. Farrer, ed. (La Salle, Ill.: Open Court, 1952).

J. L. Mackie, *The Miracle of Theism: Arguments For and Against the Existence of God* (Oxford: Clarendon Press, 1982). Excellent commentary on all the traditional proofs of God's existence.

444   Part Three · *Philosophy of Religion: Reason and Faith*

R. J. Moore and B. N. Moore, *The Cosmos, God and Philosophy* (New York: Peter Lang, 1988). Contains discussion of modern science on traditional proofs of God.

W. Paley, *Natural Theology: Selections,* Frederick Ferré, ed. (Indianapolis: Bobbs-Merrill, 1963). There is more to Paley than his famous stone and watch analogy, as the reader of this book will discover.

Alvin Plantinga, "Advice to Christian Philosophers," *Faith and Philosophy,* vol. 1, no. 3 (July 1984), pp. 253–271. Plantinga sets forth the idea that a belief in God may be a "basic belief."

James D. Proctor, ed., *Science, Religion and Human Experience* (New York: Oxford University Press, 2005). Essays on the ongoing conflict between science and religious belief.

Philip L. Quinn and Charles Taliaferro, *A Companion to Philosophy of Religion* (Malden, Mass.: Blackwell, 2002). A survey of the main issues and standpoints regarding the philosophy of religion.

B. Russell and F. C. Copleston, "The Existence of God: A Debate between Bertrand Russell and Father F. C. Copleston." This lively debate touches on several lines of proof of God, and Copleston's version of Leibniz's cosmological argument is pretty effectively worded. The debate has been anthologized in many places. See, e.g., E. L. Miller, *Philosophical and Religious Issues: Classical and Contemporary Statements* (Encino, Calif.: Dickenson, 1971).

Richard Swinburne, *The Existence of God* (New York: Oxford University Press, 1991). This edition contains a response to powerful criticisms by J. L. Mackie and considers the evidential force of recent scientific discoveries.

Anthony C. Thiselton, *A Concise Encyclopedia of the Philosophy of Religion* (Oxford: Oneworld Publications, 2002). Entries cover the issues and concepts relevant for religious philosophy.

Mary Ellen Waithe, *A History of Women Philosophers,* vol. 2, *Medieval Women Philosophers, 500–1600* (Dordrecht, Boston, and London: Kluwer Academic Publishers, 1989). Includes an article on Julian of Norwich by Elisabeth Evasdaughter.

15

Eastern Influences

The tree that brushes the heavens grew from the tiniest sprout. The most
elegant pagoda, nine stories high, rose from a small pile of earth. The
journey of a thousand miles began with but a single step.   —Lao Tzu

A sia is the world's largest continent and contains a third of earth's solid surface. It has as many inhabitants as all other continents combined. Its ancient
civilizations—China, India, Japan, Korea, Vietnam, and others—are reinventing
themselves economically, culturally, and politically. China, India, and North Korea
now have nuclear weapons. The future belongs to Asia. Is there a point to studying Eastern thinkers? Can they possibly say anything to us? The answer seems
obvious.

But familiarizing ourselves with Eastern philosophy is important not merely to
understand emerging global powers but also to know ourselves. As the German
poet Hölderlin observed, we never understand our home until we leave it. The
philosophies of other civilizations provide new vantage points from which to view
our own thought. They offer a different perspective, one from which we may reconsider and reevaluate what is important to us in our own thinking. Additionally,
they are a potential source of fresh ideas and new concepts.

For many of the Westerners who have studied it, the philosophy of ancient
Eastern thinkers has offered secure guidance to the full and contented life.

In this chapter, we consider Hinduism and Buddhism in India; Taoism, Confucianism, and Ch'an Buddhism in China; and Zen Buddhism and the samurai tradition in Japan. No effort is made to present the history of these important traditions
or to trace their evolution over the centuries. Our intent is merely to introduce these
philosophies and their most important thinkers. For a brief overview of Islamic
philosophy, see the box on page 492.

Eastern philosophy and Eastern religions are closely intertwined. Both Confucianism and Taoism took on the trappings of religion, with priests, rituals, and moral codes. Some forms of Taoism also were influenced by Chinese popular religions and superstitions. Today in Taiwan, for example, there are six levels of Taoism, including two kinds of Taoist priests, the red and the black. Only the highest level reflects the Taoist philosophy in its purest form, free from religious and superstitious add-ons.

Buddhism in China was influenced not only by Confucianism and Taoism but by popular religions as well. In India, a similar interaction took place among ancient Buddhism and various religious belief systems and practices.

HINDUISM

India, now a country of more than a billion people, more than three times the population of the United States, is also one of the oldest civilizations; remains have been found that date as far back as 50,000 B.C.E. Today, India is roughly 82 percent Hindu, 11 percent Muslim, 2 percent Sikh, about 2 percent Christian, and about 1 percent Buddhist; it has even smaller percentages of Jainists, Zoroastrians, and Jews. Islam swept into India starting in 1001, and the harshness of Islamic rulers established an antagonism between Muslims and Hindus that still exists.

The European conquest of India began in 1510, when the Portuguese seized Goa (today popular with Europeans for its beaches). The English arrived in 1612 in the form of the East India Company; initially, a power struggle among European countries vying to defend and extend their economic interests led to the stationing of troops in India by England, France, and other countries. Eventually, however, England annexed the entire country, and, as a colony of England, India became known as "the jewel in the crown." Unfortunately, the British systematically stripped India of its wealth. Some three hundred years later, in 1947, through the nonviolent resistance and disobedience of Mohandas Gandhi and his followers and the Muslim League, India was given back independence.

One element of Indian culture that is worth mentioning here is the caste system. The *Vedas,* the ancient Hindu religious texts, divided society into four classes or castes. Because the gods determined one's caste, one was meant to stay there. The highest caste were the Brahmins, the priests and teachers; next-highest were the Kshatriyas, the rulers and warriors; then came the Vaishyas, the merchants; and then the Shudras, the farmers and laborers. The largest group of all is below all of the castes. These people are known as the Parjanyas or Antyajas, or Untouchables. They are the outcasts; members of society above them were not allowed to touch them or even to enter their shadows lest they become unclean and in need of ablution. (Untouchability was abolished by the Indian constitution in 1917.)

The long history of Indian philosophy has given rise to two main schools of thought, Hinduism and Buddhism. Hinduism, for example, contains both monism and dualism. Both also have had a long list of great thinkers, such as Nagarjuna (on the foundations of Buddhism). But this text must limit itself to a brief sketch of these traditional movements. **Hinduism,** from the Urdu word for India, *Hind,* is the Western term for the religious beliefs and practices of the majority of the Indian people.

The origins of Hinduism stretch back into the unknown past. Unlike other religions, it had no founder, and there is no single religious body to judge orthodoxy. In fact, Hinduism does not even contain a unified set of doctrines—or, to the extent it does, they are given diversified interpretations. All of this makes it difficult to talk about Hinduism in a limited space. Speaking of Hinduism as a single belief system is something like speaking of philosophy in the same way. It is best to view it as a spiritual attitude that gives rise to a wide range of religious and philosophical beliefs and practices. These range from the worship of village and forest deities, which often take zoomorphic forms, to complex metaphysical theories.

Common to all forms of Hinduism, however, is acceptance of the authority of the Vedic scriptures as the basis for understanding the true hidden nature of things. The *Vedas* are the most ancient religious texts of Hinduism—indeed, they are the oldest religious texts in an Indo-European language. The *Vedas* were the literature of the Aryans, who invaded northwest India around 1500 B.C.E. Many, if not most, Hindu writings are commentaries on the Vedic scriptures.

In terms of popular religion, three contemporary movements might be mentioned. *Saivism* worships Siva as the supreme being and source of the universe; *Saktism* worships Sakti, the female part of the universe and the wife of Siva. *Vaisnavism* worships the personal god **Vishnu.** Buddha, according to orthodox Hindus, was an incarnation (*avatar*) of Vishnu.

The basis of Hindu philosophy is the belief that reality is absolutely one, that there is only one ultimate reality-being-consciousness (see the box "Ommmmm"). Six classical philosophical schools or traditions, however, interpret this reality variously: these six insights, as they are called, are *Nyāya, Vaiśesika, Sāmkhya, Yoga, Mīmāmsā,* and *Vedānta.* All are designed to lead the searcher to a knowledge of the Absolute and the liberation of the soul. Vedanta is tradition based on the *Upanishads* and is the best known in the West (*Vedanta* means "the end of the Veda").

Philosophically, the most important Vedic scripture is the last book, the **Upanishads.** The *Upanishads,* which date from about the eighth to the fifth centuries B.C.E., are the inspiration for the six systems of philosophy just mentioned. The *Upanishads* are best known for the theories of **brahman** (the ultimate cosmic principle or reality), **atman** (the inner self), and the identification of *brahman* with *atman.* There are four great sayings (*mahavakya*) of the *Upanishads,* which are all ways of saying that *brahman* and *atman* are one:

1. Consciousness is *brahman.*
2. That art thou.
3. The self is *brahman.*
4. I am *brahman.*

Brahman is considered the ultimate reality or principle and the source and sustainer of all things, including people and gods. It is absolute and eternal spirit—the supreme consciousness, the One, the One-and-only-One. A lower manifestation of

Ommmmm

During the 1960s, Indian philosophy, or what passed for it, became popular in the American youth culture, thanks in part to the Beatles' interest in it and in the music of the Indian sitar master Ravi Shankar. In San Francisco and New York and Madison, Wisconsin, it was common to see hippies chanting "*Ommmmm, ommmmm, ommmmm*" in an effort to induce a mystical state of higher consciousness.

What is "*ommm*"? It is the sound of the letters *A*, *U*, and *M*, which are the symbols in Hindu writings for the three ordinary states of consciousness: waking experience, dreaming sleep, and deep sleep. There is in addition, according to Hinduism, a fourth state (in Vedanta philosophy, *moksa*), one of higher awareness, which is described in the *Mandukya Upanishad* as "the coming to peaceful rest of all differentiated existence." *Yoga* is the general term for the spiritual disciplines in Hinduism and Buddhism that aim at attainment of this higher state. It is also the name of one of the six orthodox systems of Hindu philosophy (see text).

brahman—namely, *brahma*—may be thought of as an individual deity or personal god, but *brahman* itself is without attributes or qualities. This absolute remains the hidden, unknown, ultimate mystery.

Atman is the self, the soul, the principle of individual life. Ultimately, however, the individual must come to a realization, through meditation and contemplation, that *brahman* and *atman* are the same thing—*brahman-atman*. With the realization of this absolute oneness of all things comes recognition of the relative nonreality of the world and of the individual ego. The identification of *brahman* and *atman* is sometimes spoken of by commentators as a pantheism, but it goes beyond the claim that all things are God. In Hinduism, the gods are parts or symbolic personifications of the absolute principle, *brahman*.

Further, the identification of *brahman* and *atman* has been subject to various interpretations over the centuries. It has been looked on as both transcendent and immanent. Samkara, who is thought to have lived between 788 and 820 C.E. and who gave the most rigorous interpretation of the *Upanishads,* was a pure monist who thought that all things are one—only the ultimate principle exists, and all else is an illusion. But another way of looking at the ultimate principle or reality was introduced by Rāmānuja (b. 1027 C.E.). He believed in the ultimate principle, but he also believed that souls are real and that the world is not merely an illusion. For a time, at least, the souls and the world must be separate from the ultimate principle to be of service to it, he held.

Yet a third way of interpreting the underlying ultimate reality is represented by the outright dualism of Madhva (1199–1278), who believed that, although the ultimate principle is the cause of the world, the soul still has a separate and independent existence of its own. You can see that Hindu philosophy in fact admits a variety of viewpoints.

The metaphysical question as to what constitutes the ultimate reality is not the only philosophical concern within Hinduism. There is also the issue of the human being's relation to that ultimate principle. Human life is a journey. Humans, though basically good, are caught up in a cycle of desire and suffering that is the direct result of ignorance and ego. In short, they are miserable. The desires that torment them are many and diverse, including sensual lusts and the desire for existence. The end result is *samsara*, the cycle of being born, dying, and being reborn. The human being often goes through a series of rebirths in various forms until he or she can escape the treadmill.

That which keeps an individual imprisoned by the transmigratory cycle is **karma,** which means "action" or "deed" in Pali. It refers to the chain of causes and necessary consequences in the world of human actions. Every action inevitably has its effect, and traces of these effects can last over several lifetimes. A good action brings joy; a bad action brings sorrow. And the consequences of actions build up over a lifetime and through multiple lifetimes. It is these residues that will help determine the quality of the next **reincarnation.** Despite the fact that humans create their own limitations through their choices of actions and motives, they nonetheless have the power to continue to choose or to resist falling victim to selfish desires. Building up good karma and reducing bad karma may eventually lead a person to escape the bondage of karma altogether by surrender to God and the liberation of enlightenment.

It is the renunciation of desires and the giving up of possessions and worldly attachments that can lead to **nirvana,** or permanent liberation from the cycle of birth, death, and rebirth. *Nirvana* is the Sanskrit word for "extinction," and it means the merging of the individual, transitory existence into the ultimate reality, namely, brahman. This is a condition of bliss at the highest state of transcendent consciousness. As part of brahman, we watch *lila,* or the entire history of the world and of our lives.

Human life, then, is a journey wherein we try to control both the mind and the senses and become God-oriented in the hope of experiencing total fulfillment in oneness with God. This means going from the state of everyday, ordinary consciousness to the blissful contemplation of the divine being itself. The human being seeks God by eliminating the shadow between the two, that is, the illusion of duality and separation.

Much of the wisdom of Hinduism in all times lies in its sages. This certainly holds true for the twentieth century, whose wise men include Rabīndranāth Tagore (1861–1941), Sri Aurobindo Ghose (1872–1950), and Mohandas K. Gandhi (1869–1948) (see Chapter 16). Tagore won the Nobel Prize in 1913 for his poetry, in which he expressed the human quest for freedom and the divine. Aurobindo, who was educated in the West, sought political freedom for India. After being accused of terrorism and violence, he withdrew from political life altogether and developed a theory of spiritual evolution according to which the individual through self-effort can rise to ever-higher states of spiritual consciousness.

Gandhi, of course, is known everywhere for his use of nonviolence to help attain political freedom for India and for striving to instill a sense of self-respect in all human beings (he called the lowest caste, the Untouchables, the children of God). Through the example of his simple life and teachings, Gandhi tried to make the traditional values of Hinduism available to all.

BUDDHISM

Buddhism arose in India in the person of a prince, **Siddhartha Gautama** [sid-HAR-tuh, GO-tuh-muh], later known as **Buddha** [BOO-duh] (c. 563–c. 483 B.C.E.), "the Enlightened One." Originally, Buddhism essentially was a philosophical response to what might be called the problem of suffering—and suffering is here to be understood in the broad sense as including not merely outright pain and misery but also sorrow, disappointment, frustration, discontent, disaffection, pessimism, and the sense of unfulfillment that so often grows with the passing of the years.

Buddha

When he was twenty-nine, Siddhartha, tortured by the suffering he saw around him, abandoned a life of luxury as well as a wife and son to discover why it is that suffering exists and what its cure must be. After six years of wandering and meditation, he found enlightenment.

Buddha's answer to the problem of suffering was contained in his doctrine of the **Four Noble Truths:** (1) There is suffering; (2) suffering has specific and identifiable causes; (3) suffering can be ended; (4) the way to end suffering is through enlightened living as expressed in the Eightfold Path.

According to Buddha, suffering is in part the result of the transience and hence uncertainty of the world: indeed, all human problems are rooted in the fact of change and the uncertainty, anxiety, and fear that it causes. Suffering is also in part the result of karma. Karma, as we have seen, is the doctrine that one's point of departure in this life is determined by one's decisions and deeds in past lives and that decisions and deeds in this life determine one's beginning points in future incarnations. *Karma*, to repeat, means "action" or "deed." The intention of an action determines whether the action is morally good or bad. The effect of an action leaves a trace that extends over several lifetimes, thereby helping to determine the quality of the reincarnation.

But the most immediate causes of human suffering, according to Buddha, are ignorance, which closes the door to enlightenment, and selfish craving, which enslaves an individual to desires and passions. The individual who is ruled by desires cannot possibly be happy in an ever-changing, uncertain world, especially because what happens is so much beyond one's control. For even when life goes as is hoped for, there is no guarantee that it will continue that way, and inevitably anxiety and fear overwhelm temporary satisfaction.

According to Buddha, through meditation and self-abnegation, selfish craving can be stilled and ignorance overcome. The result of doing so is a cessation of suffering in nirvana, a permanent state of supreme enlightenment and serenity that brings the continuing cycle of reincarnation to an end for the individual.

But Buddha held that attainment of nirvana requires more than merely letting go of selfish desires. It requires understanding that what are ordinarily thought of as one's body and one's consciousness are not real, are not the true Self. This

PROFILE: Siddhartha Gautama Buddha (563–483 B.C.E.)

Siddhartha Gautama, the Buddha, was born in northeastern India. His father was a wealthy king or clan chieftain, Suddhodana by name; through his mother, Maya, he was related to the Shakya tribe of Nepal. The family enjoyed a luxurious lifestyle, and his father sought to keep Siddhartha sheltered from the dust and trouble of the outside world. The young Siddhartha was athletic, handsome, and highly intelligent. He was married at the age of sixteen to Yasodhara, who eventually gave birth to a son, Rahula.

One day on a visit to the city of Kapilavastu, Siddhartha became deeply disturbed by the sight of suffering in its various guises. First, he encountered an old man whose body showed the ravages of the years. Next, he saw a man in the throes of a virulent disease. Finally, he passed a funeral with its corpse and attendant mourners, meeting the problem of death on one hand and anguish on the other. His last experience of that eventful day was to behold a monk deep in meditation. All of these sights had a profound effect on Siddhartha, and the problem of suffering became the central focus of his thoughts. At the age of twenty-nine, he slipped away from his family during the night and entered the forest to seek a solution to the conundrum of suffering, shaving his head and taking on the raiments of poverty.

Early on in his quest, Siddhartha studied under at least two Hindu ascetics. From them he learned a form

Two gigantic statues of Buddha (the larger shown here) in the Bamiyan Valley, Afghanistan, were blown up by the Taliban in 2001. The Taliban, an Islamist movement, ruled much of Afghanistan from 1996 to 2001.

of yoga as well as the arts of breathing and motionless meditation. Later, Siddhartha joined a small band of ascetics who begged for a living. Like them, Siddhartha performed many acts of self-abnegation and self-renunciation. He grew extremely thin from excessive fasting and one day fell unconscious from his attempts to control his senses. When he awoke, he was fed milk and gruel. From that moment, it was clear to Siddhartha that ascetic practices, in and of themselves, do not lead to enlightenment.

Siddhartha dwelt in the forest for about six years. Thereafter he is thought to have sought a *middle way* between sensual indulgence and ascetic self-denial, striving for enlightenment through concentrating his mind in deep meditation. Siddhartha achieved enlightenment one day while meditating under a fig tree near the present-day town of Gaya in northeastern India. He continued to meditate for seven days. Henceforth this tree was known as the *bodhi* tree—the tree of enlightenment.

For almost fifty years Siddhartha, now the Buddha or Enlightened One, went about teaching the way of dealing with suffering. He founded a group or order, to which his wife and son ultimately belonged. Before he died, his philosophy had already found a large following. For Western readers, perhaps the most affecting account of the life of Buddha is presented by Hermann Hesse in his novel *Siddhartha*.

understanding, this totally nonegoistic perspective, is itself freedom from egoistic thoughts and desires and brings with it as well freedom from all fear and anxiety. By rejecting the fetters of egoistic craving, the individual overcomes the false self and achieves "the unsurpassed state of security . . . and utter peace" that is nirvana.

The way to the cessation of suffering is the **Eightfold Path.** In effect, the Eightfold Path sets forth the means of proper living:

1. *Right View,* which implies having adequate knowledge about those things that make human life sick and unwholesome—ignorance, selfish craving and grasping, and so on.

Islamic Philosophy

Muslim philosophy arose around the eighth century, a time when Western Europe was experiencing its Middle Ages. From the beginning, it took into account theological considerations such as the person of Mohammed, the Quran, and the schools of theology, but these were not the only sources of influence. Neoplatonism and Aristotle played important roles in shaping both the problems faced and their proposed solutions. Many translations from the Greek were made during the ninth century.

Among the concerns of the early Islamic philosophers were the nature of God (Allah), the hierarchy of creation, the nature of human beings, and their place within the universe, as well as the relationship between theology and philosophy. **Al-Kindi** [el-KIN-dee] (d. after 870) developed the idea of God as an absolute and transcendent being, which was in accord with certain Muslim ideas of the time. His definition of God took elements from both Aristotle and the Neoplatonists. He developed a cosmology based on the Neoplatonist idea of emanation, where everything evolves out of God and in some way participates in God. Al-Kindi also added the Muslim notion that God created the first being out of nothing by force of will.

Al-Fārābī [el-fuh-RAHB-ee] (875–950) further elaborated on the notion of God in terms of Plotinus's notion of the One and also the notion that everything emanates out of the One. He added Aristotle's notion of God as the first cause of everything. Al-Fārābī looked to the prophet-philosopher to gain the philosophical illumination that would be of profound meaning to his society.

Avicenna [av-uh-SEN-uh] (Abū 'Ali ibn-Sīnā, 980–1037) produced the medieval system of thought best known in the West. He envisioned God as a Necessary Being who emanated the contingent, temporal world out of himself. Everything was dependent on God, and the ultimate goal of human activity was a prophetic mind that attains an intuitive knowledge of God and his creation. For Avicenna, there was a parallelism between philosophy and theology. During this time, philosophy, and especially the mystical identification of a thinker with God, were occasionally considered a threat to Muslim orthodoxy. For example, **Al-Ghazālī** [el-guh-ZAHL-ee] (1058–1111) in his *Incoherence of the Philosophers* attacked Avicenna. Among other things, he criticized Avicenna's notion of the eternity of the world as well as the lower status given to

2. *Right Aim,* which requires overcoming selfish passions and desires by an effort of will and thus having no resentment, envy, or reason to harm another person.
3. *Right Speech,* which means refraining from lies, deceptions, harmful gossip, idle chatter or speculation about others, and so on.
4. *Right Action,* which means not responding to improper desires and cravings, including those that are sexual, and above all not taking a human life. Right Action also includes doing good deeds (described by Buddha as the "treasure" of the wise).
5. *Right Living,* which requires obtaining one's livelihood through proper means and living one's life free from selfish cravings and graspings.
6. *Right Effort,* which means struggling against immoral and corrupt conditions.
7. *Right Mindfulness,* which is the source of Right Effort. Right Mindfulness implies having a duty to attain enlightenment and to understand the nature and effects of selfish craving. The right-minded person, according to Buddha, has no sense of attachment toward body, feelings, perceptions, activities, and thought, and naturally controls all covetous longings and desires. Right Mindfulness likewise means to develop the noble principles of life, especially the six just listed. It develops a pure mind and a clear memory,

the religious law as a mere symbol of higher truths to be accessed through intuition.

The antagonism between mystical philosophy and Muslim orthodoxy represents an ongoing problem. **Averroës** [ah-VAIR-oh-eez] (1126–1198), for example, was interpreted as holding a theory of two separate truths, the truth of religion and the truth of philosophy. Averroës, who taught the idea of eternal creation, was trying to extricate Aristotle's thought from both Neoplatonic and Islamic derivations.

Perhaps what is most intriguing to modern-day Western thought is the development of Sufism. **Sufism** represents a mystical, theosophical, and ascetic strain of Muslim belief that seeks union with God (Allah). **Sadr al-Dīn als Shīrazī** (1571–1640), later known as Mulla Sadrā, sought a monistic return to the First Principle of Being. Sufism, perhaps to a greater degree than orthodox Islamic belief, was influenced by the mystical tendencies of Neoplatonism and gnosticism. There was a seeking after a direct communion with the Absolute Being, who likewise represented Absolute Beauty. Through ascetic practices and concentrated inwardness, a human being might experience a sudden illumination and a sense of ecstatic union with God (Allah). This intuition might reveal to the person his utter nothingness, on one hand, as well as his pantheistic immanence in God, on the other. It is hardly surprising that a number of Sufis during the medieval period were executed for the blasphemy of identifying themselves with God. This ongoing difficulty was to some degree mollified by Al-Ghazālī, who brought Sufism closer to orthodox Muslim belief by playing down the pantheistic elements of Sufism.

There have been four main periods of Sufism: the first period (c. 750–1050), the second period (c. 1050–1450), the modern period (c. 1450–1850), and the contemporary period (1850 to the present). There are about one hundred Sufi orders in the world today, with several million adherents. The movement has produced a number of great mystical poets; **Kabir** [kuh-BEER] (1435–1518) from Benares, India, is one of the best known in the West thanks to Robert Bly's translations. The Sufi literature, Sufi poetry, and the whirling dervishes have continued to influence the West's own contemporary pantheistic and mystical traditions.

which are necessary if our every action, no matter how seemingly trivial, is to be imbued with mindfulness. It brings all human activities under conscious control and thoughtfulness.

8. *Right Contemplation,* which is the ultimate concentration of mind, integrates the aforementioned principles in dealing with all aspects of life. It is the liberating consciousness that frees the mind from the bonds of our cravings, inclinations, and desires. Any personal consciousness is replaced by an "invisible, infinite, all-penetrating consciousness" that brings lasting peace. It is pure cognition, free from any selfishness. Buddha emphasizes that this way is achieved slowly. Deliverance is attained step by step, by constant effort in building an unshakable concentration. Right concentration is uninterrupted, blissful thoughtfulness that purifies deeds, words, and thoughts.

As you can see, the first two stages of the Eightfold Path have to do with the initial mental outlook of the individual, the next four specify appropriate behavior, and the last two pertain to the higher mental and spiritual qualities involved in a total disattachment from self.

Two additional concepts traditionally believed to have been introduced by Gautama Buddha became important for later Buddhism. The first concept Gautama

Buddhism and the West

The parallel concern of Buddhists and Stoics (see Chapter 10) with the problem of suffering is intriguing, but it is difficult to say whether there was any reciprocal influence between Buddhism and the philosophies of ancient Greece and Rome. The first major modern Western philosopher to be influenced in a significant way by Buddhist thought was Arthur Schopenhauer (1788–1860). Schopenhauer believed that human life is basically not rational and that humans are driven by blind and insatiable will. Only by overcoming one's ego and desires can a state of calm bliss be achieved, according to Schopenhauer.

After Schopenhauer, Buddhist and other Asian ideas have increasingly come to the West, mostly via Indian and Japanese gurus, monks, and martial artists. Many of these ideas are now entering the mainstream of popular culture.

Buddha identifies in his *Sayings* as "clinging to existence" (*upadana*). This clinging is an extreme form of egoistic craving or desire and must be "destroyed" if the human being is ever to reach a state of peace and imperturbability. This clinging can take different forms—a clinging to the body and its worldly pleasure, a clinging to views, a clinging to rules and rituals, and a clinging to ego beliefs. It is necessary to cultivate nonclinging or nonattachment but in such a way that there is not clinging to nonclinging.

The other important concept is silence (*moneyya*). Gautama Buddha sat and meditated under the bodhi tree to reach enlightenment. Such enlightenment requires going beyond the verbiage and logics of discursive reasoning. In the *Sayings,* Gautama Buddha is thought to have spoken of three kinds of silence: the silence of body, the silence of mind, and the silence of word. Only the person who is silent in all three ways can be said to be free of taint. Silent meditation becomes a critical way to enlightenment in later developments of Buddhism.

Buddha believed that he had found the cause of suffering in the world and a way of escaping it as well. He set forth a strategy for eliminating unnecessary fear and specified a way of living that is calming for the person but that also allows the person to be of service to others. Buddha did not believe in a divine creator or in divine salvation; thus, in his thinking, the problem of suffering is one that humans must cope with themselves.

The Indian monk Bodhidharma purportedly brought Buddhism to China about 520 C.E. There it gradually mixed with Taoism, Confucianism, and other influences and underwent a rather marked transformation (see the box "Buddhism and the West").

TAOISM

Chinese philosophy, like Indian philosophy, goes back to the prehistoric past. China's history is dominated by dynasties that at first did not extend over the entire country. Shang, the first dynasty, lasted from the seventeenth century to the eleventh century B.C.E.—enduring, you might notice, more than twice as long as the United States of America. But by the fifth century B.C.E., China had fallen into many single warring states—a period when war became "professionalized" and thus more destructive than when it was a seasonal sport of feudal lords in golden chariots. It was during this period and in response to the situation that the two great indigenous philosophical systems in China were born, **Taoism** [DOW-ism] and Confucianism [kun-FYOO-shin-ism].

Confucianism stemmed, of course, from Confucius (551–479 B.C.E.); the beginnings of Taoism are more obscure although even older. (The word *Tao* has a number of meanings but is usually translated as "the Way" in the West.) Two of the early Taoist figures were **Lao Tzu** [LAO-tsuh] (c. sixth century B.C.E.) and his chief follower, Chuang Tzu [CHWANG-tsuh] (c. fourth century B.C.E.). The dialectic between Confucianism and Taoism suffused much of Chinese history and life, from architecture and clothing styles to politics and economic strategies.

Later, during the Han dynasty (206 B.C.E.–220 A.D.), China became a centrally controlled state run by bureaucrats, which it has remained to this day, although this unity was often broken along the way. During this time, the great third religion of China, Buddhism, was introduced from India. In China, Buddhism quickly took on a unique character, in large part due to its synthesis with elements of Taoism. It was not long before the ultimate reality in Chinese Buddhism, the *Buddha dharma*, was being identified with the *Tao*.

Lao Tzu

In an oft-reported meeting between Confucius and Lao Tzu, Confucius expressed his admiration for the depth of Lao Tzu's thought. Lao Tzu, in turn, is said to have expressed doubts about the heroes of the past whom Confucius had chosen as models of behavior. Lao Tzu also tried to convince Confucius of the hopelessness of the latter's attempts to improve society by direct action.

This little story nicely illustrates an essential difference between Confucius and Lao Tzu and between Confucianism and Taoism. Confucius sought to become an advisor to a ruler and directly to change society for the better, using heroes of the past as models. Lao Tzu's vision of things and strategies for change are very different. Within the Taoist tradition, one strain of thought even uses Lao Tzu's ideas as a means cunningly to obtain and retain power (the military and political strategies of Sun Tzu might be mentioned as an example).

Lao Tzu's view of humankind is like that of the Greek philosopher Socrates in at least one respect. Both thought that even the wisest of humans is still ignorant. Both held that to act on that ignorance under the pretense that it is knowledge is folly that leads not to progress and betterment within the individual and society but to the opposite effect. It is especially here that Taoists like Lao Tzu and Chuang Tzu found Confucius wanting. They thought that he sought to impose solutions without knowledge or understanding.

According to Lao Tzu, what is needed is not interference with the world but rather humble understanding of the way it functions, namely, understanding of the Tao. Humans cannot force change on the world without injuring themselves. All

PROFILE: Lao Tzu (c. 6th Century B.C.E.)

Almost nothing is known of Lao Tzu's life, because he spent it trying to remain unknown and nameless. He is thought to have been born in the early sixth century B.C.E. and to have worked in the archives at Loyang (present-day Hunan province). Confucius is thought to have visited the older man during one of his journeys. These quotations reveal some of Lao Tzu's insights on the **Tao, or Way.**

> The Tao that can be told of is not
>   the eternal Tao;
> The name that can be named is not the eternal
>   name.
> The Nameless is the origin of Heaven and
>   Earth.
>
> Can you understand all and penetrate all with-
>   out taking any action?
> To produce and to rear them,
> To produce, but not to take possession of them,
> To act, but not to rely on one's own ability,
> To lead them, but not to
>   master them—

> This is called profound and secret
>   virtue.
> Reversion is the action of Tao.
> Weakness is the function of Tao.
> All things in the world come from
>   being.
> And being comes from non-being.
>
> Tao produced the One.
> The One produced the two.
> The two produced the three.
> And the three produced the ten
>   thousand things.
> To know that you do not know is the best.
>
> To pretend to know when you do not know
>   is a disease.
>
> The sage desires to have no desire . . . and
>   returns to what the multitude has missed
>   (Tao).
> Thus he supports all things in their natural
>   state, but does not take any action.
>
> A good traveler leaves no track or trace.

arbitrary interventions using models of the past simply lead to further disorder. The sage, he maintained, is the one who knows enough to do nothing: instead of intervening, he simply follows the patterns of the universe, of the ineffable Tao that gives order and substance to all things.

Now, the Tao, for Lao Tzu, is one, natural, and eternal (see the box "The Tao, Logos, and God"). It gives rise to the expansive forces (**yang**) in the universe, and it gives rise to the contractive forces (**yin**). The Tao is like an empty bowl that holds and yields the vital energy (*ch'i*) in all things. It is also the *means* by which things come to be, take shape, and reach fulfillment. In contrast to Confucius, who believed that the Tao can be improved on (note Confucius's remark that "it is man that can make the Way great"), Lao Tzu believed that the Tao cannot be improved on, for it *is* the natural order of things.

According to Lao Tzu, the wise person, the sage, cultivates tranquility and equilibrium in his life in order to recognize the Tao. He comes to recognize that the enduring foundation of life is peace, not strife. The harshest storm, the sage understands, can last only a short while. He frees himself of selfish desires and turns his attention to the deep-rooted Tao, where all is one, and by doing so, he acquires the secrets of both the quiet and the long-lasting life.

The Tao, Logos, and God

Ancient Chinese and Western philosophy show a striking similarity in their identification of the first principle (beginning) of all being and truth. In ancient Chinese philosophy, this first principle is the eternal Tao, the source of all necessity, meaning, order, and existence, the Way the universe functions. Yet the Tao itself, according to Taoism, remains hidden, its nature ineffable. Any attempt to define the Tao or even to describe it in words must fail. According to Lao Tzu, it is the sign of the truly wise man that he will not even try to name it. He only seeks to submit to it and follow it humbly.

In ancient Greek philosophy, a like notion was posited as the root of all things. Heraclitus (c. 540–c. 480 B.C.E.) named it *logos* and regarded it as the source of all order, lawfulness, and justice. There is no consensus on how *logos* should be translated into English, and dictionaries provide many different meanings for the term, including "reason," "proportion," "word," and others.

Logos, as Heraclitus sees it, is almost entirely unknown by earthly mortals—in part because nature loves to hide. Humans, Heraclitus thought, see the world in terms of opposites and as full of strife. But the deeper reality is the *logos*, the unity of opposites in which all is one. Seeing this deeper reality is reserved only for the gods and for those few humans who can escape conventional modes of understanding, according to Heraclitus.

The concept of God as it evolved in traditional Christian philosophy is a variation of Heraclitus's notion of *logos* as developed by Plato and Aristotle and reinterpreted by St. Augustine, St. Thomas Aquinas, and others. In fact, the "Word" that was "in the beginning" in the book of John was *logos* in the Greek text. (John's contribution to the Bible may not have been originally composed in Greek, of course.)

By following the Tao, Lao Tzu held, the behavior of the sage is natural and free, for he harbors no unfit desires and no unnatural expectations. He simply does what is appropriate in the present circumstances. Like water, he accepts the lowest places with contentment and without resistance. He deems valuable what others consider worthless and have discarded. And, because he is selfless, he seeks to care for all things and to benefit them rather than use them for his own ends.

The sage's way, maintained Lao Tzu, is modest, slow, and cautious (see the box "Lao Tzu on Virtuous Activity"). Again like water, the sage is **soft and supple** rather than hard, and (like water), while appearing to do nothing, he achieves lasting effects. To others, the results seem mysteriously produced, for they are produced without apparent effort. The sage is merely following the flow and letting events unfold at their proper time and in their own way. Further, in doing so, he seeks to remain hidden, and he takes no credit for what is achieved, for he seeks neither possession nor domination. This absence of selfish desire is his secret virtue.

Lao Tzu believed that all enduring change is brought about by weakness, not by strength; by submission, not by intervention. Like an infant, the sage conserves his vital force and progresses gradually day by day. His strength lies in his softness and flexibility. As he lives in accord with the Tao, he is preserved from harm.

Lao Tzu extended his philosophy of nonstriving to the political sphere (see the box "Lao Tzu on Government"). He recognized the disadvantages of coercion: the use of force brings retaliation, and mutual hostility quickly escalates, to the detriment of both sides. As coercion and the use of force arise from greed, he advocated a political strategy of nonacquisitiveness, in which weapons are regarded as instruments of

Lao Tzu on Virtuous Activity

Good words shall gain you honor in the marketplace, but good deeds shall gain you friends among men.

There is no guilt greater than
     to sanction unbridled
     ambition.
No calamity greater than to
     be dissatisfied with one's
     own lot.
No fault greater than to wish
     continually of receiving.

With the faithful I would keep faith; with the unfaithful I would also keep faith, in order that they may become faithful.

The ability to perceive the significance of the small things of the world is the secret of clearsightedness; the guarding of what is soft and vulnerable is the secret of strength.

The superior man hoards nothing. The more he uses for the benefit of others, the more he possesses himself. The more he gives to his fellow men, the more he has of his own.

The superior man is skillful in dealing with men, and so does not cast away anyone from his doorway.

The superior man prizes three things. The first is gentleness, the second is frugality, the third is humility. By being gentle he can be bold; by being frugal he can be liberal, and by being humble he becomes a leader among men.

The superior man anticipates tasks that are difficult while they are still easy, and does things that would become great while they are small. Therefore, the superior man, while he never does what is great, is able on that account to accomplish the greatest of things.

The superior man diminishes his actions and diminishes them again until he arrives at doing nothing on purpose.

Having arrived at this point of non-action, there is nothing that he does not do.

He who keeps his mouth open and spends his breath in the continual promotion of his affairs will never, in all his life, experience safety.

---

destruction and wars are to be fought only when absolutely necessary and then only with regret.

The wise ruler, Lao Tzu believed, understands that violence is a last resort and knows that it can often be avoided by anticipation, by reconciling potential enemies and resolving difficulties when they first arise. It is because such a ruler sidesteps problems by anticipation that his success is unfathomable to others. And because he recognizes that there is no safety in the use of force, he remains calm and unhurried in dealing with any problems that cannot be avoided. His preference is to yield rather than to attack. Gentleness brings him eventual victory with apparently no effort. His strategy is "not to advance an inch but rather to retreat a foot." Slowly he wins over the enemy without the use of weapons. And the gain is lasting because it is achieved without the destructiveness of war and therefore without the long memories of resentment.

To achieve peace and stability, the sage ruler has no wish to dominate or exploit others, Lao Tzu believed. Rather, the wise ruler encourages openness and broad-mindedness. Cognizant of the sometimes violent ways of the world, he is cautious and reserved. The very essence of his method lies in not requiting injury with injury, a practice that leads only into the endless cycle of revenge. He responds to injury with kindness. He remains faithful even to the unfaithful. In this

Lao Tzu on Government

It is the way of Heaven to take from those who have too much and give to those who have too little. But the way of man is not so. He takes away from those who have too little, to add to his own superabundance.

He who assists the ruler with Tao does not dominate the world with force.
The use of force usually brings requital.
Wherever armies are stationed, briers and thorns grow . . .
Whatever is contrary to Tao will soon perish.

Weapons are the instruments of evil, not the instruments of a good ruler.
When he uses them unavoidably, he regards calm restraint as the best principle. Even when he is victorious, he does not regard it as praiseworthy.
For to praise victory is to delight in the slaughter of men.

Tao invariably takes no action, and yet there is nothing left undone.

If kings and barons can keep it, all things will transform spontaneously.
If, after transformation, they should desire to be active,
I would restrain them with simplicity, which has no name.
Simplicity, which has no name, is free of desires.
Being free of desires, it is tranquil.
And the world will be at peace of its own accord.

Violent and fierce people do not die a natural death.
I shall make this the father [basis or starting point] of my teaching.

Govern the state with correctness.
Operate the army with surprise tactics.
Administer the empire by engaging in no activity.

---

way, he gradually and effortlessly turns people from that lower nature that tends to dominate in times of war and strife, away from aggressive ambition to thoughtfulness and the search for modest goals.

A kingdom, according to Lao Tzu, cannot be preserved by force or cunning. Further, he said, too much government only means confusion. Too many laws create disorder rather than prevent it. Too much activity upsets the balance within a state, just as it does in the life of the individual. The wise ruler does only what is absolutely necessary; because his heart is calm and nonacquisitive, his subjects are not excited to hysteria by either fear or avarice. The state achieves a stability in which all things come to completion in accordance with the Way.

In sum, according to Lao Tzu, the way of life recommended by the Tao is one of simplicity, tranquility, weakness, unselfishness, patience, and, above all, nonstriving or nonaction—allowing the world to follow its natural course. For Lao Tzu, this way of life is its own reward. Lao Tzu was concerned with this world, the world of living people; he was concerned with the human condition and not with otherworldly or supernatural subjects.

You may well think Lao Tzu's philosophy naive or idealistic. Lao Tzu was only too aware that a path of quiet nonstriving was one that few, if any, had chosen or would choose to tread. He made it quite clear that he did not expect rule by force to die out soon or quickly to be replaced by a policy of noninterference. He only drew up what he thought would be a superior way of living for any who might wish to consider his opinion in the matter.

Sun Tzu

Perhaps the oldest treatise on military strategy and methods is *The Art of War*, presumably written somewhere around 512 B.C.E. by **Sun Tzu** [SWUN-tsuh] (544–496 B.C.E.), a Chinese mercenary. According to traditional accounts, an ancient Chinese king had the good sense to hire Sun Tzu to command his forces, with the result that his kingdom became the most powerful of his period. Supposedly, ever since that time great military generals such as Napoleon and Mao Tse-tung have carefully studied *The Art of War*. Some people attribute the success of the comparatively under-armed forces of North Vietnam to their generals' following of Sun Tzu's prescriptions. Sun Tzu's philosophy reportedly is widely employed outside the military arena by those anxious to attain power or success or otherwise to advance their agendas. Luis Felipe "Big Phil" Scolari, who coached the 2002 World Cup–winning Brazilian soccer team, is said to have applied Sun Tzu to the soccer field. The film *Wall Street* (starring Michael Douglas) satirically suggested that Sun Tzu was (or is) being used by savvy corporation CEOs, and some say that the philosophy driving China, an economic juggernaut to whom the United States is billions of dollars in debt, comes not so much from Karl Marx as from Sun Tzu.

An important principle of *The Art of War* is that warfare should not be taken lightly, because it can mean the physical or financial ruin of a state as well as the death or enslavement of its inhabitants. Therefore, Sun Tzu said, all elements of a conflict must be studied carefully and all possible consequences anticipated. Merely by lasting too long, a war can ruin a country, even if the country "wins" militarily.

Another principle of Sun Tzu is that knowledge is everything. Winning requires not merely knowing one's opponent but also being realistic about oneself. Understanding only one of these options means winning only half the time; knowing neither means losing always. History provides confirmation of Sun Tzu's prediction of disaster for nations that overestimate their own abilities and underestimate their opponents.' Germany's invasion of the Soviet Union in World War II is an obvious example. Two recent Clint Eastwood films, *Flags of Our Fathers* and *Letters from Iwo Jima*, although primarily concerned with heroism, duty, and honor, show what happens when a fighting force is blinded by fanaticism.

Sun Tzu also prescribed using force only as a last resort. In fact, he rarely used the word *force* (*li*). This seems to contrast with the military strategy of von Clausewitz,[1] for whom domination is to be achieved both by force and political cunning. An oft-quoted saying in the Clausewitzian tradition is, "God is on the side of the big battalions."[2] For Sun Tzu, it was better to win before force was used and even better never to be in a position to have to use it. Battles must be won beforehand; and if violence does break out, destruction should be kept to a minimum.

---

[1] Carl Philipp Gottfried von Clausewitz (1780–1831) was a Prussian general and a military theorist. He is known for his treatise *On War*.

[2] A remark attributed to Count Roger de Bussy-Rabutin (a French writer famous for his memoirs, 1618–1693) and repeated in various forms by Voltaire, Frederick the Great, Bismarck, George Bernard Shaw, Stalin, and many others.

Sun Tzu also did not accept the idea that an enemy must be crushed utterly.[3] Decimating the enemy or the enemy's property will lead to endless hatred and an increased possibility of retaliation. Force should be used only as a last resort and with regret, he counseled.

Still, according to Sun Tzu, the enemy must taste bitterness (to quote an old Chinese proverb). But the ability to use sheer force must be tempered by keen psychological insight. One must change the opponent's mind-set from one of confidence and security to one of doubt, indecision, and fear. The decisive turning points in war are those in which these states have come to dominate the mind of the opponent.

According to Sun Tzu, decisive victories are almost always best achieved through surprise. Surprise, in turn, requires deception. Strategy in war involves mastering what today would be called mind games. To outmaneuver one's opponent, one must understand the opponent's intentions, tactics, psychology, preparation, and determination, while keeping him or her ignorant as to one's own hand. The one who is invisible will win the contest. Unpredictability is an excellent overall strategy; it induces fear and undermines determination.

Sun Tzu also thought that timing is of the essence and must be derived from analyzing the situation itself, not from wishful thinking. Patience in war is a key virtue: one must wait until exactly the right moment and then act decisively. Thus, flexibility and speed of action are also important.

According to Sun-Tzu, the strategy of war must be all-encompassing, in that war does not really begin at some fixed point nor end with the signing of a treaty. War is not limited to the battlefield, and it is not just for the generals, because it encompasses politics, economics, and societal relations as well. A wise leader, according to Sun Tzu, studies both peace and war and is especially sensitive to the long-term consequences of battle. The end of battle is not the end of war.

With this great emphasis on planning, knowledge, and psychology, it is not surprising that Sun Tzu believed that a country's thinkers are as important as its military advisers. Deep thinking across a range of variables beyond the military decide a nation's destiny, he thought.

Chuang Tzu

Chuang Tzu [CHWANG-tsuh] (c. fourth century B.C.E.), the most important Taoist next to Lao Tzu, perceived that many people live their lives as "slaves of power and riches." Chained by ambition and greed, they are unable to rest and are in constant friction with the world around them. They often feel trapped and do not know how to change their situation. They seem blind to what is happening and why it is happening. Their lives are driven and hectic, and they are in constant warfare with an indifferent world, a world that does not acquiesce to their desires.

But the world has its own wisdom, Chuang Tzu believed, as did Lao Tzu before him, and things come to fruition only at their proper time. Nature cannot be

---

[3] The main thought behind Stanley Bing's 2004 satire, *Sun Tzu Was a Sissy.*

PROFILE: Chuang Tzu (c. 4th Century B.C.E.)

Chuang Tzu was born in the fourth century B.C.E. in the kingdom of Meng, which borders present-day Shantung. He had a wife, was poor, and worked for an office connected with the city of Tsi Yuan. Little else is known about him except that he enjoyed differing with the followers of Confucius. He was not interested in holding public office, because doing so, he feared, might disturb his peace of mind. A few of his insights emerge in these quotations:

The mind of a perfect man is like a mirror. It grasps nothing. It expects nothing. It reflects but does not hold. Therefore, the perfect man can act without effort.

Proof that a man is holding fast to the beginning lies in the fact of his fearlessness.

The still mind discovers the beautiful patterns in the universe.

Flow with whatever may happen and let your mind be free: Stay centered by accepting whatever you are doing. This is the ultimate.

Only the intelligent know how to identify all things as one. Therefore he does not use [his own judgment] but abides in the common [principle]. The common means the useful and the useful means identification. Identification means being at ease with oneself. When one is at ease with himself, one is near Tao. This is to let [nature] take its own course.

Heaven and earth are one attribute; the ten thousand things [infinite things] are one horse.

When "this" or "that" have no opposites, there is the very axis of Tao.

He who knows the activities of Nature lives according to Nature. . . . How do we know that what I call Nature is not really man and what I call man is not really Nature?

Your master happened to come because it was his time, and he happened to leave because things follow along. If you are content with the time and willing to follow along, then grief and joy have no way to enter in.

forced or hurried, because nature, Chuang Tzu believed, unfolds according to the Tao: a tree's fruit must be picked only when it is ripe, not before and not after. If people choose to impose their will on the world, the result is strife, disquietude, and disruption.

Chuang Tzu also believed, as did Lao Tzu, that there is no need for people to force things for the sake of ambition or in the pursuit of profit or, indeed, for any other objective. Because it is the Tao, and not the person, that determines what is possible and what will happen, the wise individual accepts the course of events as it unfolds, with neither hope nor regret, for the Tao brings all things to fulfillment in due time (see the box "Cook Ting"). Thus, for Chuang Tzu, as for Lao Tzu, the secret of the sage—the key to freedom from fear and stress—is simply to follow the Way of things, responding to them appropriately and dwelling in nonaction. The sage is a mirror: he seeks to be utterly clear about what is before him, but he has no wish to change things.

As was true for Lao Tzu, Chuang Tzu applied his principles to statecraft, though he placed somewhat less emphasis on political affairs than did Lao Tzu. The sage ruler, Chuang Tzu believed, first gains knowledge of himself and of his subjects—gains knowledge of his and their nature and destiny—then effortlessly

Cook Ting

Chuang Tzu gave this story of Cook Ting as an illustration of the secret of the sage—to follow the Way of things, responding to them appropriately and never with force.

> Cook Ting was cutting up an ox for Lord Wen-hui. At every touch of his hand, every heave of his shoulder, every move of his feet, every thrust of his knee—zip! zoop! He slithered the knife along with a zing, and all was in perfect rhythm, as though he were performing the dance of the Mulberry Grove or keeping time to the Ching-shou music.
>
> "Ah, this is marvelous!" said Lord Wen-hui. "Imagine skill reaching such heights!"
>
> Cook Ting laid down his knife and replied, "What I care about is the Way, which goes beyond skill. When I first began cutting up oxen, all I could see was the ox itself. After three years I no longer saw the whole ox. And now—now I go at it by spirit and don't look with my eyes. Perception and understanding have come to a stop and spirit moves where it wants. I go along with the natural makeup, strike in the big hollows, guide the knife through the big openings, and follow things as they are. So I never touch the smallest ligament or tendon, much less a main joint.
>
> "A good cook changes his knife once a year—because he cuts. A mediocre cook changes his knife once a month—because he hacks. I've had this knife of mine for nineteen years and I've cut up thousands of oxen with it, and yet the blade is as good as though it had just come from the grindstone. There are spaces between the joints, and the blade of the knife has really no thickness. If you insert what has no thickness into such spaces, then there's plenty of room—more than enough for the blade to play about it. That's why after nineteen years the blade of my knife is still as good as when it first came from the grindstone.
>
> "However, whenever I come to a complicated place, I size up the difficulties, tell myself to watch out and be careful, keep my eyes on what I'm doing, work very slowly, and move the knife with the greatest subtlety, until—flop! the whole thing comes apart like a clod of earth crumbling to the ground. I stand there holding the knife and look all around me, completely satisfied and reluctant to move on, and then I wipe off the knife and put it away."
>
> "Excellent!" said Lord Wen-hui. "I have heard the words of Cook Ting and learned how to care for life!"

Cook Ting does not wear himself out by trying to force things. This would mean unnecessary friction. Like water, he seeks the empty places. When things become knotted, he only slows down and proceeds carefully. Even then, there is no need for friction or confrontation. Cook Ting's task is done by following rather than disturbing the order of things. By anticipating problems, he solves them before they become major. Total satisfaction is his reward.

"goes along with what is right for things." He permits nothing to disturb either his own inner harmony or the harmony within the state. Like a tiger trainer who anticipates the wildness of his charges, he knows how to deal with the violence of others before it arises, thus minimizing the need for force. In his fearless adherence to the Way, he remains free from selfish designs and preset goals. Because he puts forth no special effort, his success is unfathomable to others (see the box "Chuang Tzu on Virtuous Activity"). This philosophy is, of course, quite similar to that espoused by Lao Tzu. (And Chuang Tzu, like Tao Tzu before him, was quite aware that rulership in accordance with these principles would be a rare occurrence.)

Chuang Tzu's philosophy is also distinctive for the emphasis he placed on the danger of usefulness. Useful trees, like fruit and nut trees, he explained, are constantly cut back, kept small, and soon stripped of their fruit. Only "useless"

Chuang Tzu on Virtuous Activity

Chuang Tzu was fishing in the river Phu when the king of Khu sent two high officers to him with the message, "I wish to trouble you with the charge of all within my territories."

Chuang Tzu kept holding his rod without looking around and said, "I have heard that in Khu there is a magnificent tortoise shell, the wearer of which died three thousand years ago, and which the king keeps in his ancestral temple. Was it better for the tortoise to die and leave its shell to be thus honored? Or would it have been better for it to live and drag its tail after it over the mud?"

The two officers replied, "It would have been better for it to live and drag its tail through the mud."

"Go your way," said Chuang Tzu. "I will keep on dragging my tail after me through the mud."

Public spirited, and with nothing of the partisan; easy and compliant, without any selfish tendencies; following in the wake of others, without a double mind; not easily distracted because of any anxious thoughts; not scheming in the exercise of one's wisdom; not choosing between parties, but going along with all—all such courses are the path to true enlightenment.

Vacuity, tranquility, mellowness, quietness, and taking no action are the roots of all things. . . . These are the virtue of rulers and emperors when they manage things above.

If one assumes office with them [scholars] to pacify the world, his achievements will be great . . . and the empire will become unified. In tranquility he becomes a sage, and in activity he becomes a king. He takes no action and is honored. He is simple and plain and none in the world can compete with him in excellence. For such a one understands this virtue of Heaven and Earth. He is called the great foundation and the great source of all being and is in harmony with nature. One who is in accord with the world is in harmony with men. To be in harmony with men means human happiness, and to be in harmony with Nature means the happiness of Nature.

trees live out their full term of life unhindered and unsavaged—but then it is only these useless trees that are able to provide shade and beauty. Likewise, Chuang Tzu reasoned, the sage avoids becoming too useful, if he is to fulfill his destiny. These and other nuggets of Chuang Tzu's philosophy are set forth in nearby boxes.

CONFUCIANISM

Three great systems of thought dominate Chinese civilization: **Confucianism,** Taoism, and Buddhism. The predominant system is the one founded by **Confucius** [kun-FYOO-shus] (551–479 B.C.E.). Confucian political philosophy has dominated Chinese life in a way unequaled by any similar philosophy in the West.

Confucius

Confucius loved learning, and by age fifteen he had committed his life to a diligent study of the ancient wise men. In addition, he sought a better way and order of doing things. Learning and knowledge, Confucius believed, must be practical.

They must transform life for the better. The result of his own learning was a system of moral, political, and social precepts bound together by what is best called a philosophy of nature and by a faith in the perfectibility of the human character. The switch in Chinese thought from concern for the diety to concern for human effort and excellence began hundreds of years before Confucius was born. Nonetheless, it was Confucius who made humanity (*jen*) a cornerstone of Chinese philosophy. "The measure of man," he said, "is man." The nature and duties of the human being must be studied diligently and cultivated, he insisted, and humanity is to be loved.

To help others, Confucius said, one must first establish one's own humane character, which is done by imitating models of superior men from the past. Once the individual has a character that contains nothing contrary to humanity, he can rely on his humanity in all his actions. Through humanistic thinking and acting, according to Confucius, the superior man makes the Way (Tao) great.

That the human person is perfectible was a central tenet of Confucius's thinking. The human person, Confucius believed, is not always good but can become better. Betterment, he thought, comes through learning and service to others. No one begins with wisdom, but with diligence and determined study, wisdom can be acquired. And once acquired, wisdom becomes an instrument for perfecting oneself, the family, and society. Even nature itself, Confucius believed, cannot resist the power of wisdom: "It is man that can make the Way great," he said, "and not the Way that can make man great."

The Way, as here mentioned by Confucius, is a key concept in his philosophy. For Confucius, as for the Taoists, the Way, or Tao, is basically the path taken by natural events. Confucius uses the word *Way* or *Tao* often and in different senses. There is a way of the good man, a way of music, a way of proper government, and a cosmological way. Confucius even speaks of "my *tao*." Although interpreters are not in total agreement about this, it would seem that the Tao, for Confucius, is not a fixed and eternal transcendental principle that stands outside and above events and determines them. Rather, it is affected in no small part by human thought and human action. One can study the practices of the wise ancients to learn how to make the Way great in one's own time. Essentially, this means knowing how best to regulate your life. Confucius set forth ideals of human behavior based on his understanding of the Way.

For Confucius, everything "thrives according to its nature." One way in which heaven works, he thought, is through the principle of the **Mean,** which provides a standard of measure for all things. Human behavior should avoid extremes and seek moderation. In the philosophy of Confucius, when things function in accordance with this principle of the Mean, they stand in a relationship of mutual dependence. In other words, the principle essentially requires reciprocal cooperation among things—between people and between people and nature. And when the principle is followed, things flourish and nourish one another without conflict or injury.

Confucius formulated this principle of reciprocity in a general way as it applied to human affairs by saying, "Do not do to others what you would not want them to do to you." Likewise, according to Confucius, "A virtuous man wishing to establish himself seeks also to establish others, and wishing to enlighten himself,

PROFILE: Confucius (551–479 B.C.E.)

Confucius, or, in Chinese, K'ung Fu Tzu (K'ung the Great Master), was born "without rank in humble circumstances" in the small Chinese kingdom of Lu. Information about his life is scanty and is derived chiefly from the *Analects,* a collection of his sayings assembled by his disciples. Because of his father's death, he had to work at an early age to help support his mother. He was largely self-taught, and his hunger for learning was insatiable. With the exception of a brief period in which he served as prime minister of Lu, he did not have many opportunities to put his principles about statecraft into practice.

Confucius's ideas have influenced Chinese and Asian ways of life like those of no other philosopher, although their impact has varied from period to period. From the third century to the seventh, Confucianism was eclipsed by other philosophies, but under the T'ang dynasty (618–907) it became the state religion. Neoconfucianism (which incorporated a more developed metaphysics along with Taoist and Buddhist principles) emerged during the Sung dynasty (960–1279) and was the predominant stream of Chinese philosophy until its decline in the twentieth century, which was especially rapid after the Communist revolution in 1949. This was, in part, a consequence of the difference between Chinese communism and the more traditional worldviews. But it was also a side effect of the change in the system of state civil service examinations, which had formerly been based on the Chinese classic texts, including Confucius.

seeks also to enlighten others." Just as nature is built on a principle of reciprocal cooperation rather than strife, so reciprocal cooperation must reign in human affairs, he believed.

Confucius limited his investigation and concern to this changing world: his philosophy was this-worldly and not other-worldly. When he was asked about serving the spirits of the dead, he answered, "While you are not able to serve men, how can you serve their spirits?" And he said, "We don't know about life; how can we know about death?" It is in this world that the human being must live and with other people that one must associate, Confucius emphasized.

Nevertheless, Confucius understood the importance of religious ritual for the state and was fastidious in carrying out its mandates. To achieve a proper balance in this regard is the mark of a superior man, he said. "Devote yourself earnestly to the duties due to men, and respect spiritual beings but keep them at a distance. This may be called wisdom."

Another key concept in Confucius's thought is that of the **sage,** or superior man. The sage represents, in effect, an ethical ideal to which humans should aspire. To achieve the status of sage, Confucius believed, requires having intimate knowledge both of change and of the order of things; it requires, more specifically, having a correct understanding both of human relationships and of the workings of nature. A correct understanding, according to Confucius, involves, among other things, setting right in thought, or *rectifying,* what is distorted or confused, and it especially involves the correct use, or **rectification,** of names. (This meant knowing, for example, when it is legitimate to accord someone a title or rank.) The sage or superior person, according to Confucius, puts this correct understanding into action and seeks the mutual cooperation that enables others to fulfill their own destinies.

Confucius: Insight on Life

At fifteen, I began to be seriously interested in study; at thirty, I had formed my character; at forty, doubts ceased; at fifty, I understood the laws of Heavens; at sixty, nothing that I heard disturbed me; at seventy, I could do as my heart desired without breaking the moral law.

I never take a walk in the company of three persons without finding that one of them has something to teach me.

The superior man is distressed by his want of ability; he is not distressed by men's not knowing him.

The superior man understands righteousness; the inferior man understands profit.

What you do not want done to yourself, do not do to others.

A man who is strong, resolute, simple, and slow to speak is near to humanity.

The way of the superior man is threefold, but I have not been able to attain it. The man of wisdom has no perplexities; the man of humanity has no worry; the man of courage has no fear.

According to Confucius, the sage's actions are superior to those of other men because his model of behavior is superior. Specifically, he patterns his behavior on the great men of the past. In addition, he constantly learns from his own personal experience. (Confucius said that, if he were able to study change for fifty years, he would finally be free of mistakes.) Wisdom requires constant learning, and constant learning allows the superior man better to know the measure of things and to perform his duty accordingly.

Thus, in the philosophy of Confucius, the sage not only thinks correctly but also lives correctly. Indeed, according to Confucius, for the sage no discrepancy exists between thought (or speech) and action. The sage does not think (or say) one thing and do a different thing: he matches word with deed.

Further, according to Confucius, the superior man is an altruist who provides impartial and equitable service to others. He is kind and benevolent; he repays evil not with evil but rather with uprightness. His concern is with reform, not revenge. And his virtuous behavior is a matter of habit that holds even in the direst crisis. For this reason, Confucius believed, the sage can be counted on at all times. His fairness makes him a figure of trust to all, including the rulers of state.

Now, the rulers of the Chinese states of Confucius's time did not entrust their affairs to superior men; nor did the rulers themselves merit this title. Instead, these states were dominated by military regimes that ruled by force and were constantly at war with one another and whose subjects lived in a state of dread. In the opinion of Confucius, the ignoble policies of such inferior rulers were based on four root evils: greed, aggressiveness, pride, and resentment, which singly or together cause a ruler to rationalize and to excuse the most odious behavior on his part. Further, according to Confucius, a ruler is invariably the model for the behavior of his subjects, and, as a consequence, societies ruled by vicious men are themselves vicious societies (see the box "Confucius on Government").

By contrast, a state so fortunate as to be ruled by a superior man, Confucius believed, will be peaceful, secure, and prosperous. Because the superior man is

Confucius on Government

To govern means to make right. If you lead the people uprightly, who will dare not to be upright? Employ the upright and put aside all the crooked; in this way the crooked can be made to be upright. Go before the people with your example, and spare yourself not in their affairs. He who exercises government by means of his virtue may be compared with the polar star, which keeps its place, and all the stars turn toward it.

According to the nature of man, government is the greatest thing for him. There is good government when those who are near are made happy and when those who are afar are attracted.

Remember this, my children: oppressive government is more terrible than tigers. A ruler has only to be careful of what he likes and dislikes. What the ruler likes, his ministers will practice; and what superiors do, their inferiors will follow.

Guide the people with government measures and control or regulate them by the threat of punishment, and the people will try to keep out of jail but will have no sense of honor or shame.

Guide the people by virtue and control and regulate them by respect, and the people will have a sense of honor and respect.

Do not enter a tottering state nor stay in a chaotic one.

When the Way prevails in the empire, then show yourself; when it does not prevail, then hide.

Tzu-kung asked about government. Confucius said, "Sufficient food, sufficient armament, and sufficient confidence of the people." Tzu-kung said, "Forced to give up one of these, which would you abandon first?" Confucius said, "I would abandon armament." Tzu-kung said, "Forced to give up one of the remaining two, which would you abandon first?" Confucius said, "I would abandon food. There have been deaths from time immemorial, but no state can exist without the confidence of the people."

---

governed by the principle of the Mean, as a ruler he will be just and impartial and will seek to establish a fair distribution of wealth, which in turn will promote security and peace. And because his behavior will be emulated by his subjects, he will rule through virtuous example rather than by force of arms. Further, because he is conscientious in his service to all, he will act without fear or sadness.

Confucius's philosophy touched not only on the state and the individual but also on the family. In fact, for Confucius, the well-ordered family is a model for the well-ordered state and ultimately the world as a whole. The family, Confucius believed, should, like the state, be patriarchal and authoritarian.

Thus, the proper functioning of the family depends on the obedience of the subordinate members and the responsible governance of the parents (and ultimately the father) in accordance with the principle of the Mean and on the fundamental virtues of filial piety and brotherly respect. Together, these two virtues, according to Confucius, allow an optimal functioning of the five primary human relationships generally: those between ruler and subject, between parent and child, between elder and younger brother, between husband and wife, and between one friend and another. In the well-ordered family, because relationships are clearly defined, life will be stable and will provide the means for all members of the family to develop their capacities to the fullest extent.

PROFILE: Mencius (c. 371–c. 289 B.C.E.)

Mencius, or Meng-tzu, was born in what is now the Shantung province of China. He purportedly was taught by Confucius's grandson. Like Confucius, he lived in a time of political turmoil; he spent forty years traveling and teaching. His works became part of the "Four Classics" of ancient China and are based on his belief in the original goodness of human nature. These quotations reveal some of his insights.

The great end of learning is nothing else but to seek for the lost mind.

To preserve one's mental and physical constitution and *nourish one's nature* is the way to serve Heaven.

If you let people follow their feelings (original nature), they will be able to do good. This is what is meant by saying that human nature is good. If man does evil, it is not the fault of his natural endowment.

Humanity, righteousness, propriety, and wisdom are not drilled into us from outside. We originally have them with us. Only we do not think [to find them]. Therefore, it is said, "Seek and you will find it, neglect and you will lose it."

With proper nourishment and care, everything grows, whereas without proper nourishment and care, everything decays.

Those who follow the greater qualities in their nature become great men and those who follow the smaller qualities in their nature become small men.

That whereby man differs from the lower animals is small. The mass of the people cast it away, while the superior men preserve it.

The disease of men is this—that they neglect their own fields and go weed the fields of others.

Thus it may be said that what they require from others is great, while what they lay upon themselves is light.

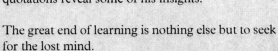

Mencius

The work of the great Confucian philosopher **Mencius** [MEN-shus] (c. 371–c. 289 B.C.E.) is regarded as second only to that of Confucius himself. Mencius, like Confucius, was very saddened by the quality of life during his time. He spoke of princes who were deaf and blind to the terrible events about them that "boom like thunder and flash like lightning." Nevertheless, a central tenet of his thought, as with Confucius, was that human beings are basically good (see the box "Mencius and Thomas Hobbes on Human Nature").

According to Mencius, the natural goodness of humans had become perverted by circumstances. Still, he said, each person has the potential for becoming perfect: doing so is a matter of recovering his lost mind and forgotten heart; it is a matter of thinking and feeling *naturally,* a matter of following intuition and conscience.

Mencius never lost his optimism about the possibility of human betterment. For him, if anything is tended properly, it will grow and thrive. Therefore, human beings should nourish the noble or superior part of themselves so that it will come to predominate. Each person, however, will decide for himself whether he will transform his life for the better.

Mencius and Thomas Hobbes on Human Nature

Mencius was quite aware that, by and large, people in his time were violent, self-serving, inclined to stop short of the mark in everything they attempted, and successful only in bringing premature death on themselves. But for Mencius, this evil came on people because circumstances had not allowed them to cultivate their inherent nobility and to search out within themselves love, wisdom, virtue, a sense of duty, and self-perfection. Human nature, according to Mencius, is inherently good, and this goodness can be actualized if people would develop their potentiality—as would happen under a just and humane regime.

Among the many Western philosophers who have also viewed people as selfish and violent, Thomas Hobbes (1588–1679) is probably the most famous. In the state of nature, Hobbes wrote, the life of man is "solitary, poor, nasty, brutish, and short." But Hobbes, unlike Mencius, attributed the ugly ways of humankind to human nature. So Hobbes believed that only through force wielded by an absolute sovereign can humans be prevented from devouring one another: *Homo lupus homini*, said Hobbes, quoting the Roman poet Plautus (c. 254–184 B.C.E.): *Man is the wolf of man.* Mencius, in contrast, believed that a wise ruler will successfully call forth the goodness inherent in human nature through mild and benevolent leadership.

Whether their malevolent actions mean that human beings, although essentially good by nature, exist in a fallen state or whether they indicate that human nature is essentially bad is a question that has not been resolved. Perhaps it is not resolvable.

For the person who has chosen to seek it, the way to self-betterment, the way to a noble existence and the upright life, according to Mencius, can be found only within oneself. Conscience, for Mencius, is "the mind that cannot bear suffering [on the part of others]." The pathway to the upright life, however, must include *self*-suffering and difficulty, he said. "When Heaven is about to confer a great office on any man," he said, "it first exercises his mind with suffering, and his sinews and bones with toil. It exposes his body to hunger and subjects him to extreme poverty. It confounds his undertakings. By all these methods, it stimulates his mind, hardens his nature, and supplies his incompetencies."

Difficulty and suffering, according to Mencius, are to be considered privileges and opportunities to develop independence, excellence, mental alertness, freedom from fear, and quietude of spirit. He goes so far as to imply that prudence and the other virtues are hardly possible for those who have not suffered deeply.

In the process of perfecting one's own life, Mencius said, one is put in a position of benefiting one's family and, through teaching and leadership, society as a whole (see the box "Mencius on Virtuous Activity"). Indeed, true happiness, he said, does not consist in ruling an empire merely for the sake of power, the desire for which is the driving ambition of the inferior mind, the mind that, like that of an animal, contains no notion of what is great or honorable. True happiness consists in seeing one's parents and family alive and free from anxiety and in helping one's society. Further, he maintained, whoever is happy in this way is happy in another way, for he need never feel shame for his actions.

Thus, it may be seen that Mencius, too, like Confucius, was concerned not only with the person but also with the state (see the box "Mencius on Government"). Disorder in a state, he believed, is often caused by a ruler who takes no

Mencius on Virtuous Activity

It is said that the superior man has two things in which he delights, and to be ruler over the empire is not one of them.

That the father and mother are both alive and that the condition of his brothers affords no cause for anxiety, this is one delight.

That when looking up he has no occasion for shame before Heaven, and below he has no occasion to blush before men—this is the second delight.

In the view of a superior man as to the ways by which men seek for riches, honors, gain, and advancement, there are few of their wives who would not be ashamed and weep together on account of them.

Men must be decided on what they will not do, and then they are able to act with vigor on what they ought.

If on self-examination I find that I am not upright, shall I not be in fear even of a poor man in loose garments of hair cloth?

If on self-examination I find that I am upright, neither thousands nor tens of thousands will stand in my path.

I have not heard of one's principles being dependent for their manifestation on other men.

Benevolence is man's mind and righteousness is man's path.

How lamentable it is to neglect the path and not pursue it, to lose the mind and not know to seek it again.

Benevolence subdues its opposite just as water subdues fire.

Those, however, who nowadays practice benevolence do it as if with one cup of water they could save a whole wagon load of fuel which was on fire, and, when the flames were not extinguished, were to say that water cannot subdue fire. This conduct greatly encourages those who are not benevolent.

notice of conditions within his own state, a ruler who—again like an animal—is indifferent to all but his own selfish interests and petty ambitions. This indifference and selfishness is a form of blindness, maintained Mencius, and a state governed without vision, he said, inevitably falls into ruin and death.

Further, according to Mencius, the subjects of the state ruled by the inferior person follow the example of their leader and also become like beasts set to devour each other. In this thought Mencius echoed Confucius. But, unlike Confucius, Mencius held that killing such a monarch is not murder, for the establishment of a humane government is not possible under such an individual.

The good ruler, Mencius maintained, is benevolent toward his subjects as a father is toward his children and will seek to establish a good order and a just regime. He displays, in addition to benevolence, three other primary virtues or attributes: righteousness, propriety, and knowledge. Further, the good ruler is mild in manner and governs with mind and heart rather than with the strong arm. Because of his mild manner, he encounters no enemies, and because he is humane and his subjects accordingly have confidence in his goodness, he will have only little opposition.

In short, this superior ruler, who has himself suffered on the path to betterment, acquires the mind that cannot bear the suffering of others, and, because it is humane and just, his governance is the foundation of all present and future good within the state.

Mencius on Government

If a man should love others and the emotion is not returned, let him turn inward and examine his own benevolence.

If a man is trying to rule others, and his government is unsuccessful, let him turn inward and examine his wisdom.

If he treats others politely and they do not return the politeness, let him turn inward and examine his own feelings of respect.

Only the benevolent ought to be in high stations. When a man destitute of benevolence is in a high station, he thereby disseminates his wickedness among all below him.

Virtue alone is not sufficient for the exercise of government; laws alone cannot carry themselves into practice.

[In a state] the people are the most important; the spirits of the land (guardians of territory) are the next; the ruler is of slight importance. Therefore to gain [the hearts of] the peasantry is the way to become emperor.

Killing a bad monarch is not murder.

If a ruler regards his ministers as hands and feet, then his ministers will regard him as their heart and mind. If the ruler regards his ministers as dogs and horses, his ministers will regard him as any other man. If a ruler regards his ministers as dirt and grass, his ministers will regard him as a bandit and an enemy.

To say that one cannot abide by humanity and follow righteousness is to throw oneself away. Humanity is the peaceful abode of man and righteousness is his straight path.

All men have the mind which cannot bear [to see the suffering of] others. . . . When a government that cannot bear to see the suffering of the people is conducted from a mind that cannot bear to see the suffering of others, the government of the empire will be as easy as making something go round in the palm.

Humanity, righteousness, loyalty, faithfulness, and the love of the good without getting tired of it constitute the nobility of Heaven, and to be a grand official, a great official, and a high official—this constitutes the nobility of man.

Mencius's philosophy exhibits the humanistic concerns and faith in human goodness and perfectibility that characterize Confucian philosophy in general. Both Mencius and Confucius were aware, however, that in practice humans are often self-seeking and that their potential for goodness must be cultivated or nurtured. As may be seen in the boxes, Mencius offers much advice and sets forth many telling maxims that, in effect, constitute a method for cultivating the better part of human nature.

Hsün Tzu

Another important Confucian philosopher, who blended Taoism with Confucianism and added his own, rather more pessimistic conception of human nature, was **Hsün Tzu** [SHWIN-tsuh] (298–238 B.C.E.). He was rationalistic and realistic in his approach, believing that the hierarchical order of society was established by following unchanging moral principles. If moral practices, laws, and the rules of propriety were followed, then order, peace, and prosperity would inevitably be the result. If they were not followed, disorder and disaster would result.

Hsün Tzu's view of the basic nature of human beings is what makes him strikingly dissimilar to other major Confucian thinkers. He did not agree with Mencius that human beings are originally good and therefore naturally inclined to goodness. Hsün Tzu believed that human beings are basically bad but that they are impelled to compensate for and overcome this defectiveness, this badness, through education and moral training. Fortunately, the human being is perfectible. Through a study of past and present sages, a human being may develop a moral understanding based on the ultimate virtues of humanity and righteousness.

For Hsün Tzu, the state, like the individual, can lose itself in seeking profit. The result is strife, violence, lewdness, and rebellion. Such an inferior state must be reconstructed through moral principles, which must come to be embodied in the person of the ruler. Hsün Tzu's thought was the official creed during the Han period (c. 206–220), and it has continued to have an important influence on Asian societies to the present.

ZEN BUDDHISM IN CHINA AND JAPAN

Zen Buddhism is one of the Buddhist sects of Japan and China. (Buddhism, it may be recalled, originated in India.) *Zen* is Japanese and *Ch'an* is Chinese, and both words derive from the Sanskrit word for meditation, ***dhyana.*** When Buddhism first came to China, it emphasized the importance of meditation, rather than any particular scripture or doctrine, as the key to ultimate reality.

Although the heading for this section is Zen Buddhism, we discuss both the Chinese and Japanese traditions, Zen and Ch'an. It should be noted that other forms of Buddhism developed as well, but the Zen tradition is the one that has awakened the most philosophical interest in the West.

The growth of **Ch'an Buddhism** (Chinese Zen Buddhism) was slow at first, and numerically it always was one of the smaller sects. But over the centuries this sect spread throughout China and into neighboring countries like Japan and Korea. In the last century, it has taken root in the United States and Europe. Its current spread in the West seems to indicate that Ch'an Buddhism responds to a need in a highly complex, technological world.

Buddhism in China and Japan has a long and rich history. Here it will only be possible to look briefly at a few of its most original and profound thinkers, the sixth patriarch of Chinese Zen, Hui Neng; Murasaki Shikibu; and Dogen Kigen, the founder of the Japanese Soto tradition. The philosophies of these thinkers complement one another and give an overall perspective on basic elements in the Zen Buddhist tradition.

Hui Neng

Hui Neng [HWAY-nung] (638–713) lost his father in childhood and had to sell firewood to keep his mother and himself alive. He was illiterate.

One day, while delivering firewood to a shop, Hui Neng heard the chanting of the Buddhist *Diamond Sutra* (perhaps the most important scripture of Chinese Buddhism, in which Buddha strips his student Subhuti of his coarse views and allows him to see the fundamental oneness of all things and the immutability of perceived phenomena; *sutra* means "secret doctrines and sacred teachings"). Hui Neng immediately grasped the deep truth latent in its words. But not until some time later did a gift of money enable him to confirm his perception of truth by seeking out Master Hung-jen, the fifth Chinese patriarch of Ch'an Buddhism, at Huang-mei Mountain in Hupei.

During the first meeting with the fifth patriarch, Hui Neng did not hesitate to manifest the unshakable strength of his vision, and he was accordingly accepted in the Huang-mei monastery. For eight months, however, he worked in the kitchen without even entering the main temple.

At this time, the fifth patriarch was seeking a successor and asked the monks to write a poem showing the depth of their insight into truth. Only the person who has a direct intuition into the truth achieves peace of mind, the Ch'an Buddhists believed, and they also thought that each person must discover this truth for himself. That all is ultimately one was a basic precept of the fifth patriarch. This one reality was thought to be our true self-nature and was held to be immanent within human beings from the beginning. To see this ever-present truth exactly as it is would require going beyond the usual way of thinking, which breaks down ultimate being into distinct entities and classifies and relates them so that they are understood only in terms of the categories to which they belong and their relationships to one another. Hence poetry rather than a normal form of discourse would be required to express insight into this truth, for normal forms of thought and language can express neither the uniqueness of the individual entity nor the underlying oneness of all things. Perhaps you are reminded here of Heidegger.

Shen-hsui, the senior monk at the monastery, was the only one who dared to write the requested poem, and the other monks doubted their ability to surpass him in depth of understanding. His contribution, however, according to tradition, only showed that he had not seen the ultimate truth and had not escaped the confines of normal thought. Hui Neng, though illiterate, is said immediately to have sensed the inadequacy of the vision conveyed by this poem when he overheard it being recited by another monk and to have composed a reply to the poem on the spot.

The monks, it is said, were astounded by the words of this twenty-three-year-old illiterate, who had not yet even been admitted into the meditation hall. The fifth patriarch was moved as well and immediately recognized Hui Neng as his successor. Perceiving the possibility of jealousy and anger among the monks, he is said to have had Hui Neng come to him in the middle of the night to receive the robe and bowl symbolic of his new status as sixth patriarch and to learn the wisdom of the *Diamond Sutra*. According to tradition, Hung-jen, the fifth patriarch, convinced that the truth of the *Buddha-Dharma* (ultimate reality) would ultimately prevail through Hui Neng, instructed Hui Neng to leave the monastery immediately and to remain in hiding until he was ready to teach.

What is the ultimate **Dharma** (reality/truth/law)? Hui Neng gave it a number of different titles: the Self-Nature, the Buddha-Dharma, the Real Nature, and the eternal and unchanging Tao (note the Taoist influence implicit in the last name).

Hui Neng on Life and Truth

As mentioned in the text, Hui Neng sought out the fifth patriarch of Ch'an Buddhism, Master Hung-jen, who eventually confirmed Hui Neng's insight into the truth and appointed him his successor. On meeting the fifth patriarch, Hui Neng is said to have said: "I confess to Your Reverence that I feel wisdom constantly springing from my own heart and mind. So long as I do not stray from my nature, I carry within me the field of bliss."

Other interesting quotations of Hui Neng as to life and truth are as follows:

> How could I expect that the self-nature is in and of itself so pure and quiet! How could I expect that the self-nature is in and of itself unborn and undying! How could I expect that the self-nature is in and of itself self-sufficient, with nothing lacking in it! How could I expect that the self-nature is in and of itself immutable and imperturbable! How could I expect that the self-nature is capable of giving birth to all dharmas [laws]!

The *Bodhi* or Wisdom, which constitutes our self-nature, is pure from the beginning. We need only use our mind to perceive it directly to attain Buddhahood.

One Reality is all Reality.

Our original nature is Buddha, and apart from this nature there is no other Buddha. Within, keep the mind in perfect harmony with the self-nature; without, respect all other men. This is surrender to and reliance of one's self.

Light and darkness are two different things in the eyes of the ordinary people. But the wise and understanding ones possess as penetrating insight that there can be no duality in the self-nature. The Non-dual nature is the Real Nature . . . both its [the Real Nature's] essence and its manifestations are in the absolute state of suchness. Eternal and unchanging, we call it the Tao.

All things, he said, are in reality one: there are no "things." Human thought and understanding, to make sense of a totality that cannot be grasped at once, impose categories, contrasts, and distinctions on reality (including thirty-six basic pairs of contrasts or opposites, such as light and darkness, yin and yang, birth and death, good and bad, and so on). But in truth there is only one thing, the Real Nature, and, as it is in itself, it exists prior to any distinctions or categorizations; it is (so to speak) beyond good and evil, permanence and impermanence, content and form. It is an absolute state of "suchness" that neither comes nor goes, neither increases nor decreases, neither is born nor dies. It is exactly as it is: it is reality and truth (see the box "Hui Neng on Life and Truth").

According to Hui Neng, though this ultimate reality or truth is in principle accessible to all, it remains hidden to many of us because we are focused on false attachments and selfish interests: in short, we lack a balanced, objective outlook. And, as a result of this imbalance in our perspective, our efforts, too, are one-sided in pursuit of our goals. Hui Neng made it his purpose to free humans from selfish, one-sided visions of reality. His recommendation was for a state of "no-thought" or "mindlessness," in which the mind does not impose itself on the truth but, rather, remains open and spontaneous—a mirror reflecting the wisdom inherent in reality, one that reflects but does not impede the flow of events.

To deepen one's spirit, he said, is to live in harmony with the true or "self-nature" of all things. When the mind is right, it thinks without bias or partiality and is thus considerate of the needs of each and every thing.

The blend of Taoist, Confucian, and Buddhist precepts is very much in evidence in Hui Neng's thought.

Buddhism in Japan

At this point, we depart China for Japan, where Zen was introduced from China. As you have seen, under Hui Neng, Zen emerged as a distinct and separate Buddhist sect that combined elements of Indian Buddhist and Chinese thought. When it spread to Japan, Zen was influenced by Japanese culture as well.

Japan is a serene and beautiful country, a collection of many islands dominated generally by volcanic mountains offering scant natural resources. Ancient legends see the Japanese as descending from the Sun Goddess, but more specific data indicate that the Japanese came from Central Asia (Mongolia today), from South China, and possibly also from the South Sea Islands of the Pacific. Because Japan consists of islands surrounded by water, it has remained relatively free of hostile invasions for long periods of its history. Its isolation has also allowed it to develop a unique style in almost every facet of life.

From early times, the Japanese borrowed ideas and practices from other cultures, often modifying them in the process. Confucius and Confucianism were particularly revered and implemented in various degrees at various times in Japanese history. Korean scholars introduced Buddhism to Japan around 552. Architecture, sculpture, painting, music, and poetry were all heavily influenced by this event, because China was the older, dominant culture of the region. The Chinese influence was furthered by the arrival of Zen Buddhism in the fourteenth century; more about this shortly. Only after the middle of the nineteenth century did modern Western influences make an impression on Japan.

Medieval Japan was a melting pot of philosophical and religious views. For men, the mixture of Asian philosophies probably was good enough, but its effect on women was less fortunate (as you will see). If there were a recipe for medieval Japanese philosophy, it would read as follows:

> 1 cup Shinto animism
> 4 Buddhist Noble Truths
> 1 yin
> 1 yang
> 1 handful Confucian virtues
> 1 Mahayana Buddhist doctrine of the void
>
> Mix all ingredients well, apply liberally to everyone. Prepares men for salvation. Prepares women for reincarnation as men.

This is intended to give a reader only a broad idea of some of the main elements in Japanese Buddhism at the time. By the late ninth century, Japanese culture reflected an unequal mixture of Shinto, Confucianism, Taoism, and Zen Buddhism (and its Mahayana branch, and *its* branches, Tendai and Shigon). What are these ingredients? You already are familiar with most of them, other than Shinto and Mahayana.

Shinto is an ancient native religion of Japan that, from the earliest times, has played a large role in Japanese culture and politics. Unlike most animistic religions, it persists even to the present day in what is now a modern society. Shinto is an animistic, nature-worshiping religion in which the sun, the moon, storm, and fire all are viewed as deities. Shinto is based on gratitude for the benevolence and beauty of nature rather than on fear of it. There are no iconic images and no angry gods to be mollified. There are also no sacred scriptures or moral codes to be followed.

Shinto related humans to the **kami,** or gods of nature, that created the universe. People were said to be just another part of the physical universe. The Japanese language did not even have a word for nature as something distinct from humans. People were regarded as "thinking reeds" completely identified with and part of the natural and divine universe. Such a view is called **animism.**

People's duties were derived through their blood relationships. One was connected to the gods of nature through one's ancestor's clan and through the divine clan of the Mikado, who was both national high priest and head of state. The Japanese word for government, *matsuri-goto,* means "things pertaining to worship." So there was no conceptual difference between religion, ethics, and government. And there was no conceptual difference between people and other natural objects.

Mahayana Buddhism was just a twist on Zen. It was introduced into Japan in the late sixth century, when Japan lost its territory in Korea and its ally, the Paekche Kingdom, suffered military defeat. Many Korean war refugees, most of them Buddhists, fled to Japan, where their religion gained acceptance among Japanese diplomats and aristocrats. Prince Shotoku (his name means "sovereign moral authority") made it the official religion of Japan, incorporating it into Shinto. Shinto connected one to one's historical, anthropological past; Mahayana Buddhism connected one to the present and to the future eternity. It incorporated the Confucian virtues of filial piety, veneration of ancestors, duties based on rank and position, honesty, and so forth. (Taoism, too, fit in nicely, with its views about the oneness of humans and nature, spiritual freedom, and peace—not to mention yin/yang emphasis on orderliness and balance.)

Mahayana saw humanity unified through spiritual enlightenment, in the worship of one god, who, as luck would have it, turned out to be the Mikado, the greatest earthly *kami.* This was the form of Buddhism adopted by Japanese aristocracy. The higher up the sociopolitical aristocracy one was, the closer one was to God— and thus the theory did not displace aristocrats.

This brings us to Murasaki.

Murasaki Shikibu

Murasaki Shikibu [MOO-ruh-sah-kee shih-kih-boo] (978?–1026?) lived at the height of the Mahayana Buddhist influence in Japan. And while all Japanese shared this philosophical heritage, not all shared social and political equality.

The Tendai sect of Mahayana Buddhism held that the closer one was to the Mikado, the greater was one's potential for moral excellence and for admission to the Western Paradise (heaven). But in Buddhism, women generally were considered to be of lesser moral worth than men. Women could achieve salvation or reach the psychological state of nirvana that would prepare them to enter the Western Paradise, but only after reincarnation as a male.

PROFILE: Murasaki Shikibu (978?–1026?)

Murasaki Shikibu, or Lady Murasaki, as she is sometimes called, is an important Japanese, Shinto, Buddhist, and feminist philosopher. Murasaki Shikibu is almost certainly not her real name, however. She was given the nickname "Murasaki" because the real author strongly resembled a character by that name in the book she wrote. Murasaki came from a literary family of the Fujiwara clan. In Japan at that time, it was forbidden for women to study Chinese characters (the original written form of Japanese language). Murasaki learned young how to read Chinese characters by hanging around when her brother was being tutored. She eventually entered court service in the entourage of the teenaged empress Joto-Mon'in Shoshi, to whom Murasaki secretly taught Chinese. Learning how to read gave Murasaki access to the forbidden literatures of religion and philosophy.

In addition to some poetry, Murasaki left two works: a diary, *Murasaki Shikibu Nikki,* and an epic philosophical novel, *Genji Monogatari.* Despite the fact that it was written centuries before the invention of the printing press, once it was printed, *Tale of Genji* (as it is also known) never went out of print. It has been translated into more than thirty languages. Murasaki's primary philosophical interest was with the moral status of women under Japanese Buddhist ethics.

The fact that one was a woman was evidence that in a past life one had been a male who was now making up for a past life lacking in virtue. In the Buddhist doctrine of reincarnation, a good woman can hope at best for reincarnation as a man. After a lifetime as a virtuous man, it would be possible to achieve salvation and enter heaven. Women, no matter their virtue, could not hope for salvation, as Murasaki says:

> But then someone with as much to atone for as myself may not qualify for salvation; there are so many things that serve to remind one of the transgressions of a former existence. Ah, the wretchedness of it all!

Murasaki's women characters illustrated just how hopeless life was for Japanese women, especially those who thought about things like self-identity, morality, free will and determinism, predestination and salvation. Judging from the popularity of her very long book, *Tale of Genji,* and the fact that it was initially circulated a chapter at a time among aristocratic women (obviously, many had learned how to read Chinese characters on the sly), a lot of Japanese women did care about these philosophical issues.

Murasaki kept the basic recipe we gave in the "Buddhism in Japan" section, but she changed the directions and added a few ingredients. Here is Murasaki's version of the recipe:

1 cup Shinto animism
4 Buddhist Noble Truths
1 yin
1 yang
1 handful Confucian virtues
1 Mahayana Buddhist doctrine of the void
1 lifetime of spiritual enlightenment

> Mix all ingredients well with a strong, feminist hand. Contemplate for a lifetime with as much detachment from worldly distractions as possible. (Become a nun if you can.) Use as an antidote to determinist misogynist elements of Tendai. With lifelong use, women may achieve salvation.

Murasaki's version of the recipe added the importance of spiritual enlightenment and contemplation. She also emphasized the virtues of simplicity and detachment from worldly possessions.

In sharp contrast to the views of women present in Buddhism and reflected in Japanese culture, Murasaki's female characters struggled with the problem that, in Japanese culture and Buddhist religion, women existed only as predestined, natural objects.

Murasaki's main character, Ukifune (which means "loose boat," "loose woman," or "person with no direction and uncertain destination"—you get the idea), becomes so depressed following a rape that she attempts to commit suicide, but she is saved by a monk, against the advice of other monks who think she should be allowed to drown.

Everyone, especially other women, has told Ukifune that she cannot do anything about the rape and its social consequences; it is just her fate. There is no hope for her other than to become a prostitute. Ukifune rages against the double injustice: first, she is just an object to a man who forcibly rapes her; second, she is punished socially for having been wronged. Rather than accept her fate, she challenges her destiny through suicide, hoping for reincarnation as a man.

But her rescue, although also attributed by the monk to fate, leads her to a path of religious contemplation. Ultimately, she becomes a nun—but not an ordinary nun performing public service. Ukifune spends her life contemplating life's meaning and seeking enlightenment. Ultimately, a lifetime of contemplation will reveal to her that she can control her destiny through self-knowledge.

Murasaki's women characters struggle to become free, responsible moral agents who assert that they have natural rights. They also assume moral responsibilities to others. Although Murasaki rejected mainstream Buddhism's view of women, her philosophy represents a minority Buddhist view that women are moral agents who, instead of blaming fate, can assume moral responsibility for their actions. Murasaki held that women should challenge their *karma* (destiny) and take control of their own lives by engaging in what were then forbidden, illegal activities such as reading the *sutras* (secret doctrines and sacred teachings) of the great Buddhist monks.

Murasaki's personal decision to become a nun and to read the *sutras* was the product of a wager that was worthy of Pascal (see Chapter 13):

> The time too is ripe. If I get much older my eyesight will surely weaken to the point that I shall be unable to read the sutras, and my spirits will fail. It may seem that I am merely going through the motions of being a true believer, but I assure you that I can think of little else at the present moment.

By understanding and living according to what Murasaki argued was the true meaning of Buddhism, women could achieve a state of contemplation that is compatible with reaching nirvana. Under Murasaki's philosophy, women need not be content to wait until they have been reincarnated as males to begin the difficult and long process of philosophical enlightenment. They can begin that process in this life by living, as do men, according to the teachings of Shinto and Buddhism. It should be taken into account that there have been more positive developments regarding women's status in Japanese Buddhism, especially recently.

Dogen Kigen

By age fourteen, **Dogen** [DOE-gen] (1200–1253) was already a monk. He eventually became dissatisfied with the decadent state of Tendai Buddhism, which, being egalitarian and anti-elitist in nature, adopted many popular rituals like chanting the name of Amitabba Buddha. **Tendai Buddhism** was a Japanese variation of the T'ien-t'ai School of Buddhism in China. It was introduced into Japan in the ninth century. Its basic notion is that all phenomena are expressions of the absolute oneness or suchness (*tathatā*). Dogen therefore sought out a Tendai monk, Eisei, who had twice traveled to China to study Ch'an Buddhism. Eisei died soon after the encounter with Dogen, but Dogen continued his studies for nine years under Eisei's successor, Myozen. Afterward, Dogen went to China himself to deepen his studies, and eventually he came under the tutelage of Ju-Ching, at T'ien T'ung Shan monastery. After five years, he returned to Japan in 1227.

Dogen continued to teach and write in monasteries in and around the old capital city of Kyoto until 1243. During this time, he came increasingly in conflict with the predominant Tendai tradition and eventually withdrew into the mountains to establish the Eiheiji monastery. To this day, Eiheiji is the principal monastery of the Soto branch of Japanese Zen Buddhism.

Many of life's numerous problems, Dogen realized, are not easily solvable. There is, for example, the problem of the impermanence of life. Life passes like the rush of a spring stream, flowing on, day after day, and then it is gone. Dogen therefore urged humans not to waste a single second. Time must be utilized in a worthy pursuit, a single objective that merits an all-out effort. The life goal must be nothing small, selfish, or narrow-minded. It must be chosen from a broad perspective and with an eye to benefiting others as well as oneself. Dogen's philosophy is, in essence, a prescription for an unwasted or noble life, a life of happiness here and now.

It is difficult, of course, Dogen realized, to choose how to live and equally difficult, if not more so, to carry out that choice. One lives in an uncertain and hurried world, and "our minds go racing about like horses running wild in the fields, while our emotions remain unmanageable like monkeys swinging in the trees." The rapidity of life and the uncertainty of its course makes people's lives full of torment and confusion. They do not understand its nature or how best to manage themselves.

Moreover, according to Dogen, the mind overwhelmed by a world not understood seeks safety in selfish and self-protective acts. Life is perceived as a succession of real and suspected dangers, and it is viewed in stark contrasts of good and bad, right and wrong, black and white. This perception of the world is what Dogen called the "Lesser Vehicle," and it arises out of ignorance and fear. The ignorant, fearful mind constructs a list of things deemed bad and to be avoided, and anger and resentment are felt toward perceived sources of danger. The individual caught in a dark and threatening world he does not understand finds little rest or peace, and doing violence to himself or others is a frequent consequence of his entrapment.

Dogen's Prescriptions for Virtuous Activity

Dogen, a Zen monk since early youth who traveled to China for further studies, gained a reputation as a strict teacher. His writings have had a profound influence up to the present day. Many of his works have been translated into English and have played an important part in the growth of Zen Buddhism. The following are his prescriptions for virtuous activity.

> To plow deep but plant shallow is the way to a natural disaster. When you help yourself and harm others, how could there be no consequence?

> Everyone has the nature of Buddha; do not foolishly demean yourself.

> Even worldly people, rather than study many things at once without really becoming accomplished in any of them, should just do one thing well and study enough to be able to do it even in the presence of others.

> While simply having the appearance of an ordinary person of the world, one who goes on harmonizing the inner mind is a genuine aspirant to the Way. Therefore as an Ancient said, "Inside empty, outside accords." What this means is to have no selfish thought in the inner mind, while the outer appearance goes along with others.

> Emperor Wen of Sui said, "Secretly cultivate virtue, await fulfillment." . . . If one just cultivates the work of the Way, the virtues of the Way will appear outwardly of their own accord.

> To practice the appropriate activity and maintain bearing means to abandon selfish clinging. . . . The essential meaning of this is to have no greed or desire.

> Students of the Way, do not think of waiting for a later day to practice the Way. Without letting this day and this moment pass by, just work from day to day, moment to moment.

> It is written (in the *Vinaya*), "What is praised as pure in character is called good; what is scorned as impure in character is called bad." It is also said, "That which would incur pain is called bad; that which should bring about happiness is called good."
> In this way should one carefully discriminate; seeing real good, one should practice it, and seeing real evil, one should shun it.

> Jade becomes a vessel by carving and polishing. A man becomes humane by cultivation and polish. What gem has highlights to begin with? What person is clever at the outset? You must carve and polish, train and cultivate them. Humble yourselves and do not relax your study of the Way.

> There is a saying of Confucius: "You can't be apart from the Way for even a second. If you think you are apart from it, that's not the Way." He also said, "As the sages have no self, everything is themselves."

This state of malcontent, according to Dogen, in which the world is perceived in terms of stark and fearful divisions, remains with the individual until he or she achieves clarification about the true nature of things. But everyone, Dogen said, has the nature of Buddha. Everyone can see the truth and live calmly and peacefully in its presence. It is simply necessary to abandon the selfish and narrow perspective in favor of the broad and unbiased view, in which the mind is expanded beyond the limitations of divisive categories like good/bad and desirable/undesirable, in which greed gives way to generosity, self-serving to other-serving. It is necessary to see things as the ancient sages did, from the perspective of the universe or "Buddha-Dharma" or "universal Self." To do this is to practice the Great Way.

Understanding from this broad perspective, Dogen thought, also involves acceptance—going along with things, following the Way. This, he said, is the wisdom

Zen Buddhism in Japan

There are two major forms of Zen Buddhism in contemporary Japan: Rinzai Zen and Soto Zen. Over the centuries, each has mutually influenced the other. The difference between the two has more to do with method than with doctrine. Both seek enlightenment apart from the scriptures.

Rinzai Zen, named after the famous Zen monk Rinzai (785–867), seeks sudden enlightenment, as preached by Hui Neng. To achieve **satori,** or the enlightenment experience, **koans** are often used in addition to sitting in meditation (**zazen**). *Koans* are illogical, even nonsensical, puzzles that are designed to break the stranglehold of conceptual thought so that the absolute, indivisible truth or reality may be suddenly and utterly seen or intuited. Among the most famous of all *koans* is "What is the sound of one hand clapping?"

The **Soto Zen** tradition places less emphasis on sudden enlightenment and tends not to use *koans*. As exemplified by Dogen, enlightenment is to be found slowly through *zazen* (meditation) and also by performing all daily duties in the same state of awareness as when sitting in *zazen*. This tradition recognizes no single moment of *satori,* for enlightenment is believed to be possible in all moments.

of emptiness—allowing things to be, without exercising any preference or desire whatsoever. The similarity to the philosophy of Chuang Tzu is evident.

How does one acquire this perspective of the universal Self? For Dogen, the answer is practice—seeking to help others without reward or praise, caring for others as a parent would. If one makes a continuous effort to do all things with a parental mind and without seeking profit or praise, then one's life will be suffused with the attitude of a "Joyful Mind," in which life takes on a buoyancy and lightness that cannot be diminished by any external event.

Dogen endeavored to set forth a way to achieve permanent joy in *this* life, a way of living that enables the human to achieve a majestic dignity, uncompromisable nobility of character, and peace. "No one or anything could ever make merit decay in any way," he said. In his precepts, Dogen continued the tradition begun by Chuang Tzu, Lao Tzu, and Hui Neng. Life does involve suffering, pain, and transience. But despite the presence of these and of evil too, life, if lived according to the Tao, should be a joyful and fulfilling event. Dogen urged, "Rejoice in your birth in the world." If one does not escape the fears and insecurities of the small self, life is a torment. But if one lives as would the Magnanimous Mind, then one is living out the truth of the Way itself—the Way of the Buddha-Dharma.

THE PHILOSOPHY OF THE SAMURAI (c. 1100–1900)

Japan's warrior class, the **samurai,** were also the ruling class for long periods of time. Their wisdom was transmitted in the form of martial precepts, the earliest dating to the twelfth century or earlier. The precepts were handed down the generations with the class, and they were often used to train the samurai and to teach them the code of **bushido,** that is, the way of the samurai. According to William Scott Wilson's *Ideals of the Samurai,* the word *bushi* ("samurai warrior") is

A samurai.

first recorded in an early history of Japan dated 97 C.E. At the time, these educated warriors served in close attendance upon the nobility. The weakness of civil government, however, led to clans and private estates developing their own armies and to increasing involvement by samurai in government. Eventually, the warrior class actually replaced the court aristocracy, and the late twelfth century marked the beginning of warrior-class rule, which lasted seven hundred years.

The literature of the samurai tradition has influenced all areas of Japanese thought and behavior. Westerners who have wished to understand the basis of the Japanese economic "miracle" since World War II have looked to such samurai classics as Miyamoto Musashi's *The Book of Five Rings* and Yamamoto Tsunetomo's *Hagakure*. The writings concerning the samurai tradition have become popular and reportedly are widely read among business executives and in business graduate schools. The film *Ghost Dog* sought to apply the teachings of the samurai to American life.

One of the most famous samurai was **Miyamoto Musashi** [Mee-yuh-moh-toh Mu-sah-shee] (1584–1645), who was perhaps the greatest swordsman and duelist ever. Among Musashi's many accomplishments apparently was the single-handed defeat of an entire band of samurai from the most prestigious school of martial arts specialists. When he was only thirteen, Musashi fought his first duel.[4] Reportedly, his opponent was armed with a *wakizashi*-style sword; Musashi had only a piece of wood. However, Musashi was sufficiently proficient with his toy

---

[4] Said to be a reliable reference on Musashi is William Scott Wilson's 2004 book, *The Lone Samurai* (Japan: Kodansha International). Not surprisingly, there is much legend surrounding Musashi.

sword to slay his opponent. As you might expect from such reports, Musashi became the subject of many unbelievable legends, such as being able to walk on air.

Beyond this, Musashi was an accomplished sculptor and artist. But he also had a keen understanding of the art, methods, and strategies of fighting. Toward the end of his life, he withdrew from society and wrote *The Book of Five Rings,* the classic treatise on *kenjutsu* (sword methods) and the martial arts in general.

The famous book has played a role in Japan similar to that played in China by Sun Tzu's *The Art of War.* It became a principal manual of military, economic, and political strategy and might have something to do with Japan's rapid rise as an economic superpower. *The Book of Five Rings* is said to be required reading in some American business colleges.

Much in this book is about weapons and techniques and how to slash heads and so forth, material that may not be useful to the average business college student. But the work goes far beyond this and is something of a primer on life strategy. According to Musashi, study and practice are everything. He thought that even trifles must be deliberated upon and understood. Nothing should escape one's gaze. "There must not be one thing you cannot see," he wrote. To achieve invulnerability, one must anticipate every possibility and understand one's opponents better than they understand themselves. The ultimate goal is to achieve "unclouded vision" of events and people, without distortions introduced by fear, prejudice, or desire. This gives rise to an intuitive and instantaneous understanding of events, which enables one to react spontaneously and decisively. The price of not being able to see and foresee everything in an instant, what Napoleon called the *coup d'oeil* (stroke of the eye), is death. Clearly, some of this has application beyond the martial arts, at least to competitive situations.

Knowledge, however, according to Musashi, is turned into action only through training and practice. Life must be constant training, and training is the practical pursuit of perfection. Because perfection is never completely achieved, one must use it to spur oneself toward improvement. Further, both body and spirit must be trained, each preventing the other from becoming lax and weak. Those who fall short in preparation will never even realize their lowest potential, let alone achieve excellence.

Training, Musashi said, develops balance, rhythm, and timing, but to do so, it must be all encompassing. The trainee must become conversant with every art and must understand all disciplines, must comprehend both the ways of peace and the ways of war. The nature of human behavior must be understood thoroughly: people's outlooks, goals, strategies, and methods all must be comprehended. The trainee must master the various arts and sciences to such a degree that they become one with his being.

Training enables one to release one's full potentiality in action, Musashi thought. Generally, people are fearful, hesitant, indecisive, and lack confidence. Thus, their actions are constrained, clumsy, and wasteful and are either procrastinated or rushed. To attain invincibility, one's actions must become lightning fast and decisive, must arise from a resolute spirit, and must be performed without hesitation.

Takuan, the Zen monk who trained Musashi, taught the way of instantaneous, untainted response. According to this perspective, the real secret is to release one's spirit from the constrictions of fear. This is what Musashi called "becoming one with the supreme power," which he regarded as the true virtue and basis of all strategizing.

But how is the spirit to be freed from fear, lack of confidence, and hesitation? How can one avoid being a "bashful monkey"? Musashi said that, to attain extraordinary ability or miraculous power, the trainee must become free of all preoccupations with the self. Musashi called this state of perfect acting the "Spirit of the Void." When a person's spirit and actions are not in the least contaminated with considerations of the self, then that is the true void. Then the warrior is no-thing, and the universe itself is no-thing to the warrior. Then there is a perfect oneness of actor, action, and the enacted, what Musashi called "just being it."

Musashi also placed emphasis on ferocity. You "must strike with all your heart and all your soul." Because the struggle with an opponent is a matter of life and death, you must not be surprised or overwhelmed when the opponent resorts to extreme measures. Likewise, you, too, must be prepared and willing to use any means to achieve victory. It is a matter of "keeping your spirit tall and your resolve strong."

Fierceness of spirit must be developed in training, he believed. The true warrior trains fiercely and thinks fiercely. Following this prescription enables ferocity to become a matter of habit. This, in turn, means that one will act swiftly and without hesitation, which will make one a formidable opponent.

But training must also emphasize dignity and bearing, he said. In *The Name of the Rose,* Umberto Eco (an Italian novelist born in 1932) wrote, "Nothing gives a fearful man more courage than another's fear." Musashi was perhaps coming at things from the reverse angle when he emphasized the importance of using body language that expresses fearlessness. Although a warrior should always be courteous and considerate, his bearing must reveal ferocity and must be unnerving, even scary.

Musashi also discussed the best strategy to defeat an enemy. The main thing is to use knowledge of the opponent to keep him or her off balance. This will ruin his timing, shake his confidence, and make him vulnerable. And once he has been misdirected and shaken, he must not be allowed to recover.

If there is another person whose name is associated with the samurai tradition, it is **Yamamoto Tsunetomo** [Yah-muh-moh-toh Tsu-neh-toh-moh] (1659–1719). Tsunetomo served only a short time as a retainer before his master died; thereafter, he withdrew from the world and lived as a recluse studying Zen Buddhism. During the final years of his life, his thoughts on the essence of the samurai way of life were written down and preserved (see the box "Samurai Insights from Yamamoto Tsunetomo, *Hagakure*"). The ideals of the samurai tradition have endured and still determine to no small extent the life and thought of modern-day Japan.

The worldview expressed in Tsunetomo's *Hagakure* will be familiar to readers of the material on Dogen. Human life at best Tsunetomo sees as "a short affair." No time may be squandered without regret and loss. Yet brevity is not what makes life so difficult and painful; this effect comes rather from life's uncertainty. Humans exist in a world of constant and unpredictable change.

When these changes are not anticipated, the result is often disastrous. Therefore, a samurai must train himself to be ready at all times for anything that may happen. He must train to anticipate all eventualities and deal with them before they become a problem. A samurai precept is "Win beforehand."

According to Tsunetomo, not only is the uncertainty of events problematic, but also human beings themselves are often flawed, ignorant, selfish, and unreasonable. Accordingly, the samurai must learn to be self-reliant. He cannot and

Samurai Insights from Yamamoto Tsunetomo, *Hagakure*

Everything in this world is a marionette show.

[The samurai] remains undistracted twenty-four hours a day.

A samurai's word is harder than metal.

The Way of the samurai is in desperateness. Ten or more men cannot kill such a man.

With an intense, fresh, and undelaying spirit, one will make his judgment within the space of seven breaths. It is a matter of being determined and having the spirit to break right through to the other side.

If one will do things for the benefit of others and meet even those whom he has met often before in a first-time manner, he will have no bad relationships.

A samurai's obstinacy should be excessive.

It is natural that one cannot understand deep and hidden things. Those things that are easily understood are rather shallow.

Courage is gritting one's teeth . . . and pushing ahead, paying no attention to the circumstances.

There is nothing other than the single purpose of the present moment.

I never knew about winning . . . but only about not being behind in a situation.

There is nothing that one should suppose cannot be done.

One must be resolved in advance.

Human life is a short affair. It is better to live doing the things that you like.

If one will rectify his mistakes, their traces will soon disappear.

At a glance, every individual's own measure of dignity is manifested just as it is.

One cannot accomplish things simply with cleverness.

By being impatient, matters are damaged and great works cannot be done. If one considers something not to be a matter of time, it will be done surprisingly quickly.

A man's life should be as toilsome as possible.

People become imbued with the idea that the world has come to an end and no longer put forth any effort. This is a shame. There is no fault in the times.

When I face the enemy, of course it is like being in the dark. But if at that time I tranquilize my mind, it becomes like a night lit by a pale moon. If I begin my attack from that point, I feel as though I will not be wounded.

It is the highest sort of victory to teach your opponent something that will be to his benefit.

Win first, fight later.

There is nothing so painful as regret.

Money is a thing that will be there when asked for. A good man is not so easily found.

Meditation on inevitable death should be performed daily. . . . It is to consider oneself as dead beforehand.

does not depend on others to act properly. He knows that human beings will not always act either reasonably or justly. He is prepared for treachery and cowardice and awaits their arrival. Only by practicing alertness and bravery can a samurai avoid wasting his life.

Because of the uncertainty of the world and the unreliability of the human character, the samurai must learn the arts of war as well as the arts of peace. Human beings, like states, must be able to defend themselves. Kuroda Nagamasa (1568–1623), known as a great military strategist, wrote, "The arts of peace and the arts of war are like the wheels of a cart which, lacking one, will have difficulty in standing."

Courage and Poetry

Samurai warriors often sought to discipline their spirit and free themselves from fear by training with Buddhist masters. At various times, samurai and Zen monks both used poetry, especially short forms of poetry like *haiku,* to test the strength and validity of their insight into truth. At a critical moment, just before death, for example, a trainee was expected spontaneously to write a poem that revealed his perfect freedom under all circumstances, as well as the depth of his insight. He was expected to remain calm, clear-headed, and imperturbable even at the point of a sword. There are stories of captured warriors being spared death if they were sufficiently intrepid and their poem manifested deep wisdom.

The greatest of all the Japanese *haiku* writers was **Basho** [Bah-sho] (1644–1694). He was deeply involved with Zen, and his death poem is regarded as profound:

Stick on a journey,
Yet over withered fields
Dreams wander on.

Dogen also gives an example of the genre:

Scarecrow in the hillock
Paddyfield
How unaware! How useful!

Here are two more poems considered to reveal the deep insight and spontaneous expression of the truly free individual:

Coming and going, life and death:
A thousand hamlets, a million houses.
Don't you get the point?
Moon in the water, blossom in the sky.
—*Gizan (1802–1878)*

Fifty-four years I've entered [taught]
Horses, donkeys, saving limitless beings.
Now farewell, farewell!
And don't forget—apply yourselves.
—*Jisso (1851–1904)*

The samurai strives to realize Confucius's notion of the complete man, who is both scholar and warrior. Life requires constant training and learning. Without learning, a person would be ignorant of what is necessary; without hard training, he would be unable to put the necessary actions into effect quickly and efficiently. The samurai works hard to know where his duty lies and to carry it out "unflinchingly." To do this, he hardens himself to suffering. He welcomes death if it comes in pursuit of duty (see the box "Courage and Poetry"). He learns to abhor luxury and considerations of money in order not to be attached to them or to life generally.

An important part of the samurai's study is past traditions, particularly the Confucian and other classical Chinese philosophies, and Zen Buddhism. These determine and shape *bushi* and are in turn unified and synthesized by *bushi* into a single, effective way of life.

The Influence of Confucius

The model of the perfect samurai closely shadows the Confucian idea of the complete man. He is a scholar warrior, literate yet deeply knowledgeable about practical affairs. He knows that life involves change and that survival depends on understanding the inner workings of change. Although a few samurai teachers emphasized the art of war and the ways of increasing courage, more usual is the view of the *Hagakure*. Here the samurai is called on to develop his knowledge of whatever might be useful, "querying every item night and day." Above all, he must understand the Confucian principle of the Mean: more than merely the middle way between two extremes, the Mean is the universal standard that determines what is right and appropriate. The wise samurai reads the sayings of the ancients as the best way to find out what the Mean recommends and how best to follow it.

For Confucius, the three basic and interrelated qualities to be pursued are humanity, wisdom, and courage. According to the samurai tradition, these virtues allow those who have them to enjoy a useful life of service as well as a life free from anxiety and fear.

As Confucius also prescribed, the samurai should be filial, making every effort to respect and honor his parents; he should be polite, discreet in manners and conduct, proper in dress and speech, and upright and sincere. He must not lie. There is the story, for example, of the samurai who refused to take an oath because the word of the samurai is more certain than any oath.

In historical Japan, those who possessed these qualities exhibited enormous dignity. The samurai's dignity displayed itself in every action and in every word. His solemn behavior and resoluteness frequently struck fear in the ordinary observer. The samurai code sought to create a character that was flawless in behavior and taut in spirit.

Another samurai virtue had its roots in the philosophy of Confucius: the samurai was to be economical and, as noted, to avoid luxury. He was to save what he could, but only with an eye to using it on campaign when it was needed.

Because of his virtues, the samurai could be expected to establish and maintain an ordered state in the midst of the most chaotic times. His own steady and unshakable behavior would then serve as a model to be trusted and followed by all others. This, of course, is a Confucian theme.

The Influence of Zen Buddhism

It is slightly ironic that members of the warrior class in Japan went to Zen monks for training, for Zen monks dedicated their lives to saving all living beings. Kamakura, a Zen center that dates back as far as the thirteenth century, was especially noted for training samurai warriors. Perhaps the most famous instance of this relationship was the influence of the Zen monk Takuan (1573–1645) on two of Japan's greatest swordsmen and strategists, Miyamoto Musashi and Yagyu Munenori [YAH-gyu mu-neh-NOH-ree] (1571–1646). All three men produced classic works that were used in the training of samurai.

The samurai, recall, were warriors who trained themselves to be ready at any moment to fight to the death. The ability to fight, of course, is frequently hampered by fear; for fear, if it does not paralyze a fighter completely, may well prevent the lightning-fast response that may be the difference between winning and losing. Though samurai engaged in ceaseless martial arts training, a state of fearlessness sometimes escaped even the best of them. Some samurai, therefore, sought out Zen masters to free themselves of their own fear.

Fear, according to the Zen Buddhist, arises from an excessive attachment or clinging to things and to life generally, a perspective of possessiveness from which anything and everything is viewed as a threat. The remedy for fear—the samurai learned from the Zen masters—is to free oneself from attachments and personal preferences, to rid oneself of the desire to possess anything, including life itself. The samurai was taught to overcome himself, so to speak—to free himself from all thoughts of gain or loss. He was taught to accept what happens without joy or sadness, without complaint, and even without resignation. This hard lesson was thought to require constant meditation on death so that the warrior was ready to "die completely without hesitation or regret."

In this way Zen training sought to rid the samurai of the self-imposed paralysis of fear. Both the Zen and the samurai traditions shared the same ideal: to attain *an unobstructed state of instant, untainted response.* For the samurai this state of mind was the key to total preparedness.

The samurai tradition therefore emphasized that, through a vigorous training of the body and the mind, the individual can perfect his character to respond immediately to any situation. Such training can create a resolute single-mindedness, in which the present moment is all there is and the present action alone is real, that is both efficient and powerful.

The ultimate goal of both Zen Buddhist and samurai training is the state of **mushin,** that is, the state of no mind, no thought. This is a state of awareness beyond calculation in which one moves "no-mindedly" in the here and now, doing exactly what is appropriate without any hesitation. This mind is the "secret" of the great swordsmen like Musashi and Yagyu Munenori.

The samurai tradition, together with Confucianism and Zen Buddhism, provided the Japanese with a noble ideal of character, a context in which the efficiency of Japanese society, and much of what is good and successful in Japan, may perhaps be understood. Certainly the vision of the noble person who trains all his life to be of benefit to others seems a fulfillment of the ideal of humanity put forward by Confucius, Zen, and the samurai. However, the chauvinist nationalism of the Japanese in World War II, the unquestioning obedience to authority, and the glorification of death may also perhaps be explained by reference to these same influences. It is interesting to speculate what these traditions might have yielded, what their effect on Japanese society might have been, if they had been stripped of their authoritarian and excessively militaristic qualities. Confucius seeks to delineate his notion of humanity (**jen**) in terms of what constitutes a superior human being.

Early in its history, Taoism had a relatively strong influence on rulers in China. But as Confucianism replaced it as the dominant value system within society, beginning with the T'ang dynasty (618–906), Taoism increasingly focused on religious functions, an area in which it eventually had to compete with Buddhism. More and more, Taoism came to encompass magic, soothsaying, and incantations for healing and for warding off evil spirits. To this day, Taoist priests perform ceremonies at funerals and on other important occasions. Reportedly, Taoist hermits are still living out the highest forms of Taoist practice in the mountains of China.

As Confucianism established itself as the dominant moral and political philosophy, the Confucian classics became the basis of civil service examination, and in this way Confucianism became even further embedded into Chinese thinking. Between the eleventh and eighteenth centuries, there was a significant Neoconfucian movement, one of whose major figures was Wang Yang-ming (1472–1529).

Confucianism received a severe blow from the Communist revolution in 1949, and Mao Tse-tung made it a repeated target for ridicule. This does not mean that Mao was not himself influenced by Confucius both in his style of writing and of ruling, nor does it mean that Mao was loath to use Confucianism to his own ends—for example, in transferring the individual's family allegiance to state allegiance. In any case, after Mao, Confucian thought is again making itself apparent.

Chinese Buddhism developed a number of different schools from the fourth to the ninth centuries. Ch'an Buddhism was especially powerful and innovative during the seventh to ninth centuries. Chinese Buddhist temples have provided religious services for the people from that time even until the present day. Further, the influence of Ch'an Buddhism spread to Japan, where Zen Buddhism and other forms of Buddhism have endured until the present. Currently, Zen Buddhism especially enjoys growing popularity in the United States and the West generally.

SELECTION 15.1

Analects

Confucius

Book I

CHAPTER I. 1. The Master said, "Is it not pleasant to learn with a constant perseverance and application?

2. "Is it not delightful to have friends coming from distant quarters?

3. "Is he not a man of complete virtue, who feels no discomposure though men may take no note of him?"

CHAP. II. 1. The philosopher Yû said, "They are few who, being filial and fraternal, are fond of offending against their superiors. There have been none, who, not liking to offend against their superiors, have been fond of stirring up confusion.

2. "The superior man bends his attention to what is radical. That being established, all practical courses naturally grow up. Filial piety and fraternal submission!—are they not the root of all benevolent actions?"

CHAP. III. The Master said, "Fine words and an insinuating appearance are seldom associated with true virtue."

CHAP. IV. The philosopher Tsa'ng said, "I daily examine myself on three points:—whether, in transacting business for others, I may have been not faithful;—whether, in intercourse with friends, I may have been not sincere;—whether I may have not mastered and practised the instructions of my teacher."

CHAP. V. The Master said, "To rule a country of a thousand chariots, there must be reverent attention to business, and sincerity; economy in expenditure, and love for men; and the employment of the people at the proper seasons."

CHAP. VI. The Master said, "A youth, when at home, should be filial, and, abroad, respectful to his elders. He should be earnest and truthful. He should overflow in love to all, and cultivate the friendship of the good. When he has time and opportunity, after the performance of these things, he should employ them in polite studies."

CHAP. VII. Tsze-hsiâ said, "If a man withdraws his mind from the love of beauty, and applies it as sincerely to the love of the virtuous; if, in serving his parents, he can exert his utmost strength; if, in serving his prince, he can devote his life; if, in his intercourse with his friends, his words are sincere:—although men say that he has not learned, I will certainly say that he has."

CHAP. VIII. 1. The Master said, "If the scholar be not grave, he will not call forth any veneration, and his learning will not be solid.

2. "Hold faithfulness and sincerity as first principles.

3. "Have no friends not equal to yourself.

4. "When you have faults, do not fear to abandon them."

CHAP. IX. The philosopher Tsaˇng said, "Let there be a careful attention *to perform the funeral rites* to parents, and let them be followed when long gone *with the ceremonies of sacrifice;*—then the virtue of the people will resume its proper excellence."

CHAP. X. 1. Tsze-ch'in asked Tsze-kung, saying, "When our master comes to any country, he does not fail to learn all about its government. Does he ask his information? Or is it given to him?"

2. Tsze-kung said, "Our master is benign, upright, courteous, temperate, and complaisant, and thus he gets his information. The master's mode of asking information!—is it not different from that of other men?"

CHAP. XI. The Master said, "While a man's father is alive, look at the bent of his will; when his father is dead, look at his conduct. If for three years he does not alter from the way of his father, he may be called filial."

CHAP. XII. 1. The philosopher Yû said, "In practising the rules of propriety, a natural ease is to be prized. In the ways prescribed by the ancient kings, this is the excellent quality, and in things small and great we follow them.

2. "Yet it is not to be observed in all cases. If one, knowing *how* such ease *should be prized*, manifests it, without regulating it by the rules of propriety, this likewise is not to be done."

CHAP. XIII. The philosopher Yû said, "When agreements are made according to what is right, what is spoken can be made good. When respect is shown according to what is proper, one keeps far from shame and disgrace. When the parties upon whom a man leans are proper persons to be intimate with, he can make them his guides and masters."

CHAP. XIV. The Master said, "He who aims to be a man of complete virtue in his food does not seek to gratify his appetite, nor in his dwelling-place does he seek the appliances of ease; he is earnest in what he is doing, and careful in his speech; he frequents the company of men of principle that he may be rectified:—such a person may be said indeed to love to learn."

CHAP. XV. 1. Tsze-kung said, "What do you pronounce concerning the poor man who yet does not flatter, and the rich man who is not proud?" The Master replied, "They will do; but they are not equal to him, who, though poor, is yet cheerful, and to him, who, though rich, loves the rules of propriety."

2. Tsze-kung replied, "It is said in the Book of Poetry, 'As you cut and then file, as you carve and then polish.'—The meaning is the same, I apprehend, as that which you have just expressed."

3. The Master said, "With one like Ts'ze, I can begin to talk about the odes. I told him one point, and he knew its proper sequence."

CHAP. XVI. The Master said, "I will not be afflicted at men's not knowing me; I will be afflicted that I do not know men."

SELECTION 15.2

The Eightfold Noble Path *

Buddha

[*The Eightfold Noble Path is at the heart of Buddhist practice, ranging from moral mandates as to how to live to the experience of the ultimate enlightenment and blissful rapture.*]

The Fourth Truth
The Noble Truth of the Path That
Leads to the Extinction of Suffering
(S.56) To give oneself up to indulgence in *Sensual Pleasure*, the base, common, vulgar, unholy, unprofitable, and also to give oneself up to *Self-mortification*, the painful, unholy, unprofitable; both these two extremes the Perfect One has avoided and found out the *Middle Path* which makes one both to

532   Part Four   ·   *Other Voices*

see and to know, which leads to peace, to discernment, to enlightenment, to Nibbana.

It is the Noble Eightfold Path, the way that leads to the extinction of suffering, namely:

1. Right Understanding, *Samma-ditthi*
2. Right Mindedness, *Samma-sankappa*
3. Right Speech, *Samma-vaca*
4. Right Action, *Samma-kammanta*
5. Right Living, *Samma-ajiva*
6. Right Effort, *Samma-vayama*
7. Right Attentiveness, *Samma-sati*
8. Right Concentration, *Samma-samadhi*

This is the Middle Path which the Perfect One has found out, which makes one both to see and to know, which leads to peace, to discernment, to enlightenment, to Nibbana.

Free from pain and torture is this path, free from groaning and suffering, it is the perfect path.
(Dhp. 274–75) Truly, like this path there is no other path to the purity of insight. If you follow this path, you will put an end to suffering.
(Dhp. 276) But each one has to struggle for himself, the Perfect Ones have only pointed out the way.
(M. 26) Give ear then, for the Immortal is found. I reveal, I set forth the Truth. As I reveal it to you, so act! And that supreme goal of the holy life, for the sake of which sons of good families go forth from home to the homeless state: this you will, in no long time, in this very life, make known to yourself, realise and attain to it.

First Step
Right Understanding
(D. 22) What now is Right Understanding?
    1. To understand suffering; 2. to understand the origin of suffering; 3. to understand the extinction of suffering; 4. to understand the path that leads to the extinction of suffering. This is called Right Understanding.
(M.9) Or, when the noble disciple understands, what demerit is and the root of demerit, what merit is and the root of merit, then he has Right Understanding.
    What now is demerit?

1. Destruction of living beings is demerit.
2. Stealing is demerit.
3. Unlawful sexual intercourse is demerit.
4. Lying is demerit.
5. Tale-bearing is demerit.

6. Harsh language is demerit.
7. Frivolous talk is demerit.
8. Covetousness is demerit.
9. Ill-will is demerit.
10. Wrong views are demerit.

And what is the root of demerit? Greed is a root of demerit; Anger is a root of demerit; Delusion is a root of demerit.
(A.X.174) Therefore, I say, these demeritorious actions are of three kinds: either due to greed, or due to anger, or due to delusion.
(M.9) What now is merit (*kusala*)?

1. To abstain from killing is merit.
2. To abstain from stealing is merit.
3. To abstain from unlawful sexual intercourse is merit.
4. To abstain from lying is merit.
5. To abstain from tale-bearing is merit.
6. To abstain from harsh language is merit.
7. To abstain from frivolous talk is merit.
8. Absence of covetousness is merit.
9. Absence of ill-will is merit.
10. Right understanding is merit.

And what is the Root of Merit? Absence of greed is a root of merit; absence of anger is a root of merit; absence of delusion is a root of merit.
(S.21 (5)) Or, when one understands that form, feeling, perception, mental formations and consciousness are transient, (subject to suffering and without an Ego) also in that case one possesses Right Understanding. . . .

Second Step
Right Mindedness
(D.22) What now is Right Mindedness?

1. The thought free from lust.
2. The thought free from ill-will.
3. The thought free from cruelty.

This is called right mindedness.
(M.117) Now, right mindedness, let me tell you, is of two kinds:

    1. The thoughts free from lust, from ill-will, and from cruelty:—this is called the Mundane Right Mindedness, which yields worldly fruits and brings good results.

2. But, whatsoever there is of thinking, considering, reasoning, thought, ratiocination, application—the mind being holy, being turned away from the world and conjoined with the path, the holy path being pursued:—these Verbal Operations of the mind are called the Ultramundane Right Mindedness, which is not of the world, but is ultramundane and conjoined with the paths.

Now, in understanding wrong-mindedness as wrong and right-mindedness as right, one practises Right Understanding; and in making efforts to overcome evil mindedness, and to arouse right mindedness, one practises Right Effort; and in overcoming evil-mindedness with attentive mind, and dwelling with attentive mind in possession of right mindedness, one practises Right Attentiveness. Hence, there are three things that accompany and follow upon right mindedness, namely: right understanding, right effort, and right attentiveness.

Third Step
Right Speech
(A.X. 176) What now is Right Speech?

1. There, someone avoids lying, and abstains from it. He speaks the truth, is devoted to the truth, reliable, worthy of confidence, is not a deceiver of men. Being at a meeting, or amongst people, or in the midst of his relatives, or in a society, or in the king's court, and called upon and asked as witness, to tell what he knows, he answers, if he knows nothing: I know nothing, and if he knows, he answers: I know; if he has seen nothing, he answers: I have seen nothing, and if he has seen, he answers: I have seen. Thus, he never knowingly speaks a lie, neither for the sake of his own advantage, nor for the sake of another person's advantage, nor for the sake of any advantage whatsoever.

2. He avoids tale-bearing, and abstains from it. What he has heard here, he does not repeat there, so as to cause dissension there; and what he has heard there, he does not repeat here, so as to cause dissension here. Thus he unites those that are divided, and those that are united he encourages. Concord gladdens him, he delights and rejoices in concord; and it is concord that he spreads by his words.

3. He avoids harsh language, and abstains from it. He speaks such words as are gentle, soothing to the ear, loving, going to the heart, courteous and dear, and agreeable to many.

4. He avoids vain talk, and abstains from it. He speaks at the right time, in accordance with facts, speaks what is useful, speaks about the law and the discipline; his speech is like a treasure, at the right moment accompanied by arguments, moderate and full of sense.

This is called right speech. . . .

Fourth Step
Right Action
What now is Right Action?

(A.X. 176) 1. There someone avoids the killing of living beings, and abstains from it. Without stick or sword, conscientious, full of sympathy, he is anxious for the welfare of all living beings.

2. He avoids stealing, and abstains from it; what another person possesses of goods and chattels in the village or in the wood, that he does not take away with thievish intent.

3. He avoids unlawful sexual intercourse, and abstains from it. He has no intercourse with such persons as are still under the protection of father, mother, brother, sister or relatives, nor with married women, nor female convicts, nor even with flower-decked (engaged) girls.

This is called right action.
(M. 117) Now right action, let me tell you, is of two kinds:

1. Abstaining from killing, from stealing, and from unlawful sexual intercourse:—this is called the Mundane Right Action, which yields worldly fruits and brings good results.

2. But the abhorrence of the practice of this three-fold wrong action, the abstaining, withholding, refraining therefrom—the mind being holy, being turned away from the world and conjoined with the path, the holy path being pursued:—this is called the Ultramundane Right Action, which is not of the world, but is ultramundane and conjoined with the paths.

Now, in understanding wrong action as wrong, and right action as right, one practises Right Understanding; and in making efforts to overcome wrong action, and to arouse right action, one practises Right Effort; and in overcoming wrong action with attentive mind, and dwelling with attentive mind in possession of right action, one practises Right Attentiveness. Hence, there are three things that accompany and follow upon right action, namely: right understanding, right effort, and right attentiveness.

Fifth Step
Right Living
(D. 22) What now is Right Living?

When the noble disciple, avoiding a wrong living, gets his livelihood by a right way of living, this is called right living.

(M. 117) Now, right living, let me tell you, is of two kinds:

1. When the noble disciple, avoiding wrong living, gets his livelihood by a right way of living:— this is called the Mundane Right Living, which yields worldly fruits and brings good results.

2. But the abhorrence of wrong living, the abstaining, withholding, refraining therefrom—the mind being holy, being turned away from the world and conjoined with the path, the holy path being pursued:—this is called the Ultramundane Right Living (*lokuttara-samma-ajiva*), which is not of the world, but is ultramundane and conjoined with the paths.

Now, in understanding wrong living as wrong, and right living as right, one practises Right Understanding; and in making efforts to overcome wrong living, to arouse right living, one practises Right Effort; and in overcoming wrong living with attentive mind, and dwelling with attentive mind in possession of right living, one practises Right Attentiveness. Hence, there are three things that accompany and follow upon right living, namely: right understanding, right effort, and right attentiveness. . . .

Eighth Step
Right Concentration
(M. 44) What now is Right Concentration?

Fixation of the mind to a single object, (lit. One-pointedness of mind);—this is concentration.

The four Fundamentals of Attentiveness;—these are the objects of concentration.

The four Great Efforts:—these are the requisites for concentration.

The practising, developing and cultivating of these things:—this is the Development of concentration.

(M. 141) Detached from sensual objects, detached from demeritorious things, the disciple enters into the first trance, which is accompanied by Verbal Thought and Rumination, is born of Detachment, and filled with Rapture and Happiness.

(M. 43) This first trance is free from five things, and five things are present: when the disciple enters the first trance, there have vanished (the 5 Hindrances): Lust, Ill-will, Torpor and Dullness, Restlessness and Mental Worry, Doubts; and there are present: Verbal Thought, Rumination, Rapture, Happiness, and Concentration.

(M. 27) And further: after the subsiding of verbal thought and rumination, and by the gaining of inward tranquillisation and oneness of mind, he enters into a state free from verbal thought and rumination, the second trance, which is born of Concentration and filled with Rapture and Happiness.

And further: after the fading away of rapture, he dwells in equanimity, attentive, clearly conscious, and he experiences in his person that feeling, of which the noble Ones say: Happy lives the man of equanimity and attentive mind—thus he enters the third trance.

And further: after the giving up of pleasure and pain, and through the disappearance of previous joy and grief, he enters into a state beyond pleasure and pain, into the fourth trance, which is purified by equanimity and attentiveness.

(S. 21 (1)) Develop your concentration; for he who has concentration understands things according to their reality. And what are these things? The arising and passing away of bodily form, of feeling, perception, mental formations and consciousness.

(M. 149) Thus these five Aggregates of existence must be wisely penetrated; delusion and craving must be wisely abandoned; Tranquility and Insight must be wisely developed.

(S. 56) This is the Middle Path which the Perfect One has discovered, which makes one both to see and to know, and which leads to peace, to discernment, to enlightenment, to Nibbana.

(Dhp. 627) And following upon this path you will put an end to suffering.

CHECKLIST

To help you review, here is a checklist of the key philosophers and terms and concepts of this chapter. The brief descriptive sentences summarize the philosophers' leading ideas. Keep in mind that some of these summary statements are oversimplifications of complex positions.

Philosophers

- **Al-Ghazālī,** a late eleventh-century and early twelfth-century Islamic philosopher, attacked Avicenna regarding the eternity of the world and the reduction of religious law to a mere symbol of higher truths. 492

- **Al-Fārābī,** a ninth-century Islamic philosopher, posited the philosopher-prophet as the one providing the necessary illumination for his society. 492

- **Al-Kindi,** a ninth-century Islamic thinker, used Greek ideas to define God as an absolute and transcendent being. 492

- **Averroës,** a twelfth-century Islamic thinker, was thought of as holding two separate truths, that of religion and that of philosophy. 493

- **Avicenna (Abū 'Ali ibn-Sīnā),** a tenth-century Islamic thinker, felt that there is a parallelism between philosophy and theology. 492

- **Basho** was the greatest Japanese *haiku* writer. 527

- **Chuang Tzu** was the most important Taoist after Lao Tzu and stressed the equality of opposites and the danger of usefulness. 501

- **Confucius,** founder of the most dominant system of Chinese thought, emphasized the perfectibility of people as well as their ability to affect things for the better. 504

- **Dogen Kigen,** a Japanese Zen monk, stressed the importance of acquiring the perspective of the universal Self, given the impermanence of life. 520

- **Hsün Tzu** was a Confucian philosopher who set forth a blend of Confucianism and Taoism. 512

- **Hui Neng,** sixth patriarch of Chinese Zen, emphasized the oneness of all things. 513

- **Kabir,** a late fifteenth- and early sixteenth-century Indian poet, was considered one of the great mystical poets in the tradition of Sufism. 493

- **Lao Tzu,** founder of Taoism, held that the Tao is ineffable and beyond our ability to alter. He emphasized the importance of effortless nonstriving. 495

- **Mencius** was a Confucian thinker second in importance to Confucius. 509

- **Miyamoto Musashi and Yamamoto Tsunetomo** were samurai writers who helped record and preserve samurai ideals of preparedness; indifference to pain, death, and material possessions; wisdom; and courage. 523, 525

- **Murasaki Shikibu,** an influential Japanese Mahayana Buddhist philosopher of the late tenth and early eleventh centuries, held that women were responsible moral agents who were capable of enlightenment and could influence their destinies, reach nirvana, and achieve salvation. 517

- **Sadr al-Dīn als Shīrazī,** a late sixteenth- and early seventeenth-century thinker who was influenced by the mystical tendencies in Neoplatonism, sought a return to the first principle of being. 493

- **Siddhartha Gautama Buddha,** an Indian prince and founder of Buddhism, sought the causes of and cures for human suffering. 490

- **Sun Tzu,** a sixth-century B.C.E. Taoist philosopher and general, applied Taoist philosophy to military strategy. 500

Key Terms and Concepts

Analects 506	*kami* 517
animism 517	karma 489
atman 487	*koan* 522
brahman 487	Mean 505
Buddhism 490	*mushin* 529
bushido 522	nirvana 489
Ch'an Buddhism 513	rectification 506
Confucianism 504	reincarnation 489
Dharma 514	Rinzai Zen 522
dhyana 513	sage 506
Eightfold Path 491	samurai 522
Four Noble	*satori* 522
Truths 590	soft and
haiku 527	supple 497
Hinduism 487	Soto Zen 522
jen 529	Sufism 593

536   Part Four   ·   *Other Voices*

17. How important is it to be self-reliant? Is total self-reliance possible?

18. Should the complete person be both wise and brave? If you wished to improve your wisdom or free yourself from fear, what would you do? How would you know if you had succeeded?

QUESTIONS FOR DISCUSSION AND REVIEW

1. Do you believe in reincarnation? Why or why not?

2. Do you agree with Confucius's belief in the goodness and perfectibility of humans? Give reasons.

3. What is the Tao?

4. Compare and contrast the philosophies of Confucius and Lao Tzu. Take sides, and determine whose prescriptions are soundest and why.

5. Evaluate Mencius's idea that difficulty and suffering are opportunities to develop independence and peace of mind.

6. Do the subjects of the state adopt the ethical standards of their leaders? Or is it the other way around?

7. "Benevolence subdues its opposite just as water subdues fire." Evaluate this claim.

8. Are Lao Tzu's prescriptions for behavior realistic and practical? Explain.

9. Are power and riches chains, or are they the keys to freedom and happiness?

10. What is the sound of one hand clapping? Is this an intelligible question?

11. Comment on Hui Neng's poem of enlightenment (see the box on page 515).

12. How did Mahayana Buddhism reinforce sexism and elitism?

13. Why would suicide help a woman achieve salvation under Mahayana Buddhism?

14. How did Murasaki Shikibu's philosophy challenge Buddhist doctrines of karma, enlightenment, and salvation?

15. How important is it to have a life goal?

16. Is it possible for a person completely to abandon selfish desires?

SUGGESTED FURTHER READINGS

Christopher Bartley, *Indian Philosophy A–Z* (Edinburgh, UK: Edinburgh University Press, 2005). A handbook of key terms and issues within Indian philosophy.

David A. Bell, ed., *Confucian Political Ethics* (Princeton, N.J.: Princeton University Press, 2008). A reconsideration of Confucian ideas and their importance for contemporary times.

John Blofield, *The Secret and Sublime* (New York: E. P. Dutton, 1973). A very readable presentation of the philosophy of Taoism, popular Taoism, Taoist mysticism, and the relationship of Taoism and yogic practices.

Daniel Bonevac, *Understanding Non-Western Philosophy* (New York: McGraw-Hill, 1993). A collection of readings from African, Asian, and southern Mediterranean philosophers.

Massimo Campanini, *An Introtduction to Islamic Philosophy* (Edinburgh, UK: Edinburgh University Press, 2008). A concise review of Islamic philosophy as it developed in the Middle Ages.

Brian Carr and Indira Mahalingam, *Companion Encyclopedia of Asian Philosophy* (New York: Routledge, 2001). Reference work concerning the philosophical traditions of the East.

Wing-tsit Chan, *A Source Book in Chinese Philosophy* (Princeton, N.J.: Princeton University Press, 1963). First-rate anthology of Chinese philosophical writings placed in historical and philosophical context.

Chuang Tzu, *The Complete Works*, Burton Watson, trans. (New York: Columbia University Press, 1968). A highly regarded translation of Chuang Tzu that is said to retain the wit of the philosopher himself.

Thomas Cleary, trans., *Classics of Buddhism and Zen* (Boston: Shambhala, 2005). A selection of important texts in Zen Buddhism.

Thomas Cleary, trans., *The Spirit of the Tao* (Boston: Shambhala, 1998). An accessible selection from the most popular Taoist classics.

Thomas Cleary, trans., *The Taoist Classics* (Boston: Shambhala, 2003). A good translation of Taoist texts.

Diane Collinson, Kathryn Plant, and Robert Wilkinson, *Fifty Eastern Thinkers* (New York: Routledge, 2001). A brief exposition of fifty major thinkers in Eastern philosophy.

Diane Collinson and Robert Wilkinson, *Thirty-Five Oriental Philosophers* (New York: Routledge, 1994). A comprehensive overview of Eastern philosophy.

Confucius, *The Analects*, Raymond Dawson, trans. (New York: Oxford University Press, 2000). Favorable reviews for this new translation.

Dogen and Kosho Uchiyama, *Refining Your Life*, Thomas Wright, trans. (New York: Weatherhill, 1983). In this short treatise on Zen cooking, Dogen provides an extraordinary method of performing any activity well and of living life as a whole.

Heinrich Dumoulin, *Zen Buddhism: A History, India and China* (Bloomington, Ind.: World Wisdom, 2005). A history of Zen Buddhism in India and China.

Heinrich Dumoulin, *Zen Buddhism: A History, Japan* (Bloomington, Ind.: World Wisdom, 2005). Classic history of Zen Buddhism in Japan.

Aislee T. Embree, ed., *The Hindu Tradition* (New York: Vintage Books, 1972). Readings that review the development of Hindu thought from the beginnings to the present.

Gavin Flood, ed., *The Blackwell Companion to Hinduism* (Malden, Mass.: Blackwell, 2003). Essays introducing the vast area of Hinduism.

Joel J. Kupperman, *Classic Asian Philosophy* (New York: Oxford University Press, 2000). Designed to give beginners a sense of the most important texts.

Lao Tzu, *Tao Te Ching* (New York: Penguin, 1973). A good and inexpensive translation of a classic.

Oliver Leaman, *Eastern Philosophy: Key Readings* (New York: Routledge, 2000). Extracts from readings on important terms in Eastern philosophy.

Oliver Leaman, *Key Concepts in Eastern Philosophy* (New York: Routledge, 1999). A glossary of main terms found in Eastern philosophy.

Trevor Leggett, *Zen and the Ways* (Rutland, Vt.: Charles E. Tuttle, 1987). Shows how the meditative calmness taught in Zen can be applied to the ways of the martial arts and of life generally.

Miyamoto Musashi, *A Book of Five Rings*, Victor Harris, trans. (New York: Bantam, 1982). Written by the most famous swordsman and samurai, this is the great book of Japanese strategy. It is a guide for making decisions and acting decisively in even the worst of times.

Murasaki Shikibu, *Tale of Genji/Genji Monogatari*. Many, many editions available at most public libraries.

Sarvepalli Radhakrishnan and Charles A. Moore, *A Source Book in Indian Philosophy* (Princeton, N.J.: Princeton University Press, 1957). A splendid historical selection of philosophical writings with background information.

D. Howard Smith, *Confucius and Confucianism* (London: Paladin, 1973). Places the teachings of Confucius in historical context and treats the interaction of Confucianism with Taoism and Buddhism.

Yamamoto Tsunetomo, *Hagakure* (Tokyo: Kodansha International, 1979). The seventeenth-century classic that encapsulates the ethics, strategies, and worldview of the samurai class. Enlightening in itself, the *Hagakure* can also be used to understand contemporary Japanese ways of thinking.

Mary Ellen Waithe, *A History of Women Philosophers*, vol. 2, *Medieval Women Philosophers, 500–1600* (Dordrecht, Boston, and London: Kluwer Academic Publishers, 1989). Includes a chapter by Waithe on Murasaki Shikibu.

Henry Clarke Warren, trans., *A Buddhist Reader* (Mineola, N.Y.: Dover, 2004). An anthology of Buddhist writings from the Theravada tradition.

Index/Glossary

Cixous, Hélène [aay-LAYN
 seek-so], 466–469, **477–480**
Class struggle (Marxism), 338
Clausewitz, Carl Philipp
 Gottfried von, 500
Clear and distinct criterion:
 René Descartes' criterion of
 truth, according to which that,
 and only that, which is
 perceived as clearly and
 distinctly as the fact of one's
 own existence is certain,
 102–103
"Clinging to existence"
 (Buddhism), 494
Cockburn [KO-burn], Catherine
 Trotter: profile, *320*
Code, Lorraine, 459
Code Pink: A third wave women's
 grassroots peace and justice
 movement that opposes any
 kind of military force, 453
Cogito, ergo sum: "I think,
 therefore I am"; the single
 indubitable truth on which
 Descartes' epistemology is
 based, 102, 408
Colonialism, history of, 538–555
Commonsense (folk):
 psychology, 230
"Commonsense metaphysics."
 See Dualism
Communism: (capital "c") The
 ideology of the Communist
 Party, 383; (lowercase "c")
 an economic system, 340,
 383, 506
Communist Manifesto (Marx and
 Engels), 336, **352–354**
Communitarian: One who
 holds that there is a common
 good defined by one's society,
 the attainment of which has
 priority over individual
 liberty, 371–376
Concept of Mind, The (Ryle), 226
Conceptualism: The theory that
 universals are concepts and
 exist only in the mind, 87
Confessions (Augustine), **90–92**
Confucianism: A philosophical
 tradition that began with
 Confucius in the sixth century
 B.C.E. and continues to the
 present day; Confucianism is a
 practical philosophy that hopes

to establish a better world
 order by means of moral
 perfection of the individual,
 485, 486, 504–513, 516, 517,
 518; Hsün Tzu, 512–513;
 Mencius, 509–512
Confucius [kun-FYOO-shus],
 496, 505–508, 510–511, 521,
 527, 528; *Analects,* 529,
 530–531; profile, *506*
Consequences and Pragmatism
 (Rorty), 192
Consequentialism: Ethical
 theories that evaluate actions
 by their consequences, 258
Conservatism: A political
 philosophy based on respect
 for established institutions
 and traditions and that
 favors preservation of the
 status quo over social
 experimentation, 383
Constant conjunction, 134
Constitution, United States,
 326–328
Continental philosophy: The
 philosophical traditions of
 continental Europe; includes
 phenomenology, existentialism,
 hermeneutics, deconstruction,
 and critical theory, 151–152,
 157, 177–178. *See also*
 individual philosophers
Continental rationalists, 117
Contingency, 191–192
Contingent truth. *See*
 Necessary/contingent pair
Contractarianism. *See*
 Contractualism
Contractarian theory: The
 political theory according to
 which a legitimate state exists
 only by virtue of an agreement
 or "contract" among the
 subjects of the state, 258,
 312–326, 364–369, 377
Contractualism: Ethical theories
 according to which right and
 wrong are established by a
 societal agreement or social
 contract, 258, 312–326,
 364–369
Conway, Anne Finch, Viscountess:
 de re modality, 108; metaphysics,
 107–109; profile, *108*
Cook Ting, 503

**Copernican revolution in
 philosophy:** A new perspective
 in epistemology, introduced by
 Immanuel Kant, according to
 which the objects of experience
 must conform in certain
 respects to our knowledge of
 them, 136
Copernicus, Nicholas, 83, 85,
 97, 136
Cosmological argument: An
 argument for the existence of
 God according to which the
 universe and its parts can be
 neither accidental nor self-
 caused and must ultimately
 have been brought into
 existence by God, 400–403,
 408, 410
Cosmology, Thomistic, 89
Counterargument: An argument
 that counters the given
 argument, 9
Counter-Reformation, The, 100
Cratylus [KRA-tuh-lus], 39,
 42, 135
Creation *ex nihilo:* creation out of
 nothing, 79–80
Creation *versus* evolution, 428–430
Critical theory: A philosophical
 method that seeks to provide a
 radical critique of knowledge
 by taking into account the
 situation and interests
 involved, 152, 178–179
Critique of Pure Reason (Kant),
 136, **144–145,** 167
Crito (Plato), **341–344**
Cultural relativism: The theory
 that what is right (and wrong)
 is what your culture believes is
 right (and wrong), 240
Cyberfeminism: The idea that
 women can resist the
 patriarchy through their
 communication links in
 computer technology, 450
Cynicism: A school of philosophy
 founded around the fifth
 century B.C.E., probably by
 Antisthenes of Diogenes; the
 Cynics sought to lead lives of
 total simplicity and naturalness
 by rejecting all comforts and
 conveniences of society,
 268–289

religion, 419–420, 421; profile, *153;* sickness-unto-death, 154
"Killing and Starving to Death" (Rachels), **384–386**
King, Martin Luther Jr., 538, 548–549; profile, *549;* "Sword That Heals, The," **558–559;** *Why We Can't Wait,* 548
Kleinman, Sherryl, **480–481;** language, sexism and, 458–459
Knowledge, theory of (Aristotle), 70–71
Knox, Ronald, 426
Koan, 522
Kripke, Saul, 231, 233–235, **241–242**
Kristeva [krisst-EH-vuh], Julia, 464–466
Kropotkin [krah-POT-kin], Piotr, 341
Kshatriyas, 486
Kuhn, Thomas, 215
Lacan, Jacques, 461–462
Language game: The context in which an utterance is made, which determines the purposes served by the utterance and hence its meaning; Wittgenstein believed that philosophical problems are due to ignoring the "game" in which certain concepts are used, 224
Langue (Saussure), 182
Lao Tzu [LAO-tsuh], 174, 485, 495–499, 501–502, 522; profile, *496*
Larmore, Charles, 274
"Laugh of the Medusa, The" (Cixous), 469, **477–480**
Law of the Father: In Lacan's theory, a system that contains encoded patriarchal values in language, 461, 462
Lawrence v. Texas: A 2003 ruling by the United States Supreme Court that a Texas law prohibiting homosexual sodomy was unconstitutional, 328
Laws (Plato), 39
"Leap of faith" (Kierkegaard), 153, 419
Lecky, W. E. H., 257
Leibniz [LIBE-nits], Gottfried Wilhelm, 107, 111–113, 117, 320, 410–412, 418, **433–434**

Leibowitz, Lila, 459
Lenin, Vladimir I., 309, 340
Leo XIII, Pope, 87, 401
Lesbian feminism, 451
Letters from Iwo Jima, 500
Leucippus [loo-SIP-us or loo-KIP-us], 30–31
Leviathan: The coiled snake or dragon in the Book of Job in the Bible; in the philosophy of Thomas Hobbes, "that mortal God, to which we owe our peace and defense"; that is, the state (or its sovereign) created by social contract, 315–318
Leviathan (Hobbes), 315–318, **348–351**
Levinas, Emmanuel, 174–175
Levi-Strauss [LAY-vee-STROWSS], Claude, 184
Lévi-Strauss [LAY-vee-STROWSS], Claude, 182
Lewis, C. S., 429
Liberal feminism, 450–451
Liberalism: A political philosophy whose basic tenet is that each individual should have the maximum freedom consistent with the freedom of others, 329–341, 338, 382–383
Liberalism and the Limits of Justice (Sandel), 372
Liberation theology, 548
Libertarian: Someone who believes in free will; alternatively, someone who upholds the principles of liberty of thought and action, 369–371
Literature and philosophy, 159–160
Locke, John, 113–116, 135, 323, 330, 366, 369, 370–371; epistemology, 113–116; *Essay Concerning Human Understanding, An,* 113; *nihil in intellectu quod prius non fuerit in sensu,* 113; political philosophy, 318–322; profile, *319;* property, theory of, 321–322, 370; representative realism, 113–114; *tabula rasa,* 113; *Two Treatises of Government,* 319
Logic: The study of correct inference, 8–9, 70–71

Logical atomism: The metaphysical theory that the world does not consist of things but of facts, that is, things having certain properties and standing in certain relationship to one another. The ultimate facts are atomic in that they are logically independent of one another and are unresolvable into simpler facts; likewise, an empirically correct description of the world will consist ultimately of logically independent and unanalyzable atomic propositions that correspond to the atomic facts, 216–218, 224
Logical form, 223
Logical Investigations (Husserl), 170
Logical positivism: The philosophy of the Vienna Circle, according to which an purported statement of fact, if not a verbal truism, is meaningless unless certain conceivable observations would serve to confirm or deny it, 176, 212, 424–425
Logicism: The thesis that the concepts of mathematics can be defined in terms of concepts of logic and that all mathematical truths can be proved from principles of formal logic, 210–211
Logocentrism: A term coined by Derrida that refers to the traditional Western ways of thinking about truth, consciousness, and reason in language, 185–186, 465
Logos, 26, 186, 496, 497
Lone Samurai, The (Wilson), 522
Love and Becoming, Theory of, in Plato, 44–46
Luther, Martin, 407, 420, 426
Machiavelli [mahk-yah-VEL-ee], Niccoló, 316
MacIntyre, Alasdair, 372, 375–376
Madhva, 488
Madness and Civilization (Foucault), 181

Theodicy: A defense of God's goodness and omnipotence in view of apparent evil, 411

Theology, Christian, 79–80

"Theology and Falsification" (Flew), **435–436**

Theology and philosophy, 87, 396–397, 404

Theoretical posits: Entities whose existence we hypothesize to explain our sensory experience, 221

Theory of Forms: Plato's central metaphysical concept, 38–41, 69, 157, 184, 187. *See also* Form

Theory of Justice, A (Rawls), 364–369, **386–387**

Thesis-antithesis-synthesis: In the philosophy of Hegel, to each thesis there is an antithesis (opposite), and the two are a unity in a higher synthesis, 140

Thick and Thin (Walzer), 373

Thing-in-itself: English for *Ding-an-sich:* a thing as it is independent of any consciousness of it, 138, 183

Third Man argument: Aristotle's criticism of Plato's Theory of Forms, according to which there must be a third thing that ties together a Form with the particular things that exemplify it, 68–69

Third wave of feminism, 452–454

This Sex Which Is Not One (Irigaray), 464

Thomas Aquinas [uh-QUINE-nuss], St., 78, 87–90, 117, 274, 374, 375, 407, 412, 418, 426; and Aristotle, 87–90; epistemology, 90; essence and existence, 87–89; ethics, 274, 276–277, 278; metaphysics, 87–90; philosophy of religion, 400–404, 412, 418; political philosophy, 313–314; profile, *401; Summa Theologica,* 92–95, **432–433**

Thompson, William, 448

Thoreau, Henry David, 159, 556

Thought: According to Descartes, the essential attribute of mind, 103

Thought experiment: Imagining a situation in order to extract a lesson of philosophical importance, 10

Timaeus (Plato), 30, 39

Time and God, 79, 109

Timocracy, 311

Tolstoy, Leo, 161, 556

Total skeptic: One who maintains nothing can be known or, alternatively, suspends judgment in all matters, 80

Towards Universal Man (Tagore), **566–567**

Tractatus Logico-Philosophicus (Wittgenstein), 217, 223–224

Trakl, Georg, 159, 173

Transcendental phenomenology: An epistemological method that seeks the certainty of a pure of consciousness of objects in the transcendental ego, 169

Translatability thesis: The idea that, in theory, statements about the world could all be translated into statements that refer to immediate sensory experience, 231

Traski, Alfred, 233

Treatise Concerning the Principles of Human Knowledge (Berkeley), 115, **124–126**

Treatise of Human Nature (Hume), 131, 135

Trial, The (Kafka), 161

Trotsky, Leon, 190

Trotter Cockburn, Catharine, 320

Truth, 191, 419, 555; antirepresentationalist, 215, 222–223; pragmatic, 189, 206

Truth, as relative, 7, 191

Tutu [too-too], Desmond, 545; profile, *544*

"Two Dogmas of Empiricism" (Quine), 231

Two-realms concept (Plato), 38–41, 79, 98

Two Treatises of Government (Locke), 319

Tyranny, 311, 312

Übermensch: In the philosophy of Nietzsche, the "Superman" who escapes the triviality of society by embracing the will to power and rejecting the

slave mentality that permeates society and dominates religion, 154, 289, 421

Ukifune, 519

Unamuno, Miguel de, 159–160

Uncaused cause of existence, 89

Universal: That which is denoted by a general word, a word (such as "chair") that applies to more than a single thing, 69, 86

Universalistic ethical hedonism: The doctrine that one ought to seek, over everything else, the greatest pleasure for the greatest number of people, 258. *See also* Utilitarianism

Universal phenomenology of consciousness: Attempts made by Hegel and Husserl to devise a pure science of knowing, 169–170

Universals, problem of, 86. *See also* Universal

Universal self, 521

Upanishads, 487–488

Upheavals of Thought: The Intelligence of Emotions (Nussbaum), 376

Utilitarianism: The doctrine that the rightness of an action is identical with the happiness it produces as its consequence, 284–288, **299–301**, 329–332, **351–352**; critique of, 367, 371

Utilitarianism (Mill, John Stuart), **299–301**, 331

Utopianism, 448

Vaisesika, 487

Vaishya, 486

Vaisnavism, 487

Value judgment: A proposition that explicitly or implicitly assigns a value to something, 238–239

Varieties of Religious Experience, The (James), 422

Vedanta, 487, 488

Vedas, 398–399

Veil of ignorance: In Indian philosophy, the perspective from which the world is viewed as a multiplicity of things; in John Rawls's philosophy, the metaphor for the conditions under which

CPSIA information can be obtained
at www.ICGtesting.com
Printed in the USA
FFOW03n2201151113
2373FF